Praise for
THE DREAM
AND THE TOMB

"An epic cast and setting. High quality, splendidly readable."
—*Boston Globe*

"The important things about Robert Payne are his sensitive, astute intelligence, his vast erudition, and his magic power over words. . . . If anyone can capture the spiritual essence of a place, of a way of life, of an exotic culture, Payne can."
—*New York Times*

"Based on wide reading in the secondary literature, organized around famous crusading leaders, and filled with romantic and anecdotal material, Payne tells an old story exceptionally well."
—*Library Journal*

"Probably no author of this century has produced so many books at such a relatively high level of scholarship."
—*The [London] Times*

THE DREAM
AND THE TOMB

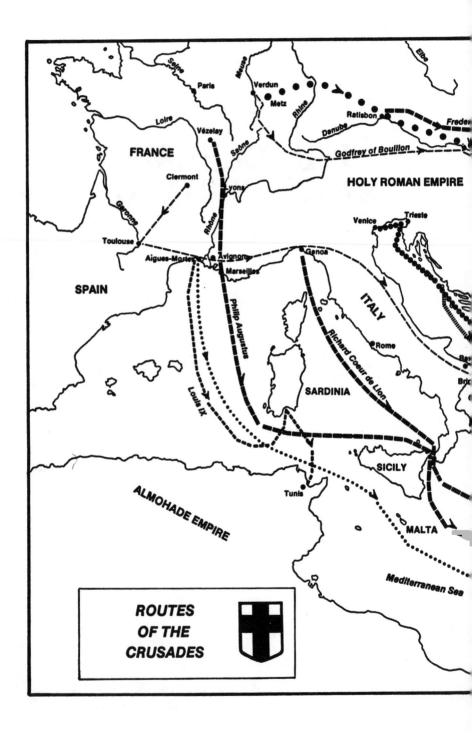

ROUTES
OF THE
CRUSADES

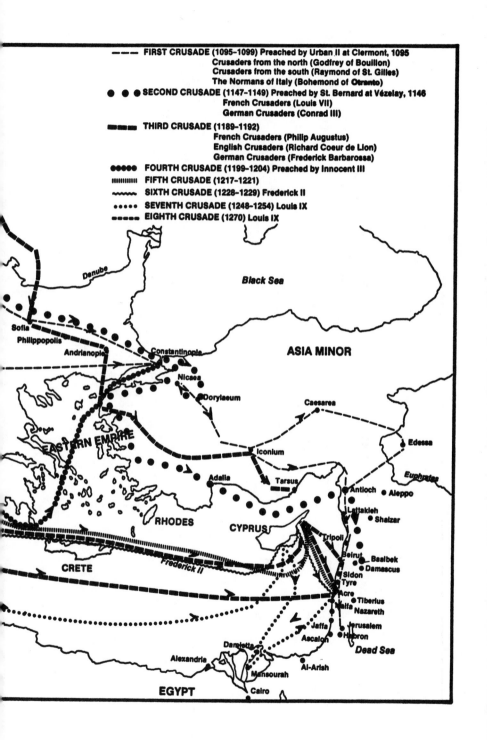

FIRST CRUSADE (1095–1099) Preached by Urban II at Clermont, 1095
Crusaders from the north (Godfrey of Bouillon)
Crusaders from the south (Raymond of St. Gilles)
The Normans of Italy (Bohemond of Otranto)
SECOND CRUSADE (1147–1149) Preached by St. Bernard at Vézelay, 1146
French Crusaders (Louis VII)
German Crusaders (Conrad III)
THIRD CRUSADE (1189–1192)
French Crusaders (Philip Augustus)
English Crusaders (Richard Coeur de Lion)
German Crusaders (Frederick Barbarossa)
FOURTH CRUSADE (1199–1204) Preached by Innocent III
FIFTH CRUSADE (1217–1221)
SIXTH CRUSADE (1228–1229) Frederick II
SEVENTH CRUSADE (1248–1254) Louis IX
EIGHTH CRUSADE (1270) Louis IX

Danube

Black Sea

Sofia
Philippopolis
Andrianople
Constantinople
Nicaea
Dorylaeum

ASIA MINOR

Caesarea

Edessa

EASTERN EMPIRE

Iconium

Euphrates

Adalia

Tarsus

Antioch
Aleppo

Lattakieh
Shaizar

RHODES

CYPRUS

Tripoli

Beirut
Baalbek
Damascus

Frederick II

Sidon
Tyre
Acre
Haifa

Tiberius
Nazareth

CRETE

Jaffa
Ascalon
Jerusalem
Hebron

Dead Sea

Damietta

Alexandria

Al-Arish

EGYPT

Mansourah
Cairo

THE DREAM
AND THE TOMB

THE DREAM
AND THE TOMB

A History of the Crusades

Robert Payne

Cooper Square Press

Maps of The Four Crusader States, The Ayubite Empire, The Crusade of St. Louis, Events in Egypt, Egypt and Syria, Homelands of Turks, Mongols, and Circassians, and The Fall of Acre are from *Soldiers of Fortune: The Story of the Mamelukes* by Sir John Glubb, reprinted courtesy of Stein and Day Publishers.

First Cooper Square Press edition 2000

This Cooper Square Press paperback edition of *The Dream and the Tomb* is an unabridged republication of the edition first published in Briarcliff Manor, New York in 1984.

Published by Cooper Square Press
An Imprint of the Rowman & Littlefield Publishing Group, Inc.
150 Fifth Avenue, Suite 911
New York, New York 10011

Distributed by National Book Network

Library of Congress Cataloging-in-Publication Data

Payne, Robert, 1911–1983
 The dream and the tomb : a history of the Crusades / Robert Payne.— 1st Cooper Square Press ed.
  p. cm.
 Originally published: New York : Stein and Day, 1984.
 Includes bibliographical references and index.
 ISBN 0-8154-1086-7 (pbk. : alk. paper)
  1. Crusades. I. Title.

D157 .P35 2000
909.07— dc21

00-057010

⊖™ The paper used in this publication meets the minimum requirements of American National Standard for Information Sciences— Permanence of Paper for Printed Library Materials, ANSI/NISO Z39.48–1992.
Manufactured in the United States of America.

This book is dedicated to
THE MARTYRS OF ALL WARS

Acknowledgments

My late husband, Robert Payne, spent close to seven years researching this book, reading both Western and Arab historians. It is, therefore, an unbiased approach to a most complex subject; it is also a vivid and colorful panorama of the first great confrontation between the Muslim East and the Christian West. In an earlier book, *The Holy Sword*, published in 1959, Robert wrote: "Out of Arabia there came a proud and august people who in their time conquered most of the known world, and there is still too little about them in our history books. Sooner or later we shall have to learn to live with them."

I hope *The Dream and the Tomb* will help people of all faiths to learn to understand each other and to live with each other. For my husband, this book was a work of love and hope.

It is not often that a major book is published so soon after an author's death. If there are any inconsistencies or omissions, I hope the reader will understand.

I am extremely grateful to Sol Stein and to Benton Arnovitz for overseeing the whole project. I am also very grateful to Patricia Day and to Toby Stein for doing a superb job of editing. My sincere thanks also go to everyone concerned for their help and support. In particular, I would like to thank The Arts of Asia Foundation and The Very Reverend James Parks Morton, Dean of the Cathedral of St. John The Divine.

Sheila Lalwani Payne

Contents

Maps

Illustrations

I

THE VOICE FROM THE TOMB

The Dream
and the Tomb

I N their hundreds of thousands the Crusaders marched to the Holy
Land, some on foot, some on donkeys, some in carts, some in armor
and on well-caparisoned horses. Perhaps a quarter of them died
on the journey and another quarter died in the wars, and many of them
suffered atrociously to defend the small strip of seacoast they called the
Kingdom of Jerusalem, a kingdom they held for less than a hundred years.
They called themselves *peregrini Christi*, pilgrims of Christ, and in their
eyes the miseries of the enterprise were outweighed by the splendor and the
glory. They came from all walks of life: kings and emperors, farm boys and
laborers, archbishops and priests, knights and foot soldiers. In wave after
wave these armored pilgrims were swept forward to the holy cities of the
Holy Land, and most especially to Jerusalem, the Church of the Holy
Sepulchre and the tomb of Christ.

Landowners abandoned their land, peasants allowed themselves to be
uprooted, princes plundered their treasuries in order to make the pilgrimage; and sometimes in old age they would return to Europe in feeble health,
having spent half a lifetime in Saracenic prisons, proud and happy that
they had been to the holy places. The odds were always against them, and
some of their happiness derived precisely from the pact they had made with
Christ and from the fact that they had accomplished an impossible task.
Jerusalem beckoned them; they answered the call, for her voice was loud
and insistent. They marched off to a country they thought they knew
intimately from reading the New Testament or hearing it read to them, and
they discovered very early that the Holy Land resembled no country they
had ever seen or ever dreamed of. The desolation of the Judaean wilderness came to them like a shock on exposed nerves; nowhere in Europe was
there a wilderness like it. Nor, when they first arrived, had they the faintest
inkling how to deal with the Saracens, who were sensual to an extraordinary degree and at the same time unbelievably hard, cruel, and ruthless.

17

They entered an unknown land inhabited by an unknown people, and the strangeness of the land entered their souls.

Today, when we look back at the Crusaders, we find ourselves marveling at their audacity and gallantry and their resourcefulness in building castles and fortresses that were works of art. When we ask ourselves why they went off in the hundreds of thousands, we discover that we do not always know why they went, or what it was all about. Certainly it was not always what the scribes and chroniclers said it was about. The more we find ourselves looking at the Crusaders, the more we shall discover that totally conflicting aims and motives were involved. There was the thirst for power and the thirst for land; there was humility and pride; there was the desire for blessedness and the desire to cut the throats of the pagans; there was malice and envy and all the remaining deadly sins. Rarely were men more sinful than when they set out to conquer the Holy Land, and rarely were they more deeply religious, more certain of their faith. Amid all the confusions and uncertainties surrounding the Crusades there existed the one absolute certainty: the Christian faith. Everything else could be argued about, but the existence of Christ as the lord of the worlds was beyond argument.

We look back at the age of the Crusades with a sense of unappeasable longing, for the world was simpler, all questions were answered, every virtue could be measured, and every vice had its appropriate penalty. The world was ordered, finite, crystal clear. However chaotic were men's lives, they fitted into an acceptable and credible pattern. Men lived the sacramental life to a degree that we can now scarcely comprehend. Christ walked by men's sides and was present in the air they breathed. One reason why it is so difficult for us to put ourselves inside the skins of the Crusaders is precisely because we lack the energy of their belief.

There was a directness in the twelfth-century mind which is lacking in our own. They were trained to it, and did not think of acting otherwise. We shall see in their wars how little they debated strategy: they were more likely to hurl themselves on the enemy than to engage in feints and ambushes or to devise elaborate stratagems. Although they were direct, logical and reasonable, they found not the slightest difficulty in believing in miracles, wonders, portents and apparitions, and the closer they came to the Holy Land the more readily they believed in them. Being simultaneously reasonable and unreasonable, they acted with an exact sense of the real world and were not in the least put out if a miracle took place in front of their eyes. They expected to see miraculous things and eagerly awaited them, while remaining the most practical of men.

Each Crusader had his own reasons for going on a Crusade; each had his own vision of what he expected to find when he reached the Holy Land. Above all, he expected to find holiness in a concrete form, something that could be seen, touched, kissed, worshipped, and even carried away. Holiness was in the pathways trodden by Christ, in the mountains and valleys seen by Christ, in the streets of Jerusalem where Christ had wandered. They had no feeling for the changing aspect of the city: the Jerusalem they saw was Christ's Jerusalem, unchanged and eternal; it never occurred to them that Jerusalem had been razed to the ground after Christ's death. The disciples had slept under the same olive trees on the Mount of Olives that the Crusaders saw. On the Mount of the Ascension they could kiss the footprint left by Christ before he ascended to heaven, and in the Church of the Holy Sepulchre they could gaze upon his tomb. All over Jerusalem there were places associated with him and with his disciples, and their closeness to these places gave them the sense of an abiding presence. He belonged to time and was outside time. Indeed, time for the Crusaders existed under two aspects: a system of dates and calendars informed them that more than a thousand years separated them from Christ, and their knowledge of Christ informed them that he was still present, that he was their contemporary, and the thousand years were as nothing.

There were fifty places in Jerusalem associated with Christ, but there was only one they regarded with absolute reverence and awe. This was Christ's tomb. To the medieval mind Christ was most present in the empty tomb. They were not obsessed with the tragedy of his death, they rarely dwelt on the Crucifixion, and the manner of his death was perhaps the least important thing about it. What absorbed their imaginations was less the tragedy of his death than the triumph of the Resurrection. This was the supreme miracle, the miracle that gave meaning to Christian life. In this small space God, wearing the shape of a man, having died, returned to life.

The tomb therefore acquired in their imaginations a very special significance: It was the relic above all relics, the icon above all icons. Here he lay dead; here he threw off the linen bands; here he sprang into the eternal life promised to all Christians. It was almost as though the shadowy tomb was a machine generating eternal life.

There was, however, something very strange and disturbing about the tomb, which had been discovered by Bishop Macarius of Jerusalem after digging through the rubble of the ancient Roman Temple of Aphrodite. The tomb had been found, according to Eusebius, "against all hope" in A.D. 325. In that same year, the Empress Helena, the mother of the Emperor Constantine, came to Jerusalem and discovered three crosses in an underground cavern about eighty feet away from the tomb. Constantine ordered a rotunda to be placed over the tomb and a basilica to be placed over the cavern. The rotunda was called the *Anastasis*, the "Resurrection," and the basilica was called the *Martyrion*, the "Place of Martyrdom." Both were sumptuously decorated with gold and jewels, and both were razed and rebuilt several times between the Persian invasion of A.D. 614 and the arrival of the Crusaders.

When the Crusaders arrived in Jerusalem, they found only the rotunda. The tomb had vanished; there was no hollowed-out rock; there was only empty space surrounded by a jewel box of delicate columns with mosaics on the circular wall. Lamps burned perpetually over a raised slab of marble intended to represent the tomb. But in the eyes of the Crusaders the tomb was still there. For them the representation corresponded to the reality. Their faith was strong enough to permit them to believe in the physical existence of a tomb that no longer existed and therefore could not be seen. They saw it with the eyes of faith.

They saw it too with the eyes of men who had traveled far to see it. They had fought their way to it, waded through blood and suffered starvation and wounds in order to come to this place, and their faith was colored by the hardships and dangers of the journey. Having suffered so much, they found what they expected to find. If the Christian doctrine was true, if Christ was lord of the worlds and the gate of eternal life, then it was necessary for the tomb to exist. According to Pope Urban II, God willed the Crusade in order that the Holy Sepulchre should be wrested from the pagans and placed firmly in the hands of the followers of Christ. God had not willed that the tomb itself should survive. God had willed that the pilgrims should be brought into the presence of Christ's death and Resurrection, and in the minds of the Crusaders there was not the least doubt that it had happened here in this small corner of Jerusalem. They did not ask for precise outlines and verifiable shapes. They asked for Christ, for they believed in him, and they knelt at his tomb, for they believed it could be nowhere else.

We understand the Crusaders better when we realize that, to them, the tomb was not of this world, that it was a divine mystery, and that they were the partakers of the mystery. The tomb was destroyed, and the tomb remained. Its destroyers hammered it into many pieces and the rubble was carted away, and because it was broken and scattered, the tomb lived all the more. Men seek shelter in the shade of a dream. The Crusaders found shelter in a tomb that was also a dream.

Thunder out
of Arabia

I
N Mecca, eight hundred miles south of Jerusalem, in a landscape as bleak and parched as the Judaean wilderness, there existed another empty tomb. This was the *kaaba,* or "cube," where according to Islamic tradition Ishmael and his mother, Hagar, Abraham's Egyptian concubine, were buried. Originally built by Abraham, it was later used as a temple for the worship of Hubal, the red-faced god of power, and al-Uzza, the goddess of the morning star, together with three hundred other gods and goddesses who formed the pantheon of the Arabs before Muhammad destroyed them. Then the *kaaba* was dedicated to Allah, the One God, lord of all universes. There was nothing in it except silver lamps, brooms for sweeping the floor, and the three teakwood columns that supported the roof. Fragments of a black meteorite were inserted in the southeastern wall, and these are kissed by the faithful who walk, and run, around the *kaaba* in obedience to Muhammad's command.

The *kaaba* is a statement of religious belief—four-square, sharp-edged, emblematic of the power believed to reside in the Arab people. Those qualities were already present in these people before the coming of Muhammad. It was their sharpness of intellect and solidity of purpose that were to make them a world power, and Muhammad was therefore justified in retaining that strange unornamented box, which had once housed so many gods, as the symbol of his own powerful faith in Allah, the One God.

The faith of Muhammad was unlike any other that existed at that time. It was compounded out of visions and dreams, the apocrypha learned along the camel routes from Mecca to Damascus, stray bits of learning and tradition, and a vast understanding of the human need for peace and salvation. The Koran, meaning "the Recitations," reads strangely to Western ears. It is a work of fierce intensity and trembling urgency. God speaks, and what he has to say is recorded in tones of absolute authority by a mind singularly equipped to reflect the utmost subtleties of the Arabic language.

The message Muhammad delivers is that God is all-powerful, his hand is everywhere, and there is no escape from him. Just as he is everywhere, so is his mercy. Into this mercy fall all men's accidents and purposes. It is not that God is benevolent—the idea of a benevolent and helping God is foreign to Muhammad's vision—but his mercy is inevitable, uncompromising, absolute. In this assurance Muhammad's followers find their peace.

Muhammad ibn-Abdullah, of the tribe of Quraysh, was born in Mecca about the year A.D. 570. His father died before he was born and his mother, Amina, died when he was a child. As a youth he traveled with the caravans that traded between Mecca and Syria, and he was twenty-five when he married Khadija, a rich widow fifteen years his senior. He was about forty when he first saw visions and heard the voice of the Angel. Out of these visions and voices came the revelations he attributed directly to God.

According to Islamic tradition, Muhammad commanded that the human figure must never be depicted, so he himself is very rarely depicted in Islamic art. On the rare occasions when he is seen, he wears a veil over his face. But his friends remembered him and described him. They spoke of a thickset man with burly shoulders, a rosy skin "like a woman's," a thick, black, curling beard. Most of all they remembered his eyes, which were very large, dark, and melting. The clue to his personality lies perhaps in his rosy skin, for he was no sun-bitten Bedouin of the desert, but a townsman with a townsman's peculiar sensibilities and perplexities.

In a cave on Mount Hira, not far from Mecca, he would spend time meditating. There he became aware one day of the presence of the Angel standing "two bow shots away," watching him. "O Muhammad, you are God's messenger and I am Gabriel," the voice thundered. From the Angel he learned that man was created from a clot of blood and lay under the protection of Allah, the Only God, the All-Merciful, whose mysteries would be revealed to him. Thereafter, day after day, in waking visions, Muhammad was visited by the Angel who expounded mysteries testifying to God's mercy and absolute power in verses that crackle and roar like a brushfire.

Half-learned in the religions of his time, impatient with all of them, Muhammad struck out into unexplored territories with a new style, a new rhythm, speaking urgently in a voice of great power:

> That which striketh!
> What is that which striketh?
> Ah, who will convey to thee what the Striking is?
> The day mankind shall become like scattered moths,
> And the mountains like tufts of carded wool.
> Then those whose scales weigh heavy shall enter Paradise,
> And those whose scales are light shall enter the Abyss.

And who shall convey to thee what the Abyss is?
A raging fire!

(*Sura* ci)

Like Jesus, Muhammad was haunted by the Last Day. The end seemed very near, but instead of simply submitting to the dissolution of the universe, there must be in this waiting time a change of heart, a total submission to God. Muhammad felt that the laws of submission must be discovered, and that men should find the way in which to hold themselves in the light of the coming flames. In these visions, dictated over a long period, Muhammad presented a cosmology of breathtaking simplicity, rounded, complete, and eminently satisfying to the Arab mind.

His torrent of visionary poetry convinced Muhammad's friends that he was indeed a prophet and a messenger of God. Soon he acquired followers and an army. Medina fell, and then Mecca, but these were only the beginnings. The furious pent-up poetry, so memorable and so naked, had the effect of inspiring the Arabs to challenge all their neighbors on behalf of the messenger of God. The Jews must be converted; so must the Christians; all the world must acknowledge the truth of the Koran. Muhammad also proved to be a gifted military commander. His successors were even more gifted. They came like thunder out of Arabia. Within a generation after Muhammad's death in A.D. 632, long-established empires fell like ninepins, and half the known world, from Spain to Persia, fell to the armies he had set in motion.

Out of the blaze of Muhammad's visionary eyes there came a force that shook the world to its foundations.

In July A.D. 640, eight years after Muhammad's death, an Arab army under Amr ibn-al-As stood outside the walls of the great university city of On, the modern Heliopolis, where the Phoenix was born and where Plato had once studied. On was the most sacred of Egyptian cities, and one of the oldest. Egypt was then a province of the Byzantine empire, and the viceroy was Cyrus, Patriarch of Alexandria. The Arabs attacked, Cyrus fled to the north, and soon the Arabs pursued him to Alexandria, where there were huge battlements and siege works and a harbor that included within its ample seawalls the largest naval base in the world. For a thousand years the Greeks and the Romans had been quietly building a city so powerful and so sumptuous that no other city could rival it. Gleaming between the sea and a lake, illuminated by the great lighthouse called the Pharos in the harbor, with powerful ships riding at anchor, and guarded by an army believed to be the best in the world. Alexandria was a bastion of Byzantine power in Africa. The scholarly and ambitious Cyrus looked upon the guerrilla army lodged outside the walls of Alexandria with cunning and distaste. He thought he could bargain with Amr ibn-al-As, while the citizens continued to receive supplies by sea, to attend the racetrack and to worship in the great cathedral of St. Mark overlooking the two harbors. Cyrus was overconfident.

In time, Alexandria fell and the Arabs rode in triumph through the Gate of the Sun and along the Canopic Way, past Alexander the Great's crystal tomb. What they did to Alexandria is described very aptly by E. M. Forster: "Though they had no intention of destroying her, they destroyed her, as a child might a watch."

The Arab army also raged through Palestine and Syria, swung eastward toward Persia, and defeated the army of the Sassanian emperor in the same year that Cyrus surrendered Alexandria. Two years later the Arabs were in command of all of Persia. The Umayyad dynasty, ruling from Damascus, derived from the Persians the habits of splendor. Luxury and corruption set in: the grandsons of the followers of Muhammad preferred to be city dwellers. The same corruption soon became evident in North Africa and Spain, which the Arabs conquered with incredible speed. In A.D. 732, a hundred years after the death of Muhammad, the Arabs poured into France, where they were defeated by the ragged army of Charles of Heristal and the bitterly cold weather.

The Arab tide was turned back, but the Arab empire now extended halfway across the known world from the Pyrenees to Persia. It had made inroads into India, and Arab armies were breaking through the Asiatic outposts of the Byzantine empire, which would endure for another seven hundred years. The Muslims regarded Constantinople, the capital of the Byzantine empire, as the eastern gateway to Europe: it must be captured and all Europe must fall under their sway.

The Christians saw in the religion of Muhammad a mortal enemy to be opposed at all costs. The name of the religion was Islam, which means "submission," "submission to God's purposes." The Christians were not prepared to submit. They regarded Islam as a heresy, a diabolic and dangerous perversion of the truths handed down by Moses, the prophets, Jesus and St. Paul. Islam was monotheism stripped bare, unclouded by ambiguities, without mysteries, without vestments, without panoply, without hierarchies of priests, democratic in its organization, abrupt and simple in its protestations of faith. There are no complex ceremonies in Islam, no Nicene Creed, no Mass, no tinkling of bells. A mosque is usually a walled space open to the sky with a pulpit, a prayer niche, and a tower from which the faithful are called to prayer; the religion, too, is open, spacious, clear-cut, without shadows. God is conceived as an abstraction of infinite power and infinite glory, the source and end of all things. That God should in some mysterious way be divided into the Father, the Son and the Holy Ghost was incomprehensible to the Muslims, who conceived of him as one and indivisible.

Although Islam reserved a special place for Jesus, the Islamic Jesus is almost unrecognizable to Christians. Muhammad tells the story of the

Virgin Birth three times and is deeply moved by it, and he is aware of something supernatural in Jesus, but he has no patience with those who proclaim his divinity. Jesus is a sign, a word, a spirit, an angel; he is also a messenger and a prophet. He could raise the dead, heal the sick, and breathe life into clay birds. He was not crucified in the flesh, for someone else was crucified in his stead. He ascended to heaven when God summoned him, and he will return in the Last Day.

No one knows where Muhammad learned about Jesus. Most likely it was from some lost Gnostic scriptures, or he may have listened to a Christian preacher during his travels. Mary and Jesus "abide in a high place full of quiet and watered with springs"; and there, very largely, they remain. They are peripheral to his main argument, which is concerned with the nature of man, the clot of blood, confronted with the stupendous presence of God, who is both far away and as close to man as his neck artery. Man is naked and defenseless; he has nothing to give God except his utter and total devotion. God, to the Muslims, has no history, while to the Christians the history of God is bound up with the history of Christ.

The two religions had no common ground, or so little that it could scarcely be perceived. It was as though Christianity and Islam were meant to engage in a death struggle, which would end only when one submitted to the other. Yet there were long periods when there was a kind of peace between them. Jerusalem, captured very early by the Arabs, was permitted to retain a Christian community, and the Church of the Holy Sepulchre remained untouched. Charlemagne conducted a long correspondence with Harun al-Rashid, Caliph of Baghdad, who acknowledged the right of the Christians to maintain their church. Harun gave the church over to Charlemagne, who was addressed as "Protector of Jerusalem." Although Charlemagne never visited Jerusalem, he sent a stream of envoys, founded a hospital and library in the Holy City, and paid for their upkeep. Throughout the ninth century, relations between Christians and Muslims were fairly amicable. The Christians demanded only that Jerusalem should be accessible to them, and that pilgrims to the Church of the Holy Sepulchre should be treated reasonably. And so it continued for another century. Even after the destruction of the church by the mad Caliph Hakim, there was peace, for the church was quickly restored. The pilgrims continued to come to Jerusalem, worshipping at the altars in the Church of the Holy Sepulchre, passing freely in and out of the city. It was as though the two religions had reached an accommodation, as though nothing would interrupt the continual flow of pilgrims.

In the middle years of the eleventh century there occurred an event that would cause a drastic change in the military posture of the Muslims in the Near East. The Seljuk Turks, advancing from Central Asia, conquered Persia. Converted to Islam, they moved with the zeal of converts, prosetyliz-ing all the tribes they came upon in their lust for conquest. They had been herdsmen; they became raiders, cavalrymen, living off the earth, setting up their tents wherever they pleased, taking pleasure in sacking cities and leaving only ashes. The once all-powerful Caliph of Baghdad became the servant of the Seljuk Sultan Alp Arslan. In August 1071, the Seljuk army under Alp Arslan confronted the much larger army of the Byzantine Emperor Romanus IV Diogenes near Menzikert north of Lake Van in Armenia. Romanus was an emperor with vast military experience, brave to excess, commanding a hundred thousand well-trained troops, including many Frankish and German mercenaries. There was, however, treachery among his officers; orders were not obeyed. The lightly armed Seljuk cavalry poured thousands of arrows into the tight formations of the Byzantine army, and when the emperor ordered a retreat at the end of the day, his flanks were exposed, his army began to disintegrate, and the Turks rushed in to fill the vacuum created by his retreating troops. Romanus fought bravely; he was seriously wounded in the arm and his horse was killed under him. Captured, he was led to the tent of Alp Arslan in chains. There he was thrown to the ground, and Alp Arslan placed his foot ceremonially on the emperor's neck. The Seljuk sultan half-admired the broad-shouldered Byzantine emperor, and two weeks later the emperor was allowed to go free. Still the defeat was so decisive, so shattering, that the emperor fell from grace in the eyes of the Byzantines, who had no difficulty deposing him. When he returned to Constantinople, he was blinded, and in the following year he died either from the injuries caused by the blinding or of a broken heart.

Although Alp Arslan himself, and his son Malek Shah, had no thought of conquering the Byzantine empire, the chieftains who served under them had different ideas. They poured into the undefended provinces of Anatolia. While the Christians remained in the towns, the invading Turks ravaged the countryside. Gone were the days when the Byzantine empire stretched from Egypt to the Danube and from the borders of Persia to southern Italy. The Turks advanced to Nicaea, less than a hundred miles from Constantinople, and occupied the city, making it the capital of the sultanate that ruled over Asia Minor. The Turks were spreading out in all directions. In the same year that saw the Byzantine defeat at Manzikert, they captured Jerusalem from the Arabs of Egypt on behalf of the Caliph of Baghdad. In 1085 Malek Shah captured Antioch from the Byzantines. Malek Shah himself came to the Palestinian shore and dipped his sword in the waters of the Mediterranean, a ceremony by which he asserted that the Mediterranean itself belonged to him.

The grandson of nomads from Central Asia, Malek Shah had the temperament of an emperor. He was more relentless, more determined, than his more famous father. He ruled in great state and saw himself as the sovereign of all the Near East. His Turks were rougher than the Egyptians; they had come like thunder from the regions north of the Caspian and they possessed to the highest degree what the historian Ibn Khaldun called *assabiya*, the determination based on a communion of interests that characterized the early Arab conquerors. The Arabs had made accommodations with the Christians; the Turks were more sure of themselves.

Christendom was reeling from the Turkish invasions. In a single generation Asia Minor had fallen into their hands. The Byzantine empire had lost the sources of its greatest wealth. Christians could no longer be assured that they could journey to Jerusalem without being arrested or sold into slavery or ill treated in other ways. The Turks were fanatical Muslims, determined to exact the last ounce of power from their victories. But their survival as a united people depended on their leader, and when Malek Shah died in 1091, the empire was divided up among his sons and nephews, whose hatred for one another contributed to the early success of the Crusaders when at last they made their way across Asia Minor in order to recover Jerusalem.

In 1081, Alexius Comnenus, who had served in the army of Romanus IV Diogenes as a general fighting against the inroads of the Turks, came to the throne at the age of thirty-three. He was an able commander in the field and uncompromising in his determination to regain the lost provinces of his empire. His daughter, Anna Comnena, wrote a history of his reign that is among the acknowledged masterpieces of Byzantine literature. Through her eyes he appears as a superb diplomat, a man who moved surefootedly amid treacheries, who knew his own value and was both forceful and humble in dealing with his friends and enemies. He reigned for thirty-seven years, recaptured some of the lost provinces, and there were few Byzantine emperors who reigned so long or fought so well.

When Alexius Comnenus came to the throne, the empire was in disarray. Although the Balkan provinces had been recaptured from Robert Guiscard, the Norman-Sicilian adventurer who founded his own kingdom in southern Italy and Sicily, he was confronted with dangers along the long Danube border from the Oghuz, Kuman, and Pecheneg Turks, half brothers to the Turks in Asia Minor, and from Slavs and Bulgars. Only a few coastal cities in Asia Minor remained in his hands. It was necessary at all costs to push back the frontiers of the sultanate of Roum. He appealed for military assistance to the pope and to the Western princes who might be sympathetic to his cause. They were asked to raise armies, to march to Constantinople and to join forces under the banner of Christendom against the infidels. He recounted the atrocities committed by the enemy and pointed to the peculiar sanctity of Constantinople as the guardian of so many relics of Christ. Constantinople and the Byzantine empire must be saved, Jerusalem must be reconquered, and the *pax Christiana* must be established in the Near East. A copy of his letter to Robert, Count of Flanders, a cousin of William the Conqueror, has been preserved. The emperor speaks with mingled anguish and pride, despair and humility, and from time to time there appears a faint note of humor.

EXCERPTS FROM A LETTER FROM THE EMPEROR ALEXIUS COMNENUS TO ROBERT, COUNT OF FLANDERS, WRITTEN FROM CONSTANTINOPLE IN A.D. 1093.

TO THE LORD AND GLORIOUS COUNT, Robert of Flanders, and to the generality of princes of the kingdom, whether lay or ecclesiastical, from Alexius Comnenus, Emperor of Byzantium.

O illustrious count and great consoler of the faith, I am writing in order to inform Your Prudence that the very saintly empire of Greek Christians is daily being persecuted by the Pechenegs and the Turks. . . . The blood of Christians flows in unheard-of scenes of carnage, amidst the most shameful insults. . . . I shall merely describe a very few of them. . . .

The enemy has the habit of circumcising young Christians and Christian babies above the baptismal font. In derision of Christ they let the blood flow into the font. Then they are forced to urinate in the font. . . . Those who refuse to do so are tortured and put to death. They carry off noble matrons and their daughters and abuse them like animals. . . .

Then, too, the Turks shamelessly commit the sin of sodomy on our men of all ages and all ranks . . . and, O misery, something that has never been seen or heard before, on bishops. . . .

Furthermore they have destroyed or fouled the holy places in all manner of ways, and they threaten to do worse. Who does not groan? Who is not filled with compassion? Who does not reel back with horror? Who does not offer his prayers to heaven? For almost the entire land has been invaded by the enemy from Jerusalem to Greece . . . right up to Thrace. Already there is almost nothing left for them to conquer except Constantinople, which they threaten to conquer any day now, unless God and the Christians of the Latin rite come quickly to our aid. They have also invaded the Propontis . . . passing below the walls of Constantinople with a fleet of two hundred ships . . . stolen from us. They forced the rowers against their will to follow the sea-roads chosen by them, and with threats and menaces, as we have said, they hoped to take possession of Constantinople either by land or by sea.

Therefore in the name of God and because of the true piety of the generality of Greek Christians, we implore you to bring to this city all the faithful soldiers of Christ . . . to bring me aid and to bring aid to the Greek Christians. . . . Before Constantinople falls into their power, you should do everything you can to be worthy of receiving heaven's benediction, an ineffable and glorious reward for your aid. It would be better that Constantinople falls into your hands than into the hands of the pagans. This city possesses the most holy relics of the Saviour [including] . . . part of the True Cross on which he was crucified. . . .

And if it should happen that these holy relics should offer no temptation to the pagans, and if they wanted only gold, then they would find in this city more gold than exists in all the rest of the world. The churches of Constantinople are loaded with a vast treasure of gold and silver, gems and precious stones, mantles and cloths of silk, sufficient to decorate all the churches of the world. . . . And then, too, there are the treasuries in the possession of our noblemen, not to speak of the treasure belonging to the merchants who are not noblemen. And what of the treasure belonging to the emperors, our predecessors? No words can describe this wealth of treasure, for it includes not only the treasuries of the emperors but also those of the ancient Roman emperors brought here and concealed in the palace. What more can I say? What can be seen by human eyes is nothing in comparison with the treasure that remains concealed.

Come, then, with all your people and give battle with all your strength, so that all this treasure shall not fall into the hands of the Turks and Pechenegs. . . . Therefore act while there is still time lest the kingdom of the Christians shall vanish from your sight and, what is more important, the Holy Sepulchre shall vanish. And in your coming you will find your reward in heaven, and if you do not come, God will condemn you.

If all this glory is not sufficient for you, remember that you will find all those treasures and also the most beautiful women of the Orient. The incomparable beauty of Greek women would seem to be a sufficient reason to attract the armies of the Franks to the plains of Thrace.

In this way, mingling allurements and enticements with intimations of the final disaster that would overwhelm the community of Christians if the Turks and Pechenegs succeeded in conquering what was left of the Byzantine empire, Alexius Comnenus appealed to Robert of Flanders to come to his aid. The letter contained admissions of terrible defeats and was sustained by a vast pride, but it also provided a picture of the world as he saw it, with its pressing dangers and wildest hopes. Two images prevailed: the atrocities committed by the enemy, and the spiritual and material wealth of Constantinople, last bastion against the Turks.

The letter was addressed not only to Robert of Flanders but to Western Christendom. Pope Urban II read it and was deeply moved. Robert of Flanders would eventually take part in the Crusade. And now very slowly and with immense difficulty there came into existence the machinery that would bring the armies of the West to Constantinople and later to Jerusalem.

In the Fields
of Clermont

HE most powerful force in Western Europe at this time was the
Church, which asserted its power in open and subtle ways. In every
village there was a priest, in every large city a bishop, in every
princedom a legate representing the pope. The work of the Church was
intertwined with the work of the government, and there were many places
where the bishop was both an earthly and spiritual ruler. Charlemagne
had called upon the clergy as well as his soldiers to create an empire. The
Church was everywhere: in men's thoughts and prayers, in the judgment
halls, in the prince's court. It was in the way men addressed one another, in
the rhythms of their writing and their speech, and it was present at their
births, their marriages and deaths. It was the all-pervading sea in which the
principalities and kingdoms swam.

The Church possessed its own momentum: it persisted even when the
popes were weak or incompetent. Between A.D. 896 and A.D. 904 eight popes
succeeded one another. But the monk Hildebrand, who reigned as Pope
Gregory VII from 1073-1086, restored the papacy to full authority. He,
too, received appeals from Constantinople to mount a Crusade against the
Turks, but he was too busy reorganizing the Church to spend his energy on
Byzantine affairs. The time was not yet ripe for the Crusade.

Then, with the coming of Urban II to the throne in 1088, the Crusade
became eminently possible. The new pope was practical, and he possessed
a peculiarly French sense of reaching to the heart of a problem. He was by
birth a French nobleman. His original name was Eudes de Lagery, and he
was born in the family castle near Châtillon-sur-Marne in about A.D. 1042.
He rose rapidly in the church hierarchy to become a canon of St. John
Lateran in Rome. Suddenly he abandoned Rome, and we next see him
wearing the habit of a simple monk at Cluny, then the intellectual center of
French Catholicism. The abbot of Cluny made him a prior and sent him on
missions to Rome. Gregory VII admired him, made him bishop of Ostia,
and then a cardinal. Cardinal Eudes was sent as a papal legate to Germany,

where he acquitted himself well. An ancient portrait shows him in his cardinal's robes, bald except for tufts of hair above his ears but with a long beard and an unusually heavy mustache. He looks singularly robust and determined. This was the man who would become Pope Urban II. This was the man who would call the Crusade into existence.

It was not by any means a sudden call based upon an emotional sympathy for the Christians who had suffered in Asia Minor and the Holy Land. It was more, and it was less. Urban II was asserting the pope's leadership in the West, he was attempting to dominate the quarreling princes of Europe by declaring a holy war in the East and the Truce of God in the West, and he was trying to give direction to a divided Europe at a time when the quarrels were becoming dangerous not only to the papacy but to the very survival of Christendom. Although Charles Martel had effectively stopped the advance of the Muslims into France, the possibility of a Muslim breakthrough from Spain was very real. To ensure that France remained free of Muslim influence, Urban II called upon the French nobility to arm themselves and attack Islam in the Near East. In the most limited sense he was concerned that French noblemen should give a good account of themselves, for he was himself a French nobleman and his chief sympathies were with France.

Thus, the character of the pope gave color to the Crusade, which remained essentially French and aristocratic throughout its two-hundred-year history. When he proclaimed the necessity of the Crusade at a general gathering of the clergy and the laity at Clermont on November 27, 1095, he was speaking as a Frenchman to Frenchmen concerning a matter of peculiar relevance to France.

"Frenchmen!" he began. "You who are chosen and beloved by God, as is shown by your many achievements, you who are set apart from all other peoples by the particular situation of your country, and also by your catholic faith and the honor of Holy Church."

The pope spoke in French, standing on a podium in the midst of an immense field crowded with people of all classes from poor peasants to princes, and around the podium stood an army of archbishops, bishops, abbots, prelates and priests. He had already spent many days in council, discussing a host of important matters concerning the machinery of the Church, the morals of princes, the right of sanctuary, and that Truce of God which was very close to his heart. By the Truce of God he meant to outlaw fighting of any kind from Sunday to Wednesday, and to put an absolute ban on fighting involving priests, monks, women, laborers, and merchants on any day of the week. At Clermont the pope was able to impose a further ban on fighting on certain religious holidays. There was some irony in the fact that the pope who called so strenuously for peace in France was also calling for a holy war in the Holy Land.

In fact, the two ideas were closely, even intimately, connected. He was aware that a war against the Turks would divert the energies expended by Christians in killing other Christians. It was a time when the princes and princelings of France were bristling with new-found powers, invading each other's territory, sacking towns, relentlessly skirmishing. There were endless dynastic disputes, and to become a prince or count meant waging war against one's own relatives. Urban II hoped to establish the principle that the Church was the supreme arbiter over earthly kingdoms with the power to authorize wars and to prevent wars, especially the wars in France.

When he spoke on that cold November day, he was about fifty-three years old, but he had the vigor of a much younger man. He had a resounding voice, which was heard across the field by thousands of people. His speech was evidently prepared with great care, and copies of it would be made available to ecclesiastical officials and the princes who attended; it was the pope's intention that his words should be heard all over France and that they should be studied and remembered. While his essential message was that the time called for a holy war against the Turks, he was also concerned with the intellectual and spiritual underpinnings of the adventure.

Urban II was deeply moved by St. Jerome's interpretation of the Prophet Daniel, and wanted his listeners to be roused by it. As St. Jerome saw it, the time would come when the Antichrist would set up his tents on the Mount of Olives and sit in Jerusalem on a throne in Solomon's Temple, "as though he were God." His first task would be to kill the three kings of Egypt, Africa, and Ethiopia, all expected to be Christian kings. Their deaths would encourage the soldiers of Christ to arise against him, and the Christians would supplant him when Jerusalem was surrendered to them. Then the Antichrist would die and the reign of Christ would be established over the earth.

But the visions of the Prophet Daniel, as interpreted by St. Jerome, were of less importance to his audience, who were instead whipped into a state of excitement by the thought of the Church of the Holy Sepulchre being in the possession of the Turks, and that Christians attempting to go there on pilgrimage were being molested and killed. Urban II referred to the Turks as Persians, and in fact the Turks had conquered Persia and had spilled over its borders to conquer vast territories in the Near East. At the beginning of his sermon he declared that the enemy was everywhere committing atrocities against the Christians, and it was necessary to put an end to these atrocities. He said:

> Distressing news has come to us . . . that the people of the Persian kingdom, an accursed race, a race utterly alienated from God, a generation that set not their heart aright and whose spirit was not steadfast with God, has invaded Christian lands and devastated them with sword, pillage and fire. Some of these Christians have been made captive and taken to Persia, and some have been

tortured to death. Many of God's churches have been violated and others have been made to serve their own religious rites. They have ruined the altars with filth and defilement. They circumsized Christians and smeared the blood on the altars or poured it into the baptismal fonts. It amused them to kill Christians by opening up their bellies and drawing out the end of their intestines, which they then tied to a stake. Then they flogged their victims and made them walk around and around the stake until their intestines had spilled out and they fell dead on the ground. Others were tied to stakes and shot through with arrows, and still others were held down with necks extended, and they would see whether it was possible to cut off a head with a single blow of a naked sword. What shall I say about the abominable rape of women? On this subject it may be worse to speak than to remain silent. . . .

Who shall avenge these wrongs, who shall recover these lands, if not you? You are the race upon whom God has bestowed glory in arms, greatness of spirit, physical energy, and the courage to humble the proud locks of those who resist you.

Rise up, then, and remember the virile deeds of your ancestors, the glory and renown of Charlemagne, of his son Louis, and all your other kings who destroyed the kingdoms of the pagans and planted the holy church in their lands. You should be especially aroused by the knowledge that the Church of the Holy Sepulchre is now in the hands of unclean nations and that the holy places are shamelessly misused and sacrilegiously defiled with their filth. Oh, most valiant knights, descendants of unconquerable ancestors, remember the courage of your forefathers and do not dishonor them!

Urban II was like another Moses, proclaiming that the knights of France were the true inheritors of the land of milk and honey, the only people deserving to be the guardians of the Church of the Holy Sepulchre.

Near him, in that vast audience, were the princes who had come to him because he had summoned them, and now he addressed them with a special vehemence. They were the men who commanded armies and were continually fighting against other Frenchmen, and he was determined that their fighting should cease in the Truce of God. He did not mince his words. He said:

Christian warriors, who continually and vainly seek pretexts for war, rejoice, for you have today found a true pretext. You, who have so often been the terror of your fellow men, go and fight against the barbarians, go and fight for the deliverance of the holy places. You, who sell for vile pay the strength of your arms to the fury of others, armed with the sword of the Machabees, go and merit an eternal reward. If you triumph over your enemies, the kingdoms of the East will be your reward. If you are conquered, you will have the glory of dying in the very same place as Jesus Christ, and God will never forget that he found you in the holy battalions.

This now is the time to prove that you are animated by true courage, the time to expiate the violence committed in the bosom of peace, the many victories purchased at the expense of justice and humanity. If you must have blood, bathe in the blood of the infidels. I speak to you with harshness because my ministry obliges me to do so. Soldiers of Hell, become soldiers of the living God!

His words were intended to shock, and also to heal. Christ's words sustained his argument. In the mythology he was developing throughout his sermon, he was relying on all those cryptic and well-known words where Christ demands that his followers should abandon their fathers, mothers, wives, and children, and for this abandonment they would be rewarded a hundredfold and enter eternal life. Significantly, it was when he was reciting these words that the crowd suddenly roared back at him: "God wills it!" *"Dieu li volt!"* cried the northerners, and the southerners cried, *"Diex le volt!"* It was at that very moment that the Crusade came into existence.

"Yes, indeed," Urban II answered. "Yes, it is the will of God. You today see the accomplishment of the word of our Saviour, who promised to be in the midst of the faithful, when assembled in his name; it is He who dictated to you the words that I have heard. Let them be your war cry, and let them announce everywhere the presence of the God of armies!"

At this point Urban II raised up the crucifix.

"It is Christ himself who comes from the tomb and presents to you his cross. It will be the sign raised among the nations, which is to gather again the dispersed children of Israel. Wear it upon your shoulders and your breasts. Let it shine upon your arms and upon your standards. It will be to you the surety of victory or the palm of martyrdom. It will increasingly remind you that Christ died for you, and that it is your duty to die for him!"

There was another uproar, a chorus of deafening voices, and then there was a hush as Cardinal Gregorio dei Guidone, who later occupied the papal throne as Innocent II, pronounced a general confession. They all fell on their knees, beat their breasts, and confessed their sins.

The first to speak after the cardinal was Adhémar of Monteil, Bishop of Le Puy, who asked that he be allowed to enter the way of God and to take the cross from the pope's hand. Urban II gave it to him. It was not a cross of wood or metal, but of cloth, which was sewed upon the right shoulder of a coat or mantle or fastened to the front of a helmet. Soon, as though from nowhere, there came strips of cloth cut in the shape of a cross, and everybody was busily sewing them on. The precise symbols of the Crusade had now been found: the cry "God wills it" and the small cross fastened to the shoulder. These symbols were important: they were simple, they evoked the idea of the Crusade, and they provided the soldiers of Christ with a war cry and an easily identifiable badge.

After Clermont, Urban II continued to travel across France, holding councils in Nimes in the south, Tours and Rouen in the north. He seemed to be everywhere. He was like an army on the march, blessing the people, encouraging all men to abandon their families and join the *militia Christi*, that army which he had summoned into existence. Bishop Adhémar was appointed papal legate to the Crusaders, charged with the ordering of the enterprise. He would be the pope's representative in the field, in theory commanding the princes and soldiers who fought against the Turks. Urban hoped that under the vigorous command of Adhémar, Bishop of Le Puy, this army of French soldiers and peasants would conquer Jerusalem in his own lifetime.

EXCERPTS FROM A LETTER FROM POPE URBAN II TO THE CRUSADERS IN FLANDERS WRITTEN IN DECEMBER 1095.

URBAN THE BISHOP, SERVANT OF THE SERVANTS of God, to all the faithful, both princes and subjects, waiting in Flanders: apostolic grace, and blessing.

We believe that your battalions have long since learned from many sources that barbarism and terror have been visited upon the churches of God and laid waste entire regions of the East. Worse still . . . the enemy has enslaved the churches and the holy city of Christ, glorified by his passion and his resurrection. Grieving over this terrible news with pious concern, we journeyed through Gaul and devoted ourselves largely to urging the princes of this land and all their subjects to free the churches of the East. . . .

We have appointed our most beloved son, Adhémar, Bishop of Le Puy, as commander of this . . . expedition, in our stead. Those who may wish to undertake the journey should therefore obey his orders, as though they were our own, and submit themselves fully to loosings or bindings, as far as they shall seem to belong to such an office. If there are any of your people whom God has inspired to this vow, let them know that the bishop with

God's help will set out on the Day of the Assumption of the Blessed Mary, and they can then attach themselves to his army.

But bishops have very rarely been able to command armies, and inevitably the Crusaders would be commanded by princes and warriors. At the same time, if many were aroused to follow warrior princes, men of proven military skill, others saw the Crusade in another light altogether. They had been excited and buoyed up by Urban's speech in the fields, but they were even more excited and buoyed up by the sermons of itinerant preachers, the most remarkable of them being Peter the Hermit. For some years he had been preaching up and down France about the need to free the Holy Sepulchre from the Turks. He claimed to have had a vision of Christ in the Church of the Holy Sepulchre itself, in which he had commanded him to rouse the people against the Turks, promising that for all those who took part in the expedition the gates of Paradise would open. Apparently without consulting the pope, Peter the Hermit ordered that all those who wished to join the Crusade should meet at Cologne the following Easter Day. He was in a hurry. Although most of these Crusaders were poor folk, untrained in war, he believed they would overcome the Turks by faith alone.

The Crusade of the Poor

WE would like to know more about Peter the Hermit, who had the honor of leading the First Crusade across Europe and into the lands of the Turks, but we have only brief glimpses of him. He led his people to total destruction, but men still revered him and continued to rely on his judgment. He was more like a force of nature than a man.

He was a very small man, insignificant in appearance, and they called him "Cucu-Peter." It has been suggested that "cucu" means "cowl," and the name meant "Cowled Peter," but it is more likely that "Cucu" was a term of endearment. He was a hermit who wore a monk's costume, but it is possible that he was neither priest nor monk. He led his followers by the strength of his character and by the strength of his belief in the necessity of saving the Holy Sepulchre from the Turks. While Pope Urban II and the Bishop of Le Puy appealed to the princes and the knights, Peter the Hermit spoke to the poor peasants, the uprooted, the prostitutes, and all those who wanted to escape from bondage. No one ever thought of Urban II as being Christlike, but in the popular imagination Peter the Hermit, with his humility and his power, was as close to Christ as it is possible to be. They believed he carried with him a letter written in heaven, summoning the people of Europe to free the Holy Sepulchre.

Only two of the chroniclers claim to have set eyes on him. One was Anna Comnena, Princess of Byzantium, and the other was Guibert de Nogent, who had the luck to see him as he left Amiens at the very beginning of his Crusade:

> . . . He was surrounded by such great throngs, received such enormous gifts, and was lauded with such fame for holiness that I do not remember anyone to have been held in like honor. He was very generous to the poor from the wealth that had been given him. He reclaimed prostitutes and provided them with husbands, not without dowry from him; and everywhere with an amazing

Visit us at
www.shutterbug.net

BUSINESS REPLY MAIL
FIRST-CLASS MAIL   PERMIT NO 273   FLAGLER BEACH FL

POSTAGE WILL BE PAID BY ADDRESSEE

shutterbug®

PO BOX 421190
PALM COAST FL   32142-7708

authority he restored peace and concord in place of strife. Whatever he did or said was regarded as little short of divine, to such an extent that hairs were snatched from his mule as relics. This we ascribe not so much to the popular love for truth as for novelty.

He wore a plain woolen shirt with a hood and over this a cloak without sleeves, both extending to his ankles, and his feet were bare. He lived on wine and fish: he hardly ever, or never, ate bread.

To understand the extraordinary influence of Peter the Hermit over the people of northern France and Germany we must go to someone like Mahatma Gandhi in our own time. A small, ugly man who walked barefoot and cared nothing for possessions, who was visibly one of the people and could talk to them in their own language and always with authority, Peter the Hermit had nothing whatsoever in common with the great princes who were beginning to arm their followers and amass the wealth necessary for the long journey to Jerusalem. Toward these princes Peter the Hermit was likely to behave as Gandhi behaved toward the maharajas. He was indifferent to them, and they lived in a world which had nothing to do with his world. He was dedicated to the idea of the Crusade, and he was able to convince the peasants that they, too, should be dedicated to it and that they could share in the glory of its success.

Peter the Hermit rode out of Amiens early in March 1096, five months before Urban had—optimistically—hoped his forces would gather at Flanders to set out. In fact they didn't set out until August 1097. He was accompanied by a huge crowd of the faithful. Women and children were in the crowd, the old and the young, the poor and the not-so-poor. They had all heard his sermons and exhortations, and they came freely, having sold their possessions except for the carts, horses, bedding, and food they needed for the journey. They were a joyful company, singing hymns, and it appears that music was played continually on the march. They came from all the provinces of France. There were even Scotsmen who came, according to Guibert de Nogent, "wearing short tunics of bristling fur which left their knees bare and with their baggage slung over their shoulders." There were also pilgrims who came from unknown lands and who indicated their desire to join the Crusade by placing one index finger over another. All of the pilgrims wore strips of cloth shaped like an X on their shoulders, in memory of the heavy cross carried by Christ to Calvary. At night they slept under tents, which were no more than swathes of cloth stretched across poles. And during this first stage of their march, they were orderly and obedient.

While Peter the Hermit remained the undisputed spiritual leader, five knights, all belonging to the same family, served as the military leaders. They were Walter de Poissy, and his four nephews—Walter, William, Matthew, and Simon. Walter de Poissy died on the march, and it was the first of these nephews, known as Walter Sans-Avoir, who served as their commander in chief, as much as a man can ever be said to command a raggle-taggle army. He had squandered his patrimony and lived for many years as a mercenary. He was not an especially good soldier but he was an admirable diplomat, a brave man, a skilled negotiator, and a faithful lieutenant to Peter the Hermit. The army reached Cologne on April 10, which was Holy Saturday. A few days later, Walter Sans-Avoir decided that the time had come to lead the first columns in the direction of Constantinople, and he set out with Peter's blessing. This was the vanguard of an army of perhaps a hundred thousand men, women, and children, all of them wearing the cross on their shoulders, all of them determined to reach the Church of the Holy Sepulchre.

Walter Sans-Avoir's column probably numbered about ten thousand men. William of Tyre tells us that there were few knights among them, and it is likely that there were no other knights at all. They had considerable sums of money, few baggage carts, only the most primitive weapons—swords, lances, axes, maces. Walter showed his diplomatic ability when the columns reached the Hungarian frontier. Hungary had only recently been converted to Christianity by St. Stephen, and Coloman, King of Hungary, had no desire to let ten thousand armed men pass through his country. Walter was able to convince him that the Crusaders offered no threat to his subjects: order would be preserved, everything would be paid for, and no harm would come to the Hungarians. On this assurance, Coloman gave his permission for them to continue their march. The people were friendly, and they reached the frontier in an orderly fashion except for a brief skirmish in a place called Semlin, where some Hungarians fell upon a handful of hapless Crusaders, beat them, stripped them, and hung their cloths and armor on the walls of the town. This small incident would have important consequences later. Meanwhile the army crossed the Save River without difficulty and marched to Belgrade in the Byzantine province of Bulgaria.

The governor of Belgrade had received no advance warning of their coming, and the sight of the ragged army made him fearful. When Walter asked permission to buy food, he was told there was none to spare, the harvest was not in, and he should seek food elsewhere. The governor was adamant. When Walter's powers of diplomacy failed him, a few of his men took matters in their own hands. They found some herds of cattle and flocks of sheep and drove them by force into their own camp. The Bulgarians took to arms to prevent the plunder. At some distance from the city they found about 150 cattle thieves in the process of carrying off cattle, and they attacked. The cattle thieves took refuge in a church and the Bulgarians set fire to it, burning all of them to death.

Walter Sans-Avoir continued his march through the forests of Bulgaria until he reached a town then known as Stralicia, which was probably Sofia.

he governor was kindly disposed to him and agreed to furnish a market
here goods could be purchased at a fair price. When they set off for
onstantinople he gave them guides, after keeping them in the town until
essengers had been sent to the emperor to warn him of their coming. The
mperor was surprised; he had been in correspondence with the princes
nd thought the Crusaders would be entering Byzantine territory in the
utumn. He seems to have known nothing whatsoever about Peter the
ermit's army of poor folk, but with his usual courtesy he received Walter
ans-Avoir in Constantinople. He offered the Crusaders lodgings and a
arketplace outside the city walls. He learned that Peter the Hermit would
on be arriving with the main army. He may have realized that the
rusade would not have the character he envisioned. If vast numbers of
oor, unarmed, or insufficiently armed people were coming to Constan-
nople on their way to Jerusalem, then it was incumbent on him to take
recautions. Above all, he could not permit them to enter the city or to
tablish any power base in the city or in the neighborhood.

Peter the Hermit's army set out from Cologne about ten days after the
anguard left. This vast, unwieldy army, soon to be augmented by Swabi-
ns and Bavarians, reached the frontiers of Hungary without incident, and
nce again King Coloman received the soldiers graciously. Peter the Her-
it gave orders that there should be no pillage, and there was none until
e Crusaders reached Semlin, where they found the arms of their friends
anging like trophies on the walls. Incensed, and perhaps believing that
any of Walter Sans-Avoir's men had been killed and that these trophies
ere deliberate provocations, they rioted. The riot turned into a pitched
attle, in which the Hungarians were defeated. This was the first big battle
aged by the Crusaders. Ironically it was fought between Christians.
bout four thousand Hungarians were killed, and the chroniclers claimed
at the Crusaders lost only a hundred men. Peter the Hermit may have
nown nothing about this massacre for many days, because he was with an
dvance column that had already entered Byzantine territory.

By this time he seems to have lost control of the army, which moved by its
wn momentum. He might give orders that the army should pay for
verything it took from the countryside, but his orders were rarely obeyed.
had become a river in flood, sweeping away everything in its path. When
e people of Belgrade saw the army coming, they fled to the mountains.
he Crusaders, feeling that the city had been abandoned to them, set fire to
. Then they set off for Nish, reaching it after a grueling seven-day march
rough the forests.

The emperor had established a large garrison at Nish, which was there-
re capable of defending itself. Once more Peter the Hermit asked for
rovisions, which were provided, and for guides, which seem also to have
en provided. The governor, however, was wary and asked for hostages
gainst their promise of good conduct. Peter the Hermit gave the hostages.

There appeared to be complete agreement between Peter and the governor
and no further incidents were expected. The Crusaders marched on, Pete
riding on a donkey at the head of the army.

But the worst of all incidents was about to happen. There were som
unruly Germans in the rear guard, and it amused them to set fire to som
country houses outside the walls of Nish and to some water mills situate
on the banks of the river. The governor was shocked and angry. He decide
to teach them a lesson, and ordered his well-trained soldiers to attacl
Peter's rear guard, capture the incendiaries, and take more hostages. Thos
captured were put to death. Then matters got out of hand. Innocent peopl
perished; baggage trains were seized; women, girls, boys, and old people
who could not keep up with the rest of the army, were arrested, yoke
together, and led into captivity. The governor, usually calm and intelli
gent, overreacted and permitted his soldiers to harass the rear guar
unmercifully. The massacre only came to an end when Peter the Hermi
hearing that something terrible had happened, rode back in search c
Byzantine officers who would be able to explain the situation to him.

Peter learned that the people who had been attacked were not entirel
innocent. They had provoked the Byzantines. The townspeople of Nisl
had rushed to aid the Byzantines in the massacre. Their pent-up hatred fo
Peter's army exploded. In the fighting, about ten thousand of Peter's me
were killed or led away into captivity by the enraged Byzantines. For thre
days the fighting continued. Peter saw his army disintegrating. There wa
little he could do but wait out the crisis. Gradually he was able to restor
order. He established his camp on a hill at some distance from Nish an
sent out heralds to seek out the broken remnants of his army. He was i
such a state of despair that he talked of giving up the expedition altogethe

Then, help came from an unexpected quarter. A messenger from th
emperor arrived at his camp with good news. Standing in the midst of th
exhausted leaders of the expedition, the messenger read from an imperia
rescript:

> Noble and illustrious men, a rumor has reached our ears that
> serious charges of an unsavory nature have been brought against
> you. They say you have done great violence to the people of our
> land who are our subjects, and that you have stirred up quarrels
> and disturbances. Therefore, if you ever hope to find favor in the
> sight of our majesty, we enjoin upon you, by our authority, that
> you do not presume to remain in any of our cities for more than
> three days, and that you will lead your expedition as quickly as
> possible to Constantinople with steady and harmonious leader-
> ship. We shall give you guides and we will cause you to be
> furnished with the necessary food at a just price.

The olive branch from the emperor came at exactly the right moment. Peter gladly accepted the invitation, and the ragged army set off for Constantinople in good heart. Money was given to him, for he had lost the baggage carts that contained his treasury; mules and horses were provided; and in all the towns they passed through they were given food. The emperor's generosity continued until at last the army reached Constantinople on or about August 1, 1096. Walter Sans-Avoir had arrived in the city two weeks earlier.

When Peter was received in audience by the emperor, he was voluble in his gratitude and convincing in his description of the trials he had passed through at the hands of the Turks when he was living in Jerusalem some years earlier. He said that a divine voice had urged him to bring a vast army to the Holy Land, and he had returned to France to organize a Crusade which would save the Church of the Holy Sepulchre for Christians. Impressed by his speech and his manner, the emperor gave him splendid gifts. Peter wanted to march against the Turks immediately. The emperor suggested that it would be wiser for him to remain in camp until the coming of the army of the princes, but Peter was determined. Five days later, at Peter's request, the remnant of the once great army of poor folk, now numbering less than thirty thousand men, women, and children, was ferried across the Bosphorus.

They pitched camp in a small place called Helenopolis. There they rested for a few days, recuperating from their adventures and receiving gifts of food from the emperor. According to William of Tyre, the emperor's bounty was so great that they were incited to arrogance by their well-being. Against the emperor's repeated warnings, they insisted on going to war against the Turks, although they were ill prepared, knew nothing about fighting the Turks and nothing about the geography of Asia Minor.

The army of the poor was not the elite army of knights the emperor had called for. Though he half-admired Peter the Hermit, he had no confidence in his leadership nor any hope that his unruly, cantankerous, pathetic soldiers would amount to anything. Integrated into the army of the princes they might serve as laborers, scouts, water-carriers, or grooms, but they were not a fighting force.

Near Helenopolis was a fortified camp formerly occupied by English mercenaries. The Greeks called it Cibotos, the Franks called it Civetot. Here the army rested and debated the coming offensive against the Turks, and when Peter the Hermit explained that this was not to be contemplated until the great army of the princes crossed the Bosphorus, they simply disregarded him and relieved him of his authority. There were some Germans and Italians in the army of the poor, and they elected a certain Rainald to be their leader, while Geoffrey Burel, who had been Peter's chief military adviser, was elected leader of the Franks. Peter was relegated to the

position of ambassador to the court of Byzantium and charged with obtain
ing as much assistance as possible for the Crusaders.

The savage momentum of the army of the poor survived its transplanta
tion to the shores of Asia. In their restlessness they began to attack sur
rounding Christian villages, murdering and plundering; then they ad
vanced farther and attacked the villages within the Turkish frontier, which
were also inhabited by Christians. All their plunder was sold to Greek
sailors at Civetot; all their success was at the expense of defenseless villager
who shared their own faith.

Thus emboldened, the Franks decided to attack Nicaea, the capital of the
Seljuk Sultan Kilij Arslan. They plundered the villages around Nicaea
drove off huge herds of sheep and cattle, caroused and murdered as the
pleased. Anna Comnena wrote that they had the unpleasant habit o
impaling babies on wooden spits and roasting them over a fire. There is ne
doubt that they were merciless. But Nicaea was a very large walled city with
huge defensive towers, a large garrison, capable commanders. A Turkish
column raced out of the city and there was a pitched battle. The Frank
were able to flee from the battlefield with much of their booty, and if the
had not conquered Nicaea, they had acquired the wealth of many villages

Then it was the turn of the Germans and Italians under Rainald, abou
six thousand men, who imagined they would do even better. They marche
beyond Nicaea to a fortress called Xerigordon, which was captured with
out any difficulty because it was undefended. Here they found all the
provisions they could wish for. They would have been well advised to tak
the stores and hurry back to Civetot. Instead, they remained in the castle
enjoying their good fortune. Then, on September 21, 1096, the Turk
arrived in force, surrounded the castle, and conquered it eight days late
massacring all those who refused to abjure their Christian faith. Th
unknown author of the *Gesta Francorum* describes the horrors of the siege

> The Turks then invested the castle and cut off the water supply.
> Our men were terribly afflicted by thirst. They bled their horses
> and asses to drink the blood. Some let their belts and handker-
> chiefs down into a cistern, and squeezed the liquid into their
> mouths, while others urinated into their fellows' cupped hands
> and drank. Still others dug up the moist earth and lay down on
> their backs and spread the earth over their breasts, being so dry
> with thirst. The bishops and priests encouraged our men and
> admonished them not to despair. . . .
> Then the commander of the Germans agreed to betray his
> companions to the Turks. Pretending to go out in order to fight
> them, he fled to them with many of his men. The remainder were
> put to death unless they were willing to betray God. Others, who
> had been captured alive, were divided among them, like sheep;

and there were some who were put up as targets and shot with arrows, and still others they sold or gave away, like animals. And they took their prisoners to their own homes, to Khorasan, Antioch, or Aleppo, wherever they lived. These men were the first to endure blessed martyrdom in the name of the Lord Jesus.

The army of the poor had suffered many disasters, but this was the worst. There remained one more disaster, and then the army would be destroyed forever as a fighting force.

At Civetot the leaders of the army burned to avenge the disaster at Xerigordon. Peter was in Constantinople, and in any case he was powerless to influence any of the leaders. Geoffrey Burel had taken command, and it was on his advice that the Crusaders marched out against the enemy. There were about twenty thousand troops. The old men, women, and children were left behind at Civetot. They marched in six columns, with standards flying and trumpets blaring, making a good deal of noise, on their way to Nicaea, where they hoped to provoke the enemy into a pitched battle. It was early in the morning, and they were of good heart.

Three miles from Civetot, the road to Nicaea entered a narrow wooded valley, where the Turks had posted scouts and were able to watch the progress of the army. Behind the scouts, in the plain beyond the valley, the Turkish army was waiting. By coincidence the Turks had decided on this day to attack Civetot and to destroy the camp and everyone in it, and they were overjoyed to see the Christians marching through the valley like lambs to the slaughter. They waited until the cavalry emerged from the valley. Then, their bowmen sent a shower of arrows into their midst. Many of the riders and many of the horses were maimed or killed, while the rest tried to flee back to Civetot. But there was no space to move in; the onward-marching infantry collided with the retreating cavalry, and the Turks, who enjoyed ambushes, raced through the woods and massacred the Christians with the greatest ease. Some fugitives reached Civetot with the Turks hard on their heels. Only about two hours had passed since the Christian army set out, and it was still early morning. A priest was celebrating mass; the Turks killed him on the altar. Some old men were still asleep in their beds. The Turks overturned the tents and went on killing, sparing only boys and girls with pleasing features who could be sold profitably into slavery. Walter Sans-Avoir was killed: seven arrows were found embedded in his body. Albert of Aix records that the Turks suffered many casualties, but this seems unlikely. The Christian army panicked from the first moment of the battle, and a panicking army inflicts few casualties.

Some Christian soldiers were able to hide in the forests and mountains. About three thousand of them reached a nearby fortress on the seashore. This ancient fortress, long since abandoned, without roof or gateway, served them well, for they were able to build a gate by throwing up rubble and stones and stout leather shields to prevent the enemy from coming in. They had slingshots, bows, and lances, and they fought desperately. The Turks had their own way of dealing with a situation like this. Since the fortress had no roof, they fired heavy arrows into the air and these arrows had the effect of knives hurtling down on the defenders. Many Christians were killed but the greater number of them survived.

They survived because the siege of the fortress became quickly known in Constantinople, because the old fortress was on the seacoast, and because Peter the Hermit urged immediate assistance. The emperor ordered part of his fleet to go to their rescue. At midnight, while the fleet was on its way, the Turks quietly lifted the siege and stole away.

The army of Peter the Hermit was a flame that had been blown out. Of the vast numbers who set out there remained only the three thousand who were taken off the coast of Asia Minor by the emperor's ships. The Crusade of the Poor was a total disaster.

If Peter the Hermit had shown himself to be incompetent militarily, he was nevertheless a legend in his own time. He went on to become a leader of the peasant militia that accompanied the army of the princes to Jerusalem, and was among the first to enter the city, although he returned to France soon afterward.

A few days after the disaster at Civetot, there arrived in Constantinople the first contingent of the army of the princes. Although the princes inevitably quarreled among themselves, they led armies that were disciplined, with clear lines of command, well trained and capable of dealing with the Turks on their own terms. To the princes went the victory denied to Peter the Hermit's rabble army.

A Pride of
Princes

HEN the medieval chroniclers set out the names of the great lords who led their armies on the Crusade, they usually began with Hugh, Count of Vermandois, who was the brother of the king of the Franks. William of Tyre calls him Hugh the Great, but he was a totally ineffective warrior, great only in his boasting, his presumption, and his love of finery. This caricature of a prince was placed first on the list only because he was the brother of a king who ruled over a large and important fragment of northern and central France.

He was not, however, the only brother of a king to set forth on the First Crusade. Robert, Duke of Normandy, was the son of William the Conqueror and the brother of King William Rufus, who ruled England ineffectively until the day when he was struck down by an unknown assailant in the New Forest. Robert was the first-born, but so exasperated his father by his rebelliousness and hot temper that he was denied the throne. He was called "Curthose," which means "Short Boots," an affectionate nickname for a man who was gregarious and mischievous and liked his creature comforts. He became grotesquely fat in his later years, but at the time of the Crusades he kept himself in good physical condition and on a few occasions he is known to have distinguished himself in battle, although he was far from being a natural leader.

Among the men who found their true vocation in the Crusades, and possessed a determination to carry through to the end, was Raymond IV, Count of Toulouse. He was also the most deeply committed. The Emperor Alexius I Comnenus, who grew very fond of him, regarded him as a man of great probity and even sanctity, vastly more intelligent and understanding than any of the other Western Europeans he encountered.

The Count of Toulouse was about fifty-six when he embarked on the Crusade. He felt he would soon die, and he hoped to die in the Holy Land, a wish that was fulfilled. He had fought against the Almoravides in Spain, and he was proud of the fact that he had lost an eye in single combat while

47

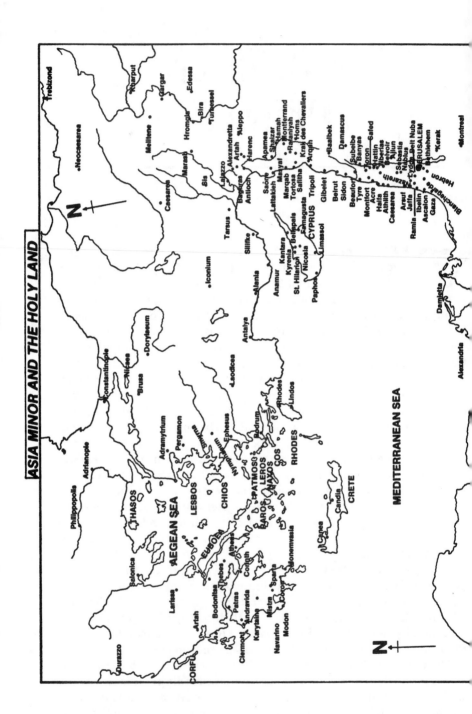

fighting the Moors. His mother was Almodis, Princess of Barcelona. The last of his many wives—for he married often and was twice excommunicated by the Church for marriages of consanguinity—was Elvira, the natural daughter of Alfonso VI, King of Leon and Castile, one of the greatest Spanish kings, who had fought implacably against the Moors. We shall not understand the half-Spanish Count of Toulouse unless we remember that he had already waged war against the Moors and throughout his life maintained his connections with Spain. Just as Alfonso VI vanquished the Moors at one end of the Mediterranean, so the Count of Toulouse intended to vanquish them at the other end. The count was a great womanizer while remaining deeply religious: he had a Spanish gravity and a Spanish sensuality. He was by far the richest of the Crusader leaders and he was the first of the princes to take the Cross.

Bohemond, Prince of Otranto, was a man of another color and of a more barbaric character. He was about forty years old when he set out on the Crusade, but he had retained a young man's fierce ambitions and ferocious temper. He was a pure Norman, with a Norman's cruelty and a Norman's belief that the whole world was ripe for conquest. His consuming ambition was the conquest of the Byzantine empire, and he had already made a serious attempt to conquer it before he embarked on the Crusade. The Byzantine emperor had reason to distrust him, realizing that he was a man who was totally unscrupulous and dangerous, capable of all manner of stratagems to accomplish his aims. Anna Comnena, the emperor's eldest daughter, who saw him when she was fourteen, described him in a famous passage in her history of her father's life and times:

> Never before had anyone set eyes on a man like this in our country, whether among the Greeks or the barbarians, for he was a marvel to behold and his reputation was terrifying. Let me describe this barbarian's appearance more particularly—he was so tall in stature that he overtopped the tallest by nearly one cubit, narrow in the waist and loins, with broad shoulders and a deep chest and powerful arms. And in the whole build of the body he was neither too slender nor overweighted with flesh, but perfectly proportioned and, one might say, built in conformity with the canon of Polycleitus. . . .
> . . . His skin all over his body was very white, and in his face the white was tempered with red. His hair was yellowish, but did not hang down to his waist like that of the other barbarians; for the man was not inordinately vain of his hair, but had it cut short to the ears. Whether his beard was reddish, or any other color I cannot say, for the razor had passed over it very closely and left a surface smoother than chalk. . . . His blue eyes indicated both a high spirit and dignity; and his nose and nostrils breathed in the

air freely; his chest corresponded to his nostrils and his nostrils explained the breadth of his chest. For by his nostrils nature had given free passage to the high spirit that bubbled up from his heart. A certain charm hung about this man but was partly marred by a general air of the horrible. For in the whole of his body the entire man showed implacable and savage both in his size and glance, or so I believe, and even his laughter sounded like roaring. He was so made in mind and body that courage and passion reared their crests within him and both inclined to war. His wit was manifold and crafty and able to find a way of escape in every emergency. In conversation he was well-informed, and the answers he gave were quite irrefutable. This man, who was of such a size and such a character, was inferior to the emperor alone in fortune and eloquence and other gifts of nature.

Anna Comnena provided no comparable portrait of the other Crusader princes. She was evidently fascinated by Bohemond, by the *terribilità* which he wore like a garment and by his extraordinary beauty. She had studied him at length, and knew him to be a merciless marauder. What, she wondered, was such a man doing on a Crusade?

It was a question which many people asked during the course of the Crusade. The Count of Toulouse asked it, and came to the same conclusion as Anna: that Bohemond was there for all the mischief he could create, and all the territory and glory he could acquire. As a result the count exerted a great deal of energy in attempting to neutralize Bohemond. They were at odds with one another throughout the campaign.

There remained the Lotharingian princes, led by Godfrey of Bouillon, and his brothers Baldwin and Eustace. They were the sons of Eustace II, Count of Boulogne, and Ida, the daughter of Duke Godfrey II of Lower Lorraine, and through their mother they were descended from Charlemagne, and it was this more than anything else that distinguished them from the other princes. To have royal blood signified a great deal at a time when kings were regarded as nearly divine. Godfrey, the second son, possessed enormous strength: once in Cilicia he wrestled with a huge bear, and when an Arab sheikh invited him to slaughter a camel, he sliced off its head with a single sword-stroke. He was deeply religious, and it was related that he accompanied the German King Henry IV on his march through Italy. He was so horrified by the sack of Rome in 1082 that he fell into a fever; when he had recovered he promised himself he would take part in no more fighting in the West; he would reserve his strength for fighting against the Saracens. He sometimes prayed for so long before a meal that his entourage complained their meals were cold by the time they were permitted to eat. He had his mother's piety and he had Charlemagne's sense of the lord's proper humility in the face of his subjects.

Once when some Arab dignitaries came to visit him in his tent, they found him sitting on the ground, resting against a tawdry sack of straw. There were no carpets, no curtains, no silk hangings, and no furniture. The dignitaries asked him why he lived like this, and he answered, "The earth serves well enough for a seat in life as it does in death."

Godfrey of Bouillon was about thirty-five years old when he set out on the Crusade, his younger brother Baldwin about thirty-two. Baldwin was originally intended for the Church and became a prebendary in various churches in Rheims, Cambrai, and Liège. Suddenly he abandoned the Church, became a soldier, married a high-born Englishwoman called Godehilde, who accompanied him on the Crusade. Baldwin gave every sign of remaining a soldier for the rest of his life. Unlike Godfrey, he enjoyed finery and never appeared in public without a mantle hanging from his shoulders. He was very grave in manner, so that they said of him that he looked more like a bishop than a warrior. His chief vice was venery; he loved women passionately. But he was also something of a scholar, and a man of exquisite manners.

Baldwin loved his older brother almost to excess. He modeled himself on Godfrey, studying his brother's every act. To the chaste and handsome Godfrey, so it seemed to him, all the virtues had been granted in double measure, and Baldwin tended to regard himself as a sinner who never came up to his own expectations for himself. Eustace, the third brother, played only a minor role in the Crusades and soon returned to manage his vast estates.

Of the three great princes who led the Crusade, one came from the south of France, another from what is now the region of Belgium and Flanders, and the third from southern Italy. They had never met and knew very little about each other. The eldest was the Count of Toulouse, the youngest was Godfrey. In the end both the Count of Toulouse and Godfrey would be offered the crown of Jerusalem and both would refuse it.

On August 15, 1097, Godfrey set out at the head of his small army for Constantinople, the staging ground for the attack on the Holy Land. No reliable figures are available, for the medieval chroniclers let their imaginations loose whenever they contemplated the size of an army. Anna Comnena, for example, says that Godfrey had ten thousand knights and seventy thousand foot soldiers when he reached Constantinople. It is more likely that he set out with about one thousand knights and gathered another five hundred during the journey along the Rhine and the Danube. There were probably about seven thousand pikemen and archers, and in addition three thousand or four thousand grooms, carters, fletchers, ironsmiths, cooks, tentmen, servants, and camp followers. Both Godfrey and Baldwin took their wives with them, and many of the knights were accompanied by their families. In medieval wars women traveled with their men, and there was always an abundance of female camp followers.

These small armies were well organized: supply problems had been worked out; there was an adequate intelligence system, and the military police saw to it that the foot soldiers obeyed orders. The army was priest-ridden: Every nobleman of substance had his private chaplain, and every company of soldiers its attendant priest.

A large number of noblemen joined Godfrey's army, among them Baldwin of Le Bourg, his kinsman, who would in time become king of Jerusalem.

In those days a count was a very important personage indeed, and the noblemen who attached themselves to the great lords could expect commensurate deference. Between the noblemen and the soldiers there was a vast gap. We shall hear very little about the deeds of the individual soldiers, for the history of the Crusades was very largely recorded by chaplains and knights.

Godfrey's army followed the Charlemagne Road, said to be the road taken by Charlemagne during his pilgrimage to Jerusalem. In fact, Charlemagne never went on pilgrimage to Jerusalem, and the road bearing his name was simply a tribute to his legendary qualities. It was a road for heroes to travel on. Peter the Hermit had followed it, and his ragtag army had suffered severely at the hands of Hungarians and Pechenegs. Godfrey was luckier. He was well armed, he was well known, and he had complete control over his men. At some time in the beginning of October, he crossed the border between Germany and Hungary, having previously sent Godfrey d'Esch, one of his noblemen, ahead on a mission to seek the king of Hungary's permission to enter the country. Godfrey d'Esch knew the king and had previously rendered him some service. He conducted his embassy intelligently, there were protracted negotiations, and soon Godfrey of Lorraine and his brother Baldwin and three hundred knights were invited to meet King Coloman at Sapron, his capital, and it was agreed that the Crusader army would be permitted to pass through Hungary on condition that they left Baldwin, his wife, and children as hostages for their good behavior. Godfrey, for his part, issued an order that anyone who committed violence of any kind on a Hungarian would immediately be put to death and all his goods would be confiscated. The order was delivered to everyone in the army by means of a herald. At all costs Godfrey was determined to pass through Hungary peacefully. "In this way, by the grace of God," wrote William of Tyre, "they traveled across the whole country without giving offence with the slightest word."

During the journey across Hungary the Crusaders were well provisioned and well guarded, for they were accompanied by Hungarian troops who had orders to see they were given everything they asked for and that none strayed from the path. This was the only uneventful part of the journey.

They paused in Belgrade to set their baggage trains in order and to regroup. King Coloman had given them extra provisions and they were in no danger of starving. Halfway between Belgrade and Nish, the Crusaders were met by envoys sent by the provincial governor to act as escorts throughout the rest of the journey to Constantinople. Thus, the army was preserved, losing no one along the way. The towns and villages they passed through were all poverty-stricken. The poverty on the Byzantine frontiers startled the Crusaders, who knew little about the endless Bulgarian wars. It was Byzantine policy to make a wasteland of the frontiers. The Crusaders reached Philippopolis, in Thrace, a city founded by Philip of Macedon, built on three hills in the midst of a vast plain, and there at last they saw a Greek city in its splendor, with its high walls, Greek temples and Christian churches. Philippopolis was a small foretaste of Constantinople, a well-ordered city run by Byzantine officials long trained in government.

It was here at Philippopolis that Godfrey received some startling information, which boded ill for the future. He learned that Hugh, Count of Vermandois, had already reached Constantinople, the first of the Crusader princes to arrive there. In a few days came rumors that Hugh had been thrown into prison. Godfrey believed the rumor and sent Henry d'Esch and Baldwin of Mons, Count of Hainault, to intercede with the emperor. Godfrey's troops marched to Adrianople and beyond. No message came from the emperor. Fearing that they, too, would be arrested and disarmed when they reached Constantinople, the leaders of the army decided upon a show of strength. They had camped in a rich pastureland and fanned out in murderous raids on the surrounding villages. The raids lasted for eight days and were called off only when Byzantine officials came hurrying to the camp with the news that Hugh the Great had been released from prison.

The Lotharingian princes continued their march to Constantinople, expecting trouble. They had no high opinion of the Byzantine officials and distrusted the emperor. They were in a foreign country where the people spoke a language they could not understand, where customs were very different, and where they were at the mercy of an army far greater than theirs. They did not know the rules of the game, but in the following months they would learn to play it well. Godfrey reached Constantinople on December 23, and he would remain there for four hectic months, waiting for the other Crusader armies to reach the staging ground.

At the emperor's orders Godfrey's army encamped on the northern bank of the Golden Horn. The high officers were billeted in monasteries and private houses, while the soldiers lived in tents. It was a bitter winter with cold winds blowing in from the Black Sea, sudden snowstorms, and it rained nearly every day. Hugh the Great came to the camp, Godfrey embraced him, and they swore to march together to Jerusalem. Hugh, now living well at the Emperor Alexius Comnenus's expense, brought a message: the emperor had invited Godfrey to visit him at the Blachernae Palace. Godfrey rejected the invitation in high dudgeon. He was Duke of Lower

Lorraine, a descendant of Charlemagne, and he did not need either the brother of a French king or a Byzantine emperor to tell him what to do. Least of all was he prepared to swear allegiance to Alexius. He knew that this would be demanded of him just as it would be demanded of all the other princes coming from the West. He regarded himself as a temporary guest on Byzantine soil, and he had no intention of being overly friendly with the landlord. He sent his trusted ambassador Henry d'Esch together with Conon de Montaigue and his own kinsman Baldwin of Le Bourg to the emperor with his excuses. The emperor was unimpressed. He was determined to exact an oath of loyalty from all the Crusader princes. Who was Godfrey that he dared to defy an emperor?

Alexius had a fair idea of what Godfrey was up to. He suspected that when all the princes reached Constantinople they would turn their weapons against him. It was not an unfounded suspicion. He knew from his officials that Godfrey was stubborn, proud, and resentful. The *émeute* below Adrianople showed that the Crusaders were capable of sudden violence. He stationed a small army of his own behind Godfrey's. One day, towards the end of March, the emperor, incensed by Godfrey's continued refusal to meet him, ordered that his food supplies be cut off, first the fodder for the horses, and then fish, and then bread. For the second time the Crusaders went on a rampage. For six days they invaded neighboring villages, capturing vast amounts of food and fodder, returning in triumph to their camp with wagonloads of provisions. They fought the troops who were guarding them, captured sixty, and put many to death. They had tasted blood and taken, as they thought, the measure of the Byzantines.

Godfrey and the Lotharingian leaders held a council of war. They decided that the time had come to attack the city in force. They were camped near the bridge that crosses the headwaters of the Golden Horn, and not more than a few hundred yards beyond the bridge, enclosed within the high city walls, lay the Blachernae Palace where the emperor was in residence. The Lotharingian army streaming across the bridge was not merely attempting to put pressure on the emperor; it was out for conquest, hoping or half-hoping to capture the palace and the emperor. With the emperor in their power, they could take possession of the empire. The attack came on Good Friday, a day when the emperor and the people of Constantinople normally observed the most solemn rites. It was unthinkable to them that men should shed blood on the day when Christ's blood was shed.

The emperor behaved in character. He had been a capable soldier and, although he was the son of an emperor, he had fought his way to power. He came from a long line of landed gentry in Cappadocia, and Cappadocians were renowned for their cunning and their patience. Wearing his jeweled robes, enthroned in a palace courtyard, surrounded by his ministers and courtiers, he waited out the Lotharingian onslaught. He would let them attack—up to a point. The movements of the Lotharingian troops could be observed from the watchtowers. He sent messages to Godfrey, "Do not attack now. If you must attack, wait until the day after the Resurrection." Godfrey appears to have regarded the messages as a sign of weakness and pressed on with the attack. A shower of metal-tipped arrows came over the high walls. An official standing beside the throne was struck in the chest. Some of these attendant officials ran for cover, but the emperor remained unmoved, sitting very straight on the throne, consoling and chiding them. His role was to resist by the sheer weight and pressure of his authority. But the Lotharingians continued to advance in the direction of the Blachernae Palace, and at last the emperor gave orders to station bowmen along the walls, adding that they should not try to kill but rather that they should shoot without taking aim, so that the enemy would be terrified by the multitude of arrows. And then, when he heard they were approaching the Romanus Gate, he ordered that a company of his nobles armed with bows and long lances should suddenly throw the gate open and advance slowly on the Lotharingians, the slow and steady march of the imperial guards which had often inspired terror in the enemies of the empire. These nobles too were ordered not to take aim at the Lotharingians, only at their horses. The emperor was desperately attempting to avoid bloodshed. At nightfall, when he gave the order for a general advance, the Lotharingians knew better than to fight. They fled back to their tents.

On the following day Hugh the Great was sent to Godfrey with another message from the emperor. He spoke of the dangers of continued resistance and the horrors of a full-scale battle. What was wrong with giving an oath of loyalty to the emperor? Godfrey answered that Hugh, from being a great prince of France, had been transformed into a slave and that there was nothing to be gained by being obedient to the emperor. To these arguments Hugh replied that indeed there was everything to be gained: the emperor could offer protection, provisions, friendship, treasure. "Matters will turn out ill for us if we disobey him," Hugh said. Godfrey, still licking his wounds from the affray of the previous day, replied stubbornly that he expected nothing from the emperor and would act as he saw fit. Hugh gave the message to the emperor, who ordered a general attack the day after Easter Sunday. For the second time Godfrey's army was in full flight.

The decision to attack Godfrey was forced on the emperor because news had come that the armies of Raymond of Toulouse and Bohemond, Prince of Otranto, were about to arrive in Constantinople. Though he had shown himself in the past to be a determined enemy of the Byzantine empire, Bohemond presented no immediate danger, for his army was pathetically small, numbering perhaps no more than two or three hundred knights and less than two thousand foot soldiers. The Count of Toulouse's army was about ten times as large, and Godfrey's was about half as large as the Provençal army. Since the new armies were coming, the emperor decided that two things must be done immediately: Godfrey's army must cross over to Asia and Godfrey himself must take the oath of allegiance. Twice defeated in battle by the Byzantines, Godfrey at last realized that all further resistance was in vain and that he would face complete destruction if he continued to make war against the emperor.

Godfrey's army was ferried across the straits. He set up his camp in Pelecanum, and in a day or two the emperor sent a ship to bring Godfrey to the Bucoleon Palace, a vast and ornate palace on the southern shore of Constantinople. This palace was sometimes known as the Great Palace, not only because it was quite simply the largest of all the palaces in the Western world, but also because it enshrined the traditions of the emperors and the relics of Christ. Here, in one of the many throne rooms, Godfrey knelt before the emperor and recited the oath of loyalty, swearing to be the emperor's vassal and promising to restore to the emperor all the cities and lands he conquered on his way to Jerusalem, those cities and lands that belonged properly to Byzantium. It was a very solemn moment as the emperor leaned forward and embraced the man who had been his enemy and was now an ally and a vassal.

There was now peace between Byzantium and the Crusaders. How long it would last no one knew, nor did the parties know exactly what was meant by peace between the Greeks and the Latins. It was a precarious peace, an armed truce, a truce in which no side trusted the other, although both sides had a common aim—the preservation of the Holy Land in Christian hands. The tragedy of the Crusades was that the Greeks and Latins never worked together wholeheartedly. If they had, the Byzantine empire and the Christian kingdom of Jerusalem might have lasted to the present day.

Under the Walls of Constantinople

WHEN the Crusaders rode up to the honey-colored walls of Constantinople, there was scarcely one of them who could have guessed at the glories within. They knew it by repute as Midgard, the center of the world. It was a city of gleaming wealth and far-reaching influence, with a dozen splendid palaces and three hundred churches, with great gardens and vast public places where the paving stones were slabs of marble and hundreds of bronze statues stood on marble pedestals. Both the palaces and the churches were decorated with sheets of mosaic. Sometimes the doors of palaces and churches were made of solid silver.

Long ago the Arabs had conquered Egypt, Palestine, and Syria, and recently the Seljuk Turks had conquered Asia Minor, but the Byzantine empire in its diminished condition was still a power to be reckoned with. The honey-colored walls, with their 370 towers, were so well designed that the city was virtually impregnable. Along the Golden Horn and the Sea of Marmora the walls went straight down to the water. The Byzantine army at full force numbered about 100,000 men, and in addition, there were multitudinous mercenaries whose chief purpose was to protect the lives of the emperor and the imperial family.

If he could have peered over the walls, the Crusader would have seen a city as busy as a beehive, throbbing with urgent life, noisy with church bells and the hammering of metal, with factories next to the churches and with the workers' tenements next to the palaces. The crowning glory of the city was Justinian's Church of Sancta Sophia, or Holy Wisdom, a church so vast, so brilliantly colored with mosaics, and so full of shimmering perspectives that a man standing under the dome could believe himself in heaven. On the south shore, facing the Sea of Marmora, stood the Great Palace, a vast complex of a hundred buildings and at least twenty chapels, set amid gardens and poplars, where the emperors had always lived in great state. This palace was also known as the Bucoleon, because a statue of a bull and a lion had stood there from earliest times. In a corner of the palace

was the small church of the Virgin of the Pharos, which served as a reliquary for the grave-clothes of Christ, the Veronica, the Crown of Thorns, the Holy Lance, the Nails, and a considerable portion of the True Cross.
Constantinople was shaped like a triangle, its sides about four miles long. At the apex of the triangle stood the Blachernae Palace, the favorite palace of the Emperor Alexius I Comnenus. Within its walls was the church of the Virgin of Blachernae, and here the Mantle and the Robe and other relics of the Virgin were preserved.
In the north were the relics of the Virgin, in the south were the relics of Christ. To the Byzantines this divine symmetry afforded divine protection, or so they hoped.
At the heart and center of the city there stood, like a powerful generator of vast and imponderable forces, the figure of the emperor, whose power was absolute in a very special way. He had many titles but the one most commonly used was *en Christo Autocrator*, meaning "Autocrat in Christ." He was more than the representative of Christ on earth: in the eyes of Orthodox believers he was very nearly an incarnation of Christ. He walked and talked in a special Christlike way; and when he was enthroned he was more especially like Christ than at any other time. He wore stiff brocaded gowns said to be copied after gowns given by the angels to Constantine, the first Christian emperor. He wore a cross in his crown, from which there dangled ropes of jewels and pearls, and there were more ropes of jewels and pearls dangling from his arms and shoulders. These ropes were intended to signify the radiance of Christ. All his public acts took on the form of ritual. Since there were rituals for every hour of the day, and on nearly every day there were public ceremonies to be performed, the wonder is that he had any time to conduct affairs of state. He possessed executive, legislative, judicial, military and religious power, and he was answerable to nobody except Christ. In theory everything that happened within the Byzantine empire took place with his permission or consent.
The theory, however, was far from the reality. The all-seeing eye and the all-judging intelligence of the emperor were at the mercy of thousands of officials who diluted his powers. They ruled in his name, and far too many of them were peculators. The civil service was corrupt. Alexius I Comnenus was one of the few emperors who was determined to stamp out corruption although he was not always aware of the extent of the corruption.
He was also one of the few emperors who was popular with the people. This hard-bitten, black-browed and black-bearded man possessed to a quite extraordinary degree a gift for government. He had spent most of his early years soldiering and he was not afraid of taking risks. With the help of the Venetians, he had prevented Robert Guiscard and his son Bohemond from establishing themselves along the Adriatic coast. Once, after losing a

battle with Bohemond, he had fled from the battlefield with a detachment of the imperial guards, with a flying column of enemy troops in hot pursuit. Suddenly he reined in his horse and shouted to a companion, "We cannot go on running like this." He then wheeled around, drew his sword, and waited for the first of his pursuers to catch up with him. The man fell with a sword-thrust in the face. The rest of the pursuers decided they were dealing with a man who was absolutely reckless, and they withdrew. Alexius returned to Constantinople, raised another army, and this time defeated Bohemond decisively, who returned to Italy.

This was the same Bohemond who was now hurrying to Constantinople, claiming to be a Crusader. Bohemond had raised his small army at his own expense. Alexius was informed of its coming, he had given permission for it to enter his territories, and he was receiving reports on its progress. Bohemond was behaving well; his troops did not plunder, and indeed they had no need to plunder, since provisions were being supplied them by imperial officials. They set out from Dyrrhachium on October 1 and Bohemond, in advance of his troops, reached Constantinople on April 9. The distance from Dyrrhachium to Constantinople, as the crow flies, is five hundred miles: they were advancing at a rate of less than a hundred miles a month. This shows that he was in no particular hurry.

For Alexius the slow march of Bohemond was something to be thankful for. If Bohemond had joined forces with Godfrey a few weeks earlier at the time of the sudden attack on the walls near the Blachernae Palace, there was no doubt that the battle would have been more hard fought, but there was also no doubt that the Byzantine forces would have been victorious.

Alexius had no illusions about Bohemond, who was capable of astonishingly audacious acts. He was a brilliant commander in the field and a relentless enemy. Even if he were friendly, it would be impossible to trust him. So he was watched carefully, and because he was well aware of being watched, he behaved in an exemplary manner and took the oath of allegiance, promising to become a proper servant of the emperor. He was playing a role and the emperor knew it. When Bohemond suggested that it might be appropriate for the emperor to appoint him Grand Domestic of the East, or Viceroy of Asia with command of all the armies to the east of Constantinople, Alexius demurred. That Bohemond should request such a position was only one more example of his astonishing audacity.

Bohemond was lodged in the monastery of St. Cosmas and St. Damian north of the city, overlooking the Golden Horn, at a short distance from the Blachernae Palace. Here the emperor kept a suite of rooms for distinguished guests. Bohemond was accompanied only by his bodyguard, ten knights who rode the best available horses. Anna Comnena tells a story about the first day Bohemond stayed at the monastery. A luxurious table had been prepared for him. A majordomo advanced and said that if Bohemond for whatever reason would prefer to have his own meals prepared rather than eat those offered by the emperor, this was perfectly understandable. The majordomo pointed to a tray of uncooked meats which were at Bohemond's disposal. Bohemond refused to touch either the cooked or the uncooked meats, though he permitted his knights to cook the meats, and the next morning he asked them how they had fared. They said they had suffered no discomfort at all. "I really thought the emperor might have poisoned the food," Bohemond told them. "I remembered the terrible wars we had fought." All this was reported to Alexius, who also remembered those wars and needed to know how suspicious and distrustful Bohemond was, in spite of all his fine words and his oath of loyalty sworn over the Crown of Thorns.

What Alexius most disliked in Bohemond was a certain coarseness, almost a cheapness. Alexius himself was too much a soldier to care about the good or bad manners of the Crusader chieftains, but he possessed a keen eye for moral qualities. Alexius ordered a room in the Blachernae Palace to be filled with treasure: rich stuffs, vessels of hammered gold and silver, an abundance of silks and jewels. The floor was covered with these objects so that it was impossible to move among them. The emperor ordered an official to lead Bohemond up to the doors, which were to be opened suddenly in order to take Bohemond by surprise. This was done, and a startled Bohemond was heard to exclaim, "If I had all this treasure, I would long ago have made myself master of many lands."

The official said, "They are all yours. The emperor has given them to you."

Bohemond, overjoyed, thanked the official and returned to his quarters in the monastery of St. Cosmas and St. Damian. Soon the entire treasure was brought to him. He gazed at it, and remembered that he was a prince of the House of Guiscard and therefore it was impossible for him to accept so large a bribe.

"I never imagined the emperor would inflict so much dishonor on me!" he said in his booming voice. "Take them away! Give them back to him who sent them!"

This was his first reaction. His second reaction was somewhat different. He was upset at the thought of the treasure's being taken away from him. Suddenly, as he watched the imperial servants dismantling the exhibition of more treasure than he had set eyes on in his life, he changed his manner abruptly. The look of horror was exchanged for smiles, compliments, and polite gestures. He told the servants he would keep the treasure and was most grateful to the emperor. The incident was reported to the emperor, who commented, "The mischief will return on the head of the mischief-maker." Anna Comnena, who recorded the story, said that Bohemond was "like a sea-polyp that changes its shape every instant." His sudden transformations were not however the most important things about Bohemond. The most important things were his courage and his cunning.

While Bohemond was changeable as a sea-polyp, the Count of Toulouse was as changeless as the Pole Star. The one-eyed soldier who led the largest army to Constantinople was quiet and reserved, sometimes obstinate but always courteous, deeply religious, and deeply attached to Adhémar of Monteil, Bishop of Le Puy. He believed in visions, miracles, and the divine power of relics to a degree that may have alarmed the bishop, who believed in none of them. Anna Comnena noted his superior wisdom, genuine sincerity, and purity of life. "He was a man," she wrote, "who valued truth above everything." He shone among the Crusaders like the sun among the lesser stars.

His army consisted of about two thousand knights and twelve thousand foot soldiers, and there were some four thousand camp servants, carters, tentmakers, camp followers, and auxiliaries. Most of the men came from Gascony and Provence. They were well armed, plentifully supplied with provisions, and extremely well disciplined. Many of the nobles of southern France accompanied the Count of Toulouse, including Francis-Lambert of Monteil and William-Hugh of Monteil, the younger brothers of Bishop Adhémar of Le Puy, who in theory was the commander in chief of the entire Crusade.

Raymond of Aguilers, the chronicler of the Count of Toulouse's army, has nothing to say about the early days of the march. We do not know where the troops assembled, although it is likely to have been in Lyons, or where exactly they crossed over into Italy. They may have crossed the Alps by the Col de Genèvre and taken the road through Lombardy and Venetia. We know they followed the coastline of Istria and Dalmatia, and were welcomed by the Byzantine envoy John Comnenus at Dyrrhachium. Thereafter they followed roughly the road taken by Bohemond. Raymond of Aguilers picks up the story as the army enters the region he calls Sclavonia, a desolate land of rugged mountains and dense forests. He has much to say about the cowardice of the Sclavonians, who would leave their villages when they saw the count's army approaching, hide in the forest until the last baggage carts and the last stragglers came in view, and then pounce on them. In this way many old and infirm people, and many who were sick, were cut off. The count was so exasperated by this maneuver that he stationed himself with the rear guard, waited until he was able to capture six Sclavonians and, in full sight of others who held back but were capable of doing much harm, he deliberately mutilated them. Some had their eyes snatched out, others had their feet cut off, and others had their noses and hands cut off. All this had to be done very quickly because the count's forces were outnumbered. He fled back to his army, having given the Sclavonians a lesson they might never forget.

This story makes a somewhat sardonic beginning to Raymond of Aguilers's narrative, a tone that can be heard throughout. He is a fine historian, because imbued with intense faith and a belief in miracles, he nevertheless shows a calm, pragmatic, sardonic eye.

Raymond was the historian attached to the Count of Toulouse, while the unknown author of the *Gesta Francorum* was just as evidently attached to the army of Bohemond. Each historian praised his own man, yet valid portraits emerge of two heroic characters so different from one another that there could scarcely be any real communication between them.

When Bohemond was commanded to take the oath of loyalty, he did so without demur, and we know that he had not the slightest intention of keeping his oath. The Count of Toulouse had refused to take the oath as a matter of principle. He was a sovereign prince, and under Adhémar of Le Puy he was the appointed leader of the Crusade. How could he be the vassal of the emperor?

The Count of Toulouse met the emperor under difficult auspices. He had reached Constantinople in advance of his army. Lodged in a palace outside the walls and treated by Byzantine officials with the respect due him, he was soon summoned to an audience with the emperor. On the way to the palace he learned that his own army, during the last stages of the march, had been raiding Byzantine villages and the imperial army had been called out to stop the Latins. The emperor was polite; the matter was not mentioned. Raymond of Aguilers suggests that the meeting was stormy; it is more likely that they spoke with excessive politeness, while the storms gathered beneath the surface. Anna Comnena, who reflected the opinions of the emperor, spoke of the Count of Toulouse's courtesy and honesty and of his aristocratic demeanor. In the end the count took a modified oath to respect the life and possessions of the emperor, to do nothing whatsoever that would harm them. The emperor grew genuinely fond of the count and respected him more than he respected any other leader of the Crusades. Two days after the oath taking, the count led his army to join all the other armies at Pelecanum. Unlike Godfrey and Bohemond, he was invited to return to the court, and he appears to have spent the two following weeks by the emperor's side.

The last army to arrive in Constantinople was led by Robert, Duke of Normandy, the fiery and intractable son of William the Conqueror. He was accompanied by Stephen, Count of Blois and Chartres. Stephen was his brother-in-law, married to Adela, the high-spirited daughter of the Conqueror, who had ordered him to embark on the Crusade, although originally he had not the least intention of doing anything so dangerous. Self-indulgent and uxorious, he was one of the wealthiest men of his time, and almost as proud and vainglorious as Hugh the Great. Robert, Duke of Normandy, had no hesitation in taking the oath of allegiance, and he was one of those who quarreled with the Count of Toulouse when he was refusing to take it.

Now all the armies had been ferried to Asia, and the emperor was satisfied at last that these barbarians from western Europe no longer threatened his empire. He had acted with finesse and intelligence under the most severe provocations; he had offered provisions and supplies, his own scouts and engineers, his own siege engines to the Crusaders; he was prepared to help them with his limited means in every way possible. He insisted only that they keep their oath of loyalty and restore to him the lost Byzantine provinces of Asia Minor.

On the last days of April or very early in May the Crusaders struck their tents in Pelecanum and set out on the second stage of their long journey to Jerusalem.

II

THE DARK
ROADS TO
THE HOLY
LAND

Journey Through the Wilderness

T̶HE city of Nicaea, where the Nicene Creed came to birth in the time of Constantine, had until recently been in the possession of the Byzantine empire. It lay some sixty miles southeast of Constantinople, and it belonged now to the empire of Kilij Arslan, the Seljuk sultan, who made it his capital, partly because it was one of the best defended cities in Asia Minor and partly because it was close to Constantinople, which he hoped to conquer. Here he kept his treasure, his wife, his children, and his best soldiers. All the refinements of Byzantine architecture had gone into the building of the city walls, which were regarded as virtually impregnable. The population was mostly Christian; there was a large and well-equipped Turkish garrison; the walls were very high, and there were two hundred and forty towers. The Emperor Alexius Comnenus seems to have had very little doubt that Nicaea could be reconquered with the help of the Crusaders and he made his plans accordingly.

Since the city lay at the western end of the Ascanian lake, the west wall rose straight out of the water, and all the remaining walls were protected by a moat fed by the lake, the capture of the city presented formidable problems. Nevertheless there were many factors working in favor of the attackers. The most important was the absence of the sultan, who was fighting a border war near Melitene nearly five hundred miles to the east against the princes of Danishmend. His intelligence system seems to have broken down and, apparently, he knew nothing about the great Crusader encampment at Pelecanum or about the coming invasion. Nicaea, though provided with a garrison force ample for its defense against a small army, was incapable of defending itself for long against a massive and well-provisioned army of Crusaders. Another factor was the desire of the Christians in Nicaea to be restored to the Byzantine empire and to communion with the Orthodox Church. There is evidence that they possessed an intelligence system of their own and were in continual touch with the emperor. Still another factor was the way the Crusading princes worked in unison; they supported one another, and refused to be deterred by the formidable task of reducing a powerful city. Later they would quarrel violently among themselves, and they would continue to pay off old scores with astonishing bitterness and contempt for one another. But during this first siege, meeting the enemy for the first time, they were on their best behavior.

One more factor needs to be mentioned: they had Byzantine advisers, for Byzantine officers accompanied them. Manuel Butumites, a seasoned general, who knew Nicaea well, acted as the emperor's representative while the emperor himself remained at Pelecanum. Butumites could call upon the emperor for supplies or ammunition or whatever was necessary.

Bohemond, the first to arrive on the scene, took up a position to the north of the city, Godfrey and the Lotharingians to the east, and the Count of Toulouse with the Provençals on the south. The troops of Robert of Normandy did not come up until much later. There was no commander in chief, but the princes met frequently and coordinated their plans. Butumites and Byzantine staff officers offered their advice. Probably Bohemond, Godfrey, the Count of Toulouse, and Butumites formed a quadrumvirate, which decided on all important issues. What is certain is that Butumites knew at every moment what the Crusaders were doing. His engineers had brought siege engines with them, and they were to play an important part in the seven-week-long siege.

When the Crusading armies reached Nicaea, they were exhausted by a long and difficult climb through the mountains. On the way, near Civetot, they passed close to the place where Peter the Hermit's ragged army had been massacred; huge heaps of bones lying by the roadside were a reminder of Turkish ferocity. Supplies gave out during the journey to Nicaea. Butumites was informed; supplies were rushed up just in time; and the troops were grateful to an emperor they half despised, because he represented in their eyes the luxury and decadence of Constantinople. According to one of the chroniclers it was the emperor himself who advised Godfrey to move cautiously over the mountains, to send scouts and engineers ahead, and to mark the track they cut through the scrub oaks with wooden crosses for the benefit of future pilgrims. The emperor also presented the Count of Toulouse with two thousand light-armed infantry under the command of Taticius, one of his most famous generals.

The first Turkish relief force to arrive on the outskirts of Nicaea found the city completely blockaded. The Count of Toulouse's army had just arrived in force and met the brunt of the attack. In a short, sharp skirmish, the Turks were hurled back, and many were killed. The Turks regrouped, attacked a second time, and were again hurled back. The Provençals discovered a cart filled with ropes and an interpreter explained that the ropes were intended for the Crusaders. They would be bound together and carried off to remote Khorassan. The chronicler of the *Gesta Francorum* wrote that the Turks were merry (*letantes*) as they came down the mountains, but their merriment was brief. "As many of them as came down remained in our hands," he wrote, "and their heads were cut off. Then we threw the heads by means of a catapult into the city, and thus wrought great terror among the Turks."

For some time the Count of Toulouse had been eyeing one of the great southern towers of the city. He decided to mine it and bring it down. His sappers advanced under a testudo, dug down to the foundation of the wall, cut away some of the stones, inserted beams and wooden joists, and then set fire to them. The sappers and crossbowmen retreated to a safer place and had the pleasure of watching the tower crumbling. By this time it was dark, and it was impossible to make an entrance into the city amid the rubble of a broken tower. In the morning when they awoke, they were surprised to see the tower standing straight and tall. The Turks had worked through the night, and they had somehow built a new tower.

Such labors testified to the determination of the garrison troops to hold out and resist to the uttermost. They, too, had advantages. Hemmed in on three sides, they were able to bring in supplies on the fourth side. The west wall, facing the lake, was provided with watergates through which passed an endless supply of food, fodder, fish, wood, and building materials. There were fishing vessels on the lake and a small fleet. The princes consulted with Butumites, and it was agreed to send messengers to Pelecanum to beg the emperor to send ships to the Ascanian lake. This meant assembling a fleet in the harbor of Civetot (which was just outside Nicaea) and then carrying the ships on bullock carts over the mountains and through the dense forests.

The emperor at once gave the order for the ships to be assembled, and in a surprisingly short time, at a secret hiding place on the shores of the lake, the ships were all brought together and prepared for launching. The launches took place at night. At dawn, from their high towers, the Turkish guards of Nicaea saw the Byzantine fleet sailing across the lake, every ship filled with soldiers. Drummers and trumpeters filled the air with their music. The ships advanced relentlessly. Raymond of Aguilers, who saw them, wrote that the appearance of the ships did more than anything else to inspire fear in the defenders and bring about the surrender.

The surrender, however, did not come about immediately. Butumites himself entered the city secretly under a safe-conduct, offering terms of surrender that were unusually generous. The emirs, the high officials, and the court nobility would receive handsome gifts from the emperor; they would be given pensions and honors according to their rank. Some of the emirs were smuggled out of the city and taken to Pelecanum, where the emperor greeted them cordially and reaffirmed that the lives of all the garrison troops would be spared and no Turk would be harmed if they surrendered. A few details of these negotiations were known to the Crusading princes but not all of them. The garrison commander held out, believing that the sultan might yet come to his aid. Butumites decided upon a show of force. A general assault was ordered. The towers with their grappling hooks were brought closer to the walls; the siege engines were brought forward; the armies took up their stations. But on the morning the assault was to begin, the Crusaders saw imperial banners waving over the city. During the night Nicaea had fallen to the negotiator.

At first the Crusaders felt cheated. They had hoped to gather up all the treasure of Nicaea and carry it with them to Jerusalem. The soldiers were hungry for loot and women. The princes, forgetting that they had sworn on oath to respect the emperor's interest in the cities that had formerly belonged to his empire, felt injured by the emperor's generosity to the garrison troops and all the Turks in Nicaea. Raymond of Aguilers calls the emperor "false an iniquitous" for permitting them to leave unharmed. It would be more accurate to say that, at Nicaea, the emperor was demonstrating his mastery of psychological warfare.

To the Crusaders the emperor was more than generous. Every Crusading soldier received a gift of food. The princes were invited to Pelecanum where they were lavishly entertained and were presented with gold and jewels from the sultan's treasure chamber.

After these ceremonies the emperor bade the Crusaders farewell. Taticius was ordered to accompany them on their march through Asia Minor. The next stage of the march would be supremely dangerous because Kilij Arslan commanded immense forces and it was inevitable that he would attempt to take revenge against the Crusaders for the fall of Nicaea and the loss of his treasury.

At a village called Leuce, on the road to Dorylaeum, the princes held a council of war and decided to divide the army into two parts. It was a dangerous move. There were now two armies marching a day's journey apart, the first led by Bohemond, who was already seeing himself as the leader of the Christian host, and the second by the Count of Toulouse. The first army was composed of the Normans of southern Italy and northern France, with Stephen of Blois and the Count of Flanders and the detachment of Byzantine troops under the command of Taticius. The Greeks provided engineers, scouts, and guides, and since many Greeks knew the country well and many of their countrymen were still living in the lands conquered by the Seljuk Turks they were able to send spies into the hinterland who returned with accurate reports. The second army, under the Count of Toulouse, was composed of Provençals and the Lotharingians under Godfrey. There was also a small French force under Hugh the Great. Godfrey and the Count of Toulouse became close friends, aiding one another whenever it was possible.

The Sultan Kilij Arslan had been following the movements of the Christian army ever since it left Nicaea. On June 30 his well-hidden army was waiting for the Crusaders in the valley of Dorylaeum. Bohemond's army was encamped on the plain on the other side of the hills. At sunrise on the following day the Turks swooped down the hills, making the loud and frightening noises that always accompanied an attack; and above these noises there could be heard very clearly the battle cry, *"Allah Akbar"*— "God is great."

Bohemond was now in extraordinary danger: his army was outnumbered by the enemy and was a day's march from the army of the Count of Toulouse. He ordered his men to form a hollow square, the knights facing outward, the infantry behind them, and the women and noncombatants at the center of the square where, as it happened, there were fountains of fresh water. "The women of our camp were a great comfort to us that day," wrote the author of the *Gesta Francorum*, "for they brought water for our soldiers to drink and they were always vehemently encouraging those who were fighting for them and defending them." From the hillside the Turks were showering arrows into Bohemond's army in such numbers that the sky darkened. The Turks were well trained at saturation firing on a massive scale, something the Crusaders had never experienced before.

Bohemond sent a messenger to the second army to make all speed to the battlefield, and it arrived just in time to save the camp from being overrun, but Bohemond was beginning to fear whether even with the two armies joined together he had the manpower to resist the endless waves of Turks who came over the mountains. He had almost lost hope when he saw a relief force, led by Bishop Adhémar of Le Puy, come over another mountain to take the Turks from the rear. The sudden appearance of a fresh army at their rear threw the Turks into a panic. They fled, leaving behind them a vast amount of booty in gold, silver, horses, camels, oxen, and sheep. Until sunset, the Turks ran, and the Christians ran after them.

At the end of the day Bohemond had to reflect that a battle he almost lost was saved by the Bishop of Le Puy, who had thought out his stratagem without help from any soldier. He had found the guides to take his troops over the mountain, and he had somehow timed his intervention in a way that would have the greatest effect on the course of the battle.

In the battle at Dorylaeum the Crusaders for the first time fought the Turks on an enormous scale, whole armies pitted against whole armies. Here they took the measure of the enemy, admiring his courage and steadfastness. The author of the *Gesta Francorum* noted that the Turks threw 360,000 men into the battle. No doubt this is how many they seemed to be. Clearly, they were worthy opponents. Taticius and his guides continued to work with the Crusaders, giving advice on the roads to be traveled and the villages where they were likely to find supplies. But supplies were running low and soon the journey across Asia Minor became a nightmare. They entered a land of salt marshes and thornbushes; they could not drink the marsh water and thornbushes were very nearly inedible. Many of their horses fell and were eaten. Some of the knights were reduced to walking on foot; others rode on oxen; sheep, goats, and dogs were employed to pull the baggage carts. It was high summer; in the pestilential heat so many fell ill that it sometimes seemed that the Crusade would have to be abandoned somewhere in the heart of Asia Minor. The Count of Toulouse was so sick that the Bishop of Orange gave him extreme unction. Godfrey, who had a passion for hunting, was wounded by a bear he had obviously hoped to eat. Even falcons and hunting dogs were eaten. Bread and water had given out. Crusaders were seen walking with their mouths open in the hope that a breath of air would cool their parched tongues. Occasionally they came upon patches of sugarcane; they squeezed out the sweet liquid and drank it ravenously.

Then the rains came, and they were more unhappy and bewildered than ever. The rain lasted for four or five days, a cold rain that numbed their senses. The animals were also numbed by it and could not move. But as they neared Iconium, the modern Konya, they came to fertile valleys and friendly villagers. Apparently there was no Turkish garrison at Konya and they entered it freely, the inhabitants helping them in every way. The author of the *Gesta Francorum* remembered that the people were especially concerned that the Crusaders carried no waterskins. They showed how the waterskins could be made, and thereafter the Christian army was never without them.

At Heraclea, the next important town on their journey, a large Turkish garrison was waiting for them. The Christians had overwhelming numbers and decided to attack immediately. Bohemond commanded the assault force, and the Turks fled, says the chronicler, "as quickly as an arrow shot by a strong hand flies from the bowstring." Here the Crusaders rested for four days. During this time they argued violently about the route to be followed to Antioch, far away in the southeast, defying the most elementary law of all armies: united they stand, but divided they fall. The divisiveness that was to become characteristic of the Crusaders had made its first appearance.

Both Tancred and Baldwin were far less interested in the Crusades than in acquiring great estates, cities, and farmlands that would produce wealth and a submissive peasantry. Tarsus, the birthplace of St. Paul, was within easy distance, and they decided independently to take possession of the city and establish themselves there. Tancred, with a hundred knights and two hundred infantry, lightly armed and therefore capable of great speed, set out from Heraclea about September 14, to be followed a few hours later by Baldwin, his cousin Baldwin of Le Bourg, and about five hundred knights and two thousand infantry. Tancred hoped to win Tarsus by speed, surprise, and sheer effrontery, while Baldwin hoped to smash the Turkish garrison troops with his heavily armed cavalry, leaving the infantrymen to mop up the survivors and take physical possession of the town. Tancred and Baldwin, both junior members of princely families, had much to win and little to lose in these dangerous adventures.

Tancred was, not surprisingly, the first to reach Tarsus, then largely inhabited by Greek and Armenian Christians who were sympathetic to the Crusaders. But the garrison troops had been ordered to stand fast. Seeing Tancred's small column advancing, the Turks took up positions outside the walls and waited. Tancred charged, there was a lot of close fighting, and the Turkish garrison was gradually thrown back on the town. Meanwhile Tancred had summoned reinforcements from Bohemond's army, which was still in Heraclea. He set up his camp outside the gates of Tarsus, and through spies he was able to learn that the Christians inside the walls were doing everything possible to ensure a Christian victory. He was afraid Baldwin would soon be arriving to snatch victory away from him. And in fact, after Tancred had been encamped for three days outside the town, Baldwin arrived and immediately offered to share the town with him. Since Baldwin's troops were far more numerous, the offer could be regarded as a friendly gesture, but it was refused. That night, without engaging in any fighting, the Turks slipped away and the people of Tarsus came streaming out of the gates to welcome the Crusaders. Even as they were being welcomed, Baldwin and Tancred quarreled bitterly; but Tancred, seeing himself vastly outnumbered, had the grace to retire and set off with his small army to capture some castles and towns in the neighborhood, while Baldwin held fast to Tarsus.

About this time the main army at Heraclea began its advance into Lesser Armenia, a province carved out of southeastern Asia Minor only a few years earlier. Armenians forced out of Armenia by the Seljuk Turks had fled under Prince Roupen over the Taurus Mountains and established themselves in an area where they believed they could defend themselves and retain their national culture. At this time Lesser Armenia consisted of many principalities under Armenian princelings who were little more than chieftains busily carving out fiefdoms for themselves. The boundaries were continually changing as the Seljuk Turks made inroads or were fought back. Lesser Armenia was in a state of permanent war with the Turks.

All through the history of the Crusades the kings of Lesser Armenia and their armies played a prominent role. They were devout Christians and superb fighters. Like the Copts and the Abyssinians they were Monophysites, and therefore at odds with both the Catholic and the Orthodox churches.

From the point of view of the Crusaders the southern march of the Armenians toward Cilicia and the areas bordering on the Euphrates was a godsend. The Armenians provided a protective wall to the north of the Holy Land. Lesser Armenia extended deep into Asia, and their farflung outposts enabled them to discern the coming invasions long before the

Seljuks were on the march. The Crusaders advanced into Lesser Armenia without too much difficulty; quite often towns were ungarrisoned. Baldwin, who abandoned Tarsus after placing a handpicked garrison in charge, began to march east, abandoning the army for adventures among the Armenian principalities. Taking only eighty knights with him and perhaps two hundred foot soldiers together with a new chaplain, the historian Fulcher of Chartres, he marched toward the Euphrates with the firm intention of becoming a prince over a principality large enough to offer him ample rewards. The leaders of the Crusade had evidently given him permission to take possession of as many principalities as he pleased on condition that they serve the purposes of the Crusaders. In fact, he obtained the principality of Edessa, one of the largest and most powerful. Baldwin became coprince with Prince Thoros, took charge of the combined army, and then conspired against Thoros, who belonged to the Orthodox Church and owed his position to the Emperor Alexius Comnenus. Historians are agreed that Thoros was unpopular because he was old, childless, did not belong to the Armenian Church, and was a loyal subject of the Byzantine emperor. But it is in the nature of princes to be unpopular, and there is no evidence that he was more unpopular than most. He had fought well against the Turks and served his people for a long time. He did not deserve the fate Baldwin had reserved for him.

Returning from a battle at Samosata that he had lost, Baldwin was determined to retain his power in Edessa. As the historian Matthew of Edessa tells the story, Prince Thoros knew there was a conspiracy against his life, and he had therefore taken refuge with his bodyguard in the citadel, and from there sent a message to Baldwin, begging to be allowed to go free on condition that he resign all his powers and become a simple citizen. Baldwin swore on the Bible and in the name of God, the archangels and the saints that the life of the prince would be spared. Thereupon the prince came out of the citadel but was promptly seized by the mob and stabbed to death. The body was thrown off a parapet and what remained of it was dragged through the streets for all to see. Prince Thoros was dead, and there was now only Prince Baldwin of Edessa.

By capturing Edessa with eighty knights Baldwin had the satisfaction of knowing that he had penetrated more deeply into Asia than any Westerner since the time of Alexander the Great. Edessa lay on an important trade route and had acquired wealth and treasure far beyond the expectation of the knights who so casually made their way to this provincial city. After the death of Thoros, Baldwin found the treasury intact. He became rich beyond his utmost dreams. His citadel was ornamented with Corinthian columns fifty feet high, and at the foot of Citadel Rock were pools once sacred to the ancient goddesses of Mesopotamia. In this exotic place, inhabited by Armenians, Turks, Jews, and merchants from Central Asia,

Baldwin established a Crusader princedom which would serve as the eastern bulwark of the Crusaders for half a century.

Meanwhile the main Crusader army under Bohemond, Godfrey, and the Count of Toulouse continued its march through Asia Minor, having more difficulty with the terrain than with the Turks. The Turks indeed refused battle. Bohemond heard of a powerful Turkish army, went in search of it, and failed to find it. Perhaps it never existed; it is more likely that it simply fled at the approach of the Crusaders, who were gathering momentum and speed for the inevitable attack on Antioch. At Coxon, where the people opened the gates and entertained the Christian army for three days, they heard rumors that the Turkish garrison had been withdrawn from Antioch and the way was thus clear to Jerusalem. The Count of Toulouse held a council of war, and it was decided to send five hundred knights ahead in order to verify the rumor, which proved to be untrue. Antioch was being heavily fortified. The Christians inside the city were being persecuted and the largest church had been desecrated, being used as stables for the reigning emir.

The worst part of the journey lay ahead, for after Coxon the Crusaders had to cross the Anti-Taurus Mountains. It was October, the rains had begun, carts and wagons filled with supplies had to be carried over great heights, horses fell over precipices, and one beast of burden would drag another down with it. The author of the *Gesta Francorum* speaks of the *diabolica montana*, the devilish mountains. They had bad maps, no protection from the weather, and knew nothing about climbing mountains. They lost more men and animals in the mountains than they lost in any battle with the Turks. Dispirited, with half their baggage trains lost, they came at last to the plains near the seacoast. They would have been even more dispirited if they had known that Yaghi-Siyan, the military governor of Antioch, had sent urgent messages to Aleppo, Damascus, Mosul, Baghdad, and as far as Persia, for reinforcements. His aim was to make Antioch impregnable by transforming the city into an armored fortress.

On October 20, four months after the battle of Nicaea, the Crusaders saw the high, biscuit-colored walls of Antioch in the distance. They were awestruck by the power and splendor of the city that stood in their way, defended by walls built by a Byzantine emperor and by a ruthless and well-organized Turkish army. They could not reach the Holy Sepulchre until Antioch was surrendered to them.

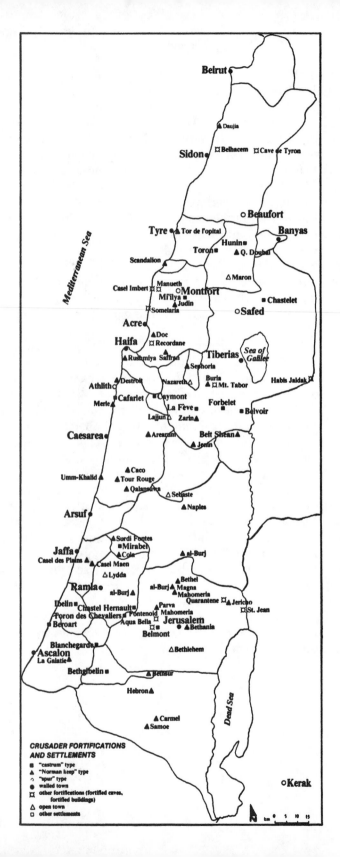

Beirut

▲ Daujia

Sidon ◻ Belhacem ◻ Cave de Tyron

○ **Beaufort**

Tyre ●▲ Tor de l'opital **Banyas**

Hunin■ **Toron**■ ▲ Q. Doubal

Scandalion▲ ▲ Maron

Casel Imbert ◻▲ Manueth■ **Montfort** ■ Chastelet
Mi'ilya■ ▲ Judin
◻ Somelaria ○ **Safed**

Acre● ▲ Doc
Haifa● ◻ Recordane

▲ Rushmiya Saffran▲ **Tiberias** ○ *Sea of Galilee*
▲ Sephoria
▲ Destroit Nazareth△ ▲ Buria **Habis Jaldak** ◻
Athlith○ **Caymont**■ ▲ ◻ Mt. Tabor

Merle▲ ▲ Cafarlet **La Fève**■ **Forbelet**
Lajjun△ Zarin▲ ▲ **Belvoir**

Caesarea ▲ Arearam **Beit Shean**▲
▲ Jenin

▲ Caco
Umm-Khalid ▲ ▲ Tour Rouge
▲ Qalansuwa △ Sebaste

Arsuf● ▲ Naples

▲ Surdi Fontes
Jaffa● ■ **Mirabel**
Casel des Plains ▲ △ Cola ▲ al-Burj
▲ Casel Maen
△ Lydda ▲ Bethel
Ramla● al-Burj ▲ al-Burj ▲ Magna
▲ Mahomeria
Ibelin● **Chastel Hernault**■ Quarantene ◻ Jericho
Toron des Chevaliers■ Fontenoid △ Parva ◻ St. Jean
■ Beroart Aqua Bella ◻ Mahomeria **Jerusalem**
Blanchegarde▲ **Belmont** ▲ Bethania

Ascalon●▲ △ Bethlehem
La Galatie▲
Bethgibelin ■ ▲ Bensur

Hebron▲

▲ Carmel
▲ Samoe

Mediterranean Sea

Dead Sea

○ **Kerak**

**CRUSADER FORTIFICATIONS
AND SETTLEMENTS**

■ "castrum" type
▲ "Norman keep" type
⌒ "spur" type
● walled town
◻ other fortifications (fortified caves,
  fortified buildings)
△ open town
□ other settlements

km 0   5   10   15

The Siege
of Antioch

NTIOCH was a city like no other in the Near East. It was once the largest in Asia; under the Romans it was the third largest of the empire; and in the time of the Crusades it was the richest and the most powerful city on the Palestinian coast. The seaport of St. Symeon, twelve miles away, was usually filled with ships, for Antioch was a vast trading center with merchants who came from North Africa, Egypt, Byzantium, from Central Asia and all the emirates in the hinterland. The city clustered at the foot of a mountain called Mount Silpius, and the fortifications extended to the top of the mountain. The river Orontes flowed just outside the city walls, which had originally been built by Justinian. Four hundred towers had been built into the walls, with the result that there was no part of the city that was not under examination by the troops stationed on the walls. Antioch, formidable in its wealth and defenses, and now made even more formidable by the determination of Yaghi-Siyan to hold it for the Muslims, was a city which in the normal course of events could resist a two-year siege without too much difficulty. It could be conquered only by treachery from within.

The military governor of Antioch was well aware that a large force of Crusaders was about to descend upon him, and he put the city in a state of defense. He was a capable commander but the Christians had no lack of equally capable commanders. For once the Christians were not quarreling excessively among themselves, and they settled down to besiege a city that by its very nature could not be completely blockaded, for there was always a way in which supplies could be brought in over those immensely long walls.

The first Christians to arrive on the Orontes River formed a small detachment under Bishop Adhémar of Le Puy. They attacked the Iron Bridge, which was heavily fortified with two huge towers, and when the bridge fell to them in a surprise assault, the road to Antioch lay open. On the following day, October 21, 1097, Bohemond came up with the vanguard of the army, and soon the entire Crusader army was deployed outside the walls of Antioch.

Even though the Crusaders could not encircle the city, they could set up their camps in places where the Turks were most vulnerable. Bohemond set up his camp opposite the Gate of St. Paul, where the mountains came down to the plain. Raymond of Toulouse, with the largest army, stood opposite the Gate of the Dog, farther to the west, while Godfrey of Bouillon commanded a position opposite the Gate of the Duke, still farther to the west. But there were no Crusaders facing the Gate of the Bridge and the Gate of St. George, and the road to the seaport of St. Symeon remained in the hands of the Turks.

At first the Crusaders simply mounted guard, with a few tentative assaults. They had spies in the city, and they felt it necessary to feel their way, to establish the geography of the place in their own minds. The Count of Toulouse characteristically demanded an immediate general attack. Bohemond, who wanted the city for himself, was more cautious. Least of all did he want an attack that would enable Adhémar and the count to claim the city for the pope. So for two weeks there was a standoff between the Turks inside the city and the Christian army outside.

During that time Yaghi-Siyan went about sending embassies for help to emirs and princes who would realize that the Crusaders must be stopped. The size of the Crusader army had surprised him.

Antioch was still a predominantly Christian city with a large population of Greeks and Armenians who were likely to go over to the enemy at the first opportunity. On the other hand, the Syrian Christians, long established in Antioch, were more loyal to Yaghi-Siyan because they had felt repressed by Byzantine rule. Yaghi-Siyan cultivated them, rewarding them handsomely for any information about the Crusaders. So the Christians within the city remained divided. If Bohemond hoped they would rise up against the Turks, whom they outnumbered, he was mistaken. Antioch would not fall like ripe fruit into their hands.

After a two-week wait Yaghi-Siyan decided to test the strength of the Christians. There were sorties, ambuscades, sudden descents from the hills above Bohemond's camp. There were some severe skirmishes, and the Christians began to lose heart. As winter came, they became increasingly fearful. They had gorged themselves on the sheep and cattle they found in the villages near Antioch; they had captured many granaries; they had taken possession of mills and bakeries; yet they had failed to make provision for the long days ahead. It was decided by the princes in council that they would have to detach some troops and march up the Orontes valley in search of provisions. Bohemond and Robert of Flanders were to lead the expedition, leaving Bishop Adhémar and the Count of Toulouse in command of the army outside the walls of Antioch. According to the chroniclers, Bohemond led twenty thousand Crusaders on this foraging expedition. This was an astonishingly large number of men to be detached from the main army, and it is possible that Bohemond was aware that a large column under Duqaq of Damascus was coming to relieve Antioch and that it was his duty to destroy it. The Turkish column encountered the column led by Robert of Flanders at Albara. Bohemond held back his forces, waiting for the first onslaught of the Turks to exhaust itself, and then hurled his own troops into battle. Robert's troops were badly mauled, but Duqaq's troops were torn to shreds. Yet there was little booty and there were almost no provisions to be found in the neighboring villages. Bohemond and Robert returned to Antioch, sadder and poorer. They had killed some Turks, and it was unlikely that Duqaq would ever again come to the relief of Antioch, but it was a hollow victory.

The days after their return from Albara were nightmarish. The earth trembled; the aurora borealis glittered in the shimmering sky; and soon the rain began to fall incessantly and the temperature dropped so low that they were all shivering. The suffering was so extreme that Bishop Adhémar ordered his army to fast for three days in the hope that God would have pity on his soldiers. The order may have seemed redundant to the starving soldiers.

Then, as the Crusaders received help from the Armenians in Cilicia and ships loaded with provisions and building materials reached the port of St. Symeon, the tide slowly began to turn. The Turks did their best to blockade the road leading to the seaport; Bohemond and the count of Toulouse broke through and some supplies were brought to the Crusader camps. But when an effort was made to bring a large caravan of supplies to Antioch, the Turks sent out strong columns to capture the caravan. The Crusaders lost three hundred men, but not the caravan. They had fought with desperation and renewed vigor because they knew that failure would mean death from starvation and the abandonment of the Crusade.

When spring came, there was a new excitement in the air. Bohemond still dreamed of making Antioch his own. He let it be known that he could no longer remain in Syria; he must return immediately to Italy. It was a ruse. He wanted the other leaders to let him set his own conditions for staying; so he said that if they gave him Antioch he would regard it as payment for his services and compensation for his absence from Italy. Bishop Adhémar, the Count of Toulouse, and Duke Godfrey remained unimpressed. Had the Crusaders come to the Holy Land for private profit? Was one man to benefit in a cause for which thousands upon thousands had died? Bohemond's followers argued that their handsome Norman had made himself the war-chieftain and deserved the prize.

In all his actions Bohemond showed that he possessed a fierce imagination and an absolute ruthlessness. When it was becoming evident that too many spies were coming out of Antioch, many of them disguised as Armenians, he acted in character. He ordered his cooks to prepare a meal of captured spies. The cooks obeyed him. The throats of the prisoners were cut, they were then spitted, and the cooks set about roasting them. When asked whether he really intended to eat Turkish spies, Bohemond answered that he was serving them up in a good cause. Everyone in the camp came running up to see the spies being turned on the spit, marveling at Bohemond's solution to a problem that had plagued the Crusader army for some time. That night all the remaining spies made their way secretly back to Antioch.

Bohemond had his own spies in Antioch among the Armenian Christians. There were some Christians who had been forced to embrace Islam and wanted to become Christians again. Among them was a certain Firouz, who commanded three towers and was in communication with Bohemond. After some coaxing, he offered to surrender his towers to Bohemond's forces. Bohemond addressed the council of princes and once more made claim to the city, saying that it was only proper to grant full possession of the city to one who conquered it or was able to bring about its downfall. The princes smelled a rat and decided against him, saying that the city should not be granted to a single man but to all, "for as we had had equal labor, so we should have equal honor."

Meanwhile, Kerbogha, Atabeg of Mosul, was at last bringing a large army to the relief of Antioch. The princes learned of the coming of Kerbogha and became frightened. There was a very real danger that they might be overwhelmed. Once more Bohemond addressed the council of princes, this time even more urgently exhorting them to grant him the city if he was the first to enter it. Adhémar appears to have demurred; the Count of Toulouse rejected the plan; Duke Godfrey accepted it. At this moment, with Kerbogha only three days' march away, Bohemond prepared to put in action the plan that had been delayed for so long. His spies went into the city, there were secret meetings with Firouz, and it was arranged that Bohemond's men should climb up a leather ladder slung from the Tower of the Two Sisters, near St. George's Gate. Antioch, attacked unsuccessfully for so many months, would be won by a single act of treachery.

Everything happened as Bohemond wanted it to happen. Sixty men climbed up the ladder, captured three towers, opened a gate, killed many Turks and caused widespread havoc even before Bohemond was aware of what was happening. Seeing that he was not on the walls, one of his soldiers went in search of him. Bohemond was surprised, followed the soldier into the city, and took command. His chief aim now was to plant his standard on the citadel, thus providing physical evidence that he possessed it. Soon the Gate of the Bridge and the Gate of St. George opened wide, and the Crusaders streamed in. It was shortly before dawn on June 3, 1098. Because Kerbogha was approaching, the Crusaders acted with the utmost speed, once they had taken the city. By the end of the day there was scarcely a single living Turk left in Antioch.

Antioch belonged to Bohemond: only the citadel refused to surrender. On the following day, the army of Kerbogha came up to the walls. It was at once obvious that this new army was large enough and strong enough to maintain a close blockade. The besiegers were now besieged. The Christians, who had suffered famine during the winter, when they were free to move about in the countryside, suffered all the more when they were enclosed within the great double walls.

From wild elation the Crusaders descended to despair. As Kerbogha's ring around the city tightened, the joy over the conquest of the city was exchanged for a melancholy knowledge that they could hold out only for a few weeks and would be forced to surrender.

There were dead Turks in all the alleyways, and the stench was so terrible that people walked about with squares of cloth covering the lower part of their faces. Astronomical prices were paid for food. Kerbogha let it be known that a special fate was reserved for the Crusaders: they would be marched to distant Khorassan and then sold in the slave markets.

On the day before Kerbogha began the encirclement of Antioch, one of the Crusader princes, Stephen, Count of Blois and Chartres, slipped out of the city, taking with him many members of his private army. He left the city partly because he was afraid, partly because he thought he could intervene with the emperor, Alexius Comnenus, and partly because he was at odds with Bohemond. In a letter to his wife he described the siege of Antioch as he saw it, before Kerbogha came to wreck the Crusaders' plans.

EXCERPTS FROM A LETTER FROM STEPHEN, COUNT OF BLOIS AND CHARTRES, TO HIS WIFE, ADELE, FROM ANTIOCH, MARCH 29, 1098.

... Together with all the chosen army of Christ, endowed with great valor by Him, we have been continually advancing for twenty-three weeks toward the home of our Lord Jesus. ...

... Hastening with great joy to the aforesaid chief city of Antioch, we besieged it and very often had many conflicts there with the Turks; and seven times with the citizens of Antioch and with the innumerable troops coming to its aid, whom we rushed to meet, we fought with the fiercest courage, under the leadership of Christ. And in all those seven battles, by the aid of the Lord God, we conquered and most assuredly killed an innumerable host of them. In those battles, indeed, and in very many attacks made upon the city, many of our brethren and followers were killed and their souls were borne to the joys of paradise.

We found the city of Antioch very extensive, fortified with incredible strength and almost impregnable. In addition, more than 5,000 bold Turkish soldiers had entered the city, not counting the Saracens, Publicans, Arabs, Turcopolitans, Syrians, Armenians and other different races of whom an infinite multitude had gathered together there. In fighting against these enemies of God and of our own we have, by God's grace, endured many sufferings and innumerable evils up to the present time. . . .

When truly Caspian, the emir of Antioch—that is, prince and lord—perceived that he was hard-pressed by us, he sent his son Sensodolo by name to the prince who holds Jerusalem, and to the prince of Calep, Rodoam, and to Docap, prince of Damascus. He also sent into Arabia to Bolianuth and to Carathania to Hemelnuth. These five emirs with 12,000 picked Turkish horsemen suddenly came to aid the inhabitants of Antioch. We, indeed, ignorant of all this, had sent many of our soldiers away to the cities and fortresses. . . . But a little before they reached the city, we attacked them at three leagues' distance with 700 soldiers on a certain plain near the "Iron Bridge." God, however, fought for us, who were faithful to Him, against our enemies. For on that day we fought with the strength given to us by God and conquered them, killing a great multitude—God was continually at our side—and we returned with more than 200 heads, so that the people might rejoice at the sight of them. . . .

On the day following Easter, while Alexander, my chaplain, was writing this letter in great haste, a party of our men were lying in wait for the Turks, fought well against them, killed sixty horsemen and brought their heads back to the army.

These things I am writing to you, dearest, are only a few of the things we have done; and because I cannot tell you, my darling, all that is in my heart, I charge you to do right and to watch carefully over your land, and to do your proper duty to your children and your vassals, for you will certainly see me as soon as I can come to you.

Farewell.

The King of
the Tafurs

I T was during the siege of Antioch that for the first time we see the
strange tribe of Tafurs. They had been there from the beginning,
invisible only because the chroniclers thought so little of them that
they were mentioned very rarely. Nearly everything we know about them
comes from the *Chanson d'Antioche,* an enormously long poem written by
Richard the Pilgrim and Graindor of Douai. There is not the least doubt
that the Tafurs existed and played an important role in the Crusade. We see
them in battle and sometimes we are aware of their presence even when
they cannot be seen clearly. Sometimes we have a glimpse of their faces:
hollow cheeks, burning eyes, ragged beards, wild hair falling to their
shoulders. If we could look closely into their eyes we would see spiritual
exaltation and terrible despair.

The Tafurs were the expendables, the poor devils who followed the army
to pick up the scraps; they were unskilled laborers, poor peasants, men who
would hold a bridle and expect a crust of bread for their pains. They were
the scavengers of the battlefield but they were also to be found among the
most daring of the warriors. They marched barefoot, sometimes naked, or
clad in rags, covered with sores and filth, too poor to afford swords and
lances, armed only with knives, clubs, pointed sticks, axes, and scythes.
They never rode on horseback and were always kept at a distance from the
main army in a kind of ghetto. In their own eyes they were the *plebs
pauperum,* the poor people of Christ, the Chosen Ones. They were never
paid, they expected no reward except the blessing of Christ and a place in
the Heavenly Jerusalem, and they fought like scrawny lions. They were the
rabble that accompanied all medieval armies, but with a difference. At a
word from their king they became shock troops, and they sometimes won
the battles that were credited to the Crusading knights.

The Tafurs were both well organized and without any visible organization. They had no training but were trained in battle. Their most remarkable quality after their poverty was their absolute indifference to danger.

They were all equal but they possessed a king, *le roi Tafur*. He was a Norman knight who had deliberately put aside sword and armor to wear sackcloth and wield a scythe. In the *Chanson d'Antioche* he appears as a formidable presence, towering over his naked rabble and leading them during their sudden onslaughts against the enemy. The king of the Tafurs had taken the vow of poverty and insisted that everyone in his army should do the same. If he found any Tafurs with money, he would order them to buy weapons and join the main army: to have money was a disgrace. A Tafur who put on the silk raiment he found in a Muslim house could expect to be drummed out of the Tafur kingdom.

Around the king of the Tafurs there gradually emerged a kind of collegium of men who were devoted to the laws of poverty and obedience. Significantly it was Bohemond, the wildest and most unscrupulous of the princes, who most often attempted to take the Tafurs under his command.

Yet the princes and the knights seem to have been in awe of the Tafurs. In battle they formed a human wave; they were mown down, but they continued to march against the enemy. When they entered a conquered town, they raped and murdered in a wild frenzy; and when the Emir of Antioch complained about their excesses, he was told, "All of us together cannot tame King Tafur."

They despised the princes who thought only of possessing principalities and kingdoms, and they despised the knights in their shining armor who rode on caparisoned horses. In their nakedness and poverty they regarded themselves as the true princes and the true knights, the only ones among the Crusaders who were sure of entering heaven. Cutthroats dressed in rags, they saw themselves as Christlike.

Guibert of Nogent is one of the few chroniclers who pays serious attention to the Tafurs. He had evidently seen them and had a deep feeling for them. Even at the time, people wondered whether they served a useful purpose or whether they were not more dangerous to the Christian army than to the Turks. Guibert of Nogent answered that they were absolutely essential to the conduct of the war against the Turks: they carried burdens uncomplainingly, guarded the pack animals, and he noted especially that they were adept at overturning the enemy's ballistas and siege engines by throwing rocks at them. They were a rabble in arms, lawless, terrible in their insolence and pride, and most terrible of all when they were in the greatest danger.

Because the Tafurs did not fit neatly into the categories of history, and because they were a living force of incalculable power and energy, they entered legend. There came a time during the siege of Antioch when the entire Christian army was living on starvation rations. Everyone suffered, even the knights, and the Tafurs suffered most of all. Desperate measures had to be taken. According to the *Chanson d'Antioche* the Tafurs resorted to cannibalism, eating dead Turks wherever they could find them:

... They flayed the Turks and removed the entrails:
By boiling and roasting they cooked the flesh.
Thus they ate while tasting no bread.

When the poet goes on to record the miracles of valor performed by the Tafurs during the siege of Antioch and again during the siege of Jerusalem, we believe him. Yet they are never mentioned in the reports the Crusader princes sent to Rome and to the kings of Christendom. We must remember that they existed, and many of the Crusader victories would have been impossible without the presence of these wild and relentless soldiers dedicated to poverty.

Bohemond, who came to appreciate the Tafurs and used them effectively, himself possessed something of their spirit. He had their ruthlessness, their cunning, their contempt for danger. With Antioch under siege and the Turks pressing hard against the walls he sometimes behaved like an army of Tafurs. At night he would race through the streets by torchlight, in search of deserters and traitors, rounding up the starving soldiers who slept in private houses, sending them to guard the walls; and sometimes he found it necessary to flush them out by burning down houses. In this way whole districts went up in flames and Bohemond would be seen with drawn sword, giving commands, cursing the imbecility of the soldiers who preferred sleep to fighting Turks.

Though he was not bedridden, the Count of Toulouse was too ill to assume the full defense of the city. He was given the task of isolating the Turkish soldiers cooped up in the citadel to prevent their escape. Bohemond was given full powers. He organized the defense of the city to the last detail, and in the same way he organized the great sortie on June 28, 1098, which led to the rout of Kerbogha and all his forces.

During those weeks in June strange things were happening in Antioch. Men suffered from hallucinations, saw divine portents in the sky, and were exhilarated by the knowledge that God would protect them against all odds. Barefoot priests walked along the ramparts, consoling the starving soldiers. It was at this time that the Holy Lance was found, bringing hope of ultimate victory, for it seemed that God had placed it among them in order to hearten them.

Early on the morning of June 28, the army of Antioch marched out through the Gate of the Bridge against the army of Kerbogha, who could have prevented them from leaving the gate by massing his troops outside it. He was so sure that he could defeat the Christian forces on the plain outside of Antioch that he permitted them to come out. He was playing chess when he heard that the Christians were pouring out of the gate. He was advised by his Arab commander to attack at once. Instead he continued his game of chess and said something about the need for the whole Christian army to appear so that he could destroy it with a single overwhelming blow.

The Christians continued their steady advance while Kerbogha ordered his troops to retreat to rougher ground, luring the Christians further from Antioch. He seemed so certain of victory that he paid scant attention to the disposition of his forces. The Christians, too, were certain of victory. The Holy Lance beckoned them on their way. Some soldiers said that on a hillside they had seen a company of horsemen with white banners, and they thought they recognized St. George, St. Mercurius, and St. Demetrius. All the portents indicated victory. Kerbogha ordered his men to set fire to the grass. This might have been dangerous to the Christians, but the wind blew toward the Turkish lines instead. While the grass crackled with flames, and the army advanced, and the Tafurs crept around the Turkish defenses, Kerbogha lost his nerve, and his army disintegrated. By the end of the morning the battle was over, Turkish dead were everywhere, and Kerbogha fled in the direction of Mosul, leaving his treasure and his stores of food and provisions to the Christians. For the first time in many weeks the Christians were well fed.

The historian Raymond of Aguilers was among those who took part in the battle. His task was to be the bearer of the Holy Lance, carrying it on a long pole so that it could be seen by all the soldiers. To the end of his life he believed the Holy Lance was the instrument of victory.

The Finding of the Holy Lance

OF the handful of men who recorded the First Crusade as it happened, the most intelligent was Raymond of Aguilers, who was a canon attached to the Cathedral of Le Puy and the chaplain of the count of Toulouse. He was a man of the Auvergne, kindly, sardonic, deeply religious, accustomed to hardship and not overtalkative, unlike the Provençal soldiers who formed the greater part of the count's army. The chief characteristics of men of the mountainous Auvergne are a certain reserve and a certain canniness in weighing up evidence. They are somewhat secretive, do not try to stand out in a crowd, and do not suffer fools gladly. Raymond liked and admired the Provençal soldiers and at the same time stood a little apart from them.

He wrote his history, which he called *Historia Francorum Qui Ceperunt Iherusalem*, with the declared purpose of correcting the errors of men who had deserted and returned to France, where they spread wild stories about the excruciating hardships undergone by the Crusaders. Raymond was not himself particularly interested in hardships and he leaves some of the most terrible passages unrecorded. He wrote in a clear, muscular style, consciously or unconsciously quoting from the Bible, and, unlike Bishop Adhémar, he was interested in relics and visions and the sudden manifestations of divinity that sometimes interrupted his care of the souls of Provençal soldiers.

So it came about that shortly after the fall of Antioch, a Provençal peasant named Peter Bartholomew came to him with a story so improbable that scarcely anyone could be expected to believe it. Peter Bartholomew said that Christ and St. Andrew had come to him four times, requesting that he should deliver an urgent message to Bishop Adhémar and the Count of Toulouse. The message was a simple one. He, Peter Bartholomew, must be allowed to present to the bishop and the count the Lance that pierced the side of the Savior. Peter Bartholomew went on to say that during the day's fighting outside the city, he had been caught between two horsemen and almost choked to death during the retreat. Finally, when he sank down, almost dead, outside the walls, lying on a rock, shivering with shock and fear, St. Andrew came to him again, with a companion. The saint said that great evil would befall Peter Bartholomew unless his message was delivered immediately.

Raymond of Aguilers was intimately acquainted with Bishop Adhémar and the Count of Toulouse, and he was sufficiently impressed to arrange a meeting. It would never have occurred to him that St. Andrew and Christ might have saved time and energy by communicating directly with the bishop and the count, for he knew that God sends messages through his humblest subjects and an authentic vision could suitably have come from a poor peasant. Peter Bartholomew was received graciously, and, in the presence of secretaries who took down his words, he said that he had received the first vision five months earlier when the Crusaders were encamped outside the walls of Antioch. On the last day of the year there had been an earthquake. At night, alone in his hut, in mortal terror because the earth was shaking, he had called upon God for aid—*"Deus adjuva me!"*

It was the cry of a soldier in battle or a man on his deathbed. The earthquake lasted for a long time, and all the while he was becoming more terrified. Then he looked up and saw two men in shining costumes. One had red hair sprinkled with white, a bushy white beard, black eyes that were well suited to his countenance, and was of medium height. The younger and taller man was beautiful beyond the sons of men. Peter Bartholomew had no doubt that the younger man was Christ. He related to the bishop and the count what had happened:

Knowing that no one was there, I cried out in great fear: "Who are you?"

Then he said: "Rise up, do not be afraid, and listen to me. I am Andrew the Apostle. . . . Follow me and I will show you the Lance of our Father, which you shall give to the Count, for indeed God has set it aside for him from the time of his birth."

I rose from my bed and followed him into Antioch, naked except for my shirt. We went through the north gate to the Church of blessed Peter the Apostle, which the Saracens had transformed into a mosque. In the church there were two lamps that shone with so much light that it was as though it was midday. And then he said: "Remain here." Then he bade me stand beside the column near the steps which lead up to the altar from the south, and his companion remained at a considerable distance, in front of the altar steps. St. Andrew reached beneath the ground and drew out the Lance, which he placed in my hands.

"Behold the Lance which pierced his side, whence came the salvation of the whole world."

While I held it in my hands, weeping for joy, I said: "Lord, if you so wish, let me take it and give it to the Count."

And he said to me: "No, wait until the time when the city is taken. And then come here with twelve men and seek it in the place where I drew it out of the earth and where I now replace it." And then he buried it. When all this had taken place, he led me over the walls to my own house and then they vanished.

Peter Bartholomew evidently spoke with great deliberation and gave all ꜰe appearance of saying something that he believed to be true. The most ꜰmous sentence reads: *Ecce lancia quae latus ejus aperuit unde totius ꜰundi salus emenavit.* It was a bold statement, saying that the lance-thrust ꜰrought about Christ's death and this in turn brought about the salvation ꜰ the whole world. To soldiers such a statement would be entirely com-ꜰehensible; it would be less comprehensible to theologians. The Crusad-ꜰs had a battle cry, *Deus vult,* but they lacked a symbolic image. Now at ꜰst a symbol was to be given to them—a lance of hammered metal only a ꜰw inches long, something one could hold in the palm of one's hand, ꜰmost insignificant in appearance, but fraught with meaning.

All this had happened many months before, and the bishop and the ꜰunt may have wondered why he was so late in relating his vision. Peter ꜰartholomew said he simply dared not at that time approach people of ꜰeat eminence. The vision had evidently terrified him, and he was even ꜰore terrified by the prospect of telling his story to the bishop and the ꜰunt. At Lent, he found himself in camp in the neighborhood of Edessa, ꜰraging for food. Once again, St. Andrew appeared to him accompanied ꜰ his silent companion. St. Andrew asked him whether he had delivered ꜰe message, and Peter Bartholomew replied that he had failed to do so out ꜰ a sense of his own poverty and insignificance. St. Andrew rebuked him ꜰernly:

> Do you not know why God brought you here, the greatness of his love for you, and above all how he made choice of you? He made you come here in order to avenge him and to avenge his people. His love for you is so great that there are saints who are now at rest and who are aware of his fondness for you that they desire to take on flesh and fight by your side. God has chosen you from all the nations just as grains of wheat are gathered from oats. In merit and grace you stand out above all who went before you or will come after you, as the price of gold exceeds that of silver.

St. Andrew's rebuke, and his vast flattery, were unavailing. Peter Barthol-ꜰew fell ill, his eyes began to trouble him, and he made a will, disposing

of his few possessions. He had taken service under a certain William Pete
and was resting in a tent overlooking the port of St. Symeon. It was the ev
of Palm Sunday. Now St. Andrew appeared for the third time, and onc
more he asked whether the message had been delivered. Peter Bartholomev
answered that he had prayed that someone else might be sent, someon
wiser, someone they might listen to. And then there was another reason
although the port of St. Symeon was close to Antioch, he was afraid of th
Turks he might encounter on the journey. St. Andrew said, "Don't b
afraid! No harm will befall you!" Then he went on to give Peter Barthol
omew precise instructions about what the Count of Toulouse should d
when he reached the River Jordan: he must not allow himself to b
baptized in the river but must take a boat to the other side, and then h
should be sprinkled while clad in a shirt and linen breeches, and thereafte
when his clothes had dried, he should put them away and keep then
together with the Holy Lance.

Peter Bartholomew returned to Antioch, made some feeble attempts t
contact the bishop and the count, and then in despair went off to the port o
Mamistra, intending to take ship to Cyprus, where there was abundan
food and where there were no Turks. Here, for the fourth time St. Andrev
encountered his unwilling messenger, warning him that he would b
severely punished if he failed to carry out the saint's orders. It was
three-day journey from Mamistra to Antioch; the countryside was infeste
with Turks, and the thought of traveling to Antioch was so depressing tha
he became hysterical. He decided to reach Cyprus at all costs. Three time
the ship set out for Cyprus, and three times it was blown back by storms
Peter Bartholomew fell ill. He realized now that he could no longer escap
from the power of St. Andrew. A few days later he heard the news tha
Antioch had fallen to the Crusaders. Ill though he was, he made his wa
back to Antioch, sought out Raymond of Aguilers, and told him the stor
of his visions.

Peter Bartholomew was not the only visionary who saw Christ and th
saints. The Crusader camp teemed with visionaries. Everywhere there wer
exhausted men starving and in terrible danger and in a state of religiou
exaltation. Raymond of Aguilers, himself no visionary, believed in Pete
Bartholomew's visions, and he also believed in the visions of a Provença
priest called Stephen of Valence.

Fearing that the Turks were about to overwhelm Antioch, Stephen o
Valence with a few companions entered the Church of St. Mary, made hi
confession, received absolution for his sins, and began to chant hymns. Hi
companions at last fell asleep, and the priest found himself saying over an
over again, "Lord, who shall abide in thy tabernacle? Who shall dwell i
thy holy mountain?" Suddenly a man of great beauty appeared to him.

"Who have entered Antioch?" the man said.

"Christians," Stephen replied.

"If they are Christians, why are they in dread of the multitudes of pagans?"

Gradually, as they were talking, Stephen began to see the form of a Cross appearing above Christ's head. It grew brighter until it shone like the sun. Out of this brightness there came a voice urging the Crusaders to turn away from sin and to remember that he was the Lord of Hosts, mighty and powerful in battle, before whom all the pagans would be compelled to bow down. Christ spoke with immense authority. His last words to the priest were, "I shall be compassionate toward you if you do what I command in five days."

Although Antioch was in Crusader hands, fear of a massive attack was uppermost in men's minds. Panic swept through the city. Some of the knights, including William of Grant-Mesnil, who was Bohemond's brother-in-law, slipped over the walls and made their way to the seacoast. Bohemond and Bishop Adhémar ordered the closing of the gates to prevent wholesale evacuation. A meteor appeared over Antioch, seemed to hover in the night sky, and at last broke up into three separate streaks of light, which all plunged into the Turkish camp. No one knew what it meant, only that it was ominous. Stephen of Valence's vision of Christ, the coming of the meteor, the paralyzing knowledge that Kerbogha was about to attack and that some of the knights and many of the soldiers were attempting to escape from the city, led Raymond of Aguilers and the Count of Toulouse to weigh the evidence. They asked themselves what Christ meant when he said, "I shall be compassionate toward you if you do what I command in five days." What did he command? In Raymond of Aguilers's mind it meant that they must search for the Holy Lance that lay somewhere below or near the high altar of the Church of St. Peter. Christ was offering them a sign: the Holy Lance, which was almost in their grasp.

On the morning of June 14, five days after Stephen of Valence had seen the vision, Raymond of Aguilers entered the Church of St. Peter, having chosen twelve of his friends to witness the finding of the Lance. The church was closed off: no one was allowed to enter or depart without the chaplain's permission. Raymond was determined that the Lance be found.

The digging went on feverishly all morning; more diggers were brought in; Peter Bartholomew explained where he expected to find it; and by evening there was nothing to show for their labor except a gaping hole below the high altar. Suddenly, when they had almost lost hope, Peter Bartholomew threw off his gown and jumped into the hole wearing only his shirt, and he summoned all those who were present to pray that the Lance would be revealed. They prayed, and Peter Bartholomew saw the point of the Lance sticking out of the earth. Raymond of Aguilers clambered down and kissed the point before the Lance was extricated from the earth. There followed wild rejoicing, the Lance was offered up on the high altar, hymns were sung, bells were rung, and on the following day the Lance was carried in procession through the city.

Raymond of Aguilers never had the slightest doubt that the true Lance had been found. Had he not seen it even before the earth had loosened its grip on it? He was confirmed in his belief that God spoke in signs and through visions and he was overwhelmed with joy. With this Lance Christ had been killed and with the help of this Lance the Crusaders would destroy the infidels who had taken possession of the Holy Sepulchre.

On the following day Peter Bartholomew had another vision. St. Andrew and Christ both appeared to him, and on the foot of Christ he saw the fresh and bloody wounds left by the nails.

The Holy Lance became the talisman of the Crusaders. Wrapped in rich brocade, and solemnly unwrapped for the benefit of those permitted to kiss it, it was shown on hundreds of occasions to the faithful. It was taken into battle in order to spur on the advance. The Count of Toulouse kept it in his private chapel, for it was the physical evidence of his authority, the demonstrable symbol of God's willingness that he should lead the Crusade. It was both a religious and political weapon, not simply an object to be worshipped and put away. In the name of the Lance, the gift of Christ and St. Andrew, Peter Bartholomew continued to prophesy the course of the war and to recount the messages he received from Christ. The Lance would continue to speak through people long after Peter Bartholomew was dead.

What the Lance said always reflected the position of the Count of Toulouse. It ordered the Crusaders to put away sin, to give alms to the Church, and to have faith in Christ's power to trample the infidels underfoot. Leaf-shaped, of hammered iron, the Lance seemed in the eyes of the Provençals a living presence.

Yet there were many, especially among the Normans, who did not believe in visions. Robert of Normandy's chaplain, Arnulf of Chocques, accepted the vision, then denied it, then accepted it again. Bishop Adhémar, who lived only a few weeks after the lance was found, did not accept the visions that led to it. Peter Bartholomew, driven to fury by the doubters, announced that there was a simple way by which he could prove the truth of his visions. "I not only desire but I beg you to light a fire," he said, "and I shall submit to the ordeal by fire with the Lance in my hands. If it is truly the Lord's Lance, then I shall emerge unburned, but if it a false Lance I shall be consumed by the fire."

On April 8, 1099, at a time when the Christian army was on its way to Jerusalem, Peter Bartholomew took the ordeal by fire. It was Good Friday. Peter Bartholomew had fasted during the four previous days. At dawn, dry olive branches were gathered and stacked up until they formed two solid rows a foot apart. The height of the stacks was given as four feet and the length as thirteen feet. At midday a crowd of some sixty thousand persons watched the ordeal. Flames were shooting into the air when Raymond of guilers offered prayers, imploring God either to confirm the visions or deny them. The bishop of Albara gave Peter Bartholomew the Lance wrapped in embroidered cloth, and there was a moment of prayer before Peter Bartholomew, barefoot and wearing only a tunic, entered the small forest of burning olive wood. Since the logs were only four feet high, his head and shoulders could sometimes be seen through the flames. They observed that, when he was about halfway, he paused; afterward he explained that Jesus had come to him in the flames and said, "You shall not cross without wounds, but you shall not see hell." Jesus had held his hands, and then let go. Thereupon Peter Bartholomew continued his journey.

At last he emerged. He waved to the crowd, held the Lance high above his head, and screamed, "God help us!" It was observed that his tunic was unscorched, and so was the embroidered cloth wrapped around the Lance. The crowd surged around him, hoping to touch him or snatch a piece of the tunic, jostling him so roughly that he was in danger of being physically harmed, and in fact he suffered three or four gashes on his legs and a cracked spine. Later, when he was examined, it was discovered that his wounds were more serious than his burns.

Even now the skeptics were not completely convinced, but there were many who believed that a man could not pass through the flames alive without God's blessing. Less than two weeks later, on April 20, Peter Bartholomew died. Raymond of Aguilers was quite certain he died as a result of the wounds inflicted on him after he had passed through the fire. He was buried in the place where he had suffered his ordeal. The Holy Lance remained in the possession of the Count of Toulouse, and it accompanied him to Jerusalem.

Of all the relics that have been handed down from generation to generation—the Crown of Thorns, the Nails, the wood of the Holy Cross, the Holy Shroud, all the skulls of the saints to be found in the churches of Rome and the monasteries of Mount Athos, and all the vast assembly of relics dispersed throughout Europe after the sack of Constantinople in A.D. 1204—the Lance remains the only relic of whose discovery we know the exact moment. Whether true or false, for the Crusaders who believed in it, it provided a poignant justification for their march on Jerusalem. It was so small that one could hold it in one's hand, and so large that it filled their imaginations. The Lance was God's promise of victory.

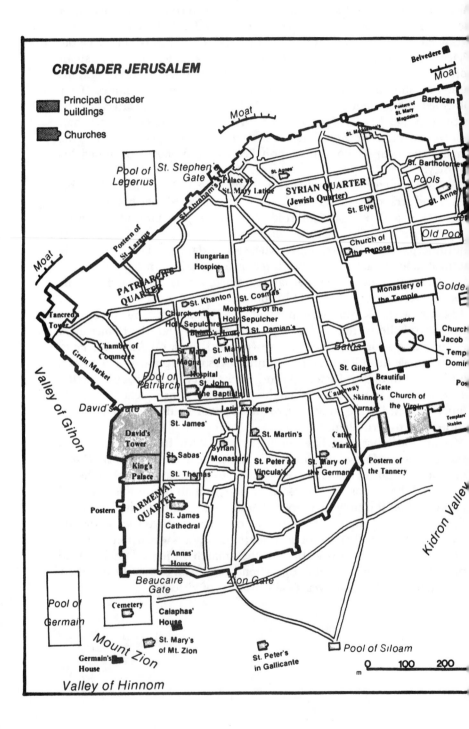

CRUSADER JERUSALEM

Principal Crusader buildings

Churches

Belvedere

Moat

Moat

Barbican

Postern of St. Mary Magdalen

St. Magdalen's

Pool of Legerius

St. Stephen's Gate

St. Agnes'

St. Bartholomew

Palace of St. Mary Latin

SYRIAN QUARTER (Jewish Quarter)

Pools

St. Anne

St. Elye

Old Pool

Moat

Postern of St. Lazarus

Hungarian Hospice

Church of the Repose

PATRIARCH'S QUARTER

St. Khanton

St. Cosmas'

Monastery of the Temple

Golde

Tancred Tower

Church of the Holy Sepulchre

Monastery of the Holy Sepulcher

Bishop's House

St. Damian's

Baptistry

Church Jacob

Chamber of Commerce

St. Mary Magna

St. Mary of the Latins

Baths

Temp Domir

Grain Market

Pool of Patriarch

Hospital St. John the Baptist

St. Giles

Beautiful Gate

Church of the Virgin

Pos

David's Gate

Latin Exchange

Skinner's Turnac

Causeway

Templars' Stables

David's Tower

St. James'

St. Martin's

King's Palace

St. Sabas'

Syrian Monastery

St. Thomas'

St. Peter ad Vincula's

Cattle Market

St. Mary of the German

Postern of the Tannery

Valley of Gihon

Postern

ARMENIAN QUARTER

St. James Cathedral

Annas' House

Kidron Valley

Beaucaire Gate

Zion Gate

Pool of Germain

Cemetery

Caiaphas' House

Mount Zion

St. Mary's of Mt. Zion

Germain's House

St. Peter's in Gallicante

Pool of Siloam

0 100 200
m

Valley of Hinnom

The Triumph

ANTIOCH had fallen to the Crusaders on June 28, 1098, but six months passed before they were able to resume their march on Jerusalem. Those six months were spent in paralyzing quarrels among the princes, while the armies rested and accustomed themselves to life in the East. There were brothels in Antioch, and the soldiers frequented them. There were defense posts to be repaired, supplies and provisions had to be found, an orderly way of life had to be discovered. Bohemond still claimed Antioch as his own, and he quarreled with the Count of Toulouse over the possession of Maarat al-Numan, a recently captured stronghold. The troops, who were well aware of these princely quarrels, took matters in their own hands: they fell on the stronghold and demolished it.

On January 13, 1099, the Count of Toulouse, having decided that the quarrels were depleting his energies and that too much time had been wasted, already set out for Jerusalem, leaving Bohemond behind to enjoy the luxuries of Antioch. The count saw himself destined to be the conqueror of Jerusalem. The march, though slow, was surprisingly easy. The emirs hastened to offer food to the great army, which would otherwise have trampled them to death. Spring came; the flowers were in bloom. As the Crusaders marched along the beautiful coastal road, they were in a frenzy of hope. Near Joppa, the modern Jaffa, the army turned inland, and began the ascent to Jerusalem.

Now Jerusalem lay before them, her yellow walls shining in the hot summer sun, banners flying from her towers. Iftikhar ad-Daula, the governor of the city and the commander of the garrison forces, had placed Jerusalem in a posture of formidable strength. He had adequate armaments and provisions for a long siege and troops who were intensely loyal to him. Moreover, an Egyptian army was on the way. The wells around the city had been poisoned, and he had had all the flocks of sheep and goats on the neighboring hills rounded up and brought into the city. The thousands of Christians living in Jerusalem were expelled and sent into the

Judaean wilderness. The Jews were permitted to remain, perhaps becaus
they possessed stores that could be made available to the defenders. From
his spies the governor learned that his own Arab and Nubian troop
outnumbered the invaders, who seemed to be ill equipped to invest a city a
large and as powerful as Jerusalem. He hoped the Egyptian army woul
arrive soon. Then the Crusading army would vanish from the face of th
earth as though it had never existed.

Iftikhar was a good general, capable of inspiring acts of heroism from
his troops. He was also a careful and cautious general, who had mad
sure that he had ample supplies of water and food. He had ordered tha
the towers should be filled with bales of cotton and hay to strengthen them
against bombardment. He acted coolly at all times and earned the admira
tion of the Crusaders.

The siege began on the day the Crusaders reached the Mosque of th
Prophet Samuel. From this hilltop, traditionally known to pilgrims a
Montjoie, the Joyous Mountain, they could see the whole of Jerusalem
lying before them. The day was June 7, 1099.

The princes had pored over maps, and considered the reports of thei
spies; in addition, they knew the lay of the land. Jerusalem was defended on
three sides—the east, south, and west—by deep ravines; the north wall wa
easily accessible, and so was Mount Zion in the southwest corner. Th
Crusaders under Robert of Normandy took up their places facing th
north wall, and those under the Count of Toulouse faced Mount Zion
Godfrey of Lorraine's troops covered the northwest angle of the city as fa
down as the Jaffa Gate, while Robert of Flanders kept watch over th
Damascus Gate. Jerusalem was not encircled; it was being besieged on tw
fronts. Yet, in a very real sense, the encirclement was complete, for all th
land around Jerusalem belonged to the invaders and the city was isolated

The first five days were spent in bringing up the carts laden with th
separate pieces of siege engines, and with the search for provisions, an
especially for water. Raymond of Aguilers, who accompanied the count'
forces at Mount Zion, describes how the men crowded around the Pool o
Siloam at the foot of the hill. The fountain gushed every third day. Thi
was one of those inexplicable things that could only be ascribed to the wil
of God. The soldiers were raging with thirst and when the fountain begar
to gush they jostled and fought with one another so violently that some fel
into it, and so did the horses and cattle brought to the watering place. H
continues:

> Those who were strong pushed and shoved their way in a
> deathly fashion through the pool, which was already choked with
> dead animals and men struggling for their lives, and in this way
> they reached the rocky mouth of the fountain, while those who
> were weaker were left behind in the filthy water. These weaker

ones sprawled on the ground beside the pool with gaping mouths, their parched tongues making them speechless, while they stretched out their hands to beg water from the more fortunate ones.

In the nearby fields horses, mules, cattle, sheep, and many other animals were standing, too weak to move. They shriveled and died of thirst, rotting where they stood, and they filled the air with the smell of death.

So the days passed in deadening heat and choking dust, and strong winds rose full of the sun's heat. There was little shade; all the trees around Jerusalem had been cut down. The Crusaders had to bring water from springs five or six miles away, and men paid small fortunes for a mouthful of water. The Saracens succeeded in ambushing some of the water-carriers.

By June 12, when the armies were settling down, the princes made a pilgrimage to the Mount of Olives and here they encountered an old hermit who said, "If you will attack the city tomorrow to the ninth hour, the Lord will deliver it into your hands!"

The princes were puzzled. The army was not yet ready for a general assault. The scaling ladders, the siege engines, and the wooden towers were not yet in place.

"The siege machinery is not here," the princes said.

The hermit replied that the siege machinery had nothing to do with it. "God is all powerful," he answered. "If He wills, you can scale the walls with a single ladder. He is on the side of those who work for the Truth."

The princes were so impressed with the hermit's argument that they did exactly as he had ordered. They commanded a general assault with improvised siege engines and, according to Raymond of Aguilers, a few Crusaders succeeded in reaching the parapets and there was continuous fighting until the third hour. Raymond of Aguilers, who had faith in hermits and miracles, reported that the attack would have been successful if it had not been for the sloth and fear of the princes who called it off too soon.

This reverse discouraged many of the soldiers, who went on foraging expeditions, searching for fodder and water for their horses, and food and water for themselves. At this moment the army became disorganized and a sortie by the defenders of Jerusalem might have destroyed the Crusaders preparing to attack along the north wall. The princes, however, regained command of their troops very quickly, announcing that there would be no further assaults until they had constructed more mangonels and siege engines. For all these they needed stout wooden timbers, but there was scarcely a tree left standing in the neighborhood of Jerusalem.

Providentially there arrived on June 17 at Jaffa six ships laden with provisions and armaments together with the tackle, ropes, nails, iron bolts, and leather hides needed for the making of siege engines. The ships also carried some timber, but not enough for the Crusaders' purpose. The Muslims were determined that these supplies should not reach the Crusader army and sent four hundred of their best Arab troops and two hundred Turks to Ramleh, a few miles inland on the road from Jaffa to Jerusalem. A certain Count Geldemar Carpenel, attached to Godfrey of Bouillon's staff, was sent with twenty knights and fifty infantrymen to secure the passage of the supplies. It was quickly realized that this might not be a sufficiently large force. Raymond Pilet with fifty knights was sent after Count Carpenel, and later still another force was sent out, consisting of William of Sabran, who belonged to the army of the Count of Toulouse. On the plain of Ramleh there was a hard-fought battle between the Crusader forces and the Muslims. Six hundred Muslims confronted seventy Christians. Five knights were killed, all the archers died, and there were about thirty survivors when the Muslims saw a cloud of dust on the horizon. Fifty additional knights were coming to the rescue. The Muslims, fearing that they would be outnumbered, fled. The Christian troops went off to Jaffa to find that the sailors had unloaded the supplies but an Egyptian fleet was blockading the port. One of the English ships succeeded in slipping past the Egyptians at night, while the remaining ships were abandoned. The sailors accompanied the knights to Jerusalem with all their stores.

Although these stores were welcome, coming at a time when the Crusaders were losing heart, they were not enough to ensure a successful siege. Water and wood had to be found. A surprisingly large amount of wood was required to build the great towers that would be set against the walls of Jerusalem. New mangonels were needed. There was also a great need for scaling ladders, as many as possible. While expeditions to get wood went farther and farther afield the princes met, debated, quarreled, and sometimes came to the conclusion that it was better not to make decisions when there was so much disagreement. The clergy disputed Tancred's claim to be lord of Bethlehem, which he had captured during a quick foray, leaving his banner waving over the Church of the Nativity as a sign of ownership. Some of the princes defended Tancred; the clergy remained adamant. In their eyes Bethlehem and its church were too holy to be under the jurisdiction of anyone except the pope. Similarly, when they discussed the future government of Jerusalem there were arguments about the title of its ruler. Should he be called King of Jerusalem? But if Christ himself had worn a crown of thorns, was it not a mockery of Christianity to grant to a mortal man a title that belonged to the Son of God? Popular feeling, backed by the clergy, insisted that no man was worthy to be called King of Jerusalem. This matter, too, was deferred.

Although the siege engines and towers, the scaling ladders and mangonels, and all the other engines of war were being constructed at a rapid pace—the army turned into a vast carpentry shop—no decision about the date of the assault had been reached by the end of June. There was a sense of urgency; but there was also the conviction that there could be no failure of equipment; the great towers must be built solidly, and everybody in the army must know what was expected of him.

Everyone was working to the point of exhaustion; something more was needed to spur them to even greater effort. What was really needed, in the eyes of Raymond of Aguilers and the Count of Toulouse and perhaps also in the eyes of the other princes, was a sure sign from God, like the discovery of the Holy Lance at Antioch.

This came on the morning of July 6 when the priest Peter Desiderius, who was known to have had visions previously, announced that the dead Bishop Adhémar of Le Puy had come to him with a message addressed to all the Crusaders. (The bishop had died of high fever in August 1098.) The bishop urged them to free themselves from the filth of the world, put sin behind them, and walk barefoot around the walls of Jerusalem. If they did all these things, then at the end of nine days, after a violent assault, the city would fall. If they did not, then God would increase their misfortunes.

Since Bishop Adhémar had been, until his death, theoretically the commander of the Crusaders and the ultimate authority under the pope, his ghostly words held special force. A general assembly was called to consider the new commandment. It was agreed that the bishop had indeed spoken through Peter Desiderius and his commandment must be obeyed. Had not Christ humbled himself by entering Jerusalem on an ass? Therefore, the Christians must humble themselves in a similar manner: they must walk meekly in the sight of the Lord, imitating Christ.

Two days later an extraordinary procession, led by priests carrying crosses and holy relics, and followed by knights and infantrymen, marched around the walls of Jerusalem. All were barefoot. Some of the soldiers brandished their weapons; the trumpeters blew on their trumpets; all were moved by the solemnity of the occasion. Raymond of Aguilers, who took part in the procession and later delivered a sermon addressed to the whole army on the Mount of Olives, remembered that it was very noisy and the Saracens on the walls amused themselves by erecting crosses on which they performed obscene acts. The crosses were supported on gibbets and could, therefore, be made to swing backward and forward when they were struck. The sight of the blasphemed crosses only stirred the Christians to firmer resolution.

The march around the walls was both a penitential procession and the celebration of a triumph. From that morning, everyone seemed to know that Jerusalem would be conquered.

A certain Gaston, Viscount of Béarn, was now placed in charge of the towers and siege engines on the northern wall, while William Embriaco was placed in charge of the construction of the towers and siege engines at Mount Zion. Huge balks of timber carried by captured Muslims could be seen making their way toward Jerusalem. Raymond of Aguilers speaks of great logs supported on the backs of fifty or sixty Muslims.

The princes worked out a timetable. On July 9 they were able to determine that the assault would take place on the night of July 13, for the great towers and siege engines were nearly completed and it only remained to put them in place. The attack would be launched simultaneously from Mount Zion and along the eastern sector of the northern wall.

At the last moment Godfrey of Bouillon and the counts of Flanders and Normandy made an abrupt change of plan. During the night, the largest tower was wheeled, with enormous difficulty, to another place a half mile away, because it was known that the Saracens were concentrating their forces where the tower had been. This tower was now facing the north wall near Herod's Gate. At Mount Zion the Count of Toulouse was offering a *denarius* to anyone who would carry three heavy stones to help to fill the dip in the land that prevented him from bringing his tower close to the walls. He paid the money out of his own purse and the dip was quickly filled.

We know surprisingly little about the fighting that took place throughout July 14. The towers closed in on the walls; the sappers were at work. The Christians battered at the walls with petraries and mangonels, instruments for hurling stones, and the huge siege engines, which could throw heavy rocks over the walls. The Saracens fought rocks and stones with fire. They hurled wooden bolts wrapped in rags aflame with burning pitch, sulfur, wax, and tow at the invaders; the bolts were provided with long nails so that they stuck to whatever they touched. The Saracens fought stubbornly. It is possible that there were too many of them—Raymond of Aguilers says there were sixty thousand of them against no more than thirteen hundred Christian knights, twelve thousand infantrymen, and workmen of all kinds—and they got in each other's way, crowding the parapets and walkways. They were less maneuverable, and perhaps less disciplined, than the Crusaders, who were attempting at many different places to claw their way up the walls with ropes and scaling ladders. The two huge towers, once they were joined to the walls, presented the greatest danger to the Muslims. It was precisely in these places, at Mount Zion and on the north wall, that the Muslims needed skilled engineers rather than soldiers. Meanwhile, they did everything they could to burn down the towers, which were covered with skins and hides to protect them from fire. The task of the Crusaders was to make a single breach in the walls through which the army could pour in.

The Muslims were well supplied with Greek fire: burning pitch and sulfur. The Crusaders used fire only with the flaming arrows they shot into the city. Sheets of flame fell on the Crusaders. Bales of hay, liberally sprinkled with oil and wax, were tossed over the walls, the hay continuing to burn long after it had reached the ground. Huge columns of smoke rose. Buildings in Jerusalem were burning, and there were pools of flame outside the walls, especially near the wooden towers, where the Muslims concentrated their fire.

So the fighting went on, all through the day and into the night. Raymond of Aguilers speaks of the incessant noise and of siege engines that were shattered by rocks, for the Saracens also had catapults trained on the machinery of the Christian army. He speaks, too, of their defensive skill, and hints at the extraordinary accuracy of the defenders, who succeeded in burning or shattering many of the siege engines. They were also using witchcraft, a weapon the Christians could not use. Two witches, he tells us, were standing on the parapet and casting spells on one of the petraries. He observes, with some satisfaction, that immediately after they had cast their spells a rock went whistling through the air and killed them.

On the morning of July 15, the Christians began to waver. They were exhausted by the continuous fighting, the lack of water, the sight of so many burnt-out siege engines. The princes met and debated whether to pull back and regroup. By this time, both towers were joined to the walls but it had been impossible to put the bridges in place, for these bridges, attached to the tops and swung into place by ropes and pulleys, were essential for making a pathway into the city. Up to this time, not a single Crusader had succeeded in entering the city. Every attempt to climb the walls had failed. An unknown knight standing on the Mount of Olives signaled with his shield to the Count of Toulouse to move forward. Raymond of Aguilers hints that the unknown knight was an angel. At this moment Godfrey of Bouillon, who was in the tower, ordered his men to throw fire on the bales of straw and cushions filled with cotton, which hung suspended from the walls, and the wind changing, huge columns of black smoke poured across the city, blinding the defenders who ran away. The Saracens had used balks of timber in an effort to keep the tower away from the walls. The Crusaders seized one of these timbers and nailed it to the tower, while the other end was secured to the battlements. Then the bridge was swung into position over the timber; at last, this narrow bridge provided a covered road into the city. Two Flemish knights, Litold and Gilbert of Tournai, had the honor of being the first to cross the bridge. They were closely followed by Godfrey of Bouillon, his brother Eustace, Robert Duke of Normandy, and the Count of Flanders. It was about noon on Friday, July 15, on the ninth day prophesied by Bishop Adhémar; and the Crusaders were aware that they were entering Jerusalem at the same hour that Christ died on the Cross.

At Mount Zion, the Count of Toulouse had succeeded in bringing his tower close to the walls but had not yet succeeded in using it as a bridge into the city. Iftikhar was commanding the Saracens fighting at Mount Zion, and he put up a powerful defense with stones, rocks, Greek fire, and incessant flights of arrows. Soon messengers came to him with news that the Crusaders under Godfrey of Bouillon had broken into Jerusalem and were already riding through the streets, killing everyone they encountered —man, woman, and child. Iftikhar shut himself up in the well-fortified Tower of David with as many of his soldiers as the tower could accommodate. He offered terms. He offered his treasure to the Count of Toulouse on condition that his life and the life of his bodyguard be spared, and that he be given safe passage to Ascalon. The count agreed. Alone among the Saracens, Iftikhar and his bodyguard survived the general massacre. They were escorted out of Jerusalem the same day.

The tower erected by the Count of Toulouse at such a vast expenditure of time and energy, and at such depletion of his own private treasury, proved unnecessary. The Provençals entered Jerusalem through the city gates; but long before they reached the Haram as-Sharif, the vast sacred enclosure which enclosed the Dome of the Rock and the al-Aqsa Mosque, Jerusalem was being drowned in blood.

Tancred and his knights were the first to reach the Haram as-Sharif. He pillaged the Dome of the Rock, removing its treasure, thus acquiring a vast fortune. The Saracens hoped to make a last stand at the al-Aqsa Mosque, but had no time to put it in a state of defense. They took refuge on the roof, hoping to be able to shoot down on the invaders, but Tancred's shock troops came on them with such speed and force that they quickly surrendered, offering to pay a large ransom for their lives. Tancred agreed to spare them, and the Saracens were allowed to raise his banner over the mosque as a sign that they were under his protection. Elsewhere in the city the Crusaders ran riot. They entered houses where they found the people cowering in corners. Caught up in a rage of destruction they killed mindlessly. The slaughter continued through the long night.

In the morning, Crusaders who had no allegiance to Tancred—probably Provençals—came upon the Saracens taking refuge in the al-Aqsa Mosque and butchered all of them. In the Temple Area, the dead lay everywhere— headless, armless, legless. Men ran over the mutilated bodies as though they were a carpet spread for them. Raymond of Aguilers, who saw the bloodletting, quotes approvingly, "This is the day the Lord has made. We shall rejoice and be glad in it."

While the Count of Toulouse was merciful to Iftikhar, he had good reasons. Here, at Mount Zion, the Saracens did not panic; they did not retreat. There was no way for the Provençals to enter the city unless the Saracens themselves opened David's Gate. The fanatical defense of the Saracens at Mount Zion threatened that, even though Jerusalem might fall, the Saracens could continue to make life intolerable for the Christians.

The massacre at Jerusalem was carried out deliberately; it was the result of settled policy. Jerusalem was to become a Christian city. The Jews, too, must be destroyed. They had all rushed to the chief synagogue, where they hoped to receive shelter and protection. The Crusaders, hungry for simple solutions, burned down the synagogue with the Jews inside.

The Crusaders ripped open the bellies of the dead Saracens, because it was learned that sometimes they swallowed gold bezants to prevent them from falling into the hands of their enemies. When, some days later, it was decided to heap the dead into great funeral pyres, the Crusaders kept watch for the melting gold that might trickle down to the bottom of the pyre.

On the night of victory, the Crusaders made their way in procession to the Church of the Holy Sepulchre. A mass was celebrated, and the priests chanted the Office of the Resurrection, candles glowed under the vaulted ceilings, knights in chain mail stood beside simple soldiers, and for a few moments, in the half-darkness of the cavernous church, there was the sense of exaltation in a common purpose achieved against overwhelming odds. The Church of the Holy Sepulchre was in Christian hands.

EXCERPTS FROM A LETTER FROM DAIMBERT, ARCH-BISHOP OF PISA, DUKE GODFREY, DEFENDER OF THE HOLY SEPULCHRE, AND RAYMOND, COUNT OF ST. GILLES, FROM JERUSALEM, AUGUST 1099.

TO LORD PASCHAL, POPE OF THE ROMAN CHURCH, to all the bishops and to the whole Christian people, the Arch-bishop of Pisa, Duke Godfrey, now by the grace of God Defender of the Holy Sepulchre, Raymond, Count of St. Gilles, and the whole army of God: greeting and prayer.

Multiply your supplications and prayers in the sight of God with joy and thanksgiving, since God has manifested His mercy in fulfilling by our hands what He has promised in ancient times. . . .

. . . the bishops and princes ordered that all with bare feet should march around the walls of the city, in order that He who entered it humbly on our behalf might be moved by our humility to open it for us and to exercise judgment upon His enemies. God was appeased by this humility and on the eighth day after we had humbled ourselves, He delivered the city and His enemies to us. It was the day indeed when the primitive church was expelled from Jerusalem, the day when the festival of the Dispersion of the Apostles is celebrated. And if you would desire to know what was done with the enemy whom we found there, know that in Solomon's Portico and in his Temple our men rode in the blood of the Saracens up to the knees of their horses.

Then when we were discussing who should hold the city, and there were some who wanted to return home for love of their fatherland, we learned that the King of Babylon had come to Ascalon with an innumerable multitude of soldiers. He said it was his purpose to lead all the Franks in Jerusalem into captivity and to take Antioch by storm. But God had determined otherwise on our behalf.

Therefore when we learned that the army of the Babylonians was in Ascalon, we went down to meet them, leaving our baggage and the sick in the care of the garrison in Jerusalem. When our army came in sight of the enemy, we fell on our knees to invoke the aid of the Lord, so that He who in all our other adversities had strengthened the Christian faith might now break the strength of the Saracens and of the Devil, and extend the Kingdom of the Church of Christ from sea to sea and over the whole world. There was no delay. God answered when we cried for help, and He provided us with such boldness that if you had seen us rush upon the enemy you would have taken us for a herd of deer hastening to slake their thirst in running water. . . . Marvellous did the Lord appear unto his servants. For before we even engaged in fighting, by our onset alone, He turned this multitude in flight and scattered all their weapons, so that if they wished to attack us later they had no weapons they could rely on. There can be no question about the spoils, for the entire treasury of the King of Babylon was captured. . . .

. . . After we had gained the victory, the army returned to Jerusalem. Leaving Duke Godfrey behind, Raymond, Count of St. Gilles, Robert, Count of Normandy, and Robert, Count of Flanders, made their way to Laodicea, where they found the fleet of the Pisans and Bohemond. After the Archbishop of Pisa had established peace between Bohemond and our leaders, Count Raymond prepared to return to Jerusalem for the sake of God and our brethren.

Therefore we call upon all you who belong to the Catholic Church of Christ and all the Latin people to exult in the wonderful courage and devotion of your brethren, in the glorious and most desirable retribution of Omnipotent God, and in the devoutly hoped for remission of all our sins through the grace of God. . . .

III

THE KINGS WHO CAME FROM ABROAD

The Quarrels
of the Princes

WO days after the conquest of Jerusalem, the princes and their chief lieutenants met in council to discuss the future administration of the city. There were urgent matters that had to be decided quickly. The city was strewn with corpses—no fewer than fifty thousand Saracens—and orders were given to dispose of the corpses by burial or by burning. The next matter of business was the apportionment of the available residences. Where would the soldiers live? Where would the priests live? Where would the princes live? Knights and ordinary soldiers had been permitted to put their names on houses they entered, thus, in theory, taking ownership of them. In fact, there were endless complications that would be sorted out in the courts. A more pressing matter was the approach of the Egyptian army. Within a few days or weeks the Crusaders could expect to have to defend Jerusalem against a powerful and well-armed army.

Other problems were hotly discussed. Was Tancred to be allowed to keep the treasure, including eight hanging lamps of solid silver, taken from the Dome of the Rock? Finally there was perhaps the most important question of all: Who would be King of Jerusalem?

There was not the least doubt that the Count of Toulouse, as the richest and most powerful of the princes who accompanied the expedition, had a claim on the title. He had not played the most heroic role in the conquest of Jerusalem, but he had fought worthily against Iftikhar at Mount Zion. Raymond of Aguilers says that the princes encouraged the Count of Toulouse to accept the title, but that he refused it, saying that he shuddered at the prospect of being addressed as King of Jerusalem. Raymond is claiming for the count more humility than he probably possessed. He was growing old, he had been very ill, he was not a good administrator, and he had reached a time in his life when he was thinking about retirement. On the other hand he had been closely associated with Bishop Adhémar, who had been vested by the pope with the leadership of the Crusade, and there were long periods when he had in fact acted as the leader in Adhémar's name. He was a master of diplomacy, as he showed in his dealings with the Byzantine emperor. Now, with Jerusalem in his grasp, he seems to have been delighted by the offer of a crown and to have been equally delighted in refusing it. Only a very proud, stubborn, and private man could have rejected so great a gift.

There remained Robert of Normandy, Robert of Flanders, and Godfrey of Bouillon, all of them able men, practical, down-to-earth, skillful in war but without much intelligence in other matters. None of them had any reputation in diplomacy; none had that elementary training in law that would permit him to be a lawgiver. Robert of Normandy was an English prince and a Norman duke, with a violent temper and a thirst for power, but his interests in England and Normandy outweighed his interest in Jerusalem. Robert of Flanders, who was a capable soldier and perhaps the bravest of the Crusader princes, had interests in Flanders and had already told the other princes that he intended to return home as soon as Jerusalem was conquered.

The debate was conducted with proper bureaucratic decorum. The clerks drew up lists of the attributes, virtues, and vices of the contenders for the crown. Their private and public lives were examined. The only fault they could find in Godfrey was an excessive piety and an excessive fondness for religious exercises. Tall, narrow-hipped, broad-shouldered, he appears to have been chosen over the others because he looked more kingly and was descended from Charlemagne. Because he was so deeply religious, he refused the crown while accepting the kingship. The title he chose for himself was "Advocate of the Holy Sepulchre." *Advocatus* means "friend" or "witness," and had the force of "protector."

In spite of his piety, Godfrey was irascible, stubborn, and devious. He picked a quarrel with the Count of Toulouse, which was totally unnecessary except as an exercise in power. The Count of Toulouse had seized the highly fortified Tower of David, and there he remained with his bodyguard and his army of retainers. Godfrey ordered him out of it. The count refused, saying that he intended to celebrate Easter in Jerusalem, and after that he would willingly surrender it. Godfrey was adamant. The tower must be surrendered, presumably because in his eyes it represented an integral part of the defense of Jerusalem. Robert of Flanders and Robert of Normandy agreed with Godfrey; so did many of the count's staff and many of his soldiers. Godfrey appears to have issued a formal order as liege lord demanding the absolute obedience of his subject, the Count of Toulouse. The Count of Toulouse attempted to avoid carrying out the order by entrusting the Tower of David temporarily to Peter of Narbonne, Bishop of Albara, to await the judgment of a properly constituted court of inquiry. The bishop accepted possession of the tower, and carried off the weapons he found in it to his own house. Then, without any qualms and without waiting for the court to meet, he handed the Tower of David over to Godfrey.

The Count of Toulouse had a high regard for his own honor; he stormed and raged. He collected some of his followers and, together with his bodyguard, he marched out of Jerusalem and made his way to Jericho to be baptized in the Jordan, remembering that Peter Bartholomew had once told him that this was necessary in the sight of God.

When the count returned to Jerusalem, the princes were meeting to elect a patriarch. Arnulf of Chocques, chaplain of Robert of Normandy, was elected. Some might say he was "the wisest and most honorable of men," but Raymond of Aguilers protested that the new patriarch had no conscience, ignored canonical decrees, and had a disgraceful birth. All of this suggests that Raymond would have been delighted if the patriarchate had been offered to him.

The patriarch's first act was to attempt to discover the True Cross, which had been concealed when the Turks conquered Jerusalem. Some Orthodox priests were rounded up and examined closely until at last, under threats of torture, they revealed its hiding place. The cross appears to have been concealed in the wall of one of the chapels of the Church of the Holy Sepulchre. This cross would later be clothed in a golden casing encrusted with jewels and would become, with the empty tomb, the most sacred object in the Kingdom of Jerusalem. It was in fact only a part of the True Cross, for a large portion of it was in the treasury of the emperor in Constantinople.

The Count of Toulouse was still bitterly upset because he had been humiliated by Godfrey, by the Bishop of Albara, and also because Arnulf, a man he despised, had been appointed to the patriarchate. He would have left Jerusalem if he had not been reminded that the Egyptian army was still on the march and the Holy City was in mortal danger. However profound his disagreements with Godfrey, he was not prepared to see Jerusalem captured by the Egyptians.

The commander in chief of the Egyptian army was al-Afdal, whose father was an Armenian slave who had risen high in the sultan's court. Al-Afdal was by this time well aware of the massacre at Jerusalem and he was determined to have his revenge. His announced plan was the massacre of all the Christians and the utter destruction of all the Christian churches and holy relics, while reserving for himself the right to capture Christian boys and girls, who would be married off to produce a race of warriors capable of defending Egypt against all her enemies.

On August 11, a Christian scouting party saw an immense cloud of dust moving toward them on the plain of Ibelin; they believed that the whole force of al-Afdal's army was about to engulf them, but stood their ground and discovered that instead of an army they were encountering something that gave them the greatest possible pleasure—a herd of sheep, cattle, and camels being moved from one pasture to another. It was a vast and unlooked-for treasure. The scouting party consisted of two hundred lightly armed cavalry, and the herds were guarded by some three hundred herdsmen and Egyptian soldiers. The lightly armed cavalry had no difficulty capturing the herd, the herdsmen, and the soldiers.

Meanwhile the Crusader army was preparing to attack al-Afdal's army. Nearly the entire army marched out of Jerusalem, leaving a pathetically small garrison behind. Peter the Hermit and the canons of the Church of the Holy Sepulchre kept vigil by the empty tomb, sang hymns, and prayed fervently for victory against the Egyptians. The army was formed into nine columns, three in the vanguard, three in the middle, and three in the rear guard. This new arrangement meant that it was possible to orchestrate nine waves of attackers, for the Crusaders knew that it would be too dangerous to remain on the defensive. They must destroy the Egyptian army or lose Jerusalem.

Carrying the Holy Lance into battle, the Count of Toulouse led his Provençals to the fertile plain north of Ascalon, where the Egyptian army was encamped. He had at least three hundred knights with him, a quarter of the total Crusader army; and with the knights were about two thousand crossbowmen, infantrymen, and camp servants. His columns were on the right flank close to the sea, while Tancred commanded the center with Robert of Normandy and Robert of Flanders, and Godfrey commanded the left flank. The princes would attack at dawn.

The Egyptians were caught by surprise. They had underestimated the strength of the Crusader army. From their spies they had learned that there were quarrels in high places, soldiers were deserting, the horses were ill fed, the army was simply a rabble. Even when they realized that a vast herd of camels, horses, sheep, and cattle had been captured by the Crusaders, they argued that they were confronted not so much with an army as with marauders and looters, a mob of utterly undisciplined troops.

Al-Afdal's army was awakened by the sound of the Crusaders' trumpets and horns. Within a few minutes the nine columns closed in on the soldiers hurrying out of their unguarded tents. Once again, there was a general massacre. No mercy was shown. The Egyptian army, which vastly outnumbered the Crusaders, was thrown back into the sea. Al-Afdal's tent was captured. It was filled with treasure of gold and silver, heaps of jewels, helmets decorated with gold inlays, ceremonial swords, and stores of grain. Al-Afdal himself escaped in an Egyptian ship, while some of his soldiers were able to escape to Ascalon.

Al-Afdal had lost his army, his treasure, his battle-standard; and he had almost lost his life. He had been defeated by a force much smaller than his own, and soon this ignominious defeat would be known throughout the Near East. The Crusaders possessed his jeweled sword, his painted tent, and the women he brought with him. The Crusaders, in their first battle after conquering Jerusalem, had shown that they were invincible. They returned to Jerusalem with a vast quantity of spoils, driving their herds before them; and exactly a month after the fall of Jerusalem they celebrated in the Church of the Holy Sepulchre a solemn mass in honor of their second victory.

The intrigues among the princes continued, the price of there being so many of them. The Count of Toulouse had fought well in the battle of Ascalon, which saw the total defeat of the Egyptian army. This was his last battle. The city of Ascalon with its high walls had not been captured; and now messengers came to the count, saying that the people of Ascalon were prepared to surrender to him, and to him alone. They remembered his fair dealing with the Saracens at the Tower of David. This matter was reported to Godfrey, who was incensed that the city should be surrendered to anyone except himself. Godfrey raged; and the count raged. Godfrey had more to lose, for the count now made his irrevocable decision to leave Jerusalem, taking his men with him.

Robert of Normandy and Robert of Flanders left about the same time, and they, too, were exasperated by Godfrey's imperious conduct. The two Roberts caught up with the army of the Count of Toulouse and they marched northward together. This was a large army, numbering about half the troops who had taken part in the battle on the plain of Ascalon, and they were treated with respect by the Muslim governors of the cities they passed through. At Jabala, just south of Lattakieh, they received bad news. They heard that a Pisan fleet was blockading Lattakieh, that Bohemond was in league with the Pisans, and that Daimbert, Archbishop of Pisa, had been appointed papal legate and was in command of the fleet. They heard, too, that the Pisans had fought a squadron of Byzantine ships and one of their ships had been captured. Bohemond, self-styled Prince of Antioch, now refused to accept the suzerainty of the emperor of Byzantium. There were all the makings of a first-class quarrel with the emperor, whose fleet was in a position to control the waters off northern Palestine, while the Egyptian fleet controlled the waters of southern Palestine. Bohemond and the Pisans were behaving stupidly, and it was necessary to prevent them from doing any more harm.

The two Roberts and the Count of Toulouse were in agreement: the blockading fleet must be withdrawn and Daimbert must be told the true state of affairs. Accordingly, Daimbert was summoned to Jabala to confront three angry princes who agreed that the alliance with the emperor must be maintained. The situation in the Holy Land was still precarious. Nothing was to be gained by insulting the emperor, whose help might be needed. Lattakieh was occupied by a Byzantine army or perhaps only by a small column of troops landed from a single ship. It was this army that was being blockaded by Bohemond and the Pisans. Daimbert saw the force of their argument, and he called off the blockade, to the immense anger of Bohemond. The Count of Toulouse then marched into the city "in the name of the emperor." His banner flew from the walls, five hundred Provençal troops were added to the garrison, and Bohemond was warned to make no further attacks on Byzantine outposts.

Robert of Normandy and Robert of Flanders sailed to Constantinople, where they were well received by the emperor, who offered them high appointments, which they quite naturally rejected with good grace. They were princes in their own countries and had no desire to serve a foreign emperor. The Count of Toulouse, who had made a vow that he would spend the remainder of his life in the Holy Land, sailed to Constantinople later in the year, and he appears to have made plans to carve out a principality of his own around Tripoli. Unlike Bohemond, the Count of Toulouse was prepared to accept the emperor as his sovereign lord. In Constantinople he was given a palace, where a special chapel was built for the Holy Lance, and we learn from the historian Odericus Vitalis that a son was born to him. The danger, of course, was that by remaining in Constantinople he was growing out of touch with affairs in the Holy Land.

The loss of the Provençals and the armies of the two Roberts had reduced Godfrey's military power dangerously. A well-equipped Muslim army under capable leadership could have destroyed the young Kingdom of Jerusalem in its infancy. Happily the Egyptian army was too busy licking its wounds, and Godfrey was adept at leading raiding parties. Thus he took Hebron with only three hundred cavalry and two thousand infantrymen. The Muslim garrison at Hebron fled to Damascus, and Godfrey found himself master of most of the northern Negev. With an even smaller army of fifty knights and perhaps three hundred infantrymen. Tancred raided the Galilee, captured Tiberias and all the towns and villages around the lake. Then it was the turn of Nazareth and Mount Tabor. Another raid took him to Beisan, which commanded the pass from the plain of Jezreel to the Jordan Valley. At Tiberias and Beisan, he strengthened the walls and left small garrisons. The Kingdom of Jerusalem was rapidly extending its borders.

Because his army was so ludicrously small and he needed allies, Godfrey welcomed the news that Bohemond and Daimbert would soon be arriving in Jerusalem. According to Fulcher of Chartres, most of Bohemond's troops were left behind to defend Antioch. Baldwin, Count of Edessa, who was temporarily abandoning his principality deep in the interior, accompanied them along the coastal road with his own small army, which probably amounted to little more than a handful of escort troops. Three princes had left Jerusalem; now two princes and a papal legate were coming to take their place. On December 21, the day of the winter solstice, they arrived at Jerusalem and immediately made their way to the Church of the Holy Sepulchre. They celebrated Christmas at Bethlehem.

For Godfrey, the importance of Bohemond's pilgrimage to Jerusalem was largely psychological. A few knights were added to his army, and the Pisan fleet brought much-needed supplies and protection from the Egyptian fleet, which continued to threaten the southern coast of Palestine. But, primarily, the presence of Bohemond and of Baldwin, Count of Edessa, added luster to his court, while the presence of Daimbert, who quickly replaced Arnulf as Patriarch of Jerusalem, brought him the comfort that the church of the kingdom was in good hands.

Bohemond and Baldwin left Jerusalem at the beginning of the year 1100, their visit so brief that it seemed scarcely worth recording in history books. Yet it was important as a gesture of friendship and understanding. From them, Godfrey was able to learn what was happening in the north and to obtain a clear picture of Muslim intentions. He appointed his brother his successor, and he saw more clearly than before that he must encourage Italian fleets to enter Palestinian waters. He would continue to send raiding parties into the interior, and with the help of the Pisan ships he could blockade and conquer the coastal cities of Ascalon, Caesarea, and Acre. Already in his lifetime, it was possible to discern the shape of the Kingdom of Jerusalem to its fullest extent. The plans were laid well. They could not have been laid at all without the help of the Pisans.

The submission of Ascalon, Caesarea, and Acre implied a kind of dual rule. The Crusaders could not yet administer these cities; the emirs remained as governors, paying tribute and raising taxes, obeying the laws of Jerusalem and the commanders of the small garrisons imposed on them. We have glimpses of Godfrey sitting among the emirs, receiving gifts of corn, fruit, and oil, and being affable and gracious. As his power increased, he appears to have become more humble, calmer, less given to sudden rages.

Tancred, who now called himself Prince of Galilee, remained firmly loyal to him, though it was clear that he was attempting to carve out a principality for himself. Daimbert, however, began to show his mettle, claiming supreme power for himself and the papacy. The patriarch demanded that the cities of Jerusalem and Jaffa should be granted to him. The knights were horrified at the prospect of the kingdom's falling into the hands of a Pisan prelate. Godfrey decided to temporize. On Easter Day, he formally endowed the patriarchate with the two cities, adding that for their own protection he would retain them to his death.

In June Godfrey was in the Galilee directing a raiding party in the Jaulan when he learned that a Venetian fleet had put in at Jaffa. Since he was well aware of the importance of sea power, he immediately left his headquarters in Tiberias and journeyed to the coast. At Caesarea, he was welcomed by the local emir and entertained with a feast. After the feast he became ill. Perhaps he was poisoned; perhaps he was stricken with typhus; perhaps he was simply worn out by the excitement of a year of battles and raids. On the following day, he was well enough to meet the admiral of the Venetian fleet and to discuss the part it might play in the defense of the city of Jerusalem. He was carried to Jerusalem, where it was thought the cooler air would help to abate his fever. Most of the time he was comatose. He could sometimes recognize people, give orders, and take nourishment, but no one doubted that he was mortally ill.

Daimbert imagined that at Godfrey's death he would become the Advocate and supreme ruler, the inheritor of the power and glory of the Kingdom of Jerusalem. But Tancred kept vigil at Godfrey's bedside and the knights were determined to prevent the kingdom from being overrun by powerful priests. The Venetians sent two separate deputations to the city to discuss the role they would play as traders and in matters of defense. Documents were drawn up. Godfrey rallied long enough to give assent to the documents. The Venetians were granted a measure of autonomy; they would receive a third of every town they helped to capture, and they would be permitted to have a church and a marketplace in every town in the kingdom. Tripoli would be handed over to them. The inevitable result of these agreements was to bring the Venetians into direct conflict with the Pisans. They were already rivals and enemies in Italy; now they would become rivals and enemies in Palestine.

Godfrey died on July 18, 1100, at age forty-one, having been Advocate of the Church of the Holy Sepulchre for exactly a year. They said of him that he was a man of great nobility, a model of Christian piety. His chief virtue as a Crusader was that he acted decisively during the attack on Jerusalem, but on him lies the whole weight of responsibility for the massacre of the Saracens and the Jews. His body lay in state for five days and he was buried in the Church of the Holy Sepulchre, not far from the empty tomb.

THE FOUR CRUSADER STATES
1099~1144

Arrival of First Crusade 1097

SELJUQS

°ANQARA

ASIA MINOR

CAESAREA

KONIA

TAURUS MTS

MARASH

TARSUS

ADANA

PRINCEDOM OF ANTIOCH

COUNTY OF EDESSA

EDESSA

ANTIOCH

°ALEPPO

R. Euphrates

CYPRUS
(BYZANTINE)

°HAMA

°HIMS

TRIPOLI

COUNTY OF TRIPOLI

SYRIA

MEDITERRANEAN SEA

°DAMASCUS

ACRE

SEA OF GALILEE

JAFFA

KINGDOM OF JERUSALEM

GAZA

JERUSALEM

THE DEAD SEA

DESERT

DAMIETTA

EGYPT

FATIMID KHALIFS

CAIRO

R. Nile

SUEZ

AQABA

SINAI

0 20 40 60 80 100
Miles

5

King Baldwin I

HE knights who had been loyal to Godfrey had their way: the kingdom was not given over to the papal legate. Just as they defended the city of Jerusalem by force of arms against the Saracens, so now they defended it by force of arms against Daimbert. They seized the Tower of David, filled it with Godfrey's bodyguard, stationed troops at the gates, and surrounded the Church of the Holy Sepulchre. According to his will, written during the previous Easter celebrations, Godfrey had granted Jerusalem and Jaffa to Daimbert and to the papacy in perpetuity. It would become a theocracy. The knights were determined that it should become an earthly kingdom.

Promptly, the knights elected their new ruler. He was Baldwin, Count of Edessa, Godfrey's younger brother, who had taken no part at all in the conquest of Antioch or Jerusalem but had spent his energy in carving out a separate principality for himself. The choice of Baldwin implied a certain antipapal posture, a feeling that the kingdom was too precious to be entrusted to priests.

Baldwin was a man who loved work, disdained idleness, and was interested in everything that happened in the kingdom. He enjoyed the panoply of kingly rule and in public always appeared with a mantle hanging from his broad shoulders. He towered above other men and had a kingly presence.

When the message came from Jerusalem saying that Godfrey was dead, and it was expected that Baldwin would succeed to the throne by hereditary right, he grieved for the death of his brother briefly, while rejoicing greatly in his inheritance. So says Fulcher of Chartres, who knew him well. In early October, Baldwin set out from Edessa with a small army of two hundred knights and seven hundred infantrymen. His intention was to reach Jerusalem in the shortest possible time, and that meant passing through territory occupied by the Turks. The Saracen intelligence system was well organized; his army was closely watched. Duqaq, Sultan of

Damascus, was determined to prevent him from reaching Jerusalem. The small army passed through Antioch—Bohemond was at this time languishing in a Turkish jail, having been captured in one of his periodic forays into the hinterland—and the people of Antioch asked Baldwin to be their regent in the absence of their sovereign prince. Baldwin refused. To be acting prince of Antioch was a small thing compared with being King of Jerusalem. He marched down the coast and was greeted civilly by the emirs who retained possession of the coastal cities. Tripoli was then ruled by Ibn-Ammar, who sent gifts of bread, wine, wild honey, and goats. Ibn-Ammar was friendly to the Christians and offered a severe warning. He had not the least doubt that Sultan Duqaq was preparing an ambush somewhere along the way. Fulcher of Chartres, who accompanied the expedition, says that Baldwin made light of the information. Baldwin was an excellent general who was inclined to believe that his enemies were aware of his excellence, and would therefore avoid him.

The ambush was laid near the Dog River, some ten miles north of Beirut, and here Baldwin fought one of the hardest battles of his life. He fell into the trap prepared for him, with seeming alacrity. His scouts had detected the presence of the Damascenes in the hills and a fleet of ships standing offshore. They reported to Baldwin that the trap was closing on them, and they were certain a large army was waiting in the hills to descend upon them. Baldwin's men remained in their tents keeping careful watch.

The enemy stormed down the hills but failed to penetrate the camp, and on the morning of the following day Baldwin ordered a retreat, taking care that the baggage train was guarded by his best knights. The line of retreat was a narrow coastal road hemmed in by the sea and the hills. At Juniye, Baldwin stopped retreating, turned around, and ordered a general attack at a place where three roads met. The attack was so sudden and so well organized that the enemy fled in panic down all the three roads and up the hills and into the sea. Victory was complete and there were many prisoners. Baldwin divided the booty among his knights and spent the following night resting in a grove of olive trees in the shadow of an abandoned castle.

The road was now open to Jerusalem. In Beirut, Tyre, Sidon, and Acre the local emirs sent food to the army. At Haifa, which had been captured by Tancred, they were able to buy bread and wine outside the city walls. Tancred at that moment was in Jerusalem, helping Daimbert against the knights. Tancred had seen his opportunity: he would become the power behind the patriarchate. When he heard that Baldwin was advancing on Jaffa, he rushed down to the seacoast to head him off, but he was too late, apart from being ineffective.

From Jaffa, Baldwin marched to Jerusalem in triumph. There was extraordinary jubilation, the people pouring out of the city to welcome him. His great height, his fiery beard, his strange pallor, marked him as a man unlike other men. While Tancred fled to the Galilee and Daimbert went into seclusion in a monastery at Mount Zion, Baldwin quietly accepted the title of King of Jerusalem and set his royal house in order. After a few days in Jerusalem Baldwin led his army out into the Judaean wilderness. He marched on Hebron and made the dramatic descent—a drop of more than four thousand feet in seventeen miles—to the Dead Sea. They were the first Crusaders to travel along the shores of the Dead Sea, which left them spellbound.

They feasted on dates and came upon strange people so blackened by the sun that they seemed inhuman; accordingly, they were left in peace. Going beyond the Dead Sea, they reached Wadi Musa, where Moses struck the rock, riding through a landscape of seething rocks, which looked as though they were still in process of formation, a shapeless and jagged landscape that might have been torn out of the moon.

They returned by way of the Dead Sea, visited Hebron again, and rode to Bethlehem, where they were met by Daimbert, who was prepared to make peace. Here, in the Church of the Nativity, Baldwin was crowned King of Jerusalem by Daimbert himself, whose change of heart was perhaps due to practicality. The knights had the power to enforce their wishes. Where Godfrey was abrupt and irascible, Baldwin was affable and courteous, using diplomacy rather than force whenever it was possible. Indeed, he had very little alternative, for although he possessed a resounding title, he could command fewer knights than many minor princes in Europe.

The Crusaders were in a pitiable position, divided among themselves, with armies so small that Bedouin raiding parties under skillful leadership could have destroyed them, and there was little income to defray the expenses of the army. More than anything else they needed to extend their territory, for new territory meant new wealth, new strategic positions, new strength.

Sometime in the early spring, Baldwin led a raiding party across the Jordan and made a night attack on an Arab encampment. He caught the Arabs by surprise, but most of the men were able to escape, leaving the women and children and all their possessions behind. Camels, asses, slaves, and treasure fell into Christian hands; the women and children were made prisoners; everything that had been in the camp, except for the swift horses on which the Arabs escaped, now belonged to Baldwin. While the prisoners were being led across the desert to Jerusalem, Baldwin learned that the wife of an Arab chieftain had given birth. She was riding in one of those woven, cagelike baskets often used by women when traveling on camelback. Baldwin ordered that she should be taken down from the camel, that a bed should be made for her, and that she should be given food and two skins of water. The wife of the chieftain asked that a maid be left with her. She lay in the shade of some trees. Two camels were left with her to provide her with milk. Baldwin himself superintended her comfort, and as a final gesture he removed his royal mantle and wrapped it around her.

Such acts of courtesy were not infrequent in Crusader times. Both sides butchered women when it suited their purpose, but the wives of princes and chieftains were generally treated with respect. Baldwin knew the Arabs would soon find her; she was in no danger. This courtesy had a happy sequel: some time later, the woman's husband would save Baldwin's life. Baldwin was happy in the desert; he had a contemplative cast of mind. His first wife, Godehilde, died during the Crusaders' march across Asia Minor, and he was now married to an Armenian princess. He could be very tender. He could also be absolutely ruthless.

Arsuf, the small seaport north of Jaffa, was in Arab hands, and it was necessary that it should be conquered. Some Genoese ships, which had been berthed at Lattakieh during the winter, sailed to Jaffa under the favorable spring winds, and the sailors made a pilgrimage to Jerusalem. Baldwin came down to Jaffa especially to greet them. There were twenty-seven galleys and five freighters, forming a formidable fleet. Baldwin offered them the same terms that had been offered to the Pisans and Venetians: a part of the spoils of captured cities, trading centers, privileges. He explained that he wanted Arsuf, and the Genoese eagerly offered their assistance. They wanted to sack the city and make off with its treasure, but Baldwin was determined that no harm should come to it. It was an important seaport. It could be used by all ships friendly to the Crusaders. He therefore wanted it intact. When Arsuf surrendered after a siege of only three days, Baldwin permitted the entire population to march out. They were allowed to take their money with them. A long column set out under a safe-conduct to Ascalon.

Merciful at Arsuf, Baldwin was merciless at Caesarea, which he also captured with the help of Genoese ships. The siege lasted fifteen days. At last the order was given to storm the walls with scaling ladders and wooden towers. This time there was a massacre of all the men. The women were spared, because, says Fulcher of Chartres, "they could be used to turn the hand mills." The emir was spared; so was the *qadi*, the chief magistrate; only because a large ransom could be expected from them. The dead Turks were burned, and by stirring among the ashes the Christians were able to find the gold bezants the Turks had swallowed to prevent them from falling into the hands of infidels. In June, the Crusaders learned that the Egyptians were massing their forces at Ascalon. They were not moving forward, but this stationary army grew rapidly during the summer.

Baldwin, always practical, decided to multiply his own army by the simple process of making every squire a knight. Thus the number of available knights increased from 130 to 260. Counting his army, Baldwin felt sure he had nine hundred infantrymen. From spies he learned that the enemy had eleven thousand knights and twenty-one thousand infantrymen. If the figures were accurate, the Crusaders were outnumbered thirty to one.

July passed, and then August, and the Egyptians were still at Ascalon. On September 6, 1101, Baldwin's army set out from Jaffa in a spirit of fearful expectation, knowing that the Egyptians would soon attack but hoping that, with God's mercy, they might be able to strike first and take the Egyptians unawares.

Baldwin himself accompanied a scouting party and saw in the distance a vast camp shimmering on the plain about eight miles from Ascalon. He raced back to his soldiers and, talking like a king who had been a priest, he told them that the gates of heaven were already opening for them, that the survivors would be blessed among men, and that those who fled the battlefield would have a long journey back to France. Then he formed his troops into six battalions and led them into battle. On a high mast, so that all could see it, shone the True Cross.

The Egyptians were not taken by surprise. What surprised them was the sheer audacity of the Crusaders, who charged straight into their massive army. The first and second columns were lost. The third column charged and held its ground without inflicting much damage on the enemy. Then Baldwin, commanding the fourth column, and mounted on his favorite Arab charger, called Gazelle, threw himself and his knights at the enemy. He fought like a man possessed. This fourth column broke the enemy line. For about an hour, there was fighting all over the plain of Ascalon, and at last the Egyptians fled back to the safety of the city walls.

Baldwin had won a great victory, but the price had been too high. He had lost nearly a third of his knights and about three hundred infantrymen. About five thousand of the enemy had been slain. The Crusaders spent the night in the Egyptians' tents, and in the morning they gathered up the huge supplies of bread, grain, and flour; even the tents were taken to Jaffa. Worn out by the battle, the Crusaders marched slowly.

A small detachment of Egyptians, who had been fighting against Baldwin's rear guard and had done some damage, reached Jaffa before them, displaying captured shields, helmets, and lances, and declaring that the Christian army had been destroyed. It was a trick to make Jaffa surrender. The trick failed, but it alarmed the people of Jaffa sufficiently to make them dispatch a message to Tancred at Antioch, urging him to send troops as quickly as possible. A few days later Tancred received another letter from Jaffa, saying that all was well, for Baldwin had returned in triumph, his pack animals laden with Egyptian booty.

The war with Egypt continued in the late spring of the following year. This time, according to Fulcher of Chartres, they came with an even larger army commanded by the son of al-Afdal. With this force the Egyptians hoped to destroy the Christians once and for all.

On May 17, 1102, Baldwin led the Christian army out of Jerusalem to join battle with the Egyptians. It would have been wiser for him to have remained in Jerusalem. When he reached Ramleh, he found the whole

Egyptian army arrayed against him. He had five hundred knights, for a small Crusading army had arrived from France to supplement his forces. The Egyptians thought at first that Baldwin's troops were the vanguard of a far greater army; they hesitated. Baldwin attacked first, as was his custom. He lost at least a quarter of his troops, and when night fell he took refuge in the fortress at Ramleh. This fortress was little more than a tower, built the previous year. Here, hemmed in on all sides by the enemy, he was as close to defeat as he had ever been. He had only a few knights with him, and he was out of touch with the rest of his army, which was in a state of total disarray. There appeared in the darkest hour of the night the Arab chieftain whose wife Baldwin had helped after she had given birth. The chieftain said that to his certain knowledge the Egyptians would attack the tower at dawn, and it was necessary that he should escape immediately. With four companions Baldwin slipped out of the tower, the chieftain leading the way. A little while later, two other knights also slipped away. All the rest were doomed, for the Egyptians heaped faggots around the tower, and were preparing to set it ablaze when, at dawn, the knights rushed out, preferring to die in battle rather than in a burning tower. A hundred knights were taken captive and perhaps another hundred were cut down.

Baldwin, King of Jerusalem, Count of Edessa, Lord of Jaffa, Arsuf, and Caesarea, was now a fugitive hiding in the hills north of Ramleh, with a price on his head. For two days and two nights he evaded Egyptian patrols. Traveling at night, he made his way safely to Arsuf.

On that same day, Hugh of Saint-Omer arrived at Arsuf with eighty knights; so from being a fugitive one day, Baldwin became the commander of a small army the next. An Englishman called Goderic offered to take the king through the Egyptian blockade to Jaffa. Baldwin accepted the invitation, and flew his royal standard from the mast of the fast-sailing ship to spite the Egyptians, whose ships were too slow and cumbersome to catch up with him. In Jaffa, he found the remnants of his army, and broke his way out of the siege to join forces with Hugh of Saint-Omer. Then he returned to Jaffa, sent messengers to Jerusalem for more knights, and was about to hurl himself on the Egyptians again when one of the largest armadas ever seen in the eastern Mediterranean came sailing into Jaffa harbor—two hundred English ships filled with soldiers and pilgrims, with stores of weapons and provisions. These pilgrims and soldiers came from all over Europe, but mostly they were English. They came at a providential time, breaking the Egyptian blockade by their sheer numbers. With this new army, only about fourteen days after his escape from Ramleh with a squire and three knights, Baldwin drove the Egyptians once more back to Ascalon.

He was determined to safeguard his kingdom, and he realized that it was above all necessary that the coastal cities should be in his possession. A master of warfare by land and sea, his general plan was to attack these cities both ways, his own knights fighting on land, while ships from Genoa, Pisa, Venice, Constantinople, England, Flanders, and Norway were used to keep the Egyptian fleet at bay, blockade the harbors, and fire flaming arrows into the cities.

Tortosa fell in 1102, Acre fell in 1104, and Tripoli in 1109. An English and Danish fleet took part in the siege of Sidon in 1107, but the siege was called off against a huge ransom because the king was in desperate need of money. Three years later he captured Beirut, and in the same year, with the help of a fleet commanded by the youthful King Sigurd of Norway, who brought fifty ships to the Holy Land, he returned to Sidon and captured it. Tyre held out. So did Ascalon. There were wars on all the frontiers. Baldwin exulted in them.

In 1115, he returned to the land he appears to have loved most, the wild and savage land below the Dead Sea, the rocks looking as though they were still heaving after volcanic explosions. On a steep, wooded hill near the village of Shobak, a hundred miles from Jerusalem in the north and Aqaba in the south, he built a castle called Montreal, the Royal Mountain, which dominated the country for miles around, and was to become in time the single most powerful castle in the region known as Beyond the Jordan or Oultrejourdain.

He was so pleased with Montreal that he visited it again the following year and then marched to Aila on the Red Sea. Having reached so far, he decided to reach farther. A little island, which the Arabs called the Island of Pharaoh, lay just off the coast. Baldwin crossed over in one of the boats abandoned by the people of Aila, and ordered the construction of a small castle on the island, which the Crusaders called the Island of Graye. He built another castle at Aila. Both castles were provided with small garrisons. The empire of the Crusaders now stretched from Edessa in northern Syria to the Island of Graye in the Red Sea, a distance of 550 miles. It was an unwieldy empire, made up of bits and pieces of territory, flourishing coastal cities, vast deserts, and princedoms. For sustenance it depended upon the charity of strangers, for without the fleets that came from western Europe at irregular intervals it could not have sustained itself. Baldwin, who spent most of his reign on the move, conducted himself like an army.

By building castles from the Island of Graye northward, and manning them with some of his best troops, he was preventing the armies of Cairo and Damascus from going to one another's assistance. The Kingdom of Jerusalem lay like a double-edged sword between them.

It would have been difficult enough to maintain the kingdom if its separate parts were at peace, but the separate parts were often intriguing against one another. Princes sometimes arrested princes. Thus the Count of Toulouse, very early in Baldwin's reign, was arrested by Tancred, who was acting as Prince of Antioch while Bohemond was the prisoner of the emir of Danishmend. The count was kept in honorable confinement and released without too much difficulty. Bohemond, released from captivity in the spring of 1103, quarreled immediately with Tancred, who felt cheated because Bohemond claimed territories that Tancred had conquered without his assistance. But in the end it was the intrepid Tancred who, while titular Prince of Galilee, inherited the princedom of Antioch. Bohemond had conceived a new plan. He would travel to the West, build up a new Crusading army in France and Italy, and throw the whole weight of it not against the Turks but against Byzantium. In October 1107, he attacked the great Byzantine fortress of Dyrrhachium with an army that included Turkish mercenaries. Unlike Baldwin, he had no understanding of seapower, and after a long siege he was himself besieged, captured, and brought before the emperor. In defeat he remained for a while superbly insolent. Anna Comnena speaks of the radiance shining from him, as though he were a god standing among mortals, able to dominate everyone around him.

Alexius knew how to deal with him. Coldly, he drew up the instrument of surrender by which Bohemond would be made to submit to the Byzantine emperor. Bohemond returned to Apulia, where he lived out the rest of his life on his estates, never returning to the East. Baldwin was the beneficiary of his absence.

Baldwin was no more modest than Bohemond, but he possessed human qualities that made him loved by his people. There was a genuine warmth in him, a genuine delight in fighting, and a genuine simplicity of manner.

In the spring of 1118 he led an expedition to Egypt, plundered Pelusium and Tanis, and was hoping to penetrate deeper into the country. One day he was walking along the banks of the Nile and came upon some knights spearing fish with their lances. He joined them, ate some of their fish, and immediately felt ill. They carried him in a litter as far as al-Arish and there he died. They cut out his intestines, salted them, and placed them in his coffin, which they carried to Jerusalem. On Palm Sunday, he was buried beside his brother Godfrey in the Church of the Holy Sepulchre.

Godfrey's short reign gave him little time for the study of kingship. Baldwin studied kingship minutely, with a cleric's passion and a soldier's courage. He had a sense of order, extraordinary courage, a feeling for the drama essential to kingship, and a flair for diplomacy. If he loved women too much, it is at least possible that they helped him remain human. Though married three times, he left no children, and the crown passed to his nephew Baldwin of Le Bourg, who happened to arrive from Edessa on the day of his funeral.

On Baldwin's tombstone it was written that he was "a second Judas Maccabaeus, whom Kedar and Egypt, Dan and Damascus dreaded." This was true, but it would have been more appropriate to say that he gave confidence to the fledgling kingdom at a time when confidence was most needed. He was the most kingly among the kings of Jerusalem.

The Armed Might of the Crusaders

WE shall not understand the Crusaders until we realize that they were different from us. They were closer to the earth, and the smells of the earth. They were closer to the brute facts of the earth; very often they were near starvation. For the most part they were peasants with a peasant's knowledge of the seasons and the rituals of the Church. They believed with a firm and intimate faith, with a medieval directness, and a rough-hewn stubbornness, that it was in their power to safeguard forever the Holy Sepulchre, which they regarded as the place of the Resurrection, offering the promise of eternal life. They knew that Christ died and rose again in the flesh; that they belonged to the kingdom of Christ; to him, they owed their ultimate allegiance.

The most enviable Crusaders were the knights, who were often only two generations removed from the peasantry. With their grooms and esquires, and their pompous trappings, they were the elite of the army, always on parade. Their horses were much heavier than those of the Saracens. Well-trained and strictly disciplined, the Crusaders were armored front-line troops with sufficient weight and power to punch holes in the enemy lines and then to wheel back and punch more holes. Their weapons were lances, which sometimes reached the length of ten feet, and a heavy double-edged sword, which they carried in a scabbard on the left side. The sword was used for hand-to-hand fighting; the lance possessed a wider range and flexibility.

From neck to waist, and from thighs to feet, knights were enclosed in chain mail made of iron links on a foundation of leather. They wore very sharp spurs and round shields with iron rims and iron bosses. Their helmets were round, flat-topped boxes of steel covering the whole head, with slits in front of the eyes and perforations in front of the mouth and nose. They were intended to look terrifying.

Once established in the Holy Land, the Crusaders had three main armies. There was the army in the service of the king, and there were the auxiliary armies of the Templars and the Hospitallers. These auxiliary armies, which became enormously powerful, grew up haphazardly, yet there were times when they became the real rulers of the kingdom. The Order of the Knights of the Temple was a military order founded by Hugh of Payens, a knight from Champagne. He appears to have been sweet-tempered, totally dedicated, and ruthless on behalf of the Faith. The Knights of the Temple were soldiers of Christ, ascetic almost to fanaticism, single-minded to the exclusion of all ideas except the worship of God and the annihilation of the Saracens. In 1118, Hugh of Payens with nine other knights sought the permission of Baldwin I to found the order. The king of Jerusalem was so delighted with the idea that he gave them part of the royal palace believed to be the Temple of Solomon. This became their headquarters and from then on they were known as Templars.

Ostensibly, the purpose of the Templars was to safeguard the lives of the pilgrims who flocked to Jerusalem and other holy places. But from the beginning, Hugh of Payens appears to have had a larger aim. The Templars quickly became an independent fighting arm of the Church, having allegiance only to the pope and the grand master. They were armed monks, priestly swordbearers, chivalrous only on behalf of God, shock troops to be thrown into every righteous battle. Their courage became legendary.

Safeguarding the comings and goings of pilgrims was difficult. How difficult we learn from the Anglo-Saxon traveler Saewulf who came to Jerusalem in 1102 and left this account of the tortuous road that leads up from the coast to Jerusalem:

> ... the Saracens ... lie in wait in mountain caves to surprise the Christians, watching both day and night to pounce on those who came in small numbers and were therefore less capable of resistance or those who were worn out with fatigue and therefore lagged behind their companions. At one moment you can see them everywhere, at another moment they are invisible, and everyone who travels in this region has observed this. . . .

Saewulf, with his Anglo-Saxon companions, arrived at a time when the Kingdom of Jerusalem had only just come into existence, when the government was still disorderly and inefficient, and when it was impossible to spare soldiers to police the road. Because the government could not guarantee the safety of the pilgrims, hundreds died even before they saw Jerusalem's golden gates.

At first, the Templars enjoyed a modest organization. Over the course of two centuries a vast body of rules and regulations would come into existence, legislating for every possible eventuality, but at the beginning they were merely monks on horseback, armed with swords and lances, sometimes so poor that two would ride on a single horse. Hugh of Payens infused the Templars with the energy of chastity and obedience. No women might enter the Temple; they were not permitted to embrace any woman, not even their sisters or their mothers. A lamp burned in their dormitories all night; their breeches were tightly laced; they were never permitted to see each other naked. They were permitted no privacy, and letters addressed to individual Templars had to be read aloud in the presence of the grand master or a chaplain. They never shaved their beards. Their spartan lives were directed toward the single end of protecting the pilgrims and the Kingdom of Jerusalem by killing the enemy.

Since they were obedient only to the pope, who was far away, they often acted independently of the king of Jerusalem. They became sophisticated soldiers, administrators, builders of castles, and owners of vast estates, not only in the Holy Land but all over Europe, for kings and princes and common people soon recognized that they possessed to an extraordinary degree the military power to secure the safety of the kingdom. They possessed, too, a vast intelligence system, sometimes working in close association with the royal government, but sometimes against it. Their own spies reported regularly from Cairo, Baghdad, Aleppo, and the other Arab capitals of the Middle East.

The headquarters of the Templars still stands in Jerusalem, for the building then known as the Temple was in fact the al-Aqsa Mosque, believed by Christians to be on the site of the Temple of Solomon. In these spacious quarters with their underground stables lived the grand master, the marshal, and the high command. Reverence was paid to the grand master as the representative of the pope. The master of the Templars was often a man who had entered the order as a youth and had spent his whole life in it. He knew no other world and was interested only in the advancement of the Templars at all costs, and if it was necessary for him to form a temporary alliance with the Saracens, he would do so without a qualm. The Templars always had the best intelligence system in the Holy Land, and very often the Saracens learned what they wanted to know through the Templars. Those hard and silent men, wearing voluminous white cloaks derived from the Cistercian robe, adorned with a large blood-red cross, played dangerous games. They brought the Crusaders some of their greatest triumphs and some of their greatest defeats.

The second army belonged to the Order of Knights of the Hospital of St. John. They were known as Hospitallers and wore a red eight-pointed cross on their black mantles. They, too, arose from humble beginnings and learned to exercise kingly powers. About the year 1070, some citizens of Amalfi established a hostel for poor pilgrims in Jerusalem, with the permission of the Egyptian governor of the city. When the Crusaders conquered Jerusalem, the master was a certain Gerard, a Benedictine priest, who escaped or was expelled from the city before its conquest. He provided the Crusaders with valuable information and was soon in the good graces of the new rulers, who endowed his hostel and encouraged his work in every way. The Church assumed control of the hostel. Like the Templars, the Hospitallers owed obedience to the pope. When Raymond of Le Puy became the new master, around 1118, the order changed direction. In Raymond's view it was not enough that the order should care for pilgrims; it must also defend them. The rule of the Hospitallers was less strict than the rule of the Templars. The Hospitallers were steadier, less adventurous, more somber. The Templars had a glitter about them while the Hospitallers seemed almost colorless. The Hospitaller army was much smaller than the Templar army and never attained the popularity of the Templars; it was also much poorer. These two rival orders vied for honor and renown. They often clashed, but when they moved in unison they performed marvelously.

Soon the orders became proud and imperious, and since the king was also likely to be proud and imperious, there were continual disputes and quarrels. In theory, they were independent of the king, owing allegiance only to Rome. In fact, the masters of the two orders had their places in the royal council chamber, and no important act was decided upon without their agreement. More and more, as the wars continued, it appeared that the kingdom was ruled by a triumvirate: the king, and the masters of the Temple and the Hospital.

King Baldwin II

HE kings of Jerusalem came in all shapes and characters. Some were devout, some made a pretense of their devotions, one was an unbeliever, another was a leper, but all were kingly in their fashion. All led their armies into battle; and because they knew battle, they knew how dangerous and desperate was the world they lived in. They learned very early that the fighting was continuous, that it might break out on many fronts, and that total victory was beyond hope.

Baldwin II was the nephew of Godfrey and Baldwin I. Originally Baldwin of Le Bourg, he became Count of Edessa. He was crowned King of Jerusalem because in the eyes of the Crusaders his experience in Edessa showed him fit to rule the kingdom, and because he was related to Baldwin I and thought to have many of his virtues.

In fact, Baldwin II was very different. He was cautious, systematic, a punctilious administrator who earned the nickname of "the Goad." He had no liking for the trappings of royalty. It was said that he was at his prayers so often that his knees were covered with calluses. In an age of license he was singularly chaste, remaining faithful to his Armenian wife.

Joscelin of Courtenay, one of Baldwin's distant relatives on his mother's side, came to the East, wandered to Edessa, asked for a fiefdom, and was given some lands west of the Euphrates, which were dominated by the castle of Turbessel. These were rich lands that had not been invaded, and Joscelin, in an incautious moment, said that he was rich enough to buy up the whole of the principality of Edessa, and that its present lord would be better served if he returned to France to live on his estates. Baldwin heard of the boasting and invited Joscelin to visit him at his capital. Baldwin lay in bed; it was rumored that he was seriously ill, and when Joscelin entered the bedroom he was convinced that he was about to be offered the entire principality. Joscelin asked him about his health. Baldwin answered, "Much better than you like!" sprang out of bed, and accused his faithless nephew of disloyalty and ingratitude, these being major crimes and deserving of great punishment. Baldwin was a just man. Instead of the entire principality, Joscelin was given a small dungeon that he could hardly move in. When Baldwin felt that Joscelin had learned his lesson, he set him free.

Joscelin, stripped of his fiefdom, made his way to Jerusalem, and being a man of extraordinary courage and address, he quickly rose to become Prince of Tiberias, an important member of the royal council. Recognizing the merits of the Count of Edessa, he was the most vociferous among the princes to urge that the count should be made King of Jerusalem. Soon Joscelin of Courtenay, formerly lord of Turbessel and Prince of Tiberias, was made Count of Edessa and lived in the palace where he had once occupied a small dungeon.

Positions changed quickly in the Kingdom of Jerusalem. A squire might be knighted one day, and on the next day he might be given charge of an immense fortress and lead an army across immense deserts. A feudal king and a feudal aristocracy ruled, but a man brilliant in warfare was likely to rise rapidly through the ranks. Just as in the Church high positions went sometimes to the sons of peasants, so the military organization of the kingdom demanded that the most talented soldiers should be given great responsibilities.

A new generation of nobles was growing up. Tancred, dying in Apulia in 1112, bequeathed the principality of Antioch to his cousin Roger, Prince of Salerno. Like all the Norman princes of Italy, Roger was a brave and ferocious warrior. He was determined to add Aleppo to his principality, and in the spring of 1119 he prepared to march out against Aleppo and called upon Baldwin II for assistance. The king counseled caution. So did Pons, Count of Tripoli, grandson of the Count of Toulouse.

An attack on Aleppo would inevitably involve the sultan of Damascus and the local emirates. Ilghazi, Emir of Mardin, commanded a powerful army said to number forty thousand men. Roger's forces were pathetically small in comparison—seven hundred knights and four thousand infantrymen. Roger hoped to take the enemy by surprise—a forlorn hope, since the enemy had spies in Antioch who knew all his movements and were able to report all the preparations for the advance upon Aleppo. Fifteen miles from Aleppo, on June 27, 1119, while the *khamsin* was blowing, the Turcoman horsemen swept down on Roger's army, encircled it, and destroyed it. The knights were slaughtered as cattle are slaughtered, deliberately, mechanically, easily. A handful were taken prisoner and displayed during Ilghazi's triumphal procession through the streets of Aleppo; while they were being displayed, they were tortured to death.

Baldwin II heard of the disaster when he was at Lattakieh on his way to Antioch. He heard that Roger was dead, that the Crusaders had lost seven thousand men, and the Turks had lost twenty. It was the most terrible defeat suffered by the Crusaders. He rushed on to Antioch with Pons close behind him. Ilghazi had been so busy celebrating his triumph that he had failed to seize Antioch when it was at his mercy. Together, Baldwin and Pons put Antioch in a state of readiness. In the middle of August they marched against Ilghazi and fought a curious battle at Tel-Danith. Neither side won; but both Christians and Turks were badly bruised. When they had disengaged, Ilghazi took pleasure in tying his prisoners to stakes, using them for target practice. Baldwin and Pons returned to Antioch to lick their wounds.

While Ilghazi showed himself to be incompetent except in battles where he commanded overwhelming forces, the king of Jerusalem seemed to be suffering from a failure of nerve. He quarreled with Pons and sent a small army against him. It was true that Pons had refused to acknowledge Baldwin II as his sovereign, but for the king to quarrel so violently with a prince was a sign that he was becoming self-indulgent: the question of sovereignty could have been postponed to a later time.

Grotesque things began to happen. Joscelin of Courtenay, made Count of Edessa at last, was caught in an ambush by Balak, the nephew of Ilghazi and a man of considerable knowledge and experience. Joscelin was once again thrown into a dungeon; this time in the castle of Kharput in the Kurdistan Mountains. Baldwin II assumed the regency of Edessa and wondered at the stupidity of Joscelin for allowing himself to be caught. Seven months later, in April 1123, Baldwin, visiting Edessa, was himself caught in an ambush while riding with a falcon on his wrist in one of the valleys of the lower Euphrates. Balak's troops fell on the king and his escort. They were all thrown into dungeons in the same castle.

Jerusalem was without a king. Fulcher of Chartres writes about these events, which he observed from Jerusalem, with a mixture of incredulity and calm. The king had vanished, but Christ was the real king. Strange events were happening far away in the Kurdistan Mountains. Reports from Edessa reached Jerusalem at irregular intervals; no one seemed to know exactly what was happening; the Egyptians were invading from the south, and all of Islam knew of the successes of Balak. What was not known until much later was that the Armenians had received a message from Joscelin of Courtenay, urging them to attack the castle at Kharput. Fifty Armenians disguised as monks or beggars, with arms concealed under their clothing, made their way from Edessa into the mountains of Kurdistan, entered the castle secretly at night, killed the guards, and then raced to the tower where Baldwin II and Joscelin were being held prisoner.

The Armenians freed the king and Joscelin, but the Turks still had a powerful army in the vicinity, and before they could escape the castle was besieged. Baldwin II had the resources of the castle at his disposal; he believed it would be possible to fight off the Turks. He urged Joscelin to escape through the enemy lines to summon help. With three Armenians to lead the way, Joscelin made his way to the Euphrates, which they crossed on inflated leather bags. It was a difficult and dangerous crossing. He had lost his shoes, his feet were bleeding, and he was exhausted. He fell asleep under a nut tree, his body hidden under bushes and brambles, for he feared the enemy was searching for him. He was awakened by an Armenian peasant, who turned out to be a former servant of his.

Soon Joscelin, riding on the peasant's ass, reached Turbessel, where Joscelin found his wife and rewarded the peasant. Almost immediately he rode off to Antioch and then to Jerusalem, where he offered some links of his prison chains as an ex-voto in the Church of the Holy Sepulchre.

A more important task was to assemble an army to rescue the king. Columns from Jerusalem, Tripoli and Antioch rode off to Turbessel, only to discover that the king was still being held in the castle. Balak offered the king a safe-conduct if he surrendered the castle. The king refused, and the fighting went on. Balak in a rage ordered that the rock on which the castle stood be mined. The Muslims were experienced tunnelers; they carved tunnels through the rock under the two principal towers, then stacked wood inside the tunnels and the wood was set on fire. The effect was to create enormous explosions which brought down the two towers. With the castle half in ruins and no longer defendable, the king was forced to surrender. Balak spared the king but took brutal vengeance on the Armenians who had helped the king conquer the fortress.

Shortly after Baldwin II was ambushed, there arrived in Palestinian waters a huge Venetian fleet commanded by the Doge Domenico Michiel. The fleet put in at Acre to learn that Jaffa was being besieged by an Egyptian fleet. Nothing could have delighted the doge more. He detached eighteen ships that looked like pilgrim ships from the main fleet and sent them to Jaffa. The Egyptians exulted at the prospect of booty. The captains of the doge's decoy ships played their roles well, pretended to be too weak to fight, and took only such evasive action as would convince the Egyptians that they were terrified. Suddenly the Venetian ships came over the horizon, their brightly colored sails filled with wind, the great banks of oars flashing in unison. The doge had ordered the Venetians to permit no Egyptians to escape. The entire Egyptian fleet was surrounded; the Venetians boarded them and massacred everyone on them. The sea turned red.

This was one of the greatest of all naval victories up to that time. It was carried out with precision and daring, with superb seamanship. Ten more Egyptian ships were found off Ascalon. They, too, were full of booty: gold and copper coins; balks of timber for making siege engines; pepper, cumin, and other spices. Those ships that succeeded in beaching themselves were burned while the rest were taken to Acre, which had never previously seen so many ships riding at anchor.

There remained Tyre, the last seaport in Muslim hands north of Ascalon. Tyre was the Mediterranean seaport for Damascus, well fortified, proud and imperious on its rocky peninsula. Toghtekin, Atabeg of Damascus, had sent in a powerful garrison. The Egyptians were attacking Jerusalem in order to make a diversion; the troops of Ascalon were confronted with the common people of Jerusalem, who fought to preserve the city without benefit of armed knights, for the chivalry was at Tyre. The land walls were surrounded by Crusading knights and crossbowmen; the seawalls were blockaded by the huge Venetian fleet, which had increased in numbers during these last days. Tyre was doomed. Toghtekin made one last despairing effort to penetrate the ring around the city, but failed. On July 7, 1124, the citizens capitulated and the Crusaders entered the city and raised the royal standard on its towers. There was some irony in this, for the king was still a prisoner in his remote castle in the Kurdistan mountains. Tyre was conquered in his name and became a part of his kingdom.

This time the conquerors behaved honorably. They permitted the Muslims to remain or to leave with all their wealth, as they pleased, according to the terms of the capitulation. This was probably due to Pons, who played an important role in the siege and was becoming increasingly respected.

Less than two months after the fall of Tyre, Baldwin was released from his prison. His enemy, Balak, had been killed in a fracas among the Muslims and was succeeded by the Emir Timurtash who offered Baldwin his freedom in exchange for some territories beyond the Orontes and a payment of eighty thousand dinars, of which only twenty thousand dinars were payable in advance. Baldwin found the terms acceptable. He was entertained at a banquet by the emir and given a royal robe, a gold cap, and embroidered buskins, like those worn by the emperor of Byzantium. He was also given his favorite charger, which had been well cared for during his imprisonment.

Baldwin repaired at once to Antioch, of which he was the regent. A new army was raised to attack Aleppo, fifty-five miles to the east of Antioch, but a five-month siege failed to reduce the city. A new Muslim commander had entered the stage. His name was Aksungur al-Bursuqi, the White Falcon, Emir of Mosul. Aleppo, Mosul, and Damascus were now allied under a brilliant commander determined to extend the limits of his frontiers at the expense of the Christians. While Baldwin returned to Jerusalem to enjoy the congratulations of his people, the White Falcon was marching toward Antioch. Baldwin hurried north, accompanied by Pons of Tripoli. At the battle of Azaz, Baldwin insisted that the Christians should employ the tactics of the enemy: a feigned retreat, a sudden wheeling about in a place which offered them the utmost advantage as attackers, and then an attack by the armored knights in massed formation. Azaz, which lies in the northeast of the principality of Antioch, offered exactly the right terrain, and the maneuver was executed faultlessly. The enemy lost as many as two thousand men; the Christians as few as twenty. The figures may be improbable, but nevertheless it was a disastrous defeat for the Muslims.

The task of the Christians was to press their advantage. Early in 1226, Baldwin moved against Damascus, assembling his troops at Tiberias. Beyond the Wadi ar-Rahub, they came to a stronghold held by Syrian Christians and a valley known as Sophar of the Meadows, where, according to tradition, the Apostle Paul had had his conversion experience. Beyond Sophar, the Atabeg Toghtekin of Damascus was waiting for them. Baldwin formed his army into twelve columns. At Tel el-Saqhab, twenty miles from Damascus, Baldwin fought one of the hardest battles of his life. He was always in the midst of the fighting, calling on his knights by name and encouraging them. The Crusaders lost their entire baggage train and the tent that served as the royal chapel. The entire army of Damascus, scenting victory, then charged—and might have won the day if Baldwin had not ordered a countercharge. Luck was with the Crusaders, for Toghtekin was unhorsed. Believing he was dead, the Muslims gave ground, panicked, and fled back to Damascus, closely followed by the Crusader army. Baldwin's forces penetrated the suburbs of Damascus, but they had been badly mauled and they had no hope of conquering the city. The king returned to Jerusalem, satisfied that the army had injured the Damascenes severely. In fact, very little was gained, there was no victory, only an enormous bloodletting.

This, of course, was the danger inherent in these indecisive border wars. The Christians could not afford to lose many men, and the Muslims with their inexhaustible manpower could always return to the attack. But the Crusaders still lived on dreams and wild hopes, miracles and portents, as men do when they are living in desperate circumstances.

Now, fifteen years after the death of the near-legendary Bohemond, his son arrived in Antioch to claim his patrimony. He was about eighteen, tall and handsome like his father, and bearing his father's name. He arrived in the port of St. Symeon in October 1126, with a fleet of ten galleys and twelve freighters laden with provisions and armaments. He was welcomed by Baldwin, who confirmed the young prince in the possession of Antioch, and to ensure that there should be a bond between them, he gave to Bohemond II his daughter Alice in marriage. In the presence of the king, all the knights of Antioch swore fealty to their new liege lord.

Alice was the king's second daughter, and it was necessary to find a husband for his eldest daughter, the imperious and wilful Melisende. Baldwin's choice fell on Count Fulk of Anjou, a distant kinsman, then living in France. There were lengthy negotiations, for it was clearly understood that Fulk would inherit the throne. Baldwin was seeking a king of Jerusalem who had never been to the East and knew very little about Jerusalem. Fulk was nearly forty, a widower with many children, calm, intelligent, and ambitious. He had made Anjou much larger by his attacks on Maine, a region in France, and therefore knew a great deal about warfare. His interests extended to England, France, and the Kingdom of Jerusalem. His son, Geoffrey Plantagenet, had recently married Matilda, the heiress to the Norman throne of England.

Fulk served Baldwin well. He possessed an exquisite loyalty, an admirable discretion. Of all those who came to rule Jerusalem he was probably the most intelligent. He reached Acre in the spring of 1129 and was greeted with great pomp and ceremony. He married Melisende on June 2. It would be a difficult marriage, for Melisende was even more ambitious than her husband and was rarely reasonable.

As far as reasonableness goes Bohemond II was no more so than his father. The people of Antioch worshipped him; his height, his beauty, and his bearing marked him out as a youth of extreme distinction. Soon after he came to the throne, he led his army against the fortress of Kafartab. There was a short siege, the people surrendered, and the young prince ordered all of them massacred. The lessons learned by Pons of Tripoli were lost on Bohemond II, who quarreled violently with Joscelin of Edessa, which would have led to war between them if Joscelin had not providentially fallen ill, thus giving Baldwin time and opportunity to heal the wounds.

Baldwin was still determined to conquer Damascus; and, with new recruits from western Europe, he amassed a large army and invaded Damascene territory. The armies of Joscelin of Edessa, Bohemond II, and Pons of Tripoli were with him, and there were many knights who came in the retinue of Fulk of Anjou. This powerful force marched against the army of Buri, son of the Atabeg Toghtekin, who had died the previous year. Buri was a capable general, but Baldwin's army pressed hard against him; he was in danger of losing Damascus when a violent storm arose, there were continuous claps of thunder, the rain fell in torrents, and the battlefield became a sea of mud. The Crusaders withdrew, defeated not by the enemy but by the weather.

This was Baldwin's last battle. Soon Bohemond II fought his last battle as well. He was leading a large raiding party in Cilicia. Amazingly careless, he appears to have thought no enemy would dare to attack him. While he was marching at a leisurely pace along the banks of a river, Danishmend Turks fell on him. The Turks killed everyone in the raiding party. When found, Bohemond's body was headless; the head had been enbalmed and sent as a present to the caliph. Bohemond was only twenty-three years old when he died.

The news of his death stunned the Antiochenes, who thought of him as their talisman, the man who would bring them luck for fifty years. He left a daughter, Constance, who was only two years old. His widow, the Princess Alice, was determined to be a sovereign princess in her own right, independent of her father.

Alice, therefore, entered into secret communication with Zengi, the

Atabeg of Aleppo, offering to marry off her daughter to a Muslim prince on condition that she remain during her lifetime the ruler of Antioch. Through a trusted messenger, she sent a superb gift to Zengi: a snow-white palfrey shod with silver, the bridle and all the trappings also of silver, the saddle covered with silver brocade. By chance Baldwin II, hurrying to Antioch as soon as he learned of the death of Bohemond, heard that the messenger had been arrested by his troops. He immediately ordered that the messenger should be brought to him. The messenger confessed everything. In a rage Baldwin II ordered that he should be put to death with every refinement of torture.

Knowing that the king was on his way, Alice ordered that the gates of Antioch be closed. There were some in Antioch who disliked Alice intensely, and they arranged that the Gate of St. Paul and the Gate of the Duke be left open. The king's troops poured in. Alice retreated to the citadel, barricading herself in the tower. She still had many followers and might have attempted to fight against her father's troops, but wiser counsel prevailed. She came out and threw herself at her father's feet, begging for mercy. She was ordered never again to assume power in any place except Lattakieh and Jabala, which were her dowry. The affairs of Antioch were entrusted to capable men of Antioch, who were made to swear on oath that they would keep Antioch for Constance, the infant princess, until she came of age. Then, very sadly, the king returned to Jerusalem.

The excitement of those days in Antioch may have hastened his death. He fell ill in Jerusalem, perhaps of typhus, and knew that he was dying. He asked to be taken from his palace to the patriarch's palace near the Church of the Holy Sepulchre, and then called Melisende and Fulk of Anjou and his three-year-old grandson Baldwin to his bedside, and abdicated in favor of the prince he had summoned from beyond the seas. He wore the habit of a canon regular of the Church of the Holy Sepulchre, and in this habit he died on August 21, 1131, in the thirteenth year of his reign. He was buried beside Godfrey and Baldwin I at Golgotha.

Baldwin was the last of the Crusader kings who fought in the First Crusade. A change was coming over the Kingdom of Jerusalem. Lotharingians, Normans, Frenchmen, and Provençals were becoming subtly orientalized. It was not that they were suffering from a lethargy of the soul or were learning the vices of the Orient, though they were sometimes lethargic and their vices were legendary. Something much more important was happening to them: they were becoming a new nation belonging to both East and West, but more to the East. They depended upon Europe, but were alienated from Europe. They had thought of conquest as a simple thing—the preservation of Jerusalem and the Church of the Holy Sepulchre—and they had discovered that conquest was ambiguous and complicated. The Crusade itself was becoming a *jihad*, a holy war, Islamic in the intensity it provoked.

On this subject, writing shortly before the death of Baldwin II, the usually rather lukewarm Fulcher of Chartres wrote with passionate feeling:

> We who were once Westerners are now Easterners, a Roman or a Frenchman in this country becomes a Galilean or a Palestinian. He who was of Rheims or Chartres has become a citizen of Tyre or Antioch. For we have already forgotten the lands of our birth, which are unknown to many of us and never mentioned among us.
>
> Some already possess homes and households and tenants by inheritance. Some have taken wives not only of their own people but of Syrians or Armenians or Saracens who have been granted the grace of baptism. . . . Those who were poor in the West, God has made rich in the East. Those who had little money there have innumerable bezants here, and a man who did not even have a house in the West now possesses a city. Why return to the West when there is an Orient like this?

Why, indeed! And why should not more people come to settle in the East under the conquering banner of the Crusaders? There were never enough settlers. The Kingdom of Jerusalem might be close to Paradise, but it was also a blood-soaked battleground, and so it would remain during the whole course of its existence.

King Fulk
of Anjou

MUCH of our knowledge of the Crusaders of this period comes from one of the greatest historians the world has known, William, Archbishop of Tyre. He writes with quite extraordinary tact and intelligence, never raising his voice, and always alert to reasonable explanations of events. He has the modern historian's gift for painting a portrait, so that we can see the characters he sets down on the page of history, and he always writes with assurance. Events follow one another in logical order, and he rejoices quietly in their logic and their orderly progression. From the pages of his history he gazes up at us with steady eyes and a look of profound understanding; he is always solemn, judicious, good-tempered. He raises good sense to the height of genius.

The title he chose for his history was *Historia Rerum in Partibus Transmarinis Gestarum*, which may be translated *A History of Deeds Done Beyond the Sea*. The title, which begs many questions, was probably chosen during one of his infrequent journeys to Rome. For him, the kingdom of Jerusalem was not "beyond the sea"; it was the place where he grew up. He was a busy man with many ecclesiastical duties, and increasingly as he grew older he was given governmental duties. He went on embassies, served as the tutor of the heir to the throne, became Chancellor of the Kingdom, was the close adviser of King Amaury, the only king of Jerusalem who was book-learned and therefore capable of discussing matters of state with a man of trained intelligence. The government of the kingdom was partly in the hands of William of Tyre, and his word counted for much in the royal court. All this he conceals quite properly in his recording of historical events. His prose rises and falls like the waves of an inland sea; events reach their crises; new crises follow; all are seen to be contained within the framework of divine providence.

One of William of Tyre's chief virtues was his understanding of the Arab mind. He was fully aware that the enemy often acted intelligently and that the Crusaders often acted stubbornly and stupidly. The intelligence of the

137

Muslims did not, of course, prevent them from being heretics who mus
necessarily live outside the mercy of God.

Fulk of Anjou came to the throne in 1131, which was probably the yea
in which William of Tyre was born. Fulk was quick, decisive, and alert
fighting on many fronts, and he had more than his fair share of trouble
with the princes who ruled over the coastal principalities. Alice of Antioch
was a thorn in his flesh. Very early in his reign, he lost Joscelin of Edessa
who died gloriously after being severely injured by falling masonry during
an attack on a Turkish fortress. As Joscelin lay close to death, a messenge
came to say that the sultan of Iconium was besieging his castle at Cresson
Joscelin summoned his son, also named Joscelin, and ordered the young
man to lead the army in an attack on the sultan's forces. The son made
excuses, saying the enemy was too large, their resources too few. In despair
Joscelin ordered that the entire army be called out; everyone who could
bear arms would attack the Muslims at Cresson. He ordered a litter to be
built and had himself strapped to it. From this litter, he took command of
his army, and they set out for Cresson. On the way, he heard that the siege
had been raised because the Turkish chieftain heard that a vast army wa
driving toward him; and so it was. Joscelin died soon afterward, still lying
in the litter and praising God for all the benefits conferred on him.

The courage of Joscelin I was not inherited by his son; Baldwin II'
intelligence was not inherited by his daughters Melisende and Alice, both
of whom were troublesome, wanted power, and would stop at nothing to
get it. Alice, the former Princess of Antioch, wanted to be princess again
She had schemed with Zengi; now she schemed with Joscelin II, which may
not have been difficult, but also with Pons of Tripoli, which shows tha
Pons had a more desperate side to his character than people generall
knew.

King Fulk rode to Antioch, where Alice had installed herself. Entering
Tripoli, the king found the way barred; Pons had sent his knights to guard
the approaches. For such matters there were always simple solutions. The
king went by boat to the mouth of the Orontes, marched on Antioch, found
the knights loyal to him, and learned that Pons had brought up an army
and was prepared to fight. At the battle of Rugia, near Antioch, a Crusade
army under King Fulk faced a Crusader army under Pons of Tripoli. It wa
a savage battle, and for a long time the issue was in doubt. At last the king
won, and the surviving soldiers of Pons's army were led in chains to
Antioch.

This was the first battle between Crusading armies; but there were to be
many more. The spirit of rebellion lay deep in the hearts of Crusaders; and
even when they were outwardly at peace, the princes of the coastal cities
were often secretly rebelling against the king. Pons fled back to Tripoli
escaping punishment. Alice was again banished. The captives from Pons'
army were released from their chains. A council of knights was established

to rule the city, but so many Antiochenes begged the king to remain that he delayed his departure for Jerusalem for some months. The main axis of the war was shifting to the north, and especially to the valley of the Orontes. The Saracens were determined to capture Antioch, thus reducing once and for all the danger to Aleppo. In Zengi, they found the first of the great Islamic strategists who were capable of uniting vast masses of people from many princedoms in a determined effort to free the country of Christians. The Arab world was stirring. A great army had crossed the Euphrates to descend upon Antioch; another army had descended on the castle of Montferrand, in Tripoli, where Pons of Tripoli was holding out. The king heard the news about Pons as he came rushing up the coastal road to help the people of Antioch. At Sidon, he was met by Pons's wife, Cecilia, Countess of Tripoli, who was the daughter of Philip I of France. She had been the wife of Tancred. The king regarded her as his sister. Now she stood beside the road, begging the king to go to the aid of Pons and his beleaguered castle. She spoke urgently and persistently. She told him Zengi himself was attacking Montferrand. The king marched to the castle, but before he reached it, Zengi fled, thinking that a large, well-trained army was descending on him. Then the king marched on Antioch.

Zengi was acting cautiously. He was assembling his main army at Qinnasrin, the ancient Chalkis. The Turks from beyond the Euphrates had not all reached the main camp, and he wanted to wait until he commanded an overwhelming force. Fulk, acting with extraordinary speed and throwing every able-bodied man in Antioch into his army, knew or sensed that Zengi was in no mood to attack until his army was at full strength. Close to Qinnasrin, near the fortress of Harim, the king assembled his forces. Scouts reported that Zengi was not ready to advance, so the king made a sudden attack, throwing the full weight of his cavalry into the enemy camp. It was a famous victory, with three thousand of the enemy killed and every imaginable kind of booty: slaves, tents, tent furnishings, horses, and flocks of sheep. For the second time, Zengi's army fled before the king.

When he returned to Antioch, the king was greeted as both conqueror and savior. Here he remained for some time, deliberating on the course he must pursue in order to safeguard Antioch now that Bohemond II was dead. Just as he had himself been brought from overseas to rule over the Kingdom of Jerusalem, so now it occurred to him to search for a French or English prince who would be strong enough to rule over Antioch and preserve it against the Saracens.

His choice fell on Raymond of Poitiers, the son of William of Poitiers, who had fought in the First Crusade. Raymond was about thirty years old, now serving in the English court, a favorite of the king of England, who had made him a knight. Everything about the young man suggested strength, determination, and courage. A messenger called Gerald Gerbarre was dispatched to England to invite him to the throne of Antioch. The messenger was sent secretly, for Alice still saw herself as the destined ruler of Antioch, and it was necessary that she should know nothing about the intended marriage of her daughter to Raymond of Poitiers.

Gerald Gerbarre carried out his mission faultlessly. He met Raymond a the court of King Henry I, conferred with him at length, and brought him safely to Antioch, where an extraordinary drama unfolded with the help o Radulph of Domfront, Patriarch of Antioch.

William of Tyre, although very young at this time, remembered the patriarch and describes him as a heavy-set man, with a military bearing, a man who looked more like a knight than a priest. He had a large popular following although it appears that he achieved the patriarchate by a ruse rather than by election.

King Fulk and Raymond of Poitiers, relying upon his famous discre tion, let him in on the secret. Radulph accordingly let it be known tha Raymond had come to marry Alice, when in fact he had come to marry her daughter. While Alice, who had returned to Antioch in defiance of her father and with the help of her sister Queen Melisende, waited in the palace for the man she thought was her betrothed, Constance was carried off to the cathedral and married to Raymond of Poitiers. By this marriage, Raymond became Prince of Antioch. Constance was then about nine years old.

Both Princess Alice and Queen Melisende were outraged by this conspi racy, which had been organized by a simoniacal patriarch, an English prince, and the king of Jerusalem. Alice and Melisende were practiced conspirators themselves: the queen was Alice's shield against the king's wrath, and Alice, it seemed, was an inveterate troublemaker, who enjoyed nothing better than flaunting her powers.

Melisende also enjoyed flaunting her powers. Earlier in Fulk's reign she had shown extraordinary favors to a certain Hugh of Le Puiset, Count o Jaffa, who was young, handsome, charming to women, and exceedingly bold. He had married a much older woman for her wealth, and was on bad terms with her sons, both of whom were well-known, powerful at court and heirs to vast estates. Fulk knew about the queen's intimacy with Hugh but tolerated it out of his deep love for his wife. Others found it les tolerable, and in the summer of 1132 one of Hugh's stepsons, Walter Garnier, rose in court and publicly accused Hugh of high treason and o conspiring to murder the king. Hugh denied the charge vehemently bu offered to submit to the judgment of the court. The matter was so seriou that the judges decreed it must be settled according to the ancient custom o the Franks, by single combat. A day was chosen. Everything was prepared for the tournament that would decide the truth or falsity of the charge. Bu on the chosen day Hugh failed to appear. He had left Jerusalem for Jaffa and then taken a ship to Ascalon, where he signed an agreement with the gyptian governor. He had now committed himself to high treason, whether or not he had acted treasonously before. The situation was now extremely dangerous, for Jaffa was the seaport of erusalem. Hugh commanded troops which began to ravage the aproaches to Jerusalem. With him were detachments of Egyptian troops. Potentially, a combined operation from Ascalon and Jaffa could take erusalem. But the governor of Ascalon was not ready to put a whole army n the field, and Hugh could not rely on his own troops. Balian, Lord of belin, who was vassal to Hugh, turned against him, fled to Jerusalem, and old the whole story to the king. To his own nobles, even the most ebellious, Fulk nearly always behaved mildly. William, Patriarch of Jerualem, was sent to Jaffa to mediate. Hugh was offered his life on condition hat he go into exile for three years. This was a light punishment, and he iccepted it readily.

Until a suitable boat could be found to take him to Apulia, he was iermitted to live in his own house in Jerusalem. He was playing chess in he Street of the Furriers when a knight of Brittany drew his sword and tabbed him repeatedly. A crowd gathered quickly; the knight was disrmed; Hugh was taken to a hospital; and the rumor spread through the ity that Hugh had been attacked at the orders of the king. These rumors nay have been inspired by Queen Melisende, who was doing everything he could to preserve the reputation of her lover at the expense of the king's eputation.

The knight from Brittany was put on trial, and the king demanded xemplary punishment. The knight was sentenced to death by mutilation: iis arms and legs would be hacked off and he would be permitted to bleed o death. Usually, in such cases, the tongue was also cut off, but this part of he punishment was rescinded by the king in the hope of a full confession. The knight from Brittany insisted to his dying breath that the king had iothing to do with the attempted assassination of Hugh of Le Puiset, and n this way the king's honor was vindicated.

Queen Melisende's desire for vengeance was not completely appeased. At ourt she made it clear that anyone who had ever said a word against Hugh vas her enemy. Such men took care to hide, for Melisende was believed to ie quite capable of having them murdered. The king, too, appeared to be rightened of her and increasingly acceded to her wishes. Meanwhile Hugh ived out the few remaining years of his life as a vassal of King Roger II of iicily.

Meanwhile, Zengi still threatened. His attention was now drawn to Fripoli. Pons had been killed in a ferocious border war, and his son Raymond had exacted a terrible revenge, torturing and massacring all the Muslims he could lay his hands on. Zengi realized that Raymond's bloodhirstiness was a sign of weakness, and that Tripoli was ripe for plunder. Ie invested the castle of Montferrand in the heights above Rafaniya.

Raymond sent an urgent call for help to the king. Montferrand was an important castle, guarding the valley of Bek'aa. The king answered that he was on his way, and Raymond set out for Montferrand with as many troops as he could raise. He was not a military genius; he fell into a trap Zengi had carefully prepared for him, and was captured. Fulk, who was a far better soldier, broke through the ring and joined the defenders inside the castle. The king's column had moved so fast that it had been unable to carry provisions. Soon the troops inside the beleaguered castle were weak from starvation, and it seemed that the time would soon come when the king would be Zengi's prisoner.

Although it was impossible to break out of the ring, it was possible to smuggle out messages. Urgent appeals were sent to the patriarch of Jerusalem, Joscelin of Edessa, and Raymond, Prince of Antioch. All answered the appeal, and the patriarch brought with him the True Cross. Out of sympathy, Raymond of Antioch led his army to Montferrand in spite of the fact that Antioch itself, in one of those turns of fortune that could only happen in the Crusades, was being besieged by the huge army of John Comnenus, the emperor of Byzantium.

Zengi continued to bombard the castle of Montferrand with huge rocks and stones, hoping with his siege engines to batter it into submission. He was so determined to destroy the castle and everyone in it that he manned his siege engines all day and all night. The castle shook continually, the noise was unendurable, and the famished defenders were unable to sleep. The king found it difficult to smuggle out any more messages, and he knew nothing about the approach of the relief forces, which had already entered the county of Tripoli. Zengi's spies reported the movements of the relief forces. They also told him that the emperor of Byzantium was at Antioch. The emperor's presence evidently weighed heavily with him, for he feared that the Byzantine army would join the Christian forces and attack Aleppo or even Damascus. He therefore decided to let the king and his starving soldiers leave the castle peacefully. In addition, he would free all the prisoners he had captured, including Raymond of Tripoli. The king and the remnants of his army withdrew with their weapons and with all the honors of war, and Zengi entered the ruined castle of Montferrand.

The relief forces were only a few miles away. Instead of attacking the castle, they returned to their own lands after a pleasant parlay with the king, who thanked them for coming to his assistance, though they had come too late.

For Raymond, Prince of Antioch, the adventure had been especially dangerous. He had no idea in what state he would find Antioch when he returned. In fact he found the situation unchanged; the emperor had made no serious attack, and the popular militia of Antioch had made a number of sallies which showed that they were a force to be reckoned with. John Comnenus, the son of Alexius and the younger brother of Anna Comnena, was a man of principle, capable of great wisdom in his dealings with nations. The people of Constantinople called him Kalojohn, from *kalos* which means "good" or "beautiful." It is possible to include him among the greatest of Byzantine emperors, for he reconquered most of Asia Minor from the Turks in a series of hard-fought annual campaigns which brought him at last to the gates of Antioch. Since the Byzantine emperors had always claimed Antioch for their own, he was merely coming to claim a city he considered as part of his empire.

Raymond, returning from his meeting with King Fulk, succeeded in breaking the blockade of the city at the north gate. The emperor, camped outside the walls, and realizing that Raymond was preparing to offer resistance, began to bombard the city with his siege engines. He hoped to break through the Gate of the Bridge, and most of his attacks were concentrated there. He was prepared to fight, but he was also prepared to accept an oath of loyalty from the prince of Antioch, and then perhaps join forces with him against the Saracens. On only one matter was he adamant: Antioch belonged by right to the Byzantine empire.

When he learned all this, Raymond sued for peace. Ambassadors from Antioch were sent to the emperor's camp, and it was agreed that Raymond should swear fealty to the emperor, who would be permitted to enter the city whenever he pleased. It was also agreed that if the emperor succeeded in taking Aleppo, Shaizar, Hama and Hims (Homs), these too should be added to the fiefdom of the prince of Antioch. In this way peace was established, Raymond knelt before the emperor, and the imperial standard flew from the tower of the citadel. The emperor returned to Cilicia, intending to spend the winter on the seacoast near Tarsus.

During the winter, plans were made for a combined Byzantine-Crusader attack on Zengi's strongholds. Shaizar was selected as the principal objective. In April, the entire Byzantine army, together with the armies of the prince of Antioch and Joscelin of Edessa, converged on Shaizar. The siege engines were set up, and thousands of heavy rocks and stones were hurled into the city. From early morning until late at night, the emperor himself, in gold helmet and breastplate, sword at his side, acted as the field commander, mingling with the soldiers and directing the men manning the siege engines. The prince of Antioch and Joscelin of Edessa, perhaps in protest against the emperor's assumption of the powers of commander in chief, remained apart from the battle. They sat in their tent, playing at dice. The emperor was furious and ordered them onto the battlefield.

After three weeks, with the news that Zengi was approaching from the east, the emperor accepted a huge indemnity from the emir in return for raising the siege.

The emperor returned to Antioch with the intention of teaching the prince of Antioch a lesson. He had not previously entered the city. Now he entered in triumph, riding on horseback, with the prince and the count walking like lowly footmen on either side of him. He provided himself with a large escort of Byzantine troops. The patriarch met him at the city gate and escorted him to the cathedral through streets hung with carpets and scented with incense. After a solemn mass, the emperor rode to the prince's palace, and it was clear that he intended to stay there. In a speech from the throne, he announced his dissatisfaction with many things seen in Antioch and Shaizar. The Byzantine army would take over the citadel, where he intended to store his own treasure and his own weapons, and henceforth Antioch would become the war capital, the center for the mobilization of a Christian army against the Saracens in Syria. The prince of Antioch was the emperor's prisoner and must henceforth do the emperor's bidding.

Help came from an unexpected corner. Joscelin of Edessa, a bad soldier but an excellent conspirator, devised a superb stratagem for getting rid of the emperor. He spread the rumor that the Byzantines would dispossess and expel the people of Antioch. He issued a call to revolt against these usurpers from overseas. Crowds formed, arms were seized; with the whole city in a frenzy, Joscelin went to the emperor. An armed mob had accused him of being a traitor, ready to sell the city to the emperor, he told the emperor.

He presented himself as an innocent spectator who had stumbled on a revolt. The emperor offered to leave Antioch for the sake of the Christian peace, and when that news spread, the revolt abated.

A few days later the emperor's army returned with him to Cilicia. Spurned by the Crusaders, John Comnenus washed his hands of them.

The man who was most pleased by the departure of the Byzantine army was Zengi, who was engrossed in a plan to seize Damascus, which was then under the government of an old Turk called Unur. Damascus was in great danger, and Unur had no hesitation in calling for help from the king of Jerusalem. Unur offered twenty thousand bezants a month, the restoration of the fortress at Banyas to the Christians, and a firm alliance against Zengi. Fulk set out for Tiberias on the Sea of Galilee, only to find part of Zengi's army parading on the farther shore. Fulk moved his army toward Damascus; and Zengi pulled out, and set up his headquarters at Baalbek. By moving toward Damascus, Fulk had shown that he could be relied upon to help Unur, who was properly grateful. The alliance between Unur and Fulk was based on a common interest and on similar habits of mind. William of Tyre describes him as "a man of much wisdom and a lover of our people." Actually, at heart Unur detested the Christians, yet he was one of the few Muslim leaders who had an understanding of them and could deal with them in a civilized manner.

Fulk invited Unur to attend his court at Acre. It was the first time that a Muslim ruler had been invited to attend the court of a king of Jerusalem. There were festivities, ceremonious exchanges of gifts, and endless diplomatic conversations. In Tiberias, there were more festivities. In Jerusalem a rather simple-minded Templar approached Unur and said, "Would you like to see God as a child?" "Yes, certainly," Unur replied. Then the Templar led the vizier to a painting of the Virgin Mary with the Christ child on her lap. "Here," said the Templar, "is God as a child." Unur said nothing; there was wisdom in his silence.

The alliance between Damascus and the Kingdom of Jerusalem continued into the reign of Fulk's successor. The battles with Zengi continued, but they were more like sustained skirmishes than real battles; and sometimes the Egyptians tested the strength of the kingdom. Once an Egyptian raiding party reached the Plain of Sharon but was forced back. Under Fulk the kingdom in alliance with Damascus seemed to be as secure as it had ever been. Fulk had learned the hard lesson that to survive at all the Crusaders must be more malleable in their attitude to the Muslims, more understanding, and more strenuous in their effort to penetrate the Muslim mind.

IV

THE KINGS BORN IN THE HOLY LAND

The Young King
Baldwin III

IN the autumn of 1142, King Fulk and Queen Melisende went on holiday to Acre, accompanied by the court. The king had a good deal of business to do in the palace, and soon the queen, bored by the ceremonial life at court and anxious to see more of her husband, suggested that they should visit a place called the Springs of the Oxen, where according to the ancient legend Adam found the oxen which enabled him to plow the earth. So they went off in a long cavalcade, the servants being sent ahead to prepare the way and to arrange for the festivities that would take place when they reached the springs. Everyone was in good spirits; it was a fine sunlit day and the plain of Acre had never looked lovelier.

It was not a hunting party; it was simply a ride into the country. But it became a hunting party when one of the servants riding ahead startled a hare lying in a furrow. Suddenly, all were chasing after the hare. The king, accompanied by his escort, dug his spurs into his horse, and with his lance at the ready he pursued the hare with wild excitement and at breakneck speed. Suddenly his horse stumbled and fell, and he was thrown head foremost over the horse's head. His saddle fell on him and crushed his skull. There was nothing to be done for him. He lingered on for three days without regaining consciousness.

The dying king was brought to Acre, where huge crowds gave expression to their grief. He died on November 10, 1142, at the age of fifty-three. A few days later King Fulk was buried in the Church of the Holy Sepulchre. He left two children: Baldwin, who was thirteen, and Amaury, who was seven.

Baldwin was crowned on Christmas day in the Church of the Holy Sepulchre, the boy-king standing beside his mother, who was crowned at the same time to emphasize her position as regent and controlling power of the kingdom. The princes and nobility of the kingdom were all present at the long and complicated ceremony, which was conducted by William, Patriarch of Jerusalem. Afterward there was a coronation feast.

The boy-king looked the part to perfection. William of Tyre, who was about the same age and knew him well, could find few faults in him. The boy-king had inherited his father's vigor and his mother's beauty. Unlike his father, who could never remember names, Baldwin III remembered the names of his lowliest servants and of everyone he met. He had a passion for books and rode a horse magnificently. He talked easily and well, possessed a sharp wit, permitted himself and others great freedom of speech, and never refused an audience. As a youth he had many mistresses but after his marriage he remained faithful to his wife. He drank little. "Excess," he liked to say, "was the touchstone for the worst crimes."

He was the first king of Jerusalem to be born in the Holy Land. His three predecessors came from the West, and brought with them certain Western prejudices and clerkly habits of mind. Although devout, he was more interested in history than in theology, and he had studied the history of the kingdom minutely. His roots were in Jerusalem; he was the son of the Judaean wilderness and the lush coastal plains. When he was daring, it was in a peculiarly straightforward, Jerusalem-like way, and when he was obstinate—he needed to be very obstinate indeed to wrest the power from his mother—then, too, he was so in a straightforward, Jerusalem-like way. He was never cunning, and this was to his advantage. They said of him that he came to the throne at exactly the right time and with exactly the right qualities and if wit, courage, intelligence, kindness, and physical beauty could have saved the kingdom, he would have saved it. But it was during his reign that there could be seen for the first time the fatal flaws that would bring about the destruction of the kingdom.

Societies decay and renew themselves continually, provided they have reasonably stable frontiers and that there exists an essential unity of purpose. Corrupt ministers and treacherous soldiers can attempt to destroy a society from within, but as long as the frontiers are held and the unity of purpose remains, the society, even though it is given a deathblow, can be resurrected. But conquest and consequent assimilation can destroy a kingdom utterly. Frontiers, therefore, are of paramount importance: they are lines drawn on a map, but they are also spiritual, enclosing arms, angelic guardians. In the Kingdom of Jerusalem, the frontiers were continually shifting. The essential unity had been in jeopardy from the beginning, from the time Bohemond took Antioch for himself, and Baldwin took Edessa. Contending principalities were ruinous, for they wasted the energy of the people. In a country where the Arabs possessed an excellent intelligence system, every dispute between the princes was quickly known to the kingdom's enemies.

The danger came from northern Syria, where the cold and calculating Prince Zengi was attempting to build up a large kingdom of his own. A bitter feud had broken out between Raymond, Prince of Antioch, and Joscelin of Courtenay, Count of Edessa. Zengi heard about the dispute and took full advantage of it. Joscelin had removed his army from Edessa, leaving the city virtually defenseless. Zengi brought up his own army, surrounded the city, and attacked it with mangonels. The defenders, though there was scarcely a trained soldier among them, fought well, and the siege was much longer than Zengi had intended. He therefore vowed that all the Franks remaining in the city would be killed without mercy. He had a very large force, having summoned troops from all over the East to besiege the city. His aim was to smother the city by sheer numbers. Food was running out; but the defenders fought on behind their massive walls. Messengers were sent to Antioch and Jerusalem to appeal for aid. The prince of Antioch refused aid, while Queen Melisende, acting as regent, sent a strong force which arrived too late to do any good. Edessa's fortress wall was mined, and Zengi's troops poured in. All the Franks were killed, but the native Christians were spared.

The loss of Edessa and the butchery of the Franks sent shock waves through the kingdom. Edessa was the northeastern anchor of the kingdom, forming a salient into enemy territory, so heavily fortified that it was believed to be impregnable. Now it was lost, and except for a very brief occupation by a Christian force a few years later, it was lost forever.

The shock waves reached Europe. The pope and the king of Jerusalem sent out appeals for help. Similar appeals had been issued often before, but this time they were more insistent, more demanding. The fall of Edessa would bring about the Second Crusade. For the first time, kings would come from Europe to the Holy Land. They would find themselves confronting someone even more crafty and cunning than Zengi—his son Nur ed-Din, who would succeed him when Zengi fell to an assassin's knife.

Meanwhile, the boy-king Baldwin III was leading a charmed life. He was genuinely loved by the people and they loved him in return. There are men who seem to be fortunate from birth, and he was one of them. In his first campaign to reclaim Val Moysis, a Crusader castle built by Baldwin II in 1127, that had been taken by Turks and local tribesmen, who had massacred the entire Crusader garrison, Baldwin III's success was crowned by the fact that he had not lost a single one of his soldiers.

But his second campaign was a disaster. It began strangely and ended in horror. A certain Altuntash, an Armenian nobleman converted to Islam, arrived in Jerusalem with a small retinue, declaring that he had come from Bosra, a town in the Hauran some forty-five miles east of Tiberias. Altuntash was the governor of Bosra. He was a tall, imposing man with a gift for easy argument and a congenial personality. He told a convincing story about his quarrel with Unur, an official whose power exceeded that of the king of Damascus. He offered to surrender Bosra to the Christians if a suitable compensation could be paid to him. In addition he offered the town of Salkhad. Queen Melisende offered to present his request to the nobles; a general conference was held, and it was unanimously agreed that this extension of Christian power into the Hauran would be acceptable to

God. Suitable compensation was provided; heralds were sent out to raise an army; the boy-king marched out of Jerusalem at the head of his troops with the now-bejeweled True Cross, the most precious object in the kingdom, held high in the hands of Robert, Archbishop of Nazareth. Altuntash was also in their company.

Although the royal councillors had discussed Altuntash's offer at great length, it appears that no one paid more than passing attention to the difficulties of the enterprise. The Hauran was a plain of volcanic ash, unexplored by the Crusaders. Even more important was the fact that the area was under the control of Damascus, and Baldwin II had signed a treaty with the king of Damascus. It was a treaty of alliance and temporary peace, which according to the custom of the time, meant a ten-year truce. By invading the Hauran, Baldwin III was breaking a solemn treaty. In a rather off-hand way the secretary of the royal court of Jerusalem wrote to Unur, explaining the king's intention, and Unur not unexpectedly wrote back that he would do everything he could to prevent the threatened invasion. Since Unur was the vizier to the king of Damascus and the chief power in the state, it might have been better if Queen Melisende had arrested Altuntash and sent him back to Bosra. Unur had shown himself to be friendly to the Christians and nothing was to be gained by making him an enemy.

Nevertheless, the army marched to Tiberias and set up camp on the shores of the Sea of Galilee. Then it set out across the waterless plain, where there had recently been a plague of locusts. Nothing grew there; the inhabitants lived in subterranean caves; and the Turks, enraged by what they regarded as the duplicity and treachery of the Christians, were already massing their armies.

Everything went wrong. There were continual skirmishes with the enemy. One day, when they were surrounded on the march, they became aware that the enemy was about to attack. Toward evening, the king ordered his men to raise their tents as though there was no enemy in sight. All night they kept a close watch. During the night more Turks came to join the solid ring formed around the Christian camp. The king held a council of war. Some spoke of retreating, others of advancing, while still others thought they could neither retreat nor advance, but must inevitably be destroyed by the enemy where they stood. Unwisely the king ordered the advance. Faith sustained them. The outnumbered Christians hurled themselves against the enemy, hacked their way through the ring, and although they were utterly exhausted and could only keep a snail's pace, they marched on to Bosra.

They were entering the terrible wasteland called Trachonitis, said to derive from the word *tracones*, meaning "underground caves." Suffering from thirst, they came upon deep wells, let down the buckets, and were not altogether surprised when the ropes were cut by men hidden in subterranean caverns. The dangling ropes were omens of disasters to come. After four days of thirst and constant skirmishes, they came in sight of Bosra, found water issuing from rocks, and rested in preparation for entering the city the following day, believing that they had earned this triumph by virtue of all the hardships they had sustained. At midnight a messenger came through the lines to the king's tent. The letter he brought was read to the nobles and the king's councillors. It said that the wife of Altuntash had already surrendered the city to Unur, who had brought up a powerful army and expelled all the Christians living there. The towers and the citadel were manned by Turkish forces. A much larger army than the one they had confronted in the wasteland of Trachonitis was now about to be thrown against them.

The medieval mind genuinely believed in miracles and wonders. It was not, therefore, surprising to discover that the king's councillors, believing in the jeweled Cross, thought that if the whole army was lost, then at least the boy-king should be saved and brought safely back to Jerusalem by the simple expedient of giving him the Cross and the fastest horse in the kingdom. How he would find his way, or what would happen if he was captured by the enemy, were not matters that concerned them, for they believed that as king and Cross-bearer, he was under the protection of Christ. The king rejected their advice, saying that he scorned to save his own life while his consecrated soldiers were likely to perish.

The likelihood of disaster was very real, for Nur ed-Din, a master strategist, was now in Bosra planning the destruction of the Christian army. The king ordered a retreat, and soon Nur ed-Din's forces were all around him. The Christians fought their way through one encirclement after another. The king gave orders that no one should be left behind; the wounded and the sick, even the dead, must be taken along. Those who could not fight must draw their swords, so that the enemy would believe they were capable of fighting. The plains were covered with thistles and brambles inflammable as tinder in that fierce summer. The Turks set fire to the brambles; the Christians were about to be engulfed in the flames when the Archbishop of Nazareth at last raised the jeweled Cross. At that moment the wind changed direction, and now it was the Turks who were in danger of being suffocated and burned. Everyone in the army had a smoke-blackened face.

The nobles thought of suing for peace and even sent an envoy to Unur to ask on what terms he would let them go free. The envoy was killed before he reached Bosra. The Christian army continued to fight its way back to the Sea of Galilee amid daily skirmishes, dust storms, and such broiling heat that the knights had to be prevented from throwing away their coats of mail. Halfway to the Galilee they encountered an unknown knight mounted on a white horse, wearing a breastplate and gauntlets reaching to his elbow, and carrying a scarlet banner. He led them by the shortest routes to water and good campsites. He spoke to no one; he was never seen in the camp. Every morning he was seen riding the white horse and every evening he brought them to a place where they could pitch their tents. He seemed to be an angel of the Lord sent down to lead them to safety. Was he an angel? Was he an apparition? William of Tyre made inquiries among the survivors of the expedition and all of them said they saw him, but never knew his name or where he had come from. No one doubted that without his help they would have been destroyed by the Turks, who followed them even when they reached the Decapolis. At last they entered Gadara on the shores of the lake, and on the following day they were in Tiberias.

There the army disbanded, the knights and the foot soldiers returning to their own homes. The king returned to Jerusalem with the jeweled Cross and the archbishop of Nazareth returned to Nazareth. In due course Altuntash, the cause of all this misery, made his way to Damascus in the hope that all would be forgiven him. He was arrested when he entered the city, and thrown into prison. Instead of putting him on trial for treacherous dealings with the Frankish enemy, the officials put him on trial on a lesser charge. Once, during a quarrel, he had put out the eyes of his brother, who now demanded that Altuntash should suffer the appropriate punishment. The family quarrel taking precedence over his treacheries, he was blinded. According to the historian Ibn al-Qalanisi, no further punishment was demanded of him, and he lived out the rest of his life as a private citizen in Damascus.

The Second Crusade

HE adventure that came to be known as the Second Crusade was another folly. It failed in its undertakings and by its failure added to the prestige of Islam; it came at the wrong time, for the wrong motives, and was led by the wrong people. But it began with high hopes, intense excitement, and a sense of destiny. It was led by two kings. Louis VII of France and Conrad III of Germany were princes in the grand tradition, possessing gifts of command and organization and a highly developed sense of the operations of government in their own countries. Once they were outside their own countries, their understanding failed them.

Louis VII came to the throne in 1137 at the age of sixteen. He was already married to Eleanor of Aquitaine. It was said of Louis VII that he was "a very Christian king but somewhat simple-minded." He attended all church ceremonies as though his very life depended on them and seemed more like a priest than a king. He liked to talk familiarly with his subjects and was always gracious and hospitable, though people were aware of a kingly reserve. Eleanor was more ebullient, delighting in dances and frolics, fine clothes and jewels, and all the secular pleasures of the court. Despite their differing temperaments, they were happy with one another. Both were under the tutelage of two singular churchmen who were among the greatest of the century. One was Abbot Suger, who presided over the Abbey Church of Saint-Denis, and the other was Bernard of Clairvaux, the greatest preacher of his time and distantly related to the house of Aquitaine.

Abbot Suger, the son of a serf, was a small man of extraordinary intelligence and great administrative power. Louis VII rarely embarked on any course of action without consulting him. Bernard of Clairvaux had a silver tongue and spoke so well that audiences were spellbound. The richly poetic words that poured out of him apparently without effort seemed divinely inspired. He was now summoning the nations of Europe to join in a Crusade. On this subject Abbot Suger had his own opinion: at all costs the young king must be prevented from leading a Crusade because it was necessary for him to attend to the affairs of France.

Apparently, Louis VII had not been attending to them very well. He had quarreled with the pope and come under an interdict. This was serious, but even more serious was his quarrel with Count Thibault of Champagne, whose territories he invaded with a large force. He set fire to a castle belonging to the count at Vitry-sur-Marne. The flames spread to the villagers' huts and then to the church where they had taken refuge. The roof collapsed and some thirteen hundred villagers were burned to death. Louis VII said later that the sight of the burning church and the screams of the dying made him a Crusader, for he had brought so much guilt on himself that his only salvation lay in asking for the pardon of Christ at the Holy Sepulchre. He would be more believable if he had not continued to ravage the land of the count with fire and sword for a few more weeks. He led his knights into battle and did much slaughtering of his fellow countrymen. The fighting ended as suddenly as it began. Louis VII fell ill. His illness was aggravated by thundering letters from Bernard of Clairvaux, who warned the king that he would be condemned to everlasting hell if he continued in his behavior. He spoke of the need for penance, and hinted strongly that the proper penance might take the form of a Crusade.

At Christmas, in 1145, Louis VII convoked an assembly of barons at Bourges. He told them that he had decided to take the Cross and wished as many of his barons as possible to follow him, but they remained strangely silent. Louis felt he was being scorned by men who did not realize that the Kingdom of Jerusalem was in danger.

At the end of Lent in the following year, the king convoked another assembly at Vézelay in Burgundy. This time he was accompanied by Bernard of Clairvaux and armed with a bull issued by Pope Eugenius III, exhorting all Christians to take up the Cross. On Palm Sunday the entire population of Vézelay was invited to hear Bernard. The crowds were so numerous that the meeting was held in an open field.

Bernard promised absolution and a heavenly reward to all those who took up the Cross. The crowd clamored for crosses, and when the supply failed, Bernard threw off his gown and asked that crosses be made from it. These badges, worn on the shoulders, were like badges of knighthood which permitted the knight of the faith to enter the New Jerusalem.

Leaving Burgundy, Bernard traveled through Lorraine and Flanders, continually preaching the Crusade. It occurred to him that the Germans, who had so far shown little interest in fighting in the Holy Land, should be introduced to the delights of battling against the infidels. Conrad III promised to lead a German army to the Holy Land in the shortest possible time. But it was not until nearly a year and a half later, in May 1148, that his army finally set out across Hungary to follow the same road which the men of the First Crusade followed fifty years earlier through Byzantine territory. Manuel Comnenus, the son of John Comnenus, was now emperor of Byzantium. He was a man with a genuine sympathy and understanding of the West, and he employed Latins in his government. He concealed a ruthless will beneath an exquisite courtesy of manner. When he learned that Conrad's army was committing depradations during its journey through Byzantine territory, the exquisite courtesy gave way to rage. It was too late to send the army back to Germany, and there was nothing to be gained by fighting it. He would let it pass through his territory, give it as little help as possible, and hope for its eventual destruction.

The army of Louis VII came close on the heels of Conrad's army. Both Louis and Conrad professed to despise the Byzantines and thought longingly of sacking Constantinople. Both were greeted with courtesy by Manuel Comnenus. Conrad was the first to pass over into Asia, following the route taken by Godfrey of Bouillon. At Dorylaeum, Conrad's guides deserted him, and the Turks were waiting. Suddenly the Turks were all over them. It was not a battle but a massacre, for the Germans were weary and dispirited after their long march; the Turks were fresh, and their aim was accurate. Conrad lost more than three-quarters of his army. He fought his way back to Nicaea, accusing the Byzantines of deliberately allowing him to enter a trap. In fact the Byzantines had warned him of the danger of crossing Asia Minor diagonally and had urged him to follow the coastal road. The German booty, the slaves and the treasure, were sold in the bazaars of the Near East for many months.

When the French army reached Nicaea, they learned of Conrad's defeat at Dorylaeum. In spite of this reversal, it was decided that the two armies should continue their march, this time along the coastal road, remaining in contact with the Byzantine fleet patroling the seacoast. They reached Ephesus without too much trouble, and there Conrad fell ill. He returned to Constantinople by sea, and Manuel Comnenus, who had some knowledge of medicine, cared for him and restored him to health. The French marched on, increasingly harried by Turks. Two days beyond Laodicea they met their greatest disaster on a pass between the snow-covered mountains that seemed to touch the sky.

Here, Geoffrey of Rancogne and Amadeus of Savoy, the king's uncle, made a fatal error. Instead of halting at the top of the pass according to orders they pitched their tents on the southern slope. They were in command of the vanguard, and it was absolutely necessary that they should keep in touch and be visible to the main army. The Turks, established on the mountaintops, shot arrows down at the Franks on both sides of the mountain; heavy stones and tree trunks followed. Then the Turks descended to cut up the survivors. It was another massacre, with no mercy given. Louis VII was almost killed The historian Odo of Deuil, who accompanied the expedition, described the king fighting off a crowd of Turks single-handedly on the mountaintop:

> During the fighting the king lost his small and famous royal guard, but he remained in good heart and nimbly and courageously scaled the side of the mountain by gripping the tree-roots that God had provided for his safety. The enemy climbed after him, hoping to capture him, and the archers in the distance continued to fire arrows at him. But God willed that his cuirass should protect him from the arrows, and to prevent himself from being captured he defended the crag with his bloody sword, cutting off many heads and hands.

The story is almost certainly true. Although Louis VII was among the worst of French kings and among the worst of generals, he was capable of feats of endurance and possessed a certain amount of courage. Kings are rarely seen defending themselves alone on lonely mountain tops, and we have a right to be grateful.

After this defeat Louis VII gave command of the army to Everard of Barre, the third master of the Temple, whose detachment of Templar troops henceforth served as a model of discipline for the army. The haphazard French army reformed and fought its way to the rocky plain of Attalia and the seacoast. From Attalia the king made his way to Antioch by sea, leaving some troops behind. The Turks swooped down on them.

The king with his knights arrived at the port of St. Symeon on March 19, where he was greeted by the prince of Antioch, and festivities were held in his honor. The prince made himself especially agreeable to Queen Eleanor, who was his niece. Out of loyalty to her uncle, the queen supported the plan that was uppermost in the prince's mind: an attack on Aleppo, Nur ed-Din's capital. Nur ed-Din's power was in the ascendant. He controlled nearly all the land east of the Orontes, and he was a perpetual danger to the survival of Antioch. The prince wanted to use all the new knights in a combined operation to capture Aleppo. The king was disinclined to lose more knights to save Antioch. He had duties to perform in Jerusalem. He exasperated the prince by saying that he had no intention of attacking Aleppo until he knew more about the situation in the Holy Land. His army left Antioch at night, in secret; the prince was unaware until it was already on the march.

By now, Conrad III had reached Jerusalem with the pathetic remnants of the German army. He was on excellent terms with Queen Melisende, who was acting as regent. To the two sovereigns the queen of Jerusalem confided her most secret desire: the conquest of Damascus, which was still guardedly in alliance with Jerusalem. This was the purest folly, as the previous attack on Bosra had demonstrated only too clearly. Strategically, an attack on Aleppo made much more sense. But Melisende was accustomed to prevail, she had set her heart on Damascus, and accordingly the army under command of three kings, Louis, Conrad, and the young Baldwin, marched out of Jerusalem to conquer the one Muslim princedom whose friendship was essential to the survival of the Christian kingdom. The attack on Damascus was a prolonged exercise in futility. Baldwin commanded the vanguard, Louis commanded the middle, Conrad commanded the rear guard. It appears that the army was abundantly provisioned and had no serious difficulty until it reached the orchards on the north and west of the city and was advancing on the river. The Damascenes on the opposite bank held up the advance, until Conrad, who came riding up to see why the army had failed to cross the river, killed a Turkish knight by slicing him through the neck and the left shoulder, so that his head, shoulder, and left arm were in one place and the rest of his body in another. Whereupon the Damascenes fled back to the safety of their walls.

The fighting continued for six days. The Crusaders chopped down the orchards and built stockades from which they could defend themselves against the continual sorties of the Muslims, who by this time had rallied, knowing that help had been summoned from far away. Then something went horribly wrong for the Crusaders. It is not possible to be sure what it was, but what seems likely is that there was a failure of nerve brought about by rumors of treachery in high places, which may have had no substance at all. Perhaps too, as the long battle continued, the Crusaders realized that nothing had been gained by the attack on Damascus, and that, even if they captured the city, they would be unable to hold it.

"From this time," wrote William of Tyre, "the condition of the Latins in the East became visibly worse."

The army withdrew from Damascus in good order on July 18. The Christians had not lost many men, but they had lost hope. Conrad III "perceived that the Lord had withdrawn favor from him," and ordered ships that would take him back to Europe. Louis VII remained for a year, staying long enough to celebrate Easter at the Church of the Holy Sepulchre.

The kings departed from the troubled kingdom ruled by Queen Melisende, who governed according to the vagaries of her whims. She knew nothing and learned nothing. Nor did the prince of Antioch apply himself to the proper government of his princedom. The people of Antioch saw him as an arbitrary ruler, who took very little interest in their fate. Proud and obstinate, despising the Muslims, he rode with a small company of men into land occupied by Nur ed-Din. Nur ed-Din's spies were everywhere. At night, Nur ed-Din's army crept up to the prince's camp, and in the morning there was a great slaughter. The prince fought well, but was hopelessly outnumbered. Nur ed-Din, who had some respect for him as a warrior, ordered that his head and right arm should be cut off and sent as a trophy to the caliph, while the rest of his mutilated body was left on the battlefield.

There was no one now in Antioch to encourage and protect the people. Nur ed-Din swept out of the hinterland, led his army past Antioch and occupied the Monastery of St. Symeon, which lay high up in the mountains between Antioch and the sea. In sight of his army he bathed in the sea, and let it be known that the sea also had been conquered by him. He seized the fortress of Harim, which was only ten miles from Antioch, provisioned it, and left a garrison which could withstand a siege of many days. Nur ed-Din was a power to be reckoned with.

Aimery of Limoges, Patriarch of Antioch, emerged at this time as the one man who could weld the people of Antioch together. He had accumulated a vast fortune, and now he placed the treasury of the patriarchate at the service of the people and the army. He spent prodigally and efficiently. When the young Baldwin III—he was now eighteen years old—arrived in Antioch, he found confidence returning. He immediately took command and pronounced himself regent.

The prince of Antioch had died fighting. Joscelin II, Count of Edessa, died ingloriously. He was on his way to Antioch with a small escort, summoned by the patriarch, when he abruptly left the path to relieve the needs of nature. Some Muslims fell on him and carried him off to Aleppo, knowing there was a price on his head. Nur ed-Din, who despised him, kept him in a dungeon, where he died nine years later. His wife continued to rule over his territories, seeing that the castles were well manned and supplied with food and weapons. She was more of a soldier than he had ever been.

Two kings of Europe had departed; a prince was killed; a count vanished into the darkness of a foreign prison. More and more power fell into the hands of Baldwin III.

King Baldwin III and the Heroic Age

O F all the kings of Jerusalem Baldwin III is the one we know best. Contemporary historians were awed by the young king who seemed to have no vices, to be at once intelligent, deeply religious, and gentle to all people. Moreover, he possessed the gift of command. He was born at exactly the right time, for his kingdom was in danger of dissolution, and only by superb ability and great gifts of mind could it be maintained. Even so, before he died he may have known that the end was in sight.

William of Tyre, who described him minutely, remembered that in his youth he was an inveterate gambler and that throughout his life he was astonishingly frank, abruptly rebuking high officers of state in public rather than in private, making enemies unnecessarily. These were dangerous elements in his character, and they were to have dangerous consequences.

One of his major gambles took place in 1152, when he quarreled violently with his mother, who had held the regency for seven years which was past the time when Baldwin should, by law, be the single sovereign. Baldwin at twenty-two performed all the military offices demanded of him, presided over the court, and acted in public as though he possessed the real power. Yet he remained under the tutelage of his formidable mother. It was an absurd situation, and the king at long last decided to assert himself.

Queen Melisende was at that time under the influence of a certain Manasses of Hierges, a clever nobleman from the region of Liège, whom she had appointed Constable of the kingdom. Manasses was rich, powerful, and insolent, determined to retain his privileged place at all costs.

Baldwin set about his assumption of real power in two stages. First, he had himself crowned secretly in the Church of the Holy Sepulchre, in the presence of only a handful of his knights, thus preventing his mother from being crowned with him. Secondly, the king decided on war. Manasses was closely besieged in his castle at Mirabel near Jaffa. He was captured, brought into the king's presence, and spared on condition that he leave the kingdom and never return. Queen Melisende fortified Jerusalem against the king's army and barricaded herself in the citadel, appealing to the people, the nobles, and the clergy for their assistance in her righteous war against her son. The people and the nobles had grown weary of her; the clergy were deeply indebted to her. After a few days of token resistance, she surrendered and was allowed to leave for Nablus on condition that she, too, never return to Jerusalem. Baldwin had been perfectly prepared to take the citadel by force; he had mounted siege engines and hurled rocks against the walls, and, if necessary, would have killed his mother. This was a gamble that had to be taken to save the kingdom.

In Antioch, the Princess Constance still ruled, headstrong, improvident, pleasure-loving, and without any skill in government. A new Prince of Antioch had to be found for her, and Baldwin presented her with a list of three noblemen who possessed the requisite qualities of courage and resourcefulness. She wanted none of them. In her own good time she would choose a husband suitable to her needs. She found such a husband in Reynald of Châtillon, the feckless younger son of the count of Gien, who had accompanied Louis VII during the Second Crusade. Reynald was young, handsome, possessed of great courage, and to all outward appearances he would have made an excellent Prince of Antioch. Constance was in love with him and appears to have married him secretly even before securing the permission of the king, who was her suzerain. Baldwin appears to have permitted the marriage reluctantly. He had hoped she would marry someone closer to her own rank.

Reynald of Châtillon was one of those men who rise from obscure origins and somehow change the course of history. He, more than anyone else, was responsible for the fall of the kingdom. He endangered everything and everyone who came near him and seemed oblivious to the damage he caused. He could be counted upon to do improbable, absurd, and terrible things with a kind of casual grace, never realizing the cost.

He proved very early that he could be extremely vicious. As Prince of Antioch he regarded himself as the sole ruler whose judgments must never be questioned. The Patriarch Aimery of Limoges sometimes did question them in private, and unhappily these private conversations were reported to the prince. Reynald had the patriarch stripped and scourged till the blood came, then had him placed on the roof of the citadel and smeared all over with honey so that flies settled all over him while the sun burned him. The patriarch was in ill-health but remarkably resilient. Somehow he survived the punishment. News of Reynald's act of revenge reached Baldwin III in Jerusalem. The king was outraged and at once sent two of his councillors posthaste to Antioch with orders that Aimery should be released from captivity and permitted to resume his patriarchal functions. Reynald obeyed. Aimery left Antioch, and it was many years before he returned.

Reynald was the prince of the second most important city in the Holy

Land. Left to itself, Antioch could have added to its great wealth and stability. Reynald, however, possessed the instincts of a bandit chieftain. The Byzantines were warring against the Armenians in Cilicia; Reynald joined the Byzantines, hoping to add Cilicia to his princedom. When it became clear that the Byzantines regarded Cilicia as their own, he turned against them and sent an expedition to Cyprus, which belonged to Byzantium. The expedition was well organized and had one purpose: to obtain booty. The Cypriot army quickly collapsed; monasteries and nunneries were seized; nuns were raped; costly vestments, gold and silver vessels, and jewels were heaped up and carted away to the waiting ships. The raiders remained on the island for only a few days, but the damage was incalculable. Manuel Comnenus, the Byzantine emperor, then busy in Europe, quietly decided to take revenge upon an insolent and treacherous prince.

Meantime, Nur ed-Din continued to attempt to forge a united Muslim army against the Christians. Like his father, Zengi, he could be cruel and implacable; unlike him, he possessed a deeply contemplative temperament. He lived like an ascetic, fasted, and sometimes found himself in a state of religious exaltation. He was a man who lived on many levels: administrator, warrior, mystic. His mysticism was perhaps given strength by his chronic ill-health, while his intense religious feeling gave strength to the holy war he conducted against the Christians.

Baldwin III had a profound understanding of his most implacable enemy. His spies gave him accurate reports, and he sometimes took advantage of the periods when Nur ed-Din was bedridden. In theory the prince of Antioch was charged with defending the northeast, while the king defended Samaria, Judaea, and the Negev. In fact Baldwin III was in overall command of Christian territory in the Holy Land.

From the beginning of his reign Baldwin III meant to conquer Ascalon, which was heavily defended by the Egyptians because it was their northernmost outpost along the Palestinian coast. The people of Ascalon were all trained in arms. High walls, barbicans, and towers protected the city on the landward side, and it was not easily approachable by sea because there were low shelving sands, the winds whipped up high waves, and there was no proper harbor. Nevertheless supplies could be brought into the city on small boats.

Baldwin proceeded with great care and intelligence. The navy of the kingdom patrolled the sea approaches; the royal fleet was under the command of Gerard of Sidon, and consisted of fifteen ships. Other ships were bought, stripped of their masts, and disassembled: from the wooden strakes they made siege engines and moving towers, covered with hides to prevent them from catching fire. On January 25, 1153, the king with his entire army, together with the grand masters of the Hospital and the Temple, the archbishops of Tyre, Caesarea, and Nazareth, and the patriarch holding high the True Cross, appeared outside the walls of Ascalon. With this formidable army it was hoped that Ascalon would yield within a month. It took much longer, for the people of Ascalon were far better prepared than the Christians had expected. They could not be starved out, they had plentiful supplies of fresh water, and no surprise night attacks were possible because they had ingeniously lit up the walls with oil-lamps which were shielded against the wind by glass containers. But more important than anything was the fact that the defenders were in high spirits and believed their walls were impregnable. They had excellent sources of information, and they knew that the army outside their gates were outnumbered two to one by their own army. One day an Egyptian fleet of seventy vessels appeared, and the small Christian fleet made no effort to attack them. The Egyptians landed supplies and provisions, and Ascalon was stronger than ever.

After two months, Baldwin III realized to his dismay that he had not even made a dent in the walls of Ascalon. That Easter, the influx of Christian pilgrims to the Holy Land was much larger than usual. The king ordered that the pilgrims and sailors must all assist in the siege of Ascalon; they would be paid from the royal treasury. All ships coming to the Holy Land must join the fleet of Gerard of Sidon. In this way, the army and the fleet increased in numbers. But three more months passed before there was any significant change.

One day toward the end of July, the defenders crept out of the city and set fire to the great wooden tower which topped the walls of Ascalon. But as the Christians watched in amazement, the wind changed and the flames began licking the walls. The Christians decided that if the walls could be burned by fires the enemy set, how much more would they burn if set by them. They heaped faggots and cordwood and wood from the surrounding orchards in the space between the burnt-out tower and the wall, poured pitch and oil on them, and then set fire to them. About dawn, as they had hoped and expected, part of the wall fell with a thunderous roar that awakened the army.

Through this breach in the wall some forty Templar knights rushed into the city, some of them standing guard to prevent any other Christians from entering. In their madness, a handful of Templars believed they could conquer the entire city. At first, the people of Ascalon took fright; then they formed ranks, and it was a simple matter to round up these proud Templars and butcher them. That night, they mended the breach in the wall with huge balks of timber from their own ships, while the bodies of the dead Templars were dangled over the walls in the full sight of the Christian army; the bodies were left there for the birds to peck at.

Ascalon seemed to be lost. A vast despair seized the Christians, who debated whether it was worth their while to continue battering a city that seemed impregnable. The army of Ascalon, thinking the Crusaders would reel back, made sorties on the third day after the Templars were hung on the walls. The Crusaders counterattacked with fury and desperation, as though all their pent-up strength and all their frustration were released in the counterattack. From their walls, the people of Ascalon, who had been so sure of themselves, so certain of ultimate victory, witnessed a massacre. The attack was so devastating that there was scarcely anyone in the city who was not bereaved. The elders of Ascalon asked for a truce to give them time to bury their dead. Having counted the dead, they sent envoys to sue for peace. Baldwin III, sitting in council, agreed that if they left the city within three days, they could take their movable belongings with them: what he required was total evacuation. On the third day they poured out of the city in the thousands, while the king's standard flew from the highest tower. He gave them guides as far as al-Arish. Beyond this town, a Turkish chieftain promised to lead them into Egypt. They followed him willingly and lived to regret it, for once the king's guides had returned to Ascalon, the chieftain attacked them and despoiled them of their possessions. When we last see them they are wandering helplessly in the desert.

The lordship of Ascalon was given to the king's younger brother Amaury, Count of Jaffa. Since Gaza had already been captured by Baldwin III, the entire coast of Syria and Palestine was in the possession of the Crusaders. Ascalon was a kingpin, and its capture spread alarm and terror in the camps of the Muslims.

The capture of Ascalon, however, was offset by the loss of Damascus to the Christians' most deadly enemy, Nur ed-Din. For many months, Nur ed-Din had been at work attempting to undermine the authority of the reigning sultan. He saw Damascus as the launching ground of an expedition that would sweep the Crusaders out of Syria. The logic of his argument appealed to the Damascenes, who were disturbed by the fall of Ascalon; and when Nur ed-Din entered Damascus, he was greeted like a conqueror who was also a friend. There were no exactions; and everything went on as before except that there was no longer any sultan. Nur ed-Din appointed one of his most trusted generals to be governor of the city.

In May 1157, Nur ed-Din attacked the Crusader castle at Banyas in the Upper Galilee. The castle occupied an important position at the foot of Mount Hermon. Nur ed-Din twice captured it, and was twice repulsed. So much blood was spilt in and around the castle, that it became a symbol of the intransigence on both sides. There were sudden surprise attacks carried out faultlessly by the king's army, and there were equally sudden surprise attacks by Nur ed-Din's army.

The massive skirmishes for Banyas showed that the Crusaders and the Muslims were evenly balanced. The logic of the situation demanded a truce. Instead they went on fighting. One small advantage was given to Baldwin III. Nur ed-Din fell ill. It was not an advantage that could be relied upon, however, for Nur ed-Din was perfectly capable of directing battles from his sickbed. On the frontiers of Antioch and in the Galilee, there were continual raids and excursions, but no real advantages were gained. The war in the Holy Land seemed to have reached a stalemate.

Baldwin, searching for new allies, had long contemplated an alliance with Byzantium. From the beginning of the Crusades, such an alliance had been discussed and for various reasons abandoned. The Emperor Manuel Comnenus was known to have a high opinion of Baldwin III and the worst possible opinion of the present prince of Antioch. It would be necessary to tread cautiously, in the Greek manner, but it was also necessary to break the stalemate. Baldwin III sent an embassy to Constantinople, asking for the hand of a Byzantine princess. Discussions went on for many weeks; at last a suitable princess was found in the person of Theodora, the daughter of Isaac Comnenus, who was Manuel's elder brother. Thirteen years old, radiantly beautiful, very tall, with thick fair hair, she possessed a natural elegance of manner. Her dowry, her bridal outfit, her wedding gown, her ropes of pearls, the coffers full of jewelry, tapestries and silken stuffs, carpets and gold vessels, were worth a fortune.

Thus equipped, and accompanied by her ladies-in-waiting and the envoys of the king of Jerusalem, she reached Tyre in September 1158. In great state she traveled to Jerusalem, where she was married to the twenty-seven-year-old Baldwin, who delighted in his bride and is said to have remained faithful to her as long as he lived.

That same autumn, the emperor set out from Constantinople at the head of an immense army, and about the beginning of December he marched into Cilicia, which the Armenians called Lesser Armenia. The emperor regarded Cilicia as a province of his empire and he was determined to take possession of it. The Armenian Prince Thoros had seized Cilicia and his army commanded strongly fortified castles. The emperor's army approached so quietly that Thoros, who was staying at Tarsus, barely had time to flee to the neighboring mountains. Reynald, Prince of Antioch, realized that he had nowhere to go. The emperor was determined to punish him for his savagery in Cyprus, and he knew that the only way to escape punishment was by making a public and humiliating submission. He therefore hurried to the emperor's camp at Mamistra in Cilicia, where he appeared, barefoot, wearing a woolen tunic cut short at the elbows, with a rope around his neck, and a sword with the point resting on his breast and the hilt turned outward in his hand. The emperor took the sword by the hilt, whereupon Reynald flung himself violently to the ground, where he lay prostrate for a long time. The emperor was pleased by this self-indulgent theatrical display because he believed in the sincerity of the prince's submission. He did not know that Reynald submitted to no authority except his own.

Baldwin III arrived in Mamistra a few days later with a large retinue. The emperor gave the king the kiss of peace. They spent ten days together. Among the subjects they discussed was the Armenian Prince Thoros, who was brave and had fought many battles against the Turks. The king acted as mediator; Thoros was permitted to retain Cilicia after swearing fealty to the emperor, who saw himself in those days as the kindly, all-forgiving father of an empire so powerful that he could afford to be kindly and all-forgiving.

The king returned to Antioch, while the emperor spent Easter in Cilicia. In April 1159, the emperor descended upon Antioch accompanied by his army, wearing the imperial jeweled cap with pendants and an embroidered robe so weighted with jewels he could hardly move. Trumpets blared; drums boomed; flags waved; and all the dignitaries of Antioch came out to meet the emperor, riding stiffly on horseback, with Reynald of Châtillon, Prince of Antioch, walking by his side and holding the bridle in token of complete submission. Behind the emperor rode the king of Jerusalem and his brother Amaury. The day of the emperor's triumphal entry into Antioch was one of intense celebration and festivity, with gifts showered on the people and everyone vying for the honor of being able to set eyes on the man who possessed such vast power and an empire so ancient that it seemed to be a permanent fixture on earth. All favor and honor flowed from the emperor. During those days he was lord of Antioch, suzerain of the king of Jerusalem and all the Christian principalities of the Holy Land.

The emperor enjoyed the baths of Antioch, which were among the most luxurious of their time; he also enjoyed hunting. One day, when he was hunting with King Baldwin, there was an accident. The king's horse, racing over rough ground covered with low-growing shrubs, stumbled and threw Baldwin headlong to the ground. His arm was broken; suddenly the emperor hurried up, knelt beside him, and began to tend the broken arm like a doctor. The emperor prided himself on his knowledge of medicine and he liked to put his knowledge to use.

These hunting parties, processions, feasts, and visits to the bathhouses emphasized the bonds between Byzantium and the Holy Land. It was felt that the eight days spent by the emperor in Antioch implied the promise of immediate military assistance. Yet it was not so. He had not the least intention of throwing his army against the Turks; he had come to demonstrate the imperial power of Byzantium to Christian and Turk alike. He made the motions of beginning an advance on Aleppo, leading the combined forces of Antioch, Jerusalem, and the Byzantine empire, and then halted abruptly. Through envoys, he arranged a truce with Nur ed-Din, who promised an exchange of prisoners, and then, hearing of a plot against him in Constantinople, he began the homeward march across Asia Minor.

That he had shown himself without engaging in battle was entirely in the Byzantine character. The Byzantines were skilled diplomats, masters of many ruses, and they knew that a show of force was sometimes more effective than force itself. The emperor's tactic offered little consolation to the king of Jerusalem and the prince of Antioch.

The wild and daring Reynald decided to take matters in his own hands and march at the head of a column into the territory of Nur ed-Din's brother in the Marash region. Someone told him that there were immense herds of sheep and goats, many Christians, and almost no Turks. This was true, but his progress had been watched and reported to Aleppo. All their lightly armed cavalry was sent against him. The Turks found him in camp, laden with booty. He could have abandoned the treasure, fled, and saved himself. Instead he elected to fight, and he had the bad luck to be captured. Slung on the back of a camel, he was carried off to a dungeon in Aleppo where he spent the next sixteen years of his life. They did not kill him only because they believed he might prove useful in future bargaining. Neither the king nor the emperor made any effort to ransom him, knowing perhaps that the ransom would be so large that they could not afford to pay it. The king became regent of Antioch, and little more was heard of Constance, Reynald's wife.

The chessboard was being swept clean. Queen Melisende died of a lingering illness; the king was inconsolable. A few months later the king fell ill while on a journey through Tripoli, and died, possibly poisoned by a doctor sent by the count of Tripoli to attend him. His body was borne to Jerusalem with the appropriate pomp and ceremony, to be buried beside the other kings of Jerusalem in the Church of the Holy Sepulchre. His subjects stood beside the road in silence; and Muslims came down from the hills to wail and lament his passing. For eight days the cortege made its way to Jerusalem amid sighs and lamentations. It was reported that Nur ed-Din was advised by his captains to attack the kingdom during these prolonged ceremonies. William of Tyre tells us that Nur ed-Din refused, saying, "We should pity them, for they have lost such a prince as the world no longer possesses." It is possible that he said these words; it is also possible that it was he who paid to have the king poisoned.

With Baldwin III's death in January 1162, the heroic age of the Crusades came to an end. He became a legend. In him, there had been combined a youthful gentleness and a youthful cruelty, reasoned audacity, a kingly beauty. He was soldier and statesman, student and philosopher, and William of Tyre was only exaggerating a little when he wrote, "There is no record in any history, nor does any man now living recall, that such deep and poignant sorrow was ever felt over the death of any other prince of our own or other nations."

King Amaury I

KING Amaury, Baldwin III's younger brother, came at the end of a line of heroic kings. There was about him a certain princely air, that of a man who knows his own importance. However, he had none of his older brother's ease and affability, and was rarely at peace with himself or his fellowmen. His reign was full of glamorous exploits and resounding victories, yet the victories were hollow because Amaury remained at odds with the kingdom he served well and even brilliantly.

The young monarch never spoke to anyone if he could avoid it. William of Tyre remembered that it was easier for him to give good counsel than to tell a story. Far more than his predecessors, he had the royal vices of lechery and greed for money. If he was more intelligent and reflective than other kings of Jerusalem, he was also possessed of a deep sense of curiosity about the people he ruled over and was insatiably curious about the mysterious lands of the Orient. Travelers arriving at his seaports would find themselves invited to his palace to discourse on everything they had seen and known. Many months later he would mention some exotic detail he remembered to William of Tyre, who was astonished to find himself among the king's closest advisers.

They liked each other and worked well together, but it is possible that they never understood one another. William of Tyre was profoundly shocked by the king's lechery. Even more shocking was the king's questioning of certain established teachings of the Church.

Fascinated by the king who was so strange, so close, and yet so distant, William of Tyre speaks of his "rare beauty," which was perhaps a beauty of manner rather than of physical features, or perhaps it was the beauty of his strangeness. It was not Amaury's fault that there should emerge during his reign an adversary of power and genius, Saladin, who never doubted the validity of *his* faith.

Amaury's first task was to harass Egypt, and he went about it with his usual intelligence. He sent a reconnaissance expedition to Egypt in September 1163, reaching Bilbeis after nearly annihilating an Egyptian army outside the city. The survivors fled behind the walls of Bilbeis, and Amaury made a show of besieging the city until the Egyptians opened the dikes. In danger of being drowned by the flooding Nile, the Christian army retired with more than enough prisoners and booty to defray the cost of the expedition.

In the spring of the following year, Nur ed-Din sent an army across the desert in the hope of adding Egypt to his growing empire. The army was commanded by a Kurdish chieftain called Shirkuh, a general of formidable military accomplishments, who captured Bilbeis.

Shawar, Vizier of Egypt, in alliance with King Amaury, besieged Shirkuh. The combined armies of the Kingdom of Jerusalem and Egypt were so large, so well disciplined, and so determined that Shirkuh was in danger of being overwhelmed. But just at this time Nur ed-Din succeeded in capturing the fortress of Harim near Antioch and the fortress of Banyas on the frontier of the territory of Damascus. Instead of continuing the siege of Bilbeis, King Amaury sent envoys to Shirkuh suggesting that both the Christian army and the army of Damascus should retire from Egypt. Shirkuh, in danger of losing his army, agreed. The siege was lifted, and both armies set out from Bilbeis, the Christians following the coastal road, Shirkuh marching across the desert. Shawar, now sultan of Egypt, returned to Cairo to meditate on the fact that he was now, as a result of the king's stratagem, master of his own country with no enemies in sight.

Shawar was a trusting man. He was perfectly prepared to live at peace with the Crusaders, whom he no longer feared because he regarded them as allies against the dreaded army of Damascus. Early in 1167, Shirkuh, maneuvering his army in great secrecy across the desert, set out for Egypt again. Shawar called on the king of Jerusalem for help. The king led his troops to Cairo to find Shirkuh already besieging the city. Shirkuh, seeing that his army was hopelessly outnumbered, withdrew across the Nile and set up his camp at Giza in the shadow of the pyramids. The Crusaders set up their camp in the eastern suburbs, while Shawar and the king discussed a treaty of perpetual peace and the gift of four hundred thousand pieces of gold if the king would guarantee not to depart from Egypt until the army of Shirkuh was destroyed or driven from the country.

This was the first time a king of Jerusalem had been in Cairo. The Crusaders were amazed by the size and splendor of the city. Only two Crusaders entered the palace of the Fatimid Caliph, the ultimate spiritual and temporal ruler of Egypt. They were Hugh of Caesarea and Geoffrey Fulcher, a Templar knight, who probably served as an interpreter. Hugh of Caesarea was charged with the mission of seeing that the caliph himself put his hand to the treaty.

The huge fortress-palace of al-Kahira was one of the great wonders of the world, more luxurious than any other palace known to history. William of

Tyre heard about it from Hugh of Caesarea: the colonnades, the gilded ceilings and marble fishpools, the aviaries full of strange singing birds, and the menageries with animals never seen or imagined before, and the seemingly endless corridors leading at last to the throne room. A curtain of gold cloth heavily ornamented with pearls was suddenly drawn, and there, on a golden throne, with his councillors and eunuchs beside him, sat the youthful caliph in all his splendor.

The sixteen-year-old caliph was the fountain of religious truth, the ultimate judge, and the owner of all Egypt. Shawar, although he was the sultan, treated the caliph with respect bordering on abject terror, making all the proper prostrations while wearing a sword hanging from his neck as a sign of submission. The proceedings were long-drawn; the caliph's councillors were puzzled by the demeanor of the Crusaders, who talked so freely to their caliph. He stretched out his gloved hand to Hugh of Caesarea, a sign of friendship and a token of agreement. Hugh of Caesarea quite properly suspected there might be some significance in a gloved hand. He pointed out that a naked hand ensured true friendship, while a covered hand suggested reservations and a lack of sincerity. The caliph, finally, yielded; "with extreme unwillingness, as if it detracted from his majesty, yet with a slight smile that greatly aggrieved the Egyptians, he put his uncovered hand into that of Hugh."

This was a moment of some importance in the history of the Crusades: a moment when caliph and Crusader met, explored each other's understanding and willpower, and remained on equal terms. Out of this common need to defeat Shirkuh a real friendship was growing. If Sultan Shawar and the Caliph al-Adid had lived, the alliance of Egypt and the Kingdom of Jerusalem might have survived.

Nur ed-Din and Shirkuh were determined that Shawar should not survive. Shirkuh's army was still on the other side of the Nile. The allied armies made several efforts to do battle with him, but he slipped away into Upper Egypt. At a place called Beben, at the edge of the desert, the allies caught up with him, only to discover that Shirkuh occupied some low hills, which gave him an advantage, and between the two armies there was a stretch of sand difficult for the heavily armored knights to cross on horseback. There was heavy hand-to-hand fighting. Here, at Beben, the young Saladin, in command of a division, first distinguished himself. Hugh of Caesarea, with a large number of knights, attacked Saladin's army and was completely overwhelmed; many of his knights succeeded in escaping from the battlefield, but Hugh was taken prisoner. King Amaury's army drove back the enemy, or at least thought they were driving back the enemy, until it became clear that they had fallen into a trap. They had advanced far beyond the Egyptian army, which was being chopped up by Shirkuh's forces. The king's army wheeled around, rode back to the assistance of the Egyptians, finding them with difficulty among the desert dunes. When at last the armies met, the king set up his standard on a high place, reformed his troops, drew them up in close formation, and marched straight toward Shirkuh's troops, which were established on two hills. The Christians marched between the hills with the enemy on either side of them. Shirkuh could have ordered his troops to race down the slopes and savage the Christians, but there was something about the way they marched, in tight order and perfect discipline, which suggested that it would not be easy to break this column, where the most heavily armed rode on the outside to protect those within. He therefore made no attempt to bar their progress to Cairo. He had made his own secret plans. He would race north, capture Alexandria, establish himself there, and make the seaport his base for the conquest of Egypt.

He had not counted on the combined fleets of the sultan and the king, which prevented any help coming by sea. The land walls of the city were surrounded by the king's troops, who waited quietly until Alexandria showed signs of dying of starvation. The orchards outside Alexandria were leveled: the wood was used for the making of siege engines. Shirkuh decided that diversionary tactics were necessary. With a large part of his army he slipped out of Alexandria at night, leaving Saladin in charge of the city with only a thousand knights. Shirkuh went on a rampage, took property and treasure wherever he could find it, and advanced on Cairo, which was held by a strong force. Was he strong enough to conquer Cairo? Unsure of himself, he invited Hugh of Caesarea, his prisoner, for a discussion. It appeared that Shirkuh was prepared to leave Egypt once again, leaving Alexandria to the king, who in turn would give the city to Shawar. The king would march back to Jerusalem, Shirkuh to Damascus. All prisoners would be exchanged, no indemnity would be paid, and once the treaty was signed the people of Alexandria would be free of punishment and molestation by the soldiers.

But Shawar decided that the Alexandrians must be punished for allowing themselves to be conquered by Shirkuh. He demanded a vast indemnity and condemned to death all those who had worked actively with Shirkuh. To others he distributed favors with kindly largesse. He appeared to regard the surrender of Alexandria as the inevitable result of his carefully wrought policies.

Saladin was a welcome visitor to the camp of King Amaury. He appears to have stayed several days with the king, but William of Tyre does not tell us what they discussed. The Kurdish emir was given a bodyguard, for it was feared that he might be insulted or even assassinated by someone who had suffered at the hands of his soldiers. The king offered to provide ships so that the wounded could be taken back by sea to Syria; Saladin accepted the offer gratefully. There were the customary exchanges of gifts. Outwardly they were friends, while at a deeper level they remained mortal enemies.

In Alexandria there were scenes of festivity. Crusaders walked about the city like sightseers, gaping at the mosques and churches, the battlements, the ornamental gates, the colonnades, the many fountains, and the Pharos, the great lighthouse, which lay at the end of a little tongue of land jutting into the sea. But after a few days the Crusaders who came by sea returned home in their ships, and the others took the coastal road with all its dangers.

Having, as he thought, contracted a treaty of friendship and perpetual peace with Egypt, Amaury decided that the time had come for a similar treaty with Byzantium. Ambassadors were sent to Constantinople to negotiate for a Byzantine princess. The emperor was agreeable, and the bride chosen for Amaury was Maria Comnena, who could not by any means be considered beautiful, but she was the emperor's grandniece. She arrived with her attendants at Tyre; the marriage was performed with great fanfare in the cathedral, and she was crowned Queen of Jerusalem. She brought with her in her retinue two high officials of the Byzantine court, who were empowered to conduct negotiations leading to an alliance.

About this time, a certain Andronicus Comnenus, a cousin of the emperor, arrived in the Holy Land bent on mischief. He had been the Byzantine governor of Cilicia, had amassed considerable wealth, and seemed to believe that it might be possible to marry the young widow of Baldwin III and thus establish himself in a very high position in the Kingdom of Jerusalem. He made himself very agreeable to Amaury, who gave him Beirut as his personal fiefdom. From Beirut he journeyed to Acre, which belonged to the dowager Queen Theodora, now twenty-one and more beautiful than ever. Andronicus and Theodora fell in love, and the queen came to Beirut to be with her lover. It was a great scandal. The emperor was incensed; the king of Jerusalem was all the more angry because he was seeking the emperor's goodwill. The emperor demanded that Andronicus should be extradited. Andronicus and Theodora fled to Damascus, where they were cordially received by Nur ed-Din, who sought to find some way to put a dowager queen of Jerusalem to some use. They were permitted to visit Baghdad. A Muslim emir gave Andronicus a castle on the Paphlagonian border, where he practiced the trade of a professional bandit. When Theodora and their two sons were captured by the emperor, he begged permission to join them in prison. Soon he charmed the emperor into giving him another governorship. It was his custom to rise high and to fall low. When the Emperor Manuel died, leaving the eleven-year-old Alexius II to rule the empire, he saw his opportunity, marched on Constantinople, which had just witnessed an appalling massacre of the Latin inhabitants, and seized the throne. Alexius II was murdered, and Andronicus proclaimed himself emperor.

It is worthwhile dwelling for a moment on this extraordinary man, who by his guile and audacity did much to weaken the Byzantine empire. At first he ruled well, protected the poor, ensured that the rich paid their taxes in full, made a covenant with Venice that included an indemnity for their losses during the massacre, built a church of the Latin rite in the midst of Constantinople, the heart and center of Orthodoxy, and struck down the power of the aristocracy. No emperor had ever been so popular with the people. Then Theodora died and he married the twelve-year-old Princess Agnes of France, the daughter of Louis VII. He was now aged sixty-two. Slowly, he grew more arbitrary in his judgments; his police used torture; the people began to murmur against him. In 1185, a Sicilian army attacked Thessalonica; his army deserted him; his bodyguard refused to guard him. He tried to flee to Asia but was caught in Constantinople and tortured to death by his own people, who had grown to hate him as avidly as they had once admired him.

Earlier, in 1168, when Andronicus was a refugee in Baghdad, Manuel Comnenus was still the emperor and the empire was stable. Amaury was coming to the belief that Egypt, riddled with conspiracies, would have to be completely annexed if it was to present no problem to the southern border of the Kingdom of Jerusalem. Shawar was becoming weak and undependable. A concerted attack against Egypt by the Crusaders and the Byzantine army was an idea that appealed to him. He therefore sent William of Tyre to Constantinople to open negotiations, while various groups within the kingdom and the principalities debated the issue. The Hospitallers were for the invasion, the Templars against it. Some of the important knights wondered why it was necessary to share the treasure of Egypt with the Byzantines. The Templar fortress at Gaza commanded the southern frontier. The Templars saw no urgent need for an invasion; they had their own agents at the court, and there was substantial trade, often financed by the Templars, between Egypt and the Italian seaports. The Templars, well informed about the affairs of Egypt, regarded an invasion as an invitation to disaster.

Without waiting for news from William of Tyre, Amaury marched out of Ascalon at the head of his army and ten days later he was outside the walls of Bilbeis, demanding immediate surrender. The garrison troops refused, Amaury brought up all his siege engines, and three days later he was master of the city. Just as Godfrey of Bouillon had employed terror in order to conquer Jerusalem, the Crusaders employed terror at Bilbeis in the hope of terrifying all Egypt into submission. Men, women, and children were hacked to pieces in the onslaught, and every soldier was free to take whatever loot he wanted. Bilbeis became a desert. Shawar was shocked into making overtures to Nur ed-Din, whom he had regarded until recently as his mortal enemy. At the same time he offered the king a huge indemnity if only he would get out of Egypt. The king was adamant. He marched on to Cairo, set up his siege engines, and erected wickerwork screens so that the inhabitants would have no idea what was happening behind them while fearing the worst. A son and a nephew of Shawar had been captured at

Bilbeis. Shawar offered two million pieces of gold for their release. The king was tempted by this vast sum; the knights were tempted by the promise of loot to be obtained during the sack of Cairo. Only a small part of the money was paid, and the army was never able to plunder Cairo, for on Shawar's orders a large part of the city was set on fire. A few days later the king and his army returned to Palestine. Immediately after the king left Egypt, another enemy arrived. It was Shirkuh, at the head of a large army, and in his retinue was his nephew Saladin. Thereafter, events happened very quickly. Nur ed-Din, too, wanted to annex Egypt, and within a few days, almost without effort, the annexation took place. Shawar, who had shown himself to be a resourceful general in the defense of Cairo, showed that he possessed some virtues dangerous to himself. He was trusting and generous, and it never seems to have occurred to him that his life was in danger. On January 18, 1169, ten days after Shirkuh's forces had set up their camp outside Cairo, Shawar was invited to accompany some emirs from Damascus in a pilgrimage to the shrine of a local saint. It was an invitation he could hardly refuse; such pilgrimages were holy acts, and it was unthinkable that any harm would come to him. Shawar rode beside Saladin, and they had scarcely set out on the pilgrimage when Saladin leaned over, seized Shawar by the collar, and ordered him placed under arrest and taken to the camp. There Shawar was beheaded.

Egypt, which a few days earlier had almost fallen to the army of the king of Jerusalem, now fell into the hands of Shirkuh and his chief adviser, Saladin. It had been an easy and treacherous victory, and it would never have happened if Amaury had taken the advice of the Templars.

Muslim authority now stretched from the Euphrates to the Sudan; the kingdom was confronted with a disaster of incalculable proportions. There was only one thing the Crusaders could do. They called on the Byzantine empire and all the kings and princes of Europe for immediate help.

But help was slow in coming. The Emperor Manuel Comnenus, who realized the gravity of the situation, took a long time to assemble a fleet for the combined attack on Egypt. About 225 ships arrived at Tyre at the end of September 1169. By this time Saladin had destroyed the last remnants of opposition to his rule in Egypt and was the master of a land with enormous wealth and vast human resources.

This was the testing time: the fate of the kingdom was now being decided in Cairo by a thirty-one-year-old general who said openly, "When God gave me Egypt, I felt sure he intended to give me Palestine as well." Shirkuh had died. Power streamed out of Saladin's five-bladed hands. By his willpower and his strategies, the kingdom would be tested as it had never been tested before.

The tragedy of the kingdom was that it produced at this time no one who was a match for Saladin. Amaury was slow, dogmatic, fearful unless he possessed overwhelming forces. Shawar had been too trusting and too confident for his own good; Amaury showed too little confidence and too little trust in his advisers. The Crusaders had decided on a direct attack on Damietta. But when the army had marched out of Ascalon, and the huge Byzantine fleet was patrolling Egyptian waters, and they came in sight of Damietta, Amaury became afraid. He ordered a delay. The admiral of the Byzantine fleet wanted an immediate attack: his own ships were in the Nile, Damietta had been caught by surprise and was not equipped with a powerful defense force, and all the advantages lay with the assault force. But Amaury, looking up at the huge towers of Damietta, counseled caution; and from too much caution Damietta was lost to them. Delay worked in favor of Saladin, who had time to rush troops to Damietta and to concentrate on the defense of the fortress that guarded the approach to Cairo.

Amaury proposed to batter Damietta into submission. A huge tower, seven stories high, was erected overlooking the walls with a clear view of everything taking place in the city. Huge battering rams hammered at the walls; sappers attempted to mine the walls; the bombardment was continual, and it was all in vain. The Byzantine ships were running short of provisions; nor was the army of the Kingdom of Jerusalem in much better shape. Rain fell nearly every day; the camp became a flooded lake, and the soldiers had to waste their energies digging ditches to drain the floodwaters away. On rainless days, the Damiettans sent fireships—small boats filled with dry wood, pitch, and naphtha—against the Byzantine fleet, with the result that six of their great galleys were burned to the waterline. The king of Jerusalem himself took part in the fire fighting, and he led his troops when the Egyptians made sorties from a postern gate. The Grand Duke Alexius Contostephanos, who commanded the Byzantine fleet, also fought with the army. For about seven weeks the siege continued. Saladin was able to send provisions into the city without any serious interference. The defenders were of good heart. Together, Contostephanos and Amaury made the decision to raise the siege.

The troops who marched back to Ascalon were luckier than the sailors who sailed back to Constantinople. Most of the fleet was wrecked in storms, and the bodies of drowned sailors cluttered the shores of Egypt and Palestine.

In the following year, Jabala and Lattakieh on the coast were almost destroyed by earthquakes. Aleppo, Shaizar, Hama, Hims, and nearly all the fortress towns of Syria suffered. In June, Tripoli was struck with an earthquake so violent that nearly the entire population perished, and the huge fortress towers of Tyre crumbled and fell. Men came to believe that God was speaking to them out of the whirlwind, and for a few months there was a truce between the Christians and the Muslims, while the earth trembled and more towers fell. Then, in December, Saladin led his forces against Daron, a fortress near Gaza. The king succeeded in relieving Daron, whereupon Saladin attacked Gaza and massacred everyone in the city except the knights who had taken refuge in the fortress. Then Saladin marched back to Egypt, having shown that the southern defenses of the kingdom were more vulnerable than the king had believed.

Once again the king turned to the emperor for help. He decided that the matter was so important that he would go himself to Constantinople to plead for the men, ships, and provisions he needed. He set out from Acre on March 10, 1171, and he was away from his kingdom for nearly a hundred days. The emperor entertained him royally, first at the Bucoleon Palace on the seashore, and then at the Blachernae Palace set in the northern corner of the city. There were urgent affairs to attend to; but Amaury went sightseeing.

Various promises were made, various agreements were signed; and Amaury returned with the feeling that another massive expedition against Egypt with Byzantine help would be far more successful than the last. The documents have not survived, and we do not know what Amaury promised in return. Nor, for the moment, was there any need of Byzantine help. Saladin and Nur ed-Din had quarreled, and to this extent the kingdom was safe again, holding the balance of power between Damascus and Cairo. Nur ed-Din ordered an attack on Kerak of Moab, and Saladin obliged, then raised the siege when he heard that Nur ed-Din was leading his army out of Damascus. Saladin excused himself by saying that his father was dangerously ill in Egypt. This was true, but it was not the whole truth. Saladin by his ambition and scrupulous independence had incurred the enmity of Nur ed-Din. In the spring of 1174, Nur ed-Din died suddenly in Damascus; and in the summer, Amaury died in Jerusalem. The heir to the Crusader throne was a thirteen-year-old boy, the son of Amaury's first wife, Agnes of Courtenay. The young boy stammered a little like his father. He had another defect which is rarely associated with kings: he was a leper.

V

THE YOUNG KING'S VALOR AND THE FALL OF JERUSALEM

Baldwin IV:
The Leper King

HE was the bravest, the most intelligent, the most understanding of the kings of Jerusalem, and it is possible to feel for him a respect one has for none of the other kings. He was kindly and solicitous toward others, he understood exactly what was demanded of him, and he was learned about all the affairs of the Levant, but what was most important about him during his brief reign was a certain style, a way of looking at life with eagerness and grace. For most of his life he fought against terrible odds: his sickness, the declining energies of the kingdom, the quarrels within the royal family, the sense that the Arabs were acquiring the upper hand. Yet he knew at all times what he must do, and he was one of the very few who succeeded in cutting Saladin's army to pieces.

Baldwin IV was thirteen years old when he came to the throne, and it is worth noting that, in spite of the fact that Baldwin IV had been suffering from leprosy for at least four years, and this was known to all the nobles at court, there was not a single dissenting voice at his coronation in the Church of the Holy Sepulchre. He was consecrated and crowned four days after his father's death, and thereafter, as long as he was conscious, he commanded the loyalties of the kingdom.

The historian William of Tyre, who was his tutor, had known the king as a boy, taught him his letters, instructed him in his religious duties, and superintended every aspect of his education. One day when the boy was about nine years old, William of Tyre was told of a strange incident that occurred when the prince was playing with noblemen of his own age. The boys were pinching each other's arms and hands to see which one could bear the pain longest, and they realized to their astonishment that Baldwin could bear any amount of pain, not because he was brave, but because he was insensitive; he seemed to have no nerves in his right arm and right hand. William of Tyre immediately consulted the medical books and found in the works of Hippocrates some words that indicated that lack of feeling was an indication of a very grave and dangerous sickness. King Amaury had to be told, the best doctors were consulted, fomentations were applied, oils of various kinds were rubbed into his skin, and even more severe medicaments were given to him, including some that contained poisons. But nothing availed. The illness continued on its course, attacking especially the face and limbs. What made it all the more horrible was that the boy was handsome, gifted, and possessed a rare refinement and delicacy of manner. Fortunately, he also had an inner strength, which permitted him to endure his sickness without complaint. William of Tyre says that he resembled his father; even his way of walking and the tone of his voice were exactly like his father's. He had very bright eyes, an aquiline nose, blond hair drawn back from his forehead and reaching to his shoulders, and he laughed quickly and sometimes explosively, his whole body shaking. His father was a man who measured his words; Baldwin IV measured them even more carefully either because he disliked attracting attention to himself or because he wanted to think carefully before he spoke, knowing that as a king his words would have special significance.

The knowledge that the young king was suffering from leprosy made very little difference to the life of the court. It was as though they expected him to recover miraculously; meanwhile the disease was not to be talked about, it was not to be included in their plans, it did not exist. For a few years, until he came of age, he reigned but did not rule. A *bailli*, or guardian, was found. This was Miles of Plancy, the husband of Stephanie of Kerak, a man who relished his high position and had been very close to King Amaury, but was totally ineffective in directing the affairs of the kingdom. William of Tyre described him as a man so proud that he scorned all the other barons. He was lavish in high-sounding speech, and openly admitted that he relied on the advice of the commander of the citadel of Jerusalem to the extent that he blamed the commander for the errors he made himself.

There were many who realized that Miles of Plancy's ineffectiveness threatened the kingdom. One day, in the autumn of 1174, after being *bailli* for only two or three months, he was stabbed in a public street in Acre. The murder took place at dusk and the assailants got away, but not before the body of the proud nobleman had been submitted to terrible indignities. Since William of Tyre was in a position to know everything that could possibly be known about him, and could not decide whether he was assassinated because he was thought to be excessively loyal to the king or because he was himself attempting to seize the throne, the real reason must remain uncertain. What is certain is that Stephanie of Kerak, now twice-widowed, felt that the assassination had been ordered by Count Raymond of Tripoli, who succeeded her husband as *bailli* of the kingdom.

Raymond of Tripoli was a far more impressive character, hard, reserved, efficient, and capable of prompt action. It was remembered of him that he could be generous to strangers when it served his diplomatic purpose, but was not in the least lavish toward his familiars. He possessed the gift of equanimity. In the feverish court of the leper king, which was full of intrigues, the gift of equanimity was especially valuable. The Arabs regarded him as the ablest Crusader of his time.

Not that Raymond of Tripoli was a paragon, for he had many faults. He had foresight, but did not always see far enough. His relationship with the king was firm but not affectionate, and he could do very little to exorcise the dark spirits which crowded round the head of the king, who knew he was dying even before he was raised to the throne. Raymond of Tripoli's appointment to the guardianship augured well for the kingdom.

It is one of the fictions of history that men gifted with foresight, intelligence, and sobriety will bend history to their will more effectively than those who are lacking in these virtues. They are men who can be relied upon to act decisively; they will not make terrible errors. Yet Raymond of Tripoli, always acting reasonably, with far more understanding of the real problems of Syria and Palestine than anyone else in his time, contributed as much as any man to the downfall of the kingdom.

There was a moment shortly before Baldwin IV ascended the throne when Raymond of Tripoli made one of the greatest mistakes of his life. If he was aware of it, he thought it was something that could easily be repaired. A Flemish knight called Gerard of Ridfort, just arrived from Flanders, entered his service. He was strongly built, handsome, audacious, quite obviously one of those young men who would amount to something. King Amaury was also impressed with him. Here was someone who could be trained for high position, but needed a more or less prolonged period of discipline. In character he was exactly the opposite of Raymond, and this may account for the attraction between them. Since Gerard of Ridfort had no fortune, Raymond in an unguarded moment promised, or half-promised, him the first good marriage that would become available within his territory. Some months passed, and a certain Guillaume Dorel, Lord of Botrun, died, leaving a daughter by his first wife. Gerard asked for the hand of the daughter, who was an heiress and very beautiful. He was refused. It so happened that a certain merchant from Pisa, having recently arrived in Tripoli, became violently enamored of Lucia of Botrun and offered to pay her weight in gold in order to be permitted to marry her. Raymond accepted the offer, put her on the scales, watched as the merchant heaped ten thousand bezants in the other pan, and accepted the offer. In these feudal times, the property of the underlords at their deaths fell by right of inheritance to the overlords, and there was nothing remarkable in the fact that Lucia of Botrun should be sold in this way. But it would have been better for the safety of the kingdom if the merchant from Pisa and all his money had been thrown into the sea.

For Raymond had made a mortal enemy of Gerard of Ridfort. Raymond was not himself a man who bore grudges, and it is possible that he knew nothing whatever about Gerard's infatuation with Lucia, or very little. It was something that could be explained away; the young knight had asked for something quite impossible and easily forgotten. But Gerard of Ridfort swore vengeance.

At about this time the affairs of the kingdom were no longer in the control of the king: the fate of the kingdom depended upon the decisions of Saladin, who, possessing both Cairo and Damascus, needed only Aleppo to make himself master of an Islamic empire. Accordingly he laid siege to Aleppo with a powerful army composed of troops from both Egypt and Damascus. He expected Aleppo to fall; so did many of its citizens. But the governor of the city called upon the Crusaders and the Assassins for help and their indirect intervention. The Assassins, in their headquarters at Masyaf, a fortress in the Nosairi mountains, belonged to a heretical sect which believed that murder was a legitimate political weapon. They were at this time ruled by a certain Sheikh Sinan, known as the Old Man of the Mountain, who possessed authority over perhaps a thousand men trained in political assassination. This word derives from hashish, and it was widely believed that the youthful Assassins were high on drugs when they committed murder.

The Assassins sent out their cutthroats in disguise to attempt to kill Saladin, and the Crusaders attacked the fortress of Hims as a diversionary measure and forced Saladin to raise the siege. Gumushtekin, Governor of Aleppo, was so delighted with the assistance offered him by the king's army that he released Reynald of Châtillon who had been languishing in a dungeon for sixteen years.

The strange alliance between the Assassins and the Crusaders lasted a little while longer. Saladin attacked Masyaf but then thought better of it, being convinced that the Old Man of the Mountain possessed magic powers. Once an Assassin slipped into his tent while he was sleeping and would have killed him if Saladin had not been wearing chain mail under his turban. At another time, he found a poisoned dagger on his bed and was convinced that the Old Man of the Mountain had himself entered his tent. He conducted a correspondence with Sinan and made an accommodation with him: they agreed not to enter each other's territory, to respect each other's rights, and to negotiate such differences as might arise. Even so, Sinan continued to help the Crusaders as long as it served his purpose.

While Saladin was besieging Aleppo, the combined armies of Raymond of Tripoli and the king converged on the Bek'aa, the fertile valley which leads to the city of Baalbek. The valley was being defended by Turanshah, the brother of Saladin, and here the Crusaders won a signal victory. Turanshah's army was crushed, a vast amount of booty was taken, and the Christians returned to Tyre to divide the booty. The king had shown himself to be a very capable military commander.

There followed a period of truce, while Saladin regrouped his forces and

e young king set about strengthening his position by repairing his
rtresses and by urging the princes of Europe to join the Crusade.
Since it was obvious that Baldwin IV would not enjoy a long life, the
uestion of the succession arose quite early in his reign. By the law of
rusalem, his elder sister Sibylla would become queen at his death, and
er husband would become king. It was, therefore, of the utmost impor-
nce that a husband worthy of kingship should be found for her. Sibylla
as impetuous, with no understanding of royal responsibilities; she
eeded to be tamed. A suitable tamer was found in William Long-Sword, a
n of the marquis of Montferrat, who had the reputation of being a good
mmander. He had a fierce temper, but could be very calm and judicious
hen it served his purpose. William Long-Sword was eminently a man
ho could control Sibylla and rule a kingdom.

Unfortunately, three months after the marriage, William died of mala-
a, leaving a pregnant Sibylla. The succession was once more in doubt,
d messages were sent all over Europe in the hope of securing another
idegroom. The king himself was very ill with malaria, and was expected
die at any moment. The choice of a new king therefore presented
nsiderable urgency.

Not long after the death of William Long-Sword, there arrived in Acre
e very personable and illustrious Philip of Alsace, Count of Flanders. He
as accompanied by an impressive retinue of knights, a considerable
nount of wealth, and a reputation nearly as exalted as that of William
ong-Sword. His father, Thierry of Alsace, Count of Flanders, had taken
art in earlier Crusades and his mother, Sibylla of Anjou, was a notable
nefactor of the Holy Land. Philip was met in Jerusalem by the king, who
me hurrying up from Ascalon while still weak from his long bout with
alaria. Deeply impressed by the count of Flanders, the king summoned
assembly, which included the patriarch of Jerusalem, the archbishops,
shops, abbots, priors, the chief members of the laity, and the masters of
e Hospital and the Temple, and it was agreed that Philip should become
gent "without restraint." He was to be given full powers to administer
e kingdom in peace and war, in internal affairs and in foreign affairs, and
e treasury and revenues of the kingdom were to be placed at his disposal.
he count rejected this royal gift, saying that he had come to Jerusalem not
seek power, but in order to devote himself to divine service. In fact, as
admitted later, the real reason for his coming was to marry off two of his
usins, Sybilla and Isabelle, to the sons of a nobleman called Robert of
thune. The barons of Jerusalem were aghast when they heard that, and
ey said openly that they thought he had come for the sake of the Holy
pulchre, not to act as the marriage broker of two young women. Philip,
stressed by so many baronial admonitions, threatened to leave Jeru-
lem.

This was a bad time for leaving, because the Emperor Manuel Comnenus, in a gesture that showed he had forgiven the loss of an entire fleet, wa preparing to offer the king of Jerusalem another fleet for the conquest o Egypt, but only on condition that Philip lead the expedition. Philip studied the situation and concluded that this new invasion of Egypt would be suicidal. He had evidently read reports by the captains of the previous invasion and talked to the survivors. He spoke a little too loudly. The emperor's ambassadors heard of it, and William of Tyre, who acted as the chief negotiator, felt that Philip was being unnecessarily frivolous. Philip thereupon offered to obey the king in all things, even to leading the Egyptian expedition; but then he retracted the offer, saying that he had no interest in fighting but only in making pilgrimages.

Having lost hope that Philip would serve in any notable capacity, and being desperately in need of a captain-general who would take command of the kingdom in the absence of the king or when the king was incapacitated by his illness, the barons with the king's assent began to search for a new regent. Their choice fell on Reynald of Châtillon, the former prince of Antioch, who was described by William of Tyre as "a man of proven loyalty and remarkable steadfastness." He became regent of the kingdom and commander in chief of the army, and it was declared that he would be assisted by Raymond of Tripoli, the implication being that Raymond would share the power with him. Power, therefore, was divided between three men: the king, Reynald of Châtillon and Raymond of Tripoli. This was an unworkable division of power, and in fact the power remained in the hands of the king, who recovered from his malaria, although his leprosy progressed apace.

When Raymond and Philip joined forces to attack Hims and Hama— Philip could hardly return home without taking part in fighting against the enemy—the king as a mark of his goodwill lent them a thousand knights and two thousand foot soldiers. This was a mistake for, according to William of Tyre, the king was now left with a pathetically small army numbering no more than 375 men "including all ranks and conditions."

While Philip and Raymond were fighting in the north, Saladin decided to attack from the south. He had an excellent intelligence system, knew that the king's army was pathetically small, and believed he had been presented with an opportunity to destroy the kingdom once and for all with the help of an army so large, so overwhelming, and so well provisioned that the Crusaders would be quite unable to stand up against it. William of Tyre says his army consisted of twenty-six thousand light-armed cavalry, at least eight thousand men on camels or beasts of burden, and another thousand men who served as Saladin's bodyguard, all of them wearing yellow silk over their breastplates like Saladin himself.

The king also possessed an excellent intelligence system. He knew that Saladin, with his huge army, was marching on Ascalon. With Bishop

Albert of Bethlehem holding up the True Cross, the king's army rushed to Ascalon, occupying it only a few hours before Saladin came up to the city's walls and began to lay siege to it. Then Saladin had second thoughts. There was no need to lay siege. Knowing how many men were hidden behind the walls, Saladin decided that it was possible to bypass and thus isolate them. All Judaea lay before him. Jerusalem and the coastal cities were at his mercy, or so he thought.

The main body of the Egyptian army swept onward to Ramleh, which they burned, and on to Lydda, where the entire population took refuge in the Church of St. George, and to the outskirts of Jerusalem, where the population crowded into the Tower of David. Farms were burned, villagers were massacred, stragglers were cut down, while Saladin, supremely confident of his power, prepared to lay siege to Jerusalem.

Meanwhile, Baldwin IV summoned the knights defending Gaza, which Saladin had also bypassed, and slipped out of Ascalon with all the forces he could muster, marching up the coastal road and preparing to do battle with Saladin against all odds, for the alternative was to see all of Judaea in the hands of the conqueror. He came with perhaps two hundred knights and five hundred infantrymen. They saw the burning villages and were determined to hurl themselves at Saladin's army wherever they could find it.

On November 25, 1177, Saladin's army was crossing the bed of a wadi near the castle of Montgisard, only a few miles southeast of Ramleh, when the Christians fell upon them. The crossing of the wadi was a confused and ill-organized operation. The Muslims felt so safe that they posted no guards. The heavily armed knights charged into them and, like a great hammer striking them at the point of greatest weakness, they shattered the Egyptian army. The hammer came from the north, the least expected direction. From the neighborhood of the castle of Montgisard, the remnants of Saladin's army fled in wild disorder. The Christian soldiers spent days retrieving the treasure scattered by the Muslims, including enough swords and lances to equip an army twenty times larger than their own. Saladin's army was pursued for twelve miles; the Christians showed very little mercy. The region south of Ramleh was filled with Egyptians wandering, weaponless, in the direction of Egypt.

On the following day, and for the ten succeeding days, the rains fell. There were thunderstorms, the temperature dropped, and the Egyptians died of hunger. Most of them were on foot, for they had lost their horses. Day after day, prisoners were brought in from the forests and mountains, even from the desert. Those who reached al-Arish were plundered by the Bedouin. Some Egyptians, lost in the Holy Land, begged for food from villagers, who either killed them or handed them over to the military.

Saladin, Sultan of Egypt and Damascus, drawing his troops from all over the Arab world, with a vast army of Egyptians, Turks, Nubians,

Kurds, Sudanese and even Ethiopians, fled before two hundred knights and a leper king. The victory seemed to be a gift from God. Had the king not dismounted from his horse and thrown himself down on the ground before the True Cross, pleading for divine intervention, while tears ran down his face? His soldiers had been moved to tears by the sight of the king prostrate before the Cross. Later some of them would say that they had seen the Cross glowing above them, so huge that it touched the walls of heaven, and there were some who said they saw St. George fighting at their sides. The king was now seventeen years old, wasted by disease, his face white and corpselike, and he fought in the vanguard.

Saladin was well aware that he had suffered a major defeat. He wrote a famous poem to his brother Turanshah in Damascus:

> I thought of thee, amid the thrusting
>   of their spears,
> While the straight browned blades
>   quenched their thirst in our blood.

He went on, "Again and again we were on the verge of destruction; nor would God have delivered us save for some future duty."

Three months later, he was at the head of his army in Syria. There were a few raids, but the main fighting was now localized around Banyas and a place called Jacob's Ford on the Upper Jordan, between Lake Huleh and the Sea of Galilee, where the king had built a castle on an eminence. The castle commanded the road that runs from Tiberias to Qoneitra, although there was an unwritten understanding that the Christians would not build a castle there because Muslim merchants often traveled along this road. The castle was, therefore, an affront to Saladin, as the king well knew.

When the fortress was completed, the king learned that some Muslims, searching for new pastures, had incautiously led their flocks and herds into a forest near Banyas. He ordered a night march, and in the morning the sheep and cattle were captured. It is possible that the booty was the bait, for suddenly the Christians who found themselves in a narrow space were being shot at from all sides. The king was in great danger, and was saved only by Humphrey of Toron, the Constable of the kingdom, an elderly man, who threw himself in front of the king and saved his life at the cost of his own.

Saladin then turned his attention to the great fortress built at Jacob's Ford, which was very nearly impregnable. Arrows fell like rain on the fortress. There were massive assaults on the walls. The Christians held firm, and one of the chief emirs was killed, with the result that the Muslim army panicked and fled in confusion.

Leaving the River Jordan, Saladin decided to destroy the harvests between Beirut and Sidon. The king quickly learned that farms and vil-

ges were being put to the flames, marshaled his army at Tiberias, and set
f in pursuit of the raiders, catching up with Saladin's main army when
ey themselves were exhausted after a long march. Saladin's army
vooped down on them. In the first engagement the Christians were
ctorious, but a second engagement showed that Saladin had not lost his
astery of his troops, and he hurled the remnants of his beaten army
gainst the Christians with devastating effect. The Christians fled, lost
emselves in a defile with steep cliffs on either side, and were butchered by
e pursuing Muslims. There was worse to come, for Saladin advanced on
e castle of Jacob's Ford, now defended only by garrison troops, captured
, massacred everyone in it, and razed the castle to the ground.

These Christian reverses—the great battle near Banyas and the loss of the
stle of Jacob's Ford—might have been more damaging if Saladin's forces
ere not also suffering from exhaustion. On both sides there were heavy
sses. So it happened that Saladin and Baldwin IV concluded a two-year
uce, confirmed by solemn oaths and seals. Hunger was stalking the
uslim lands; bad harvests and drought were sapping Saladin's strength.
e needed a period of rest, and the dying king also needed to rest. But the
uce signed in the summer of 1180 provided only a brief hiatus before the
ost disastrous battle fought by the Christians in the Holy Land.

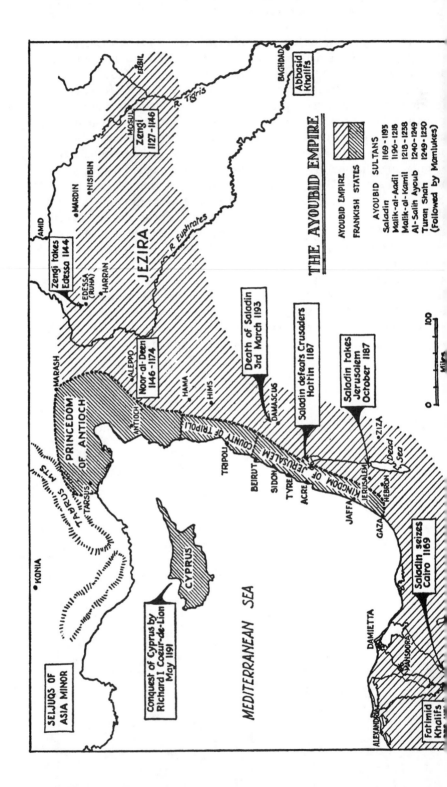

THE AYOUBID EMPIRE

AYOUBID EMPIRE
FRANKISH STATES

AYOUBID SULTANS
Saladin   1169 - 1193
Malik-al-Aadil   1196 - 1218
Malik-al-Kamil   1215 - 1238
Al-Salih Ayoub   1240 - 1249
Turan Shah   1249 - 1250
(Followed by Mamlukes)

0   100
└────────┘
        Miles

SELJUQS OF ASIA MINOR

Conquest of Cyprus by Richard I Cœur-de-Lion May 1191

Zengi takes Edessa 1144

Zengi 1127 - 1146

Noor-al-Deen 1146 - 1174

Death of Saladin 3rd March 1193

Saladin defeats Crusaders Hattin 1187

Saladin takes Jerusalem October 1187

Saladin seizes Cairo 1169

Abbasid Khalifs

Fatimid Khalifs

PRINCEDOM OF ANTIOCH

COUNTY OF TRIPOLI

KINGDOM OF JERUSALEM

JEZIRA

MEDITERRANEAN SEA

CYPRUS

TABUS MTS

KONIA

MARASH

TARSUS

ANTIOCH

ALEPPO

HAMA

HIMS

TRIPOLI

BEIRUT

SIDON

TYRE

ACRE

JAFFA

GAZA

HEBRON

JERUSALEM

ZIZA

Dead Sea

DAMASCUS

AMID

MARDIN

NISIBIN

MOSUL

ERBIL

EDESSA (RUHA)

HARRAN

BAGHDAD

R. Tigris

R. Euphrates

ALEXANDRIA

DAMIETTA

MANSOORA

church, Peter the Hermit and Arnous, chaplain of the Duke of Normandy,
ch the Crusade while men go to confession. *(Bibliotheque Nationale, Ms. Fr.
, f. 91vo)*

Egyptians and Turks taken prisoner by the Crusaders at a port. *(from* Livres des Passages d'Outremer, *15th century ms., Bibliotheque Nationale, Ms. Fr. 5594, f. 143vo)*

The 1390 Genoese and French expedition to Barbary. *(The British Library Board, Ms. 4379, f. 60b)*

The Turkish siege of Constantinople (1453). *(Bibliotheque Nationale, Ms. Fr. 9087, F. 207vo)*

Crusaders approach Nica
bombard the city with the
of their captives. (*From Le*
tories d'Outremer, *13th*
ms., Bibliotheque Nationale, N
2630, f. 63v, 38v, and 22v)

The King of France's departure from the west for the crusades. (Bibliotheque Nationale, Ms. Fr. 9087, f. 9)

Bertrandon de la Brocquiere offers a translation of the Koran and the history of Mohammed to Philip the Good as he leaves the abbey of Pothieres during the siege of Mussy-l'Eveque (1433). *(Bibliotheque Nationale, Ms. Fr. 9087, f. 152vo)*

Battle scenes. *(Top left)* A party led by
Robert, Count of Flanders, attacks during
the First Crusade. *(Bottom left)* Combat at
Thessalonica. *(Top right)* Crusaders routing
enemies. *(Bottom right)* The Siege of Antioch, October 21, 1097, to June 3, 1098,
ended when Bohemond's men climbed a
ladder, captured three towers, killed many
Turks, and opened a gate to their fellow
Crusaders. *(New York Public Library)*

m a 15th century ms., *School of Bourguignone, New York Public Library Picture Collection)*

The Siege of Ascalon *(Bibliotheque National, Ms. Fr. 5594)*

Crusaders battle with Saladin's forces. *(Bibliotheque Nationale, Ms. Fr. 5594, f. 197)*

Massacre of the Witnesses *(from an apocalypse, 13th century, British Library Board, Ms. Add. 42555, f. 30v)*

Christ leading the crusaders. *(from an apocalyse, 14th century, British Library Board, Ms. Roy.19/B xv, f*

Crusaders besieging a walled town. (*from* Chroniques de France, *late 14th century,* The British Library Board, Ms. Roy. 20, c. vii, f. 100v)

Crusader heavy infantry with archer support wait to assault a city when guns breach the walls. *(British Library Board)*

The Turks attack the army of Louis VII on a mountain in Anatolia. The advan
guard, commanded by Geoffroy de Rancon, goes back down the mountain a
sets up its camp. *(Bibliotheque Nationale, Ms. Fr. 5594, f. 143vo)*

Crusaders sally from a walled city to engage Muslims. "The very noble and excellent history of the holy chronicles of foreign lands and noble chevaliers, written and commentated on by the brave, valiant, and holy man Godefroy de Bouillon." (14th century) *(Bibliotheque Nationale, Ms. Fr. 352, f. 49)*

A 19th- or early 20th-century rendering of an unnamed Crusader battle. *(New York Public Library Picture Collection)*

Crusader column crossing the field of a previous battle. *(New York Public Library Picture Collection)*

usaders at prayer at an encampment in the Levant. *(New York Public Library ure Collection)*

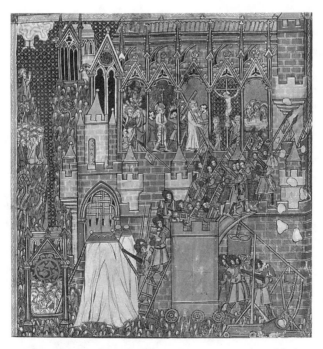

The taking of Jerusalem, 1099, as envisioned by a 14th century French artist. *(Bibliotheque Nationale)*

The seal of Richard the Lion
Hearted *(The Public Record
Office, London)*

The seal of the Templars *(The British Library Board, seal cxxv 4 and 3)*

Crusader doing homage. *(From an English 13th century psalter, The British Library Board, Ms. Roy. 2A XXII, f. 220)*

The sea castle of Sidon, built by the Crusaders to protect the harbor in the winter of 1227-28. *(National Council of Tourism in Lebanon)*

Beaufort Castle. The site was captured from the Emir Shehab al-Din by King Fulk of Anjou in 1139 and handed over to the Frankish seigneurs of Sidon, who built the castle. *(National Council of Tourism in Lebanon)*

The Horns of Hattin, scene of the most devastating Crusader defeat. The Sea of Galilee is in the foreground. *(Bar-David Agency)*

Refectory of the Order of St. John in Acre. *(Bar-David Agency)*

Knight's Hall of Belvoir fortress
(Bar-David Agency)

David's Tower, Jerusalem *(Bar-David Agency)*

Lions' Gate, Jerusalem *(Bar-David Agency)*

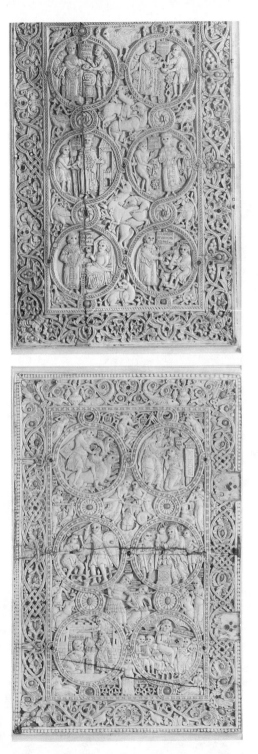

The ivory covers of the Melisend Psalter (1131-43) depicting a king performing acts of mercy. They are the only surviving works in ivory from the Crusader domains. *(The British Library Board, Ms. Egerton 1139)*

(left) An illustration of the adoration of the Magi from the Melisend Psalter. *(The British Library Board, Ms. Egerton 1139, f.2)*

(below) Crusader art eventually began to manifest a strong Islamic influence. *(Freer Gallery Art, the Smithsonian Institution)*

King Baldwin IV Against Saladin

HE star of Saladin was in the ascendant, and the star of the king of Jerusalem was waning. For all his courage and intelligence, the young king of Jerusalem, now emaciated, his hands and face eaten away by his disease, could no longer dominate his affairs, while Saladin was in the prime of life.

Saladin was not his real name. It was a name he gave himself: Salah al-Din, meaning "Rectifier of the Faith." His real name was Yusuf ibn Ayyub (Joseph, son of Job). He was a slender man of middle height, dark-bearded and dark-eyed, dark-complexioned, and given to dark thoughts. Saladin was learned in theology and liked nothing better than listening to theologians as they propounded the Koran, engaging in their discussions. He was not indifferent to the pleasures of life: it was simply that he viewed his responsibilities with the gravity that seemed to place him beyond corruption.

In this respect, he differed from nearly all the caliphs and sultans of the East. Even when they were perfectly aware that by being corrupt they endangered their power, they usually permitted themselves to be seduced. Hence their short-lived dynasties, and the fierce battles over the succession. Saladin detested the panoply of power, lived unostentatiously, and deliberately arranged his life so that he could die poor. In Egypt, for example, he lived in a house not very much larger than a cottage, although, if it had pleased him, he could have lived in sumptuous magnificence in a palace with four thousand rooms. Within the palace were storerooms full of jewels; he gave them away or endowed schools, colleges, and hospitals with them or used them to pay the army.

He was accessible to all men, listened patiently to petitioners, and saw that no one left his presence without satisfaction. He forbade flattery, saying it was a waste of time and an insult to the intelligence, and if by accident or design someone acted too freely toward him, he usually laughed it off.

From the stories told about him by his companions we receive a clear picture of him: gentle, kindly, compassionate. Yet this same man was capable of a blind bloodlust against Crusaders who fell into his hands; even though a moment later he might treat them with exquisite courtesy, remembering that they were men like himself. His detestation of the Crusaders, especially when they broke their promises and their oaths, was so deep-rooted that he threatened to pursue them back to their own cities. One day he told his friend Baha ad-Din: "I think that when God grants me victory over the rest of Palestine, I shall divide my territories, make a will stating my wishes, then set sail on this sea for their far-off lands and pursue the Franks there, so as to free the earth from anyone who does not believe in Allah, or die in the attempt."

Baha ad-Din was not in the least astonished by the sultan's threat to wage war through Europe; what amazed him was the thought of Saladin sailing on a ship through mountainous waves. "You, who are the bulwark of Islam, should not risk your life on shipboard," he told Saladin.

"Now," said Saladin, "I shall put a question to you. What is the most noble death?"

"Death in the path of Allah."

"Well then, the worst that can befall me is the most noble of deaths."

This exchange is perhaps the most revealing of all the recorded conversations with Saladin. His passion and his motives are both revealed, and so is the intensity of his faith. In Saladin's eyes the glory was not so much in ridding the Holy Land of the Crusaders as in following them to their lairs beyond the seas and exterminating them. He failed to do this, but there is very little doubt that such was his intention.

Almost from the beginning, Saladin was pictured in the West under a dual aspect: the harsh conqueror, the man of mercy and chivalry. But because the medieval mind was rarely capable of believing that men were made up of contradictions, there were many Christians who believed that he was the perfect knight, the soul of chivalry.

Unlike Saladin, who came to power by killing the sultan of Egypt, Baldwin IV was never treacherous. And he was certainly as complex, as noble, as commanding as Saladin. When his face and features were no longer recognizable, when there came from him only halting whispers, and when he was carried on a litter because he could no longer walk, he was braver than any of his knights and more intelligent than any of his advisers.

There were, however, problems which could not be solved by intelligence alone. The problem of the succession weighed heavily on the barons; it also weighed heavily on the king. When the prince of Antioch and the count of Tripoli came to Jerusalem in 1180 to perform their private devotions in the Church of the Holy Sepulchre, he suspected that their real intention was to depose him, and he had them watched carefully. His sister

Sibylla was the rightful claimant to the throne in the event of his death. Since her husband, William of Montferrat, had died, it became necessary to find a husband for her who would be at least as commanding and personable as William. While a search for a suitable husband was continuing among the courts of Europe, Sibylla made her own choice. She chose Guy of Lusignan, the younger son of the count of Lusignan, a lady's man accomplished in the arts of flattery, without experience in war or government. The king permitted the marriage to take place, although with extreme reluctance, and granted to his new brother-in-law the counties of Ascalon and Jaffa. Henceforth, until he became king, Guy of Lusignan was generally known as the Count of Jaffa.

To the barons of the Kingdom of Jerusalem, the coming of Guy to a position of prominence was a disaster scarcely to be tolerated. But Sibylla doted on him, and the king, who was slowly dying, and going blind, acquiesced sufficiently to hold out the hand of friendship to him.

The king had another half sister, Isabelle, who was described by the poet Ambrose as "exceedingly fair and lovely." He decided to marry her to Humphrey of Toron, the grandson of the great Constable, and in October 1180 there was an announcement of the engagement of Humphrey and Isabelle, who was then eight years old. The marriage would take place three years later. Humphrey was a scholar of Arabic, and in later years he would be sent on embassies to the enemy camps, Saladin would compliment him on his use of Arabic, and he would become the translator of all the chief Arabic texts addressed to the Kingdom of Jerusalem. The barons appear to have despised him because he was not a soldier like his famous grandfather, and they accused him of effeminacy, of being "soft in gestures and fruitful of speech." What is certain is that Humphrey was among the very small group of people who had access to the king and was in the king's trust, and that he exerted in his own way considerable influence on the course of events.

While Humphrey of Toron was always helpful, Reynald of Châtillon, formerly prince of Antioch and later Nur ed-Din's prisoner in an Aleppo jail, proved to be as unhelpful as it was possible to be. He had married Stephanie, the widow of Miles of Plancy and the heiress of the whole region of Oultrejourdain (Beyond the Jordan) stretching from Hebron to the Red Sea and including the two great castles of Kerak and Montreal and the lesser castles of Petra and Val Moysis. Embittered by his long imprisonment and exulting in his newfound power, Reynald defied the king's truce with Saladin. It occurred to him to invade Arabia, to destroy the tomb of Muhammad at Medina and to sack Mecca and raze to the ground the sacred Kaaba. In the summer of 1181, he attacked and captured a caravan that was traveling peacefully to Mecca, taking possession of all the pilgrims, their animals, provisions, and goods. Later in the year he embarked on a daring escapade against Medina and Mecca. Only about three hundred Franks and perhaps an equal number of renegade Muslims took part in the disastrous expedition, but their depredations were out of all proportion to their numbers. They brought fire and sword to the Red Sea, which was hitherto a safe and protected region of the world. Saladin swore that if he could lay his hands on Reynald he would kill him.

While the raid on the Red Sea invited a counterraid of equal proportions, it was not the only incitement to Saladin's rage. Reynald was capturing all the caravans passing through his territory. These caravans were now heavily armed for protection. It did them no good to be well armed: Reynald could always capture them. He captured a great caravan traveling from Damascus to Mecca, and it was said that Saladin's aunt was among the passengers. For Saladin the capture of this caravan was a crime almost as great as Reynald's desecrations around the Red Sea.

Baldwin IV, who had inaugurated the truce with Saladin and meant to keep to it, remonstrated with Reynald, ordered him to restore all the prisoners and all the booty to Saladin, and was laughed at for his pains. The king received letters from Saladin asking for an explanation, and had to admit that he was powerless regarding Reynald. While flouting the king's authority, Reynald was digging his own grave—which was not perhaps a matter of great importance. What was more important was that he was digging the grave of the Kingdom of Jerusalem.

The kingdom was breaking up, for the lines of authority were tangled, obscure, or stretched to breaking point. It was as though the kingdom too, like the king, suffered from leprosy.

On June 12, 1183, Aleppo fell to the forces of Saladin, and with its capture Saladin became the most powerful man of Islam, ruling from the Tigris to the Nile, from the frontiers of Ethiopia to the frontiers of Persia. He was an emperor in all but name, styling himself King of All the Kingdoms of the Orient. Such a man could scarcely be expected to tolerate the existence of Christian enclaves along the seacoast of Palestine and Syria. In August he marched out of Damascus with the intention of driving the Christians into the sea.

The battle intended by Saladin to be the last of his battles with the Christians took place in the Plain of Esdraelon near the castle of La Fève. Thirteen hundred knights and fifteen thousand foot soldiers, well armed and aware that they were fighting a battle that might be decisive in the history of the kingdom, were confronted by a somewhat larger number of Muslims. The Christian force, which included Reynald of Châtillon, was led by Guy of Lusignan, whom the dying king appointed *bailli* or regent. Guy, who generally distinguished himself by his lack of distinction, his irresolution, and inefficiency, fought surprising well that day. It was not so much a battle as a hard-fought hand-to-hand struggle, a vast *mêlée*, with neither side gaining victory.

Exhausted, the armies disengaged and took up positions facing each other at Tubaniya and at the Pools of Goliath, with a stream flowing between them. For five days they regarded one another. The Christian army was reinforced with hundreds of sailors from ships that had just come to port, all clamoring to join the army. Reynald of Châtillon was disputing the authority of the regent. He wanted to attack; Guy wanted to retreat to a stronger position. Saladin attempted to lure the Christians out of their encampment. He failed. On October 8, he withdrew beyond the Jordan, his rage against Reynald intact.

Once the armies had withdrawn, Reynald hurried off to his seemingly impregnable castle, Kerak of Moab, the launching ground for all his adventures. Knowing that Reynald was scheming behind its walls, Saladin wanted it more than he wanted Jerusalem, and he would not rest until he had taken it.

For nearly two months Saladin attacked the castle, using seven powerful mangonels to batter at the walls. But the castle was well provisioned— Reynald was as much a master of defense as of attack—and in December, confessing failure, Saladin withdrew his army to Damascus. It was in fact his fourth attempt to reduce the castle.

In the summer of the following year he returned, more powerfully armed than before, swearing to take the castle and to kill Reynald with his own hands. On the day he arrived, Humphrey of Toron was celebrating his marriage to the Princess Isabelle, the king's half sister, now eleven years old. The marriage was taking place in the castle because Reynald had married Humphrey's mother, the Lady Stephanie of Milly. Saladin attacked the small town which clustered around the castle, separated by a great ditch from the castle gates. Most of the people in the town had made their way to the safety of the castle, bringing their sheep and cattle with them. Saladin might have led his troops up to the walls of the castle, but for a single knight who commanded the bridge over the ditch and kept the Muslims at bay. This time Saladin had brought nine mangonels, and the noise of rocks being hurled against stone walls continued day and night.

The chronicler Ernoul, who continues the story of the Crusades where William of Tyre leaves off, tells a strange story about the Lady Stephanie on the wedding night of her son:

> She sent to Saladin bread and wine, sheep and cattle in celebra-tion of her son's wedding, reminding him that he used to carry her in his arms when she was a child and he was a slave in the castle. And when Saladin received these gifts, he was exceedingly de-lighted and gave thanks to those who brought them very effu-sively, and he asked where the bride and bridegroom were staying: their tower was pointed out to him. Thereupon Saladin gave orders throughout his army that no attack and no bombardment should be directed at this tower.

Nevertheless he continued to attack the rest of the castle.

The story is intriguing because there exists no other source for the enslavement of Saladin. In the many Arabic accounts of Saladin's life there is no mention of his capture or of his being a slave in the castle. The story however is not improbable. In the forays and skirmishes of the time, a ten-year-old boy might be captured, and if his appearance were pleasing he might find himself transformed into a castle servant until he grew weary of the task and made his escape. The Muslim chroniclers would probably go to some lengths to conceal such a story.

Saladin's forces were so powerful that it became necessary to send a relief column from Jerusalem. The king, now virtually a living corpse, quickly organized the expedition and led it. He was carried on a litter. When his small army was south of the Dead Sea, his strength failed, and he turned over the command to Raymond of Tripoli. Saladin, hearing of the advance of the royal forces, abruptly lifted the siege. The king entered Reynald's castle like a conqueror. He was greeted by everyone as though he had been sent by God.

The following spring, in Jerusalem, with all his nobles around him, he died. He was blind, faceless, his hands and feet eaten away; but to the end he remained kingly. He was only twenty-four years old when he was buried in the Church of the Holy Sepulchre. The Christians revered him; the Muslims respected him. It was a Muslim chronicler, Imad ed-Din of Isfahan, who wrote of him, "The leper child knew how to make his authority respected."

Under Baldwin IV the Crusaders experienced a resurgence of strength. The boy-king, in his long martyrdom, quickened the people with his high spirits, his defiance, his intelligence, his courage. The boy with the halting tongue and the burned-out eyes, so helpless in appearance, and so full of intellectual energy, represented all that was best in Western Europe, though he had never seen the West. He was the last of his dynasty, and of his kind. After him, the little men came out from under the stones.

The Horns
of Hattin

DURING the last months of his life the leper-king was embroiled in a strange conflict with Guy of Lusignan, because the king was determined that Guy should not inherit the throne. The king seemed to know that, if Guy was permitted to rule, he would be fatally dangerous to the kingdom. He went to astonishing lengths to neutralize Guy and to attempt to destroy the marriage that gave a kind of legitimacy to Guy's claims.

Returning from his triumph at Reynald's castle, the king ordered Guy to appear before him in Jerusalem. The urgent summons was resisted; Guy pleaded illness. The summons was repeated. When Guy absolutely refused to leave Ascalon, the king decided to go to him, but he found the gates of the city closed.

In a rage the king rode off to Jaffa, which was governed by one of Guy's lieutenants. This time the gate was opened for him without any difficulty. The king appointed a new governor and went off to Acre, where he summoned a general council to discuss the succession. The king was concerned with the fortunes of the kingdom, and he was aware at this time of the pressing dangers and the need to find a king who would defend the kingdom to the uttermost.

The general council took place in January 1185. Guy did not attend, but he possessed powerful protectors. They included the Patriarch Heraclius of Jerusalem, Gerard of Ridfort, who was master of the Temple, Reynald of Châtillon, and Joscelin of Courtenay. Heraclius had reached his high position by intrigue; he was barely literate but wielded enormous powers. He was especially close to Guy of Lusignan, Reynald of Châtillon, and the members of the young, new nobility, who had assumed high positions by their charm and daring. William of Tyre, who belonged to the old order, warned against the growing power of the newcomers, who had no roots in the Holy Land, and who were concerned only with their own fortunes.

At the general council in Acre, Heraclius, Ridfort, and others appealed to the king to abandon the feud with Guy of Lusignan, and to forgive whatever crimes he imputed to his brother-in-law. The king was adamant. He rejected their pleas, and he seems to have been unperturbed when they left the council chamber in high dudgeon. He had already decided that, when he died, the kingdom should be ruled by Raymond of Tripoli acting as regent for Sibylla's young son by William of Montferrat. The boy was then five or six years old and in delicate health. And so it happened that when Baldwin IV died in March 1185, he was succeeded by Baldwin V, who was crowned in the Church of the Holy Sepulchre.

In this way, Guy of Lusignan was disinherited and Raymond became king in all but name.

Raymond was a man of many talents. A superb diplomat, he arranged a truce with Saladin to last for four years. When a famine threatened the Holy Land, he even arranged that Saladin should supply him with corn and grain. Saladin himself fell ill, and during his illness conspiracies flourished in his court. He was believed to be dying, but by the end of the year he had recovered, and once again he set in motion his plans for destroying the Kingdom of Jerusalem, as well as those who had conspired against him. He had respect for Raymond of Tripoli but none for Guy of Lusignan.

When Guy heard that he had been disinherited, he wreaked his vengeance not on the dying king but on some harmless Arab shepherds who, under the king's protection, pastured their flocks outside the castle of Daron. He captured the shepherds, seized the flocks and drove them all to Ascalon. It was his way of telling the king, "You cannot protect anyone."

In August 1186 young Baldwin V died in Acre. It is possible that he died of natural causes. It is also possible that he died of poison. Raymond of Tripoli and Joscelin of Courtenay were present at the deathbed, and while Joscelin undertook to conduct the body to Jerusalem, Raymond hurried off to Tiberias to assemble the forces of the kingdom. While Raymond was making his way to the Galilee, Joscelin, Sibylla, and Guy of Lusignan hurried to Jerusalem. The city fell to them. The Patriarch Heraclius brought them the support of the clergy. Reynald came up from his castle with an army.

The barons met at Nablus under Raymond of Tripoli and issued a proclamation denouncing Sibylla's claim to be the legitimate heiress of the kings of Jerusalem, for had not Baldwin IV annulled her claim by royal edict? Had not Guy of Lusignan fought against the legitimate power of Baldwin IV? The parliament at Nablus called upon the people of Jerusalem to overthrow the government installed by means of a *coup d'état*. Heraclius was commanded not to crown Guy of Lusignan as the rightful king. The patriarch ignored the injunction of the barons and crowned Sibylla, who turned to her husband, removed the crown from her head, gave it to him as he knelt before her, and permitted him to crown himself.

In this way Guy of Lusignan, the handsome and impecunious son of the count of Lusignan, with his courtly gestures and unfathomable ignorance, became king of Jerusalem.

Gerard of Ridfort, Master of the Temple, regarded himself as the kingmaker, for he had thrown the forces of the Temple on the side of the new king. What pleased him more than anything else was the rebuke to Raymond of Tripoli, still sitting with his parliament at Nablus, still regarding himself as the lawful regent. He remembered in particular the time when the fiefdom of Botrun had been given to a merchant who could pay the bride price. "This crown," he said, "is well worth the reversion of Botrun." He spoke as one who felt he was on the eve of many triumphs. In fact he was on the eve of many defeats. The prophecy of Baldwin of Ramleh, one of the great barons of the kingdom, would prove accurate: "The new king will not last a year! The kingdom is lost!"

In Nablus the barons devised a simple and quite impractical solution to the problem. Humphrey of Toron, the husband of the Princess Isabelle, was offered the throne. According to the chronicler, Humphrey behaved ignobly. He was so terrified by the weight of kingship that he slipped out of Nablus and made his way to Jerusalem, where he sought out Sibylla and blurted that it was not his fault that he had been offered the crown. Sibylla is supposed to have said, "Well then, I shall forgive you, but now you must go and do your homage to the king."

It probably happened differently. Humphrey was intelligent: he knew that if he assumed the crown, he would have provoked a civil war. He may have genuinely believed that he did not have the makings of a king. Related by marriage to Sibylla, it is possible that he felt more loyalty to her than to the barons, who had placed him in an intolerable position. The king was commander in chief of the kingdom's military forces, and Humphrey had reason to doubt his military ability. Only a little while before, he had raised a column to go to the relief of Baldwin IV. Saladin's forces swept down on the column, most of his soldiers were killed, and he had escaped with difficulty. The memory of that disaster may have been with him when he refused the kingship.

Indeed, it was a time of many disasters. The barons remained at Nablus, while King Guy remained in Jerusalem. Within a few days Guy was thinking of attacking the barons, thus ending once and for all the dispute over the succession. Wiser counsel prevailed. Meanwhile Raymond of Tripoli was in correspondence with Saladin, and he succeeded in arranging a truce which applied to his own territories in Tripoli and the Galilee. It was a separate peace, and he would claim that it was absolutely necessary for the survival of his principalities. Guy assumed Raymond was in treacherous communication with the enemy.

In these ominous times, with Saladin building up his forces in a deliberate effort to bring about the destruction of the kingdom, with a king in

Jerusalem and a regent in Tiberias, a man was needed who could in some way unify the kingdom. But no such man appeared. Instead the Crusader princes so conducted themselves that the worst prevailed. At a time when a spark could have caused a war and it was incumbent on the Christians to prepare their forces carefully and patiently, a spirit of wild impatience was gripping their leaders, and they acted carelessly and intemperately. Reynald of Chatillon chose this particular moment to provoke a war with Saladin.

The hard-pressed Saladin had agreed to a truce with his archenemy Reynald, who agreed to exact customs dues from the travelers and pilgrims passing through his territory rather than order outright confiscation and the ransom of prisoners. But when, at the beginning of 1187, his spies reported that an especially large caravan was traveling from Cairo to Damascus, he was incapable of resisting the temptation to acquire booty. He laid an ambush, captured the entire convoy, threw the Muslims into his dungeons and all the wealth of the caravan into his storehouses.

When Saladin heard that the caravan had vanished into Reynald's possession, he sent a peremptory letter demanding their release. He received a curt refusal. Saladin appealed to King Guy, who seemed to realize the gravity of the situation and begged Reynald to surrender the captured caravan. Reynald rejected the appeal for the same reason that he had rejected an earlier appeal from Baldwin IV: it was not the king's business to give him orders. He regarded himself as beyond the law of Jerusalem. It was a fatal error.

In May 1187, Saladin again surrounded Kerak of Moab and ravaged all of Transjordan. Then he made plans for an attack on the Kingdom of Jerusalem, first asking for permission to enter the Galilee, this permission to be given by Raymond of Tripoli according to the treaty worked out between them. He asked that a column of seven thousand men be permitted to have free passage across the Galilee. The request was, in fact, a demand. Raymond demurred. He could not grant it because he would be acquiescing in the defeat of the kingdom; and he could not refuse it without endangering his own troops. He therefore resorted to negotiations, finally granting Saladin the right to make a show of strength across the Galilee with his troops, the demonstration to last for a single day from sunrise to sunset. Saladin agreed to these terms. At this moment King Guy sent to Tiberias a delegation of high officials to ensure that Raymond would grant as little as possible to Saladin, but they failed to reach Tiberias in time.

Seven thousand of Saladin's troops, under the command of Saladin's son al-Afdal, entered the Galilee at dawn and departed at sunset without harming a single Christian living in the towns and villages of the Galilee. Yet the march of al-Afdal was full of menace, and far from peaceful. The Muslim army was near Nazareth, at the Springs of Cresson, when Gerard of Ridfort, at the head of a hundred and fifty men, including forty Templars and ten Hospitallers, fell upon it. The Muslims, watering their horses, were taken by surprise, and at first Gerard's column did a good deal of damage. But there were seven thousand Muslims, and soon the Christian knights were lost in the vast crowd. The rash and impudent attack was doomed to failure. Of the hundred and fifty knights who charged down the hill, all except three were captured or slain. Gerard of Ridfort fled the battlefield. Wounded, he made his way to Nazareth, where he went into hiding. Later that day, Raymond of Tripoli, looking down from the walls of his castle at Tiberias, saw the seven thousand riding by. On the tips of their lances they carried the heads of the Templars and Hospitallers they had slain that morning.

Seeing those heads, Raymond realized that it was no longer possible to reach an understanding with Saladin. He was enraged when he learned about Gerard of Ridfort's attack on the Muslim army on a day of truce. Nor was it possible for him any longer to regard himself as regent. He rode to Saint Job, near Jenin, where King Guy received him. Raymond knelt before the king and was lifted up and given the kiss of peace. The king was well aware of the gravity of the situation, for Saladin was gathering an immense army "as numberless as the waves of the ocean" in the Hauran. Raymond and the king agreed to gather all their available forces at Sephoria, not far from the Springs of Cresson; this would be their staging area. Their combined armies totaled about fifteen hundred knights and perhaps twenty thousand infantry. They could almost feel the breath of Saladin's advancing horde on their faces.

The time for a decisive battle was at hand, and they were ready for it. There were experienced soldiers, with excellent battle equipment, and they had large sums of money including some sent by King Henry II of England in expiation for the murder of Thomas à Becket. Although nearly forty Templars had been killed at the Springs of Cresson, the remaining Templars in the kingdom could be massed into a formidable body of shock troops quite capable of carving up a Muslim army. Crusader morale was still high; they had a healthy fear of Saladin, but were not in awe of him; and most of them seem to have believed that Saladin and all his army could be pushed back into the Hauran.

Yet for the Christians one thing of incalculable importance was missing: the design of victory. Guy of Lusignan, King of Jerusalem, possessed no skill in warfare, and his adversary, Saladin, had more skill than anyone of his generation.

Saladin's purpose was clearly to march along the shores of the Sea of Galilee, take Tiberias, and then wage war against the king's army on grounds most favorable to himself. What he could not have anticipated was that the Christians would provide him with grounds as though they were bent on destroying themselves; nor could he have anticipated that

King Guy would be so lacking in generalship that he would commit errors that a six-year-old schoolboy would avoid.

Raymond of Tripoli, always astute, saw clearly that the coming battle should be waged on grounds favorable to the Christians, and that nothing was to be gained by marching to the Sea of Galilee to save Tiberias. It was now July, the hottest time of the year, when the lightly armed cavalry of Saladin had advantage over the armored knights of the kingdom. Their task, therefore, was to wear down Saladin's forces, avoid battle until the enemy was exhausted, and even then retain as defensive a posture as possible. No purpose would be served by fighting for Tiberias. The chronicler Ernoul tells us Raymond begged King Guy to let Tiberias be taken:

> Tiberias is mine, and the Lady of Tiberias is my wife, and our children are in the castle together with all our possessions, and if it falls, no one will lose as much as I. I know that if the Saracens take it, they cannot hold it, and if they raze the walls, I shall build them up again. If they take my wife and my children and my possessions, I can ransom them back again. If they attack my city, I shall in time make it strong again. And to me there is more advantage that Tiberias be taken and destroyed and my wife and children and my possessions in enemy hands than that this entire land should be lost to us. For I know that if you go to the help of Tiberias, you will all be taken or killed, you and all your army. I shall tell you why. Between here and Tiberias there is no water except only a little spring called the Spring of Cresson, which cannot water a whole army. Your men and your horses will be dead of thirst before the multitudes of the Moslems have hemmed you in!

King Guy was impressed by the incontrovertible argument. Gerard of Ridfort, ever the apostle of violent and dangerous acts, cursed Raymond, but the barons were in agreement with him. It was nearly midnight; the council of war broke up.

Later that night—it was the night of July 2-3, 1187—Gerard went to the king's tent and convinced him that he must act now to save Tiberias. The count of Tripoli was plotting against the kingdom.

"Have no faith, Sire, in the count," he said. "He is a traitor, and you know he has no love for you and wishes to dishonor you and take the kingdom from you!"

King Guy, who was likely to be influenced by the last man he spoke to, was appalled by the sudden allegation of Raymond's untrustworthiness. Gerard's arguments seemed conclusive. What should he do?

"Sire," replied Gerard, "you should sound the alarm throughout the army. Let everyone take up his place in battle formation and follow the banner of the Holy Cross!"

King Guy immediately ordered the trumpeters to sound the call to arms. The sleeping camp awoke; the barons hurried to the king's tent; they asked why there had been this sudden change of plans, and the king responded by saying that he alone was responsible and their task was to obey. There was no possibility of defying his order. Only Raymond was of sufficient stature to lead a mutiny, but he had no taste for it.

At dawn the army left Sephoria. The hot night was followed by a burning day. Raymond led the vanguard, the king led the center, Gerard of Ridfort led the rear guard. The army marched across the plain of Sephoria and then wound its way up the hills that guard the western shores of the Sea of Galilee. The hills, a thousand feet above sea level, were covered with burned scrub and wild grasses, with no trees to provide shade. There were no water-carts, and the men carried leather bottles filled with water; as the heat grew fiercer, the bottles grew lighter. For the armored knights, especially, the heat was almost unendurable.

The columns marched in silence, for the men were despondent. Soon after they set out, Muslim skirmishers attacked them, pouring arrows into their midst as soon as they were in bowshot, then racing away on their swift horses. While these skirmishers did little physical harm, they slowed up the march and wore down the Christians. From Sephoria to Tiberias is only about fifteen miles, as the crow flies, but it was perhaps ten miles longer by the road they traveled. The vanguard under Raymond of Tripoli reached the Horns of Hattin by midafternoon, seeing the blue lake below them. By this time the lightly armed Muslim cavalry was worrying the rear guard, which was forced to stand and fight the enemy. The Templars sent a message to King Guy, saying that they could go no further. The king ordered them to press on as quickly as possible, while the barons urged the king to order a forced march on Tiberias, which was burning, for Saladin had put the city to the flames.

Because the Templars in the rear guard were still fighting off the Muslim skirmishers, and because he felt it necessary to keep his army intact, the king ordered the army to halt for the night. They camped on the brow of a wavelike mountain overlooking the Sea of Galilee, between two slight eminences called the Horns of Hattin. In all that neighborhood there was no worse ground for fighting. They were in fact standing in the partly broken-down crater of an extinct volcano, strewn with bombs of black basalt, treacherous to men and horses, for these stones were hidden below the dry grasses. Hattin was a dried-up lava flow, an impossible terrain for heavily armed horsemen. They were flies stuck to the flypaper. Down below, the army of Saladin was deployed along the shores of the lake, waiting for them. Small columns of Muslim cavalry were climbing into the hills; stragglers were being picked off; scouts were reporting every movement of the Christian army, but by nightfall, the Templars had beaten off the skirmishers and had joined the main army.

For the Christians it was a night of brooding terror. It was as though the day's journey had been designed to bring them closer to death. The night was nearly as hot as the day. From these heights they could see the lake glimmering in the starlight and the Muslims moving in the darkness below. Around the royal tent of red silk the guards kept watch on the king, who could not sleep. All the news that reached the tent was ominous.

During the night, Saladin moved up his men. Toward morning, when an easterly wind was blowing, a Muslim set fire to the dry grass, sending clouds of suffocating smoke into the Christian camp; and to the prayers of the Crusaders and the ululations of the Muslims, there was added the sinister crackling of grass. By dawn the Christians were surrounded on all sides by implacable Muslims thirsting to destroy them.

At dawn the Saracen archers attacked. The Christian infantry fought badly; they were dying of thirst and nearly uncontrollable in their desire to drink the water of the lake. When they saw the Muslims all around them, they raced to the top of a hill to escape from Muslim arrows and lances. King Guy ordered them to rejoin the cavalry, but they refused.

While the infantry behaved badly, the knights behaved heroically. They charged continually, wheeled back, resumed the charge. They hoped to break through the enemy lines. The Muslims were impressed by their extraordinary courage. They were at the limits of their strength, yet they fought on. Their thirst, their dry throats and parched tongues, already marked them for defeat, but they continued to fight with the energy of despair. Their desperate charges were like hammer blows that dented the encircling army but were never able to break through the encirclement.

The battle lasted all day, high up on the level ground between the Horns of Hattin, spilling over the slopes, reaching at times close to the lake. The wind changed; there were no more clouds of suffocating smoke from burning grass; and during the afternoon the battle seems to have slackened. The Muslims were cautious, conscious that the Christians possessed reserves of strength and might even now carve a passageway to the lake. According to Imad ed-Din, the mangled Christian army spent the night on the mountain, rejoicing because they had captured one of Saladin's emirs and struck off his head.

The battle raged through the following morning. During the night the infantry had regained their courage, which was the courage of despair. Sometimes the billowing clouds of smoke proved advantageous to the defenders, but more often the smoke helped the Saracens who infiltrated Crusader lines. Infantry and cavalry clung together. There were fewer charges. Raymond of Tripoli, who had shown himself to be dauntless and whose knights were among the most fearless, continued to search for a chink in the enemy lines. Nevertheless, five of his knights went over to the enemy and begged the Saracens to kill them in order to end their misery. At midmorning, Raymond led his knights in an attack on the battalions commanded by el-Modhaffer Taki ed-Din, Saladin's nephew. It was one of those sudden hurtling charges of heavily armored knights which the Saracens feared, and it succeeded. Once he had broken through, Raymond decided to abandon the battlefield and make his way to Tripoli in order to fight another day. King Guy had given his blessing to this maneuver, for it seemed unlikely that anyone would be left to fight future battles unless some of the knights and infantrymen escaped. The king had lost about a quarter of his best knights; yet he ordered another charge immediately. The Saracens wondered how the Christians could find the strength to fight without food, without water, and without hope, for they were still hemmed in on all sides.

The bishop of Acre, who had been carrying the jeweled True Cross, was killed in the battle. After his death the Cross was carried by the bishop of St. George of Lydda, who was so fearless or so foolish that he advanced close to the enemy and was captured. Nothing more was ever heard of the Cross, except the rumor that it eventually passed into the possession of the Great Mosque in Damascus, where it was buried under the threshold so that every Muslim stepping into the mosque stepped on the True Cross.

Saladin's young son, al-Afdal, whose first battle this was, recorded the last moments of the battle, as the remaining knights and infantrymen gathered around the king's red tent, high on one of the Horns of Hattin, and kept on charging until they could charge no more. Finally he writes, ". . . we saw the tent come down; then my father dismounted, prostrated himself to the earth in thanks to Allah, and wept tears of joy." The battle of Hattin was over. The Christians were so exhausted that they simply lay on the ground, almost beyond caring, too weary even to perform the formalities of surrender.

Saladin had won more than a battle; he had triumphed over the Kingdom of Jerusalem. Thereafter, people might speak of the kingdom, but the kingdom no longer existed. Kings and queens of Jerusalem would continue to be crowned while the kingdom itself became a mirage, a ghostly shape which continued to haunt the imaginations of the Crusaders. They remained in the Holy Land for another hundred years, but the kingdom and Jerusalem itself were lost to them. At the Horns of Hattin, on a midsummer day, among the lava rocks and the creeping grass fires, the heart had gone out of them.

Islam Takes Jerusalem

SALADIN, famous for his chivalry, showed very little toward the Christian army he defeated at the Horns of Hattin. It was Saladin's pleasure that all the surviving infantrymen should be immediately sent off to Damascus to be sold in the slave market. A different fate was reserved for the knights: they were killed not by soldiers but by the mullahs who accompanied him everywhere. A few, very few, of the leaders were spared and allowed to live in dungeons in Damascus until suitable ransoms were paid for them.

The battle had ended about noon. That afternoon, Saladin ordered his tent to be erected near the battlefield. Standing outside the tent, he held a review of his prisoners, who included Gerard of Ridfort, the Master of the Temple, leading a small number of Templars and Hospitallers. King Guy, his brother Geoffrey, Hughes of Jebail, Humphrey of Toron, and Reynald of Châtillon were among the first of the Crusader lords to fall into enemy hands. Saladin had promised himself that he would kill Reynald the moment he set eyes on him, but now he was savoring his victory. He permitted the great lords of the former Kingdom of Jerusalem to enter the shade of his tent. He engaged them in conversation, and probably young Humphrey of Toron served as his interpreter. King Guy was suffering terribly from thirst, and Saladin handed him a goblet of water cooled by the snows of Mount Hermon. Suddenly he raged against Reynald, saying that the lord of Kerak had broken every promise he had ever made and every agreement he had signed. Reynald answered, "I did only what princes have always done. I followed the well-trodden path." This was a surprisingly adroit defense, for Saladin had also broken promises and treated agreements with disdain. Saladin was sitting next to the king; Reynald sat on the king's far side. Saladin was watching them closely. When the king handed the goblet to Reynald, who was also suffering terribly from thirst, Saladin made no effort to prevent him from drinking; but he pointed out to the king that the gift of cool water to Reynald had been made without asking his permission. "I am therefore not bound to protect his life," he said, reminding the king that Reynald had committed too many crimes to receive the benefits of Arab hospitality. A stranger who has received drink or food in an Arab's tent is under the protection of his host: he cannot be killed or maimed in any way. The confrontation between Saladin and the king was high drama. Everyone was watching them closely. Both the king and Reynald were trembling, probably not so much from fear as from exhaustion, hunger, and a thirst that could not be quenched by a goblet of snow-cooled water. Saladin had not yet decided what he would do with his high-ranking prisoners. Quite suddenly he left the tent and rode off on his horse for a tour of the battlefield. He was probably accompanied by Imad ed-Din, who is known to have ridden over the battlefield that afternoon, and who wrote:

I rode across the battlefield, and learned many lessons. I saw what the elect have done to those who are entirely rejected, and the fate inflicted on their leaders provided me with a moral. I saw heads lying far from their bodies, eyes gouged out, bodies coated with powdery ashes, their beauty marred by the clawmarks of birds of prey, limbs mangled in battle and scattered and scattered about, naked, torn, shreds of flesh, stumps of flesh, crushed skulls, cloven necks, loins smashed, sliced heads, feet cut off, noses cut off, extremities hacked away, empty eyes, open bellies, bodies cut in two, shrivelled mouths, gaping foreheads out of which eyes trickled, twisted necks, all lifeless and contorted among the stones and as rigid as the stones. And what a moral this conveys! These faces glued to the earth, no longer animated by desires, made me think of the words of the Koran: *The infidel shall say: Would to God that I might become dust.* And yet what a sweet odour rises from this charnel house.

Imad ed-Din was a moralist of the old order, ready to find lessons in brooks and stones and crushed skulls. Saladin's ride over the battlefield led him, too, to some moral conclusions. The infidel must die, and he must make an example of Reynald with his own hands. Returning to his tent, he summoned Reynald into his presence and immediately stabbed him in the throat, killing him. Saladin then ordered that his head be cut off and the headless body dragged in front of the king. Pointing to Reynald's body, Saladin said, "This man was guilty of unimaginable crimes. His perfidy and insolence brought about his death. You should have no fear, for a king does not kill a king." The trunk was then thrown out of the tent but the head was kept. Stuck on a lance, it would decorate Saladin's triumphal march through Damascus.

On July 5, the day following the battle, Saladin rested. His only known act on that day was to send a chivalrous message to the countess of Tripoli, who had remained in the heavily fortified castle at Tiberias, offering her safe-conduct through the Galilee to rejoin her husband. Her servants, her bodyguard, her soldiers, and all her possessions were allowed free passage through the country.

On Monday, July 6, he put into action the moral conclusions he had reached two days earlier. He was prepared now, after long contemplation, to murder his captives. The Knights Templar and the Knights Hospitaller were sentenced to be killed by the mullahs and religious teachers who accompanied his army. Imad ed-Din, who watched the executions, describes them as "men of pious and austere sentiments, devout sufis, men of the law, learned and initiated in asceticism and mystical knowledge." Some two hundred knights were drawn up outside Saladin's tent; each mullah and religious teacher was given a sword. Saladin spoke briefly about the harm done by the knights and how the world must be set free from these people who represented the worst of the infidels. Then, one by one, the knights were killed. It took a long time. Some executioners did a good job and were applauded, some botched it and were excused, and some put on such a ridiculous performance that they had to be replaced. Imad ed-Din, standing close by, observed the smiling Saladin, and pondered the merit granted to him by Allah for cutting off so many heads.

The same day, Saladin sent an order to the governor of Damascus to cut off the heads of all the knights imprisoned in his dungeons. The only people he spared were the king, his brother, Humphrey of Toron, Hughes of Jebail and Gerard of Ridfort, the Master of the Temple, and the other knights of noble blood. They were all sent to Damascus except for Balian of Ibelin, who asked permission to go to Jerusalem on parole to look after his wife, Maria Comnena, the former queen of Jerusalem, the widow of Amaury I. Kingship weighed heavily on Saladin. It seemed to him that even Christian kings and queens received their titles from God and were under divine protection. He therefore permitted Balian to make the journey to Jerusalem.

After Hattin, Saladin's chief task was to secure the coast of Palestine. Acting with great speed, his army reached the walls of Acre four days after the battle of Hattin. Three days later, Saladin attended public prayers in the mosque, which had been a church for three generations. He freed four thousand Muslim captives and acquired the wealth of the richest city on the Palestinian coast. He summoned his brother al-Adil (Saphadin) to help him reduce all Palestine with his Egyptian army. Al-Adil marched up the coast to Jaffa and laid siege to the city, which refused to surrender. He therefore took it by storm, and the entire population was made captive, to be sold eventually in the slave markets of Aleppo. In Acre the Christians fared better for they were allowed to leave unharmed with their private possessions.

From Acre, Saladin's forces fanned out over the Galilee and Samaria, receiving the surrender of Nazareth and Sephoria, while others marched along the coast to capture Haifa and Caesarea. Nablus fell, and so did Toron, which was besieged for six days. By the first week in August, Saladin was master of Sidon, Beirut, and Jebail. Beirut alone put up stiff resistance, holding out for eight days. In these cities Saladin offered the same terms he had offered to Acre: the citizens could leave freely. Only Jerusalem, Tyre, and Ascalon remained in Christian hands, and Jerusalem was doomed.

Tyre survived because Saladin was in no hurry to capture it. This was a mistake. Conrad of Montferrat, who had been in the service of the Byzantine emperor, left Constantinople suddenly as a result of a blood feud and sailed in his own ship first to Acre, then, as soon as he realized that Saladin's army was in possession of the city, he sailed to Tyre, where he found the Christians downcast by the defeat at Hattin and disturbed by Reynald of Sidon, who was preparing to surrender the city to Saladin. Conrad took command, expelled Reynald, and issued orders that everyone in the city must man the defenses. Conrad was fiery, ruthless, and absolutely determined.

Saladin brought up his army and attacked. Tyre proved to be impregnable. By order of Saladin the old marquis of Montferrat, Conrad's father, was brought from his dungeon in Damascus, paraded outside the city walls, and threatened with death unless the city surrendered. Conrad answered that he would not bargain over his father's life; he would not surrender. Saladin permitted the old marquis to return to his dungeon, and continued the attack.

The defense of Tyre was crucial to the survival of the Crusaders. Conrad knew this, and fought all the more ardently. At last Saladin pulled out his army and sent it against Ascalon, where there was no one like Conrad capable of stirring up the population to uncompromising defiance of the enemy. Just as the old marquis had been brought to Tyre to be shown to the people standing on the walls, so now before the walls of Ascalon Saladin paraded the king and the master of the Temple, who had been brought from Damascus, promising them their liberty if Ascalon surrendered. But Ascalon refused to surrender and continued to fight for another two weeks. Then, when it became clear that Saladin would take the city by assault and that such assaults were generally accompanied by a general massacre, the king intervened, and on his authority the city surrendered. He was not given his liberty immediately. Instead he was imprisoned in Nablus, where he was permitted to see Queen Sibylla. The following summer, he was released with his brother together with all the nobles captured at the battle of Hattin.

None of these excursions was so important to Saladin as the certain surrender of Jerusalem, to which he now turned his attention. Jerusalem had no army capable of defending it, and no commander capable of arousing the people in a *levée en masse*. Heraclius, who was in command was distrusted by the inhabitants, and detested by the clergy and the captains of the garrison. On the day Ascalon surrendered—it was September 4, 1187—there took place a partial eclipse of the sun. On this day, in near darkness, Saladin received a delegation from Jerusalem, fifty miles away, consisting of its leading citizens. Saladin asked them when they were prepared to surrender the city. They answered that they would defend it to the very end. Angrily, he sent them home, reminding them that he had the power to capture Jerusalem and destroy all the Christians in it.

Balian of Ibelin took command of the Christian forces. He had been captured at Hattin, and was well aware that, as a prisoner on parole, he was in an ambiguous position. He wrote to Saladin, explaining the circum stances under which he had assumed command of the city, begging forgiveness for breaking his parole, and urging Saladin to spare the city. This was something Saladin could not do. Balian of Ibelin made a heroic effort to place the city in a state of defense. Every boy who could prove noble descent and was capable of bearing arms was made a knight, and some thirty citizens were also knighted. The Tower of David contained a plentiful supply of arms. Balian took possession of the treasury and stripped the silver from the roof of the Church of the Holy Sepulchre. Raiding parties brought in corn from the surrounding villages. The city was swollen with refugees, most of them women and children. Balian had no illusions about the difficulty of defending Jerusalem.

Saladin's army marched on Jerusalem like a slow and steady machine destroying everything in its path. On September 26, he was on the Mount of Olives, looking down on Jerusalem. He had already sent siege engines against the city, with little effect. The Christians surged out of the city and destroyed them. Under Balian's command Jerusalem had become a city of men so desperate that they were prepared to die rather than submit to the conqueror. Saladin realized that he would have to take each street of Jerusalem, house by house. He was not averse to a general massacre, but preferred a peaceful surrender. On September 30, Balian appeared in his tent to sue for terms.

Saladin rejoiced in his triumph. Simply to have Balian standing there as a suppliant was a boundless joy. Saladin pointed to his own standard flying from the walls of Jerusalem and said, "The city is captured. You cannot sue for terms."

Balian answered that a single flag on the walls meant nothing, the fighting would go on, and there was more than the city at stake. There were five thousand Muslims in Christian hands, and thousands upon thousands of Christians would slaughter themselves to avoid being killed by the Muslims. He threatened to set Jerusalem on fire, to destroy all the holy places including the Dome of the Rock and the al-Aqsa Mosque. All the treasure would be destroyed, and every living creature. He described the new Jerusalem vividly, a city of ashes and flames. Outside the city walls, the Christians who could bear arms would hurl themselves at the Muslims. All would die, but in dying each would take a Muslim with him. He painted a picture of Doomsday.

Saladin, alarmed and convinced that Balian meant exactly what he said, agreed to terms. He would regard the population as prisoners who must pay a ransom: each man ten pieces of gold, a woman five pieces of gold, and a child one piece of gold. As for the poor, they could be released on payment of the thirty thousand bezants that remained in the keeping of the Hospitallers from the treasure of King Henry II. The people were given forty days to pay the ransom money. Those who failed to pay and remained behind would become slaves of the Muslims.

Saladin set his guards at the gates. They examined everyone who passed through the gates, exacting the appropriate tribute. Saracenic merchants came flocking to Jerusalem to see what they could buy for a few gold coins—a house, a bed, a slave girl—and there was much cheating on the part of Christians and Muslims. Christians were fair bait and quickly dispossessed of their goods. Some, like Heraclius, paid their ten pieces of gold and walked out of Jerusalem laden with treasure. Heraclius took with him the gold plate of the churches of Jerusalem, even the gold plate of the Church of the Holy Sepulchre, and nobody stopped him. Saladin, told that the patriarch was going off with all the gold treasure remaining in Jerusalem, commented mildly that he must be allowed to do what he pleased: no one must lay a finger on the patriarch. Al-Adil, Saladin's brother, interceded for some poor Christians, saying, "Sire, I have helped you by God's grace to conquer the land and this city, and therefore I pray that you give me a thousand slaves from among the poor people." Saladin granted his wish, and al-Adil set them free as an offering to God. Saladin himself proclaimed that old people who could not pay the ransom would be allowed to go free. Saladin's lieutenants reminded him frequently of the bloody massacres committed by the Crusaders when they first conquered Jerusalem, yet his mercy was widespread. The wives and daughters of knights, after paying their ransom, marched out of Jerusalem to Saladin's tent and cried out that their husbands and fathers should be returned to them. Some had died in battle, others were in prison. Saladin ordered that the women whose husbands had died should be paid from his treasury, and he ordered scribes to take down the names of the prisoners, promising that as soon as he could go to the prisons he would set them free. What was most extraordinary about the meeting was that Saladin wept when he saw the women weeping.

He could afford to be compassionate: to have Jerusalem in his grasp was his supreme achievement. By showing at last that the Christian kingdom could be struck a deathblow at its heart, he had demonstrated the power of

Islam to overcome all obstacles. He played his role with intelligence and sensibility. He had a simple aim and knew what he was doing, unlike the Christians who had blundered like sleepwalkers to defeat. Saladin, sitting in his tent, possessed the power of the Caesars. The East lay in the hollow of his hand and he could do what he wanted with it. He was the master of the Arabic world and was more than king. He had become an emperor, a man who ruled over many nations, disdaining the panoply of power, very quiet and singular.

But although the kingdom died, it lived on in the minds of the Christians who lived in fear, huddled along the seacoast of Palestine. In their eyes, a lost city was all the more vivid because it was lost. Jerusalem captured was Jerusalem freed from all ambiguity. A lost city, like an empty tomb, was all the more real, all the more desirable, because it was unattainable.

Three Letters

EXCERPTS FROM A LETTER FROM TERENCE, MASTER OF THE TEMPLE, TO ALL COMMANDERS AND BRETHREN OF THE ORDER, FROM TYRE, NOVEMBER 1187

BROTHER TERENCE, known as Grand Master of the most impoverished house of the Temple, himself the most impoverished of all the brethren, and that brotherhood almost completely destroyed, to all commanders and brethren of the Temple, greetings! May they utter sighs to God, at whom the sun and the moon are astounded!

The wrath of God has lately permitted us to be scourged by innumerable calamities which our sins have brought down to us. Neither in writing nor in the language of tears, so unhappy is our fate, can we tell the full measure of these things. Know that the Turks assembled an immense multitude of their people and with bitter hostility they invaded the territories of the Christians. . . . They spread themselves over nearly all the land: Jerusalem, Tyre, Ascalon and Beirout being all that is left to us and to Christendom. Since nearly all the citizens of these cities have been slain, we shall not be able to hold them unless we speedily receive divine assistance and the aid you can bring to us. At the present moment they are besieging Tyre relentlessly by day and night, and they are so numerous that they cover the entire land from Tyre to Jerusalem and Gaza, like swarms of ants.

Grant us, we beseech you, your aid with all possible speed. Grant succour to us and to Christendom, which is now all but ruined in the East, that with God's aid and by the great merits of the brotherhood and with your help, we may be able to save the few remaining cities. Farewell.

EXCERPTS FROM A LETTER FROM THE EMPEROR

FREDERICK I BARBAROSSA TO SALADIN, KING OF EGYPT, WRITTEN BEFORE THE FALL OF JERUSALEM WAS KNOWN IN THE WEST.

FREDERICK BY THE GRACE OF GOD Emperor of the Romans, the ever august and glorious victor over the enemies of the Empire and the fortunate ruler of the entire kingdom, to Saladin, the illustrious Governor of the Saracens. May he take warning from Pharaoh and touch not Jerusalem!

. . . [Y]ou have profaned the Holy Land over which we, by the authority of the Eternal King, bear rule, as guardian of Judaea, Samaria and Palestine, [and] solicitude for our imperial office admonishes us to proceed with due rigour against such presumptuous and criminal audacity. Wherefore, unless, before all things, you restore the land which you have seized, . . . [within] a period of twelve months, . . . you will experience the fortune of war, in the field of Zoan, by the virtue of the life-giving Cross and in the name of the true Joseph.

We can scarcely believe that you are ignorant of that which all antiquity and the writings of the ancients testify. . . . That . . . innumerable . . . countries have been subject to our sway?

All this is well known to those kings in whose blood the Roman sword has been so often steeped: and you, God willing, shall learn by experience the might of our victorious eagles, and be made acquainted with our troops of many nations. You will learn the anger of the Teutons who take up arms even in time of peace. You will know the inhabitants of the Rhineland and the youth of Istria, who never flee from battle, the towering Bavarians, the proud and cunning Suabians, the cautious Franconians, the Saxons who sport with their swords, Thuringians, Westphalians, the energetic men of Brabant and the men of Lorraine who are unaccustomed to peace, the fiery Burgundians, the nimble mountain men of the Alps, the Frisians with their javelins, the Bohemians who know how to die joyfully, the Poles fiercer than the beasts of the forest, the Austrians, the Istrians, the Illyrians, the Tuscans, the Venetians and the Pisans—and lastly, also, you will assuredly be taught how our own right hand, which you suppose to be enfeebled by old age, can still wield the sword on that day of reverence and gladness which has been appointed for the triumph of Christ's cause.

EXCERPTS FROM A LETTER FROM SALADIN TO FREDERICK I BARBAROSSA, WRITTEN AFTER THE FALL OF JERUSALEM.

TO THE GREAT KING, HIS SINCERE FRIEND, the illustrious Frederick, King of Germany, in the name of God the
merciful, by the grace of the one God, the powerful, the almighty,
the victorious, the everlasting of whose Kingdom there is no
end. . . .

We make it known to the sincere and powerful King, our great
and amicable friend, the King of Germany, that a certain man
called Henry came to us professing to be your envoy, and he gave
us a letter which he said was from your hand. We caused the letter
to be read, and we heard him speak by word of mouth, and by the
words which he spoke by word of mouth, we answered also in
words. Here, therefore, is the answer to your letter:

You enumerate all those who are leagued with you against us,
you name them and say—the king of this land and the king of that
land—this count and that count, and the archbishops, marquises
and knights. But we wished to enumerate those who are in our
service and who listen to our commands and obey our words and
would fight for us, this is a list which could not be reduced to
writing. If you reckon up the names of the Christians, the Saracens are more numerous than the Christians. If the sea lies
between us and those whom you call Christians, then no sea
separates the Saracens who cannot be numbered: between us and
those who will come to aid us there is no impediment. The
Bedouin are with us, and they alone would be sufficient to oppose
all our enemies. And the Turkomans alone could also destroy
them, and our peasants at our orders would fight bravely against
any nations that invaded us and despoil them of their riches and
exterminate them. And then we have the soldiers who opened up
the land and took possession of it, and drove out our enemies.
These together with all the kings of Islam will not be slow when
we summon them, nor will they delay when we call them.

Whenever your armies are assembled, as you say in your letter,
and whenever you lead them, as your messenger tells us, we will
meet you in the power of God. We will not be satisfied with the
land on the seacoast, but we will cross over with God's good
pleasure and take from you all your lands in the strength of the
Lord. For if you come, you will come with all your forces and will
be present with all your people, and we know that there will be
none remaining at home to defend themselves or fight for their
country. And when the Lord, by his power, shall have given us
victory over you, nothing will remain for us to do but freely to
take your lands by His power and with His good pleasure.

The army of the Christian faith has twice come against us in
Babylon, once in Damietta and again in Alexandria; the Chris-

tian army reached into the land of Jerusalem, and toward Damascus, and into the land of the Saracens; in every fortress there was a lord who studied his own advantage. You know how the Christians returned every time and what happened to them. . . .

By the virtue and power of God we have taken possession of Jerusalem and its territories; and of the three cities that still remain in the hands of the Christians: Tyre, Tripoli, and Antioch, nothing remains but that we shall occupy them also. But if you desire war, we shall meet you with the power of God, who wills of his good pleasure that we shall occupy the whole land of the Christians. If you want peace, you have only to command the captains of these three cities to deliver them up to us, and we shall restore to you the Holy Cross, and we shall liberate the Christian captives in all our territory, and we will be at peace with you. We will allow you one priest at the Holy Sepulchre and we will restore the abbeys to their former state and we will do good to them. We will permit the pilgrims to come throughout our lifetime and we will be at peace with you.

If the letter that came to us by the hand of Henry is indeed the letter of a king, we have written this letter in reply and may God give us council according to His will. This letter is written in the year of the coming of the Prophet Muhammad 584, by the grace of the only God. And may God save our Prophet Muhammad, granting the salvation of our saviour, our illustrious lord and victorious king, the giver of unity, the true word, the adorner of the standard of truth, the corrector of the world and of the law—from the Sultan of the Saracens and the infidels, the servant of the two holy houses and the holy house of Jerusalem, father of victories, YUSUF son of AYYUB.

VI

THE RAGES OF KING RICHARD

A Journey
to Joachim

KING Richard I of England was one of those princes who inevitably command respect. He was tall, long-limbed, square-shouldered, possessing a peculiar grace of movement and an enchanting capacity to put people at their ease. He had the carriage of a king and the mind of a *condottiere*, clean-cut, ruthless, unyielding. In the Holy Land he would find a worthy enemy in Saladin.

King Richard I inherited his good looks from his mother, Eleanor of Aquitaine, and from his father, King Henry II, he inherited demonic energy. Richard was an excellent poet and a superb musician, while his principal talents lay in military architecture and military strategy. He was proclaimed Duke of Aquitaine when he was fifteen, and thereafter he was constantly at war with neighboring principalities.

He was twenty-one when he undertook the most impressive of his early campaigns, an attack on the castle of Taillebourg, which was virtually impregnable, being surrounded by a triple ditch and triple walls, with a garrison of over a thousand well-armed men and provisions for a long siege. Richard set fire to the village that clustered about its walls and to all the other villages in the neighborhood. He had the insolence and bravado to pitch his own tents close to the castle. When at last the garrison troops made a fierce sortie, he was ready for them, attacked them mercilessly, and followed them through the castle gates. Afterward the survivors and his own troops tore down the castle until there remained only a heap of rubble. He was not yet Richard Coeur de Lion; he was Richard the Ruthless, without the least mercy or sympathy.

His mercy and sympathy were aroused in 1187, when he heard about the disaster at Hattin. Although the battle took place on July 7, he did not hear about it until the end of October. He took the Cross immediately, vowing to reconquer Jerusalem, to the surprise of his father, King Henry II, and the displeasure of his prospective father-in-law, King Philip of France.

In a field near Gisors, Philip and Henry met to discuss a host of misunderstandings. The archbishop of Tyre, who was visiting Western Europe to seek support for a new Crusade, arrived at Gisors just at this moment, and began to speak movingly about the loss of the Holy Sepulchre and the precarious situation of the Christians now clinging to a few fortresses on the shores of Palestine. He spoke so well that Philip and Henry forgot about all the problems that bedeviled them and listened intently to the archbishop, whose eloquence stirred them to take the Cross. Heaven favored the archbishop, for a huge Cross had appeared in the sky while he was speaking.

Once more, as in the days of Urban II, France was caught up in a wave of wild enthusiasm. Thousands took the Cross. It was agreed that the English should wear white crosses, the French red ones, the Flemings green.

These preliminaries were interrupted, however, when war broke out between the English and the French. Richard found himself embroiled in rebellions south of Aquitaine, and Henry fell ill at Chinon with his army in disarray, while Philip rode high in the saddle, dictating terms. Henry died miserably, muttering, "Shame, shame, on a conquered king."

With Henry's death, Richard acquired England. For him, England was booty. He had little interest in the country except as a source of revenue, of able-bodied men capable of fighting in Palestine, and of shipbuilders and shipwrights capable of building a fleet that would take them there. When he returned to England to be crowned at Westminster, the English thought he had come to stay. They could not have been more mistaken. He had come to loot in the name of the Crusade. He sold offices and titles to the highest bidder. He removed all sheriffs from their positions, and then ordered them under threat of imprisonment to buy back their sheriffdoms. Told that one of his acts of merchandising the state was particularly flagrant, he answered, "I would sell London if I could."

He was able, by such dubious means, to raise a sum of money sufficient to pay for a fleet of nearly 250 ships and to buy thousands of horses, which were conveyed overland to Marseilles. He was in England only about four months, raging through the country like a giant predatory insect, and then he was off to his own dominions in France, having left England almost in ruins, and having proclaimed a general amnesty with the result that the prison gates opened wide and all the other thieves were allowed to depart freely.

For the same reason that Richard showed himself to be an admirable military architect and strategist, he could also, when it suited his purpose, be an admirable diplomat. King Philip of France was intensely aware of his responsibility to enlarge the frontiers of his kingdom until it was as large as Charlemagne's. In particular, he wanted Aquitaine, Champagne, and Flanders. That made him and Richard natural enemies; yet when the Crusade finally set out from Vézelay, Richard made the overtures that gave them the appearance of being perfect friends. They rode side by side, ate their meals together, engaged in endless friendly discussions, and slept in the same tent. Anyone who watched them together observed that they were in perfect agreement on all subjects and wonderfully gentle to one another, although in fact each would have liked to see the other dead.

In the history of the Crusades there was never quite such a procession as the one that left Vézelay on July 4, 1190. It was a very long procession, for it was estimated that a hundred thousand men took part in it. There were Englishmen, Frenchmen, Angevins, and Normans, a raucous and happy crowd, singing their Crusader songs with great relish far from the battle-fields. The procession made its way through towns and villages, until the marchers reached Lyons. Villagers came out of their houses to offer bread and wine and cool water from the wells, and when they saw a great knight approaching on his caparisoned horse, with nodding plumes and silk cape flowing in the wind, they held up their babies to be touched in the belief that these lordly men on their way to the Holy Sepulchre possessed a special grace. At least a thousand black-robed priests accompanied the procession, the most colorful that had ever passed through France.

At Lyons, the two kings parted. Both Richard and Philip were terrified by sea voyages, but Philip was the more terrified. He, therefore, decided to take his army over the Alps and march along the Italian coast to Genoa. Richard, trusting that his immense fleet which had set out months earlier from Dartmouth would soon arrive in Marseilles, decided to march along the left bank of the Rhone until he reached the sea. On the whole, Richard was in a kindly mood during the journey through Provence, but when he reached Marseilles, and discovered the English fleet had not arrived, he was enraged.

The two kings had solemnly agreed to meet in Messina, at the foot of Italy, and the first one to arrive would wait for the other. Although they had also agreed that they should divide the spoils equally between them, they must have known that such an agreement was impractical; it was intended chiefly as testimony to their outward friendship.

Enraged because his fleet, together with the greater part of his army, had failed to arrive, Richard quickly hired two large transports and twenty well-armed galleys for the household troops who had accompanied him along the Rhone Valley, and sailed to Genoa, the ships keeping close to the shore.

Philip had already arrived in Genoa, and was ill and in low spirits. He had had a difficult journey over the Alps; moreover, he had recently learned that Frederick Barbarossa, the emperor of Germany, had been drowned in the Calycadmus River in Cilicia while on his way to the Holy Land, and thereafter his army had disintegrated. Only a few were able to reach Germany; the rest were slaughtered by the Turks or died of plague. Never had a powerful army vanished so quickly. The news weighed heavily on Philip, but Richard was not unduly alarmed. He spent a day comforting

Philip and sailed off to Portofino and a leisurely jaunt down the Italian coast. He was at Salerno when he learned that his fleet had overtaken him, and was already approaching Messina.

Like all the kings who took part in the Crusades, Richard suffered from a strange dilatoriness. He had vowed to safeguard the Holy Sepulchre, but he was in no hurry. He spent ten days in Naples, rode to Salerno, visited the famous medical college. He acted as though he were on holiday. But when he finally reached the Sicilian shore and was rowed out to his ships, he assumed the stance of a conqueror. From his flagship he gave orders that the entire fleet should wheel around and make for the harbor, and he further ordered his sailors and soldiers to make such a sound with their clarions and trumpets that the white walls of Messina would quake and tremble as though in an earthquake. His loud and memorable entry into the city struck terror into the hearts of the inhabitants.

Philip welcomed Richard with the kiss of peace. He had recovered from his fever, and was in a mood to set out at once to the Holy Land. On that same day, or the day following, Philip ordered his fleet to set sail; but the wind shifted and he was forced to turn back. With their fleets riding at anchor, the two kings contronted one another, vying for advantage. Philip, having reached Messina first, occupied the royal palace, while Richard with his entourage occupied a villa surrounded by vineyards in the outskirts of the city.

Messina at this time was inhabited by three different peoples: Greeks, descendants of the early settlers of southern Italy; Italians; and Saracens. The Greeks had a special dislike for the Crusaders; they were in close contact with Constantinople, and they may have feared that Richard and Philip had designs upon Byzantium. The English and Angevin troops were camped on the seashore outside the city walls. There were frequent brawls. Some of the Crusaders had been killed. It would have been very easy to provide a provocative incident that would start a full-scale battle. Richard, already regarding himself as chief justice, set up a gallows in his camp and proceeded to hang all thieves and murderers, whether they were "Greeks" or his own soldiers.

It seemed that Philip never took the law in his own hands. From such superficial judgments, the two kings became known as "the Lion and the Lamb." In fact, Philip could be just as lawless as Richard when it suited his purpose.

From Tancred, King of Sicily, who ruled from Palermo, there soon arrived the present that Richard desired most—his favorite sister, Joanna, who was beautiful and accomplished. She was the dowager queen of Sicily, having been married to King William II. She had been kept a virtual prisoner by Tancred. She now came with her "bed gear" and a million terzini, in lieu of her dowry. Richard demanded the rest of her dowry, which included a gilded table more than twelve feet long, a golden chair, and a dinner service of twenty-four gold and silver plates and cups. He also demanded the legacy bequeathed by William II to his sister. It was obvious that he doted on his sister Joanna, who was now twenty-five years old, and he also wanted some of this money and treasure for himself. As King of England, Duke of Normandy and Aquitaine, and Earl of Anjou, he felt responsible for the young dowager queen of Sicily, who was also an English princess. In the course of time he would extract from Tancred every penny he felt was owed to him or to his sister.

To safeguard Joanna he seized the castle at La Bagnara, which was well fortified, and installed her in it, leaving some knights and men-at-arms to see that she came to no harm. His next step was to seize the monastery lying on an island in the Faro River; he expelled the monks and their servants, and filled the monastery with military provisions, which would not be needed until the spring, for it was quite evident that it was already too late in the year for ships to sail to the Holy Land. He would winter in Sicily, and he would seize Messina, if he could.

All he needed was an act of provocation, and these were happening daily. A squabble between English soldiers and a woman breadseller led to violent quarrels; the English took to arms, the Messinians closed their gates, mounted their walls, and prepared to defend their city. Richard arrived from his villa, made a tour of the outer walls, observed an unguarded postern gate, entered it with two of his soldiers by the simple process of breaking down the gate with a hatchet. While the English were still attacking outside, Richard was already inside the city. It was dark now; they were unobserved as they crept along the curtain wall, and they quickly reached the main gate, which was unattended. Richard with his two soldiers opened the gate and let the army in.

To celebrate the conquest of Messina, Richard ran up his own flag over the main gate of the city and around the walls, to the discomfiture of King Philip, who had watched the battle from the royal palace in Messina. Had they not formally agreed that all the spoils should be held in common? Richard was reluctant but he decided to order that the French flag be run up beside the flag of England. King Philip felt that the cause of friendship had been served by flying the two flags together.

Richard distrusted and feared the people of Messina for good cause. How could he make sure that they would never desire to try to avenge themselves? Richard hit on a remarkable expedient. He had brought siege engines with him, and now he erected one of these huge towers with a drawbridge at the very summit close to the walls. This tower, which he called "Mategriffon" ("the Greek-killer") had a profound psychological effect, for the tower overtopped the walls and appeared to be watching everyone in the city.

On October 8, two weeks after his arrival in Messina, Richard invited Philip to attend a council of war, which would deal with all matters concerning the Crusade. They swore friendship over holy relics; each army would help the other; both in going and in coming they would defend each other; and they would observe the laws of the Crusade which had never previously been promulgated. There must be no gambling except by knights and clergy, no knight or clerk was permitted to lose more than twenty shillings. If they lost more, they must pay a fine of a hundred shillings. This law did not apply to kings. Sailors, soldiers, and common men, when found gambling, would be whipped naked through the army for three days or thrown into the sea on three consecutive mornings. No one was permitted to hoard goods; no one in the army might buy bread to sell for profit. The price of bread was fixed at a penny a loaf. The price of wine was regulated, profits on all sales must not exceed 10 percent, and there was an express injunction against the purchase of dough. The laws were harsh and probably unenforceable. Richard had amused himself at Chinon before setting out for Vézelay by drawing up a code of laws for his seamen. If a sailor murdered another, he was to be bound to the murdered man and hurled into the sea. If a sailor cursed, swore, or reviled another sailor, he must pay an ounce of silver. A sailor who stole would have his head shaven, boiling pitch would be poured over him, and chicken feathers would be shaken on the pitch, so that he could be recognized for what he was, and at the next port he would be cast ashore. Richard enjoyed punishing.

By conquering Messina Richard forced Tancred, the King of Sicily, to come to terms over the matter of Joanna's dowry. They met at Cefalù, a small seaport on the northern coast of Sicily graced with a magnificent cathedral possessing the finest Norman mosaics of the time, and once again there were protestations of friendship. Tancred offered Richard forty thousand ounces of gold, half of this sum to represent the dowry of Joanna and the other half as the dowry of one of Tancred's daughters, whom he wished betrothed to Arthur, Duke of Brittany. Arthur was the son of Richard's dead elder brother, Geoffrey, and at this time he was three years old. He had some claim to being heir to the English throne. Tancred seems to have been delighted at the idea of having a future queen of England among his daughters, and he was perhaps even more delighted by the possibility that he could play Richard against Philip and retain his throne, which had seemed only a few days before to be in great danger.

The long winter was filled with diplomatic maneuvers, alarms and excursions. Richard was busy reorganizing his army, beaching his ships and examining them for dry rot and wormholes, conducting an interminable correspondence with the pope, the various crowned heads of Europe, and his own family. He also arranged to perform penance for certain sins of the flesh in the privacy of the chapel attached to his villa. The archbishops and bishops gathered in Messina were invited to watch the king, barefoot and wearing a simple shift, advance toward the altar, strip off his shift, and kneel before the assembled churchmen, while pleading for God's mercy in his nakedness. "From that hour forward," wrote the chronicler Roger of Hoveden, "he became a man and feared God, and abandoned what was evil and did good."

Although one may doubt whether there was a true conversion to a life of pure morality, there is no doubt that Richard was, for the first time in his life, turning to the comforts of religion. A certain Joachim of Floris, a preacher of great eloquence and the possessor of prophetic powers, was at this time abbot of the monastery of Corazzo in Calabria. Richard appears to have been fascinated by this visionary. He summoned Joachim to Messina and engaged him in a long discussion, a major portion of which had to do with the coming of the Antichrist. Joachim was sure that the Antichrist would take the form of a pope. Having brought a number of archbishops with him, Richard was able to argue the case in favor of an Antiochene or Babylonian Antichrist. But both felt he was so close that they could feel his breath, and he had to be reckoned with. Richard or Joachim—it is not clear from Roger of Hoveden's account who is speaking—describes the Antichrist in chilling terms:

> He shall cause persecution in every clime against the Christians and all the elect, and he shall raise himself up against the faithful in three ways—by terror, by gifts and by miracles.
>
> To those who believe in him he will give abundance of gold and silver; those whom he shall not be able to corrupt by bribes he will conquer with terror; those whom he shall not be able to conquer by terror, he will be able to lead astray by signs and miracles; and those he cannot lead astray by signs and miracles, he will torment, and in the sight of all he will destroy them by a cruel death.
>
> Then there will come tribulations such as the earth has never seen since the time of the nations, and those who are in the field will flee to the mountains and none shall come down from the mountains into their houses to take what belongs to them.

Although the tribulations were extreme and most men would perish in them, there was one saving grace: this time of trouble would last exactly three and a half years, and afterward the kingdom of God would be established.

Richard's conversation with Joachim of Floris was important because it revealed the apocalyptic strain running through the Crusades. The aim of the Crusade was not only to safeguard the Holy Sepulchre and the holy places but, in the eyes of many who took part in it, the aim was also to hasten the time of the establishment of God's kingdom on earth. There, at Armageddon, or Antioch, or Babylon, or Jerusalem, the Christians would fight the final battle with the Antichrist and overthrow him. According to Joachim of Floris, speaking in the winter of 1190, a state of perfect blessedness would descend on the earth in about fifteen years, and Richard was expected to play an important role in the conquest of the Antichrist. His immediate task, however, was the conquest of Saladin, the sixth of the seven kings.

Richard was well aware of his responsibilities, but Joachim's voice was not the only one he heard. He heard claps of thunder louder and more terrifying than any he had heard in France, saw lightning flashes brighter than any he had ever seen, and he was puzzled and frightened by them. One of his ships was struck by lightning, split apart, and sank to the bottom of the sea. They were signs and portents of the coming war with Saladin and the Antichrist.

Meanwhile, he attempted to placate his enemies and comfort his friends. He gave the people of Messina a charter, and, from being murderous, became kind to them. On Christmas day, he entertained King Philip at an immense banquet held outside the walls of Messina in the shadow of Mategriffon, the towering siege engine. He gave King Tancred a sword, which he claimed to be the original Excalibur worn by King Arthur of England. He seemed to be mellowing.

Slow Boat
to Acre

HE winter season was coming to an end, but Richard remained in Messina. One of his most important affairs was to attend to the continuity of his line by marrying and having offspring. At the end of February 1191, news came that his mother, Eleanor of Aquitaine, was in the south of France on her way to Messina, acting as the duenna of Princess Berengaria of Navarre. Berengaria had so charmed Richard when she was young that now the king of Navarre had entrusted her to Queen Eleanor to prepare her for marriage.

The coming of Eleanor and Berengaria to Messina might have presented difficulties. Richard was determined to keep the peace with Philip of France, who meant him to marry Aloysia. Unfortunately for Philip, Aloysia had been sent to the court of Henry II, and there was very little doubt that Henry had used his royal power to seduce the intended bride of his son. There was even some documentary proof of this, or so Richard seemed to believe. Philip was understandably dismayed when he was shown the evidence; but he was now convinced that the Crusade was more important than the fate of his sister, and he issued a proclamation in which he maintained, in the name of the holy and undivided Trinity, that he had no quarrel with Richard over Aloysia and that they had established a firm peace and friendship. Philip set sail for Acre on March 30 and Richard, according to custom, accompanied the French fleet a few miles out to sea.

A few days later, Queen Eleanor arrived in Messina with the young Spanish princess, and a few days of festivity celebrated their coming. Then Queen Eleanor, having accomplished her mission, left for England, and the princess was given into the care of Joanna, the Dowager Queen of Sicily. It was too late to arrange a marriage ceremony; the fleet was about to sail for the East, and Berengaria and Joanna, with their servants and well-armed guards, were given a ship of their own.

The fleet sailed out of Messina on April 10. Richard commanded a fleet of over two hundred ships of all sizes, from great men-of-war to cargo vessels, some with sails, some with banks of oars, and some with both sails and oars. We must not imagine that these sailing ships bore any resemblance to the clippers of the Victorian age. The art of sailing was still in its infancy. The admiral of the fleet, Robert of Turnham, gave orders by trumpet and the beating of a great drum, so that any ship out of earshot of the flagship might wind up in trouble. For this reason the ships were bunched together as much as possible.

They were two days out of Messina when a violent storm sprang up and the ships were scattered. Twenty-five ships were lost without a trace. Richard prayed fervently on the main deck of his war galley; he was still praying when, suddenly, in the middle of the night, the storm abated.

A week after leaving Messina, he anchored off Crete; there was no sign of the galley bearing his princess. It terrified him that she might have been drowned. The loss of the princess meant also the loss of his treasure, which had been stowed away on her ship. In fact, her ship had been blown far to the south with several other ships, and they were now making their way north.

Two of these ships were shipwrecked; the survivors reached the shore and were captured near Amathus by the troops of Isaac Comnenus, the self-appointed despot of Cyprus. Some failed to reach the shore and were drowned; among them was Roger Malchen, Richard's vice-chancellor, who carried the royal seal around his neck. His body and the seal drifted on shore, and Isaac Comnenus soon realized that the ships belonged to Richard's fleet and that he was in a position to hold the survivors as hostages. He also learned that the third ship contained the princess. He did everything possible to induce the princess and her entourage to step on shore. He was aware that Richard had a very large fleet; it was advisable to have as many hostages as possible.

He was still sending rowboats out to the princess's ship, inviting her ashore, when Richard's fleet suddenly appeared over the horizon. The princess was saved, but Isaac Comnenus had taken many shipwrecked sailors prisoner, and he had taken possession of the treasure that had been washed ashore.

Richard sent envoys demanding the return of the prisoners and the treasure. When his demand was rejected three times, Richard decided to invade the island. Isaac Comnenus saw the attack coming, quickly threw up a barricade made of logs, beams, chests, and benches, armed his men as best he could, and waited for the attack. Richard was a far better strategist than Isaac Comnenus, and the Anglo-Norman army made a landing without any difficulty, with Richard, armed with an ax, among the first to reach the shore. The barricades were quickly torn down, the bowmen fired their arrows, and then it was the turn of the lancers, swordsmen, and mace-carriers to grapple with an enemy that had no stomach for fighting. In the late afternoon, as dusk was falling, the despot abandoned the city, taking his household troops with him. Richard, entering in triumph, found plentiful supplies of oil, wine, corn, and meat. About five miles away, Isaac Comnenus set up his tents in a thickly forested valley and waited for an opportunity to recapture the city.

The news that Isaac Comnenus was hiding in a nearby secluded valley was brought to Richard in the middle of the night. Richard decided to destroy Isaac Comnenus's camp and, if possible, capture him. He very nearly succeeded. There was a quick, bloody battle in the valley, all Isaac Comnenus's horses, weapons, and treasure were captured, together with his splendid tents and his gold-embroidered battle-standard. The despot leaped naked from his bed and fled into the forest.

Three days later, there arrived at Limassol a small fleet of well-armed galleys from Acre. On board was Guy of Lusignan, King of Jerusalem, and all his chief nobles. What they wanted, on any conditions whatsoever, was a clear declaration from Richard that he would immediately bring his vast fleet to the sorely pressed Holy Land. Richard demanded that they should all swear fealty to him, and they assented. He promised to bring his fleet to Acre as soon as he had taken care of several important matters.

The first was the coronation of Berengaria, who was crowned Queen of England in the chapel of the castle of Limassol, with two kings in attendance, all Richard's officers of state, and half the nobility of the Holy Land. The wedding ceremony was as long, complex, and spectacular as the coronation. There followed the inevitable feast, but as soon as it was over, Richard was on the march again, in search of Isaac Comnenus and the remnants of his army.

Isaac Comnenus was in Nicosia, building up an army to recapture the city he had lost, hoping that Richard was in too much of a hurry to reach the Holy Land and would not waste time for him.

Richard, however, wanted to fight him, but the master of the Hospital thought there were advantages in making him an ally. The master was so insistent that Richard finally agreed to a meeting with Isaac Comnenus on a field near Limassol. There he confronted Isaac Comnenus with an ultimatum. If he behaved well, the island and all its fortresses would be restored to him. But he must first convince Richard of his good intentions by swearing fealty and by sending five hundred of his knights to the Holy Land under Richard's command. In addition, he must place all his castles and fortresses on the island of Cyprus at the king's disposition and pay an indemnity of 3,500 marks for the men who had been plundered when they were shipwrecked on the island. Isaac Comnenus agreed to all this, feeling sure that Richard would soon leave and everything would be restored to him. Richard returned to him the ornamental tent that had been captured during the night foray and gave him the kiss of peace.

The meeting came to naught. Isaac Comnenus fled to Famagusta, fearing that Richard would arrest him; he hoped that he could build up a large enough army to keep Richard at bay. Guy of Lusignan, King of Jerusalem, was placed in charge of the expeditionary force sent to hunt him down; Richard made his way to Famagusta by sea. Isaac Comnenus had vanished. There were thick forests nearby; the pathways were known to the Greeks; there were many castles where the despot might have taken refuge.

Richard was sitting in a tent on the seashore at Famagusta when he saw a ship arriving from the east. When it came closer, he saw that it carried the flag of the Kingdom of Jerusalem: five black crosses on a white ground. On board were envoys from King Philip of France. Troops were needed for the siege of Acre, Philip's messengers complained; why was Richard wasting his time in Cyprus? King Philip had already been in the camp outside Acre for a month, waiting for Richard. How many more months would he have to wait? Richard, who was not accustomed to anyone making peremptory demands on him, flew into a rage. He announced that the capture of Cyprus was necessary for the defense of the Holy Land, and they were fools who thought otherwise. He sent them away and turned his attention to Nicosia, where, according to his spies, Isaac Comnenus was mounting a large army. The spies also said Isaac was hoping Richard would march on Nicosia and fall into an ambush prepared for him somewhere along the road. Richard was pleased. It meant that there would be a battle, perhaps the one that would put an end to Isaac. So they marched out of Famagusta in battle order, with Richard in the rear, to guard against the ambush promised by the spies.

There was no battle: only a series of skirmishes, intended to harass the army. Once Isaac Comnenus drew close enough to Richard to fire poisoned arrows at him. They did no harm, glancing off his armor; but when Richard discovered that the arrows had poisoned tips, his anger blazed up again, he dug his spurs into his horse, and went in pursuit. Isaac Comnenus had the fastest horse in Cyprus, a bay called Fauvel, which "bore him away with the swiftness of a stag straight to the castle of Kantara." Wisely, Richard reined in his horse, returned to his army, and set out for Nicosia.

There the people came out to meet him and to acknowledge him as their new sovereign lord, and he ordered the Greek nobles to shave off their beards as a sign that they were under a new dispensation. Isaac Comnenus, infuriated by the capture of Nicosia and by the order that everyone be beardless, tortured the few Anglo-Normans who fell into his hands, mutilating them, plucking out their eyes, or cutting off their noses.

Richard fell ill, the conquest was left in abeyance for a few days while forces were assembled by Guy of Lusignan for attacks on the great Byzantine fortresses of Kyrenia, Dieu d'Amour, and Buffavento. In Kyrenia, they found the daughter of Isaac Comnenus and made her prisoner. This fortress had been attacked by land and sea, with the help of guides who knew the way, and its capture was surprisingly easy. Dieu d'Amour was far more difficult, being set on crags 2,400 feet high; it could only be reached by narrow pathways that favored the defense. Guy of Lusignan's forces came close to the summit only to find themselves the targets of well-directed arrows and huge rocks.

When the fortress at last capitulated, it was decided that this was the most secure place in all of Cyprus, and accordingly the daughter of the despot was brought there. Richard himself attacked the fortress of Buffavento, which was also nearly unreachable, but Isaac Comnenus was not there. He was hiding in a fortified monastery at Cape St. Andrew. There, a few days later, Richard rode to receive his surrender.

In the presence of the king, Isaac Comnenus threw himself down on his knees and begged for his life. His only request was that he should not be put in iron chains. Richard agreed to this request and was fairly hospitable to the former despot. Then he ordered that chains of silver would serve instead of iron chains. Isaac Comnenus, in silver chains, was sent to Tripoli and thrown into a dungeon in the fortress of Margat, which belonged to the Templars.

The queen of England, the dowager queen of Sicily, and the daughter of the despot were sent to Acre with the greater part of the Anglo-Norman fleet. A few days later, on June 5, 1191, Richard himself set sail for the Holy Land.

He was a man who never lacked for adventures. His ships encountered a ship flying the French colors, but there was something suspicious about it and he sent two galleys with envoys to speak to the captain, who told them the ship had come from Antioch to take part in the siege of Acre. Richard was still suspicious, and he turned out to be right. They were not what they said they were. The ship was manned by Saracens. Richard gave the order to attack. The Saracens poured Greek fire on their attackers, but they were surrounded on every side by quick Anglo-Norman ships, whose eager sailors had been promised all the booty on board. The wooden sides of the Saracen ship were hit by the iron beaks of Richard's ships. The ship began to sink, but not before Richard's men had crawled over it like ants and found their promised booty. Many of the fourteen hundred men aboard threw themselves naked off the sinking ship, only to be engulfed in Greek fire. Some Saracens were taken prisoner, but most of them were drowned.

Having already established himself as a conqueror, Richard came to the camp outside of Acre.

Richard
and Saladin

RICHARD spent sixteen months in the Holy Land, and accomplished miracles. If he had stayed longer, he might have accomplished more miracles, but it is just as likely that he would have fallen into the traps the Saracens were preparing for him. In those sixteen months he provided a new vigor, a new way of looking at life, one that was violent, self-assured, flamboyant, and sometimes chivalrous. It was as though the strength and determination of the early Crusaders had returned to the Holy Land.

At first the prospects were far from promising. He landed his troops near Acre, established a campsite, and immediately examined the troops stationed around the high walls of the city, who were preparing to attack as soon as the generals felt sure they could take them by assault. The siege had begun two years earlier when Guy of Lusignan had boldly struck out from the north with a pathetically small army and established his lines around the place, cutting off the people of Acre from the hinterland. On the hills above Acre, Saladin had assembled a powerful force. The besiegers were therefore in danger of being caught in a vise, for if Saladin descended on them and the army of Acre sallied forth at the same time, the Crusaders were lost. But Saladin had never felt strong enough for a massive descent from the hills, and the besieged never felt strong enough to make a massive sortie.

So there was a stalemate. The Crusaders were taking great risks, but they had advantages denied to the enemy. They already possessed powerful siege engines, they were receiving detailed reports about the situation in Acre through their spies, and they had a new confidence, born since Richard's arrival. It was almost as though they expected the walls to fall simply because Richard was present.

The last details for the assault were being drawn up when Richard fell seriously ill with what was perhaps an aggravated form of malaria. Though weak and listless, he had himself carried to the forward lines on a tour of inspection and shot arrows up at the watchmen on the towers. We are told that his face and lips were wasted with a sickness called *leonardie*, and one of the consequences of this illness was that the skin peeled off. All through the siege of Acre, Richard suffered in varying degrees from this sickness. Saladin heard that he was ill and chivalrously sent him fruit and snow.

Although Richard was very ill, he was still capable of carrying on diplomatic offensives in all directions, against King Philip and especially against Saladin. He heard that King Philip was paying his men three gold bezants a month; he offered four to any knight who entered his service. Pisans and Genoese flocked to his colors, but he refused to take on the Genoese who had pledged themselves to the French king. Henry of Champagne, who was Richard's nephew, found himself in desperate need of money, asked King Philip for a loan, and was told that he would receive the loan only if he pledged Champagne as a surety for it. Henry had no intention of surrendering Champagne and turned to Richard for assistance. Richard enjoyed making grand gestures, and he offered Henry of Champagne £4,000, together with food for his men and horses, without any surety at all. Apart from making grand gestures, Richard would always seize on an opportunity to undermine King Philip's position.

Richard also hoped to undermine Saladin's position. He sent a message to Saladin urging an interview. Saladin answered uncompromisingly, pointing out that, according to tradition, kings met only after terms of peace had been arranged. He did however delegate his brother Saphadin to meet with Richard, during a three-day truce, in a tent erected on the plain between the two camps.

There was no meeting, for Richard was by this time too ill. Saladin sent him a present of a Negro slave: a dubious gift for the slave could easily have been a spy. Saladin was also sending scouts into the English tents at night, hoping to take prisoners. Anyone who resisted had his throat cut. Those captured could expect to be tortured until they had revealed everything they knew, unless they died before that. Saladin was often merciless to his prisoners. Richard was even more merciless.

On June 14, King Philip ordered a general assault on the walls of Acre. Richard was distressed, fearing that the assault might be successful and he would have no part in the victory because he was so ill. The French army was massed against the Accursed Tower, and near this tower the French, the Pisans, and the Templars succeeded in making a breach in the walls. But the Muslims counterattacked, pouring through the breach, and this first assault came to nothing. While the fighting for the walls was going on, the Anglo-Norman army kept watch on Saladin's army in the hills. There was an agreement between the two kings that while one attacked, the other would safeguard the rear. This was a sensible arrangement, which would have been more profitable if Richard and Philip had not felt so contemptuous of one another, and if their armies had not despised one another. In such circumstances, lines of communication often failed, and the absence of a single commander in chief made their efforts more difficult.

Philip ordered a second attack on June 17. This time the Muslims on the walls saw what was coming and warned Saladin, far off on the hills, by shouts and loud banging of plates and basins, cymbals and kettledrums. Saladin sent a large force against the Anglo-Normans, whose commander was Geoffrey of Lusignan, the brother of Guy. Geoffrey distinguished himself by dashing against the enemy with an ax, slaughtering ten of them, and taking many prisoners. There was hard and vicious fighting against Saladin and against the Muslims of Acre, who employed Greek fire with devastating effect. The Christians won no victories that day. Geoffrey of Lusignan's feats were extolled, but there were mountains of dead, Christian and Saracen alike, to be thrown into the ditches.

Richard had brought with him the great siege engine, Mategriffon. Philip, too, had his siege engines, one of them of monstrous size called "Bad Neighbor," which battled against a similar engine mounted on the walls called "Evil Kinsman." There were continuous duels between "Bad Neighbor" and "Evil Kinsman." From time to time "Bad Neighbor" would be damaged, and then it would be repaired. Finally, it was completely destroyed, and King Philip, scarcely recovered from malaria, fell ill of vexation. Philip's engineers designed a new form of scaling ladder called "the Cat," and when this was also destroyed by Greek fire, the king's vexation grew boundless; he cursed everyone in sight and threatened the most terrible vengeance on the Saracens.

On July 2, Philip ordered another assault on Acre, and this time he achieved some results. The French had succeeded in making a tunnel under the Accursed Tower; they had shored it up with timbers and were preparing to set fire to the timbers. The Anglo-Normans had also mined the walls, while the Saracens in turn were digging countermines. Saladin, knowing that the Crusaders were on the verge of a massive attack, sent his chief lieutenant down into the plain with orders to destroy the Crusader rear guard at all costs. There was hand-to-hand fighting of the fiercest kind, but the Crusaders held their ground.

Meanwhile the attempt to scale the walls with ladders continued, and a certain Alberic Clements, who was the military commander directly under the king, swore that he would enter Acre that day, or perish. He held up the king's standard, gathered a large number of soldiers and officers around him, charged against the walls, and began, with the help of scaling ladders, to climb the walls. The Saracens let down a gigantic grappling hook and pulled him up for the pleasure of killing him. At about the same time, they threw down a multitude of heavy rocks which killed forty of the men who came charging up to the walls. To annoy the attackers still more, a Saracen paraded along the wall wearing the armor of Alberic Clements. Richard, though still sick and lying on a silken mattress, aimed with his crossbow and shot the man in the heart.

Then it was the turn of the Pisans to scale the Accursed Tower, only to meet resistance so desperate and at the same time so effective that the Crusaders found themselves marveling at the intelligence and energy of the enemy, half-starved, blockaded by sea, without any reserves of ammunition, yet continuing to defend ragged walls which were blackened by fire, mined, and broken. Saladin, who was waiting for fresh troops from Egypt, had refused to send his main army into the plain, but the defenders of Acre were now desperate. They begged for a truce, which would allow them some communication with Saladin. He must be made to realize that Acre would have to surrender unless he sent more aid. Saladin was at that moment trying to distract the Christians with marauding expeditions. On July 8, he burned Haifa. On the two following days he uprooted all the vineyards and cut down all the fruit trees around Acre. He appears to have thought the Christians would send out flying columns, which he could cut down at leisure. Instead they held firm. For two years they had been besieging Acre and the prize was almost in their hands.

The Saracens who came out from Acre to bargain for a truce offered to surrender the city and everything in it if they were permitted to march out alive with only the clothes they were wearing. King Philip was prepared to accept this offer; but Richard rejected it outright, saying that after such a long and difficult siege he refused to enter a deserted city. He wanted bloodshed. There were six thousand Saracens in the beleaguered city and he was determined that many should die.

He was determined, too, to extract from Saladin as many concessions as possible. The True Cross must be given back to the Christians; fifteen hundred prisoners in Saladin's hands must be released; Philip and Richard were each to receive an indemnity of 100,000 bezants, while Conrad of Montferrat, regarded as a contender for the crown of Jerusalem, would receive 1400 bezants. At a great meeting held at the Templar camp, Richard's terms were agreed upon. On July 12, a little more than a month after Richard's arrival, Acre formally surrendered.

Richard took up residence in the palace with his wife, Berengaria, and his favorite sister, Joanna. Philip took up residence in the Templar stronghold. Leopold, Duke of Austria, whose German troops played a minor role in the campaign, set up his standard beside Richard's and was offended when the flag was torn down by the Anglo-Normans and thrown into a ditch. Leopold thus became Richard's mortal enemy and would later have his revenge on Richard. Once Acre was captured, many laid claim to the spoils. Philip claimed half of everything, former Christian owners of houses and establishments in the city claimed possession of their property, the Templars and Hospitallers claimed their estates, and the churchmen claimed the churches, which had been converted into mosques, and the estates that went with the churches. The Templars succeeded in keeping order between the factions, but only with the greatest difficulty. Those who had the greatest claim—the fighting men who had endured a two-year siege—received nothing. They were fobbed off with promises, while the kings and princes took the lion's share.

Richard had recovered his health and was flushed with victory. He proposed that the two kings make a vow to remain in the Holy Land for three years: time enough for them to destroy the armies of Islam. Philip, who was now suffering from dysentery, had no stomach for three years of campaigning, and there were urgent matters summoning him to France. He distrusted Richard's intentions and did not believe that the Holy Land could be conquered. When the bishop of Beauvais and the duke of Burgundy, who had brought Richard's plan to Philip, and had to listen to Philip's diatribes against Richard returned, Richard saw Philip's answer in their faces. He said, "It will be a shame and a disgrace for my lord if he goes away without having completed the business on which he came hither. But still, if he finds himself ailing, or in bad health, and is afraid lest he should die here, his will be done." "And is afraid lest he should die here" contains more than a little malice, since it was the duty of a Crusader to die, if necessary, in the Holy Land.

Philip and Richard had to decide on many issues while there was still time. One of the more important issues concerned the King of Jerusalem. Which of the two contenders was the real king? Guy of Lusignan claimed the title by virtue of his marriage to Sybilla. Guy of Lusignan had led the Christian army to defeat on the Horns of Hattin, and had therefore, as some believed, forfeited the crown by his stupidity and ineptitude. Richard, remembering how well Guy of Lusignan had fought on Cyprus, was not inclined to believe that Hattin was entirely his fault. Conrad of Montferrat claimed the title by virtue of his marriage to Isabelle. Philip favored his claim because the marquis had fought with the French army before the walls of Acre. So they struck a balance. Guy of Lusignan was confirmed with the title, but was allowed to possess it only during his lifetime; after Guy's death Conrad would possess the title, and if he had a son by Isabelle, this son would in due course be crowned King of Jerusalem. Meanwhile Conrad was given the fiefs of Tyre, Sidon and Beirut, and the royal revenues would be shared equally between Guy and Conrad. In this way the pragmatic medieval mind resolved a problem that seemed almost beyond resolution.

At last, on July 31, Philip departed from Acre and made his way to Tyre where he found three Genoese galleys waiting to take him to Apulia. Wars were raging in France; he had excellent reasons for returning to his own country; Richard was glad to see him go.

As King of England, Richard carried little weight with the great body of

Frankish Crusaders. As Duke of Aquitaine, he carried a little more. As a man he was admired, worshipped, and feared. But it never occurred to him that Philip, however ungainly and maladroit, had an advantage he could never possess. Simply by being King of France, Philip was loved by the Frankish army.

At this time Leopold of Austria also left the Holy Land, unloved and unwanted. He had done too little to justify his existence there; he was quarrelsome and proud, and almost insanely jealous of the two kings who possessed the preponderance of power. Inside the walls of Acre the chief command went to the duke of Burgundy, who was closer to Richard than to Philip.

The kings, as usual, were remembered by the chroniclers. Sometimes, but very rarely, we hear of the exploits of the common soldiers. During the last clash with Saladin's forces, according to the Arab chronicler Baha ad-Din, an enormous Frank standing on a parapet drove off the Muslim attackers. He stood there, hurling stones with deadly accuracy, being helped by his fellows who handed him more stones as soon as one was aimed. He had received fifty wounds from arrows and stones thrown by the enemy. He was so covered with blood that he seemed to have turned scarlet, but he continued to throw stones to the very end. At last one of the Muslim officers was able to pitch a bottle of naphtha at him. It exploded, burning him alive.

The battle for Acre was, like all battles, ugly; but it possessed a special ugliness. The long siege reduced everyone to exhaustion and desperation. The Christians, hemmed in between the walls of Acre and the hills where Saladin's troops were waiting, forced to fight on two fronts simultaneously, became utterly merciless; and the Muslims inside the walls were equally merciless. On both sides the main body of the troops lived in misery and squalor. The prices of food on the Christian side are known. An egg cost a silver penny, which could also buy thirteen beans. A sack of grain cost exactly a hundred gold pieces. For ten copper pennies one could buy a stew of horse entrails. Strips of leather were shredded and boiled; a dead horse provided a hundred men with small feasts for a week. Bone meal, grasses, leaves, bark, earth were eaten. Soldiers died of starvation, scurvy, typhus, and the strange disease called *leonardie*, which reduced men to helpless lethargy. Saladin suffered from terrible boils from the waist downward, so that he could neither sleep nor rest; and one of the reasons why he did not attack the Christian camp may have been that he was too ill, and his army was too ill, to mount an attack. Corpses that lay unburied were devoured by rats or black clouds of flies settled on them; vultures and scavenging dogs were given splendid feasts. Scorching heat and rain, winter frosts and mud, made life nearly impossible. Like the Tafurs who had taken part in the siege of Antioch nearly a hundred years earlier, the majority of the Christian soldiers were living in total fear and squalor.

Even when they achieved victory, even when Acre surrendered, they were still starving, and only the knights received a few tidbits from the kings.

Richard announced that he was prepared to parlay with Saladin. He would return the prisoners in exchange for the True Cross, the Christian captives, and a large ransom. Saladin temporized. He sent costly presents and hoped to prolong the argument until fresh troops came up and a sudden descent on the Christian forces would decide the issue once and for all. Richard demanded that a list of important Christian captives should be supplied to him. Saladin possessed such a list but refused to supply it. The terms of surrender, which had been accepted by the garrison in Acre, seemed to Saladin to be merely the basis for an agreement to be arrived at later. Richard had set a time limit: the exchange of prisoners was to take place within a month. A month passed: the ransom money had not been received, the Christian prisoners had not been released; and though Christian ambassadors had been allowed to see the True Cross, which was hidden away in the treasury somewhere within Saladin's camp, its surrender had not taken place. Saladin was temporizing so obviously now that Richard lost all patience. He could not leave the prisoners in Acre and he could not take them with him to Jaffa, which lay seventy miles to the south. Jaffa was the seaport of Jerusalem, and would serve as a supply base for an attack on the Judaean hills. Richard decided that Saladin had no intention of keeping the agreement, and deserved exemplary punishment. On the morning of August 20, he ordered the killing of all the prisoners. He himself directed the massacre which took place a few miles from Acre on a hill called Ayyadieh. Richard's butchery was deliberately carried out in full view of the Muslim army. More than three thousand men, women, and children were killed on the hill of Ayyadieh. It was a remarkably clear summer day, and Saladin, from his field headquarters on the second range of hills, could see everything that was happening on Ayyadieh. He saw the parade of armored knights and thousands of infantrymen, and he saw the long train of Muslim prisoners bound together with ropes. Then he saw the flashing of swords and axes and lance heads, and the prisoners falling.

His army saw what he saw, and went charging down the hills, howling for revenge. But it was too late. The massacre had been conducted expeditiously; there were no survivors. Though the Muslims charged again and again, they were turned back. There came a rumor that many of the prisoners had swallowed gold coins, and while some of the Anglo-Normans were fighting off the Muslims, others were slitting open the bodies to find the gold. In the afternoon Richard simply abandoned the hill, and his army marched back in the direction of Acre. He had choreographed the massacre to the last detail. He was not surprised to hear that Saladin had made no effort to follow him.

Of all Richard's actions, the massacre was the most terrible. The portrait of the chivalrous Crusader king who behaved always with courtesy has no foundation in fact: At Ayyadieh, he employed the tactics of terror in the modern way, with efficiency, cunning, and a sense of drama. Still, we should remember that massacre was the order of the day, and when the Saracens captured a fortress they were accustomed to massacring the captives, except for the leading knights, whose lives would be saved by the offer of a ransom. An unwritten code of war demanded that high officers on both sides were treated with courtesy and gentility, while the rest were treated like animals fit only for slaughter.

All that night the Muslim soldiers could be heard wailing over the headless corpses of the men, women, and children who had bravely withstood the siege of Acre for two years.

All hope of regaining the True Cross vanished after the massacre; it was rumored that Saladin, who had long been carrying it for safekeeping in his treasury, sent it to Damascus, where it was said to be buried under the portals of the chief mosque. The Christian prisoners held in Damascus were killed at Saladin's orders.

At dawn on August 24, Richard led his army out of Acre. Provisions for his troops, his siege engines, and the heavier instruments of war were carried by his ships, which sailed slowly, close to the shore.

A Famous
Victory

HE army that moved along the coastal road to Jaffa was one of the most powerful the Crusaders had ever put in the field. It numbered about eighty-five thousand men, who were well armed and well equipped; but it was powerful mainly because it was under the protection of the fleet, because it was well organized, and because it was under the influence of a single well-wrought military mind. Richard and his general staff had thought out the problems of marching along the coastal road, knowing that an equally large Saracen army would be marching inland parallel to the Crusaders. There would be skirmishes and harassing attacks all along the way. There would be attempts to cut through the army, to separate its various parts, and to inflict damage where it was weakest. Richard, therefore, had to provide an order of march such that no part would be weaker than any other, and at the same time he had to arrange his troops so that they could take battle positions at a few moments' notice. In all this he succeeded brilliantly.

It is one of the few occasions when we can observe his mind working quietly and dispassionately. No doubt he had the assistance of the Templars, who were famous both for their daring and for their mastery of tactics. Since he had never previously traveled these roads, he relied on the experience of travelers, studied maps, and interrogated prisoners. His army was organized in twelve brigades and grouped in five divisions; each brigade included cavalry and infantry. They marched in three columns. On the right, near the seashore, were the pack animals and the human carriers, for there was never enough animal power and human beings could be made to carry enormous burdens. In the center rode the cavalry, and on the left the infantry. The Hospitallers and Templars formed the advance guard and rear guard. Richard rode up and down the lines as he pleased. The army had rested after the fall of Acre, and the men were in good spirits.

Baha ad-Din, the friend and chronicler of Saladin, watched Richard's army from the high ground and could not conceal his admiration for its discipline and order. Here he is describing what he saw on August 31, 1191, when he took part in a hit-and-run attack by Saladin's light cavalry:

> . . . the Moslems sent in volleys of arrows from all sides, deliberately trying to irritate the knights and force them to come out from behind the wall of infantry. But it was all in vain. The knights kept their temper admirably and went on their way without the least hurry, while their fleet sailed along the coast parallel with them until they arrived at their camping ground for the night.
>
> They never marched a long stage, for they had to spare the foot-soldiers. Half of the infantry, when not actually engaged, carried the baggage and the tents, for there was a great lack of beasts of burden. It was impossible not to admire the patience shown by these people. They bore crushing fatigue, even though they had no proper military administration and derived no personal advantage. And so they finally pitched their camp on the farther side of the river of Caesarea.

Baha ad-Din's testimony to the solidity and fortitude of the Crusader army obviously reflects the opinion of Saladin, who had prepared what he hoped would be an ambush in which the entire army would be destroyed. Meanwhile, there were incessant skirmishes. By this time Saladin had acquired some Nubian troops, who, unarmed except for scimitars and shields, had a way of slipping into the camps at night and doing much damage. But the chief damage, as usual, came from the lightly armed cavalry, who swooped down whenever they saw an opportunity. Mostly they attacked the rear guard, where it was easier to pick off the lame, the halt, and the wounded.

The army marched only in the early hours of the morning, for about three hours. They seldom made more than eight or ten miles a day, and on alternate days they rested in camp. They encountered no fortresses, for Saladin had destroyed the fortifications of the captured towns and castles. The progress of this large, steady, well-oiled and relentless machine was so slow that it took nineteen days to cover the eighty miles between Acre and Jaffa. Once Jaffa had been fortified, the army would march inland and try to conquer Jerusalem.

At one time, the coastal road had been a great paved highway that allowed carts and chariots to drive quickly from Acre to Jaffa and beyond. Built by the Romans, paved with local stone from the hills, it had represented imperial power. Now it was lost under the burning white sand or appeared as little more than a track through the dry bush. The foot soldiers were scratched and torn by thorns, their faces were cut by the thick reed-forests growing along the shore, or they fell up their knees in soft sand. Though there were no dangerous animals, there were dangerous insects. The Crusaders were attacked at night by tarantulas, which stung them and left a painful swelling. The knights could go to the doctors, who prepared sweet oils and balms that healed the swellings. The foot soldiers could not afford these unguents, but found a simpler way to deal with tarantulas. Someone discovered that tarantulas detested loud noises, and so they made the night miserable with the banging of drums, clashing of helmets, and the beating of basins, caldrons, and whatever metallic objects lay at hand. There was very little sleep during those nights when the tarantulas came out of the ground.

Sometimes, too, the nights were made sleepless with prayers. It was the custom, once they had settled down for the night, to send one of the king's heralds among the tents with the cry, "Sanctum Sepulchrum, adjuva!" "On hearing these words," says the chronicler, "the whole multitude would take up the cry, stretching out their hands to heaven and with copious tears praying God for aid and mercy." Usually the herald would make the same cry three times, and there would be the answering cry from the thousands in the camp. But sometimes, especially at moments of grave danger, there would be cries and prayers all through the night.

The decisive battle took place on September 7, 1191, at Arsuf, not far from the half-ruined town of Caesarea, as the army wandered over the sand dunes in the direction of Jaffa, about thirty miles away. More than half the journey was done. Here at Arsuf the wooded hills came down to the sea, providing deep cover for the Saracens, who expected to burst upon the Christians and cut them to pieces. Richard was forewarned. He had studied the topography of the region, and he had long since regarded Arsuf as the place where he would expect to stand and fight. Although weary of skirmishing, he was in good spirits, and looking forward to battle. His men were perhaps less ardent, for a surprisingly large number were coming down with fever, and the Templars were complaining that so many of their horses were crippled by arrows that they could scarcely be expected to mount a charge.

That morning, Richard issued a proclamation throughout the camp that he expected to do battle during the day. He ordered the Templars in the vanguard; then came the Bretons and Angevins; then the Poitevins under King Guy; then the Anglo-Normans in the center around the cart bearing the royal standard; and the Hospitallers brought up the rear, the most dangerous position of all. The duke of Burgundy and some French knights rode up and down the line, to see that the troops maintained the positions assigned to them. Henry of Champagne was charged with the duty of keeping close to the hills, to watch for the moment when the Saracens would emerge, and to signal the rest of the army.

The Saracens came out of the woods with a noise like Doomsday:

clarions, horns, trumpets, gongs, cymbals, high-pitched yells, all intended to exalt their own spirits and terrify their enemy. This first attack came shortly before nine o'clock. The main charge was directed at the Hospitallers in the rear guard, but the whole army felt the weight of the attack. At first there were foot soldiers, Negroes, Nubians, and Bedouin, shooting arrows and hurling javelins, throwing themselves on the first line of infantry, who were shaken but held their positions with bolts from their crossbows as they protected the cavalry. Then it was the turn of the Saracen cavalry, armed with axes, swords, and lances. They raised a cloud of dust that obscured the sky. There came wave after wave of them, until there seemed to be no more room. "For the space of two miles," writes the author of the *Itinerarium*, "you could not see as much earth as could be taken up in one's hand, so numerous were the Turks in that place." The sheer weight of numbers on the narrow shore threatened to drive the Christians into the sea. All the time the Christians were pressing forward on their march to Jaffa. The hammering of the Hospitallers in the rear guard continued. Saladin's aim was to chop it to pieces or to halt its forward march, thus cutting it off from the main body of the troops. Once a gap was formed, the process of cutting up the army could be continued indefinitely. Richard was determined to keep the army in one piece at all costs. The crossbowmen in the rear guard fought while marching backward, their faces turned to the enemy. But men cannot walk backward at the same pace they march forward, and there was the danger that the rear guard, moving at an alarmingly slow pace, would open up a gap that could never be filled except by the enemy. The fighting here was at such close quarters that the sound of battle, according to the chronicler, was like the battering of countless hammers upon blacksmiths' anvils. The Hospitallers sent messengers to Richard, begging for permission to unleash their cavalry on the enemy, pointing out that there might not be any horses left unless they acted now, for so many of them had been brought down by enemy arrows. Richard refused to listen to the messengers. He wanted his cavalry intact until he would let them all loose.

It was a day of cloudless skies and terrible heat, and the Hospitallers were beside themselves with fear that the battle would be lost unless the cavalry mounted a charge. Garnier of Nablus, Master of the Hospitallers, was impelled to seek out the king. "My lord king," he said. "We are being violently oppressed by the enemy and in danger of eternal infamy, if we lack the courage to answer them blow for blow! As it is, we shall soon lose all our horses! Why should we endure them any more?" "My good Master," replied the king, "it must be endured, for we cannot be everywhere at once." This exchange, recorded in the *Itinerarium*, has a truthful ring. For Richard, endurance was everything. He was still determined that the knights should hold back so that they could deliver the *coup de grâce* at a moment chosen by him.

In the Christian army orders were delivered by trumpet blasts. There were two trumpeters with the vanguard, two at the center, and two in the rear guard. The trumpet notes for a general charge by the cavalry were well known, and every cavalryman was listening for them. But they were not heard. Two of the Hospitallers, including the marshal and an Anglo-Norman knight called Baldwin of Carron, decided in a fury of impatience to act as though the trumpeters had already sounded the advance. They forced their way through the infantry, shouted "St. George!" at the top of their voices, and hurled themselves at the enemy.

At this particular moment, the lightly armed Saracen cavalry had dismounted so that they could aim more accurately at the infantry, and the knights plowed through them with swords and lances, while the infantry, coming after them, like modern foot soldiers with fixed bayonets following closely behind heavily armored tanks, cut off the heads of the unmounted cavalrymen. Richard's order to wait for the trumpet blasts had been disobeyed, but he showed no anger. He joined the Hospitallers. "Then the king, the fierce, the extraordinary king, cut down the Turks in every direction, and none could escape the force of his arm, for wherever he turned, brandishing his sword, he carved a wide path for himself." Richard had a habit of throwing himself into the thick of battle with a recklessness rarely to be found in a commander in chief. He had an exceptionally long reach and that helped him to keep his adversaries at a proper distance. He was riding Fauvel, the famous bay horse that had once belonged to Isaac Comnenus, and he was riding it harder than he had ever ridden it before.

There were more charges and countercharges, but after the Hospitaller cavalry broke through the protecting wall of infantry, the issue was never in doubt. Seven thousand Saracens were slain; the Crusaders lost perhaps a thousand men.

The battle was won when the Saracens fled back into the woods. Some of them hid in the branches of trees, and the crossbowmen amused themselves by shooting them down. Yet the strategical advantages of the victory were few compared with the psychological advantages. Saladin's army remained intact; he could, and would, continue to harass the Christians. Baha ad-Din records that Saladin was deeply disturbed by his defeat, withdrawing into himself, keeping strangely silent, scarcely moving, sunk in prolonged meditations. He seemed not to hear his emirs when they attempted to comfort him.

The Christians reached the small seacoast village of Arsuf without any further fighting. There they rested for a whole day before setting out for Jaffa. The harassment by the light cavalry continued until they reached the walls of Jaffa; here, at last, the Crusaders could really rest. The Christian army encamped in an olive grove just outside the walls because the city of Jaffa had been destroyed by Saladin.

Marches and Countermarches

NEVER again would Richard score such a resounding victory over Saladin. From this height there would be only a downward passage. Richard would soon realize that a victory for him did not mean defeat for Saladin, who could call upon inexhaustible resources in men and treasure; Richard would realize, too, that all victories in the Holy Land were precarious.

Meanwhile, the Christian army fortified Jaffa, throwing up a new wall and digging a ditch in front of it. The city was partially rebuilt: Richard did not think it was worth rebuilding and argued with the Franks, saying that it was more important to attack the enemy at Ascalon than to pile brick upon brick. Yet there was no doubting the way the army felt. They wanted to stay in Jaffa, where there was an abundance of fruit, and where a man might stretch his legs a little leisurely, knowing that he was close to Jerusalem. Richard, who hated leisure, had other thoughts. He wanted action, and was continually on the move.

One day, with a small escort, he went out hawking, intending to fall upon any small group of Saracens he met on the journey. After a long ride, he dismounted and fell asleep. His companions also slept, and when the armed Saracens found them, Richard had enough time only to gird on his sword and mount Fauvel before the attack came. Richard rushed upon them, wielding his sword, and suddenly the Saracens took flight and the Christians went hurrying after them. An ambush had been skillfully prepared, and all the Christians fell into it. The Saracens thought they recognized the king and surrounded him. At this moment one of Richard's closest friends, William of Pratelles, shouted in their language, "I am the king! I am the *melech*!" The Saracens turned around, captured William of Pratelles, and rode off with him: for the king was worth a king's ransom. Four knights were killed in this engagement, and although Richard attempted to pursue the Saracens, they were already too far away by the time the Christian army could be summoned to go after them.

The nobles of the Kingdom of Jerusalem begged Richard never to go out again without a heavily armed escort. He listened to them politely and went on doing as he pleased. What pleased him most was the thought of conquering Jerusalem. His plans were far advanced. He proposed to mount a massive attack on Jerusalem after transforming Jaffa into an impregnable base of operations. He had calculated the exact date of his arrival: January 13, 1192.

A LETTER FROM RICHARD I, COEUR DE LION, KING OF ENGLAND, TO HIS FAITHFUL SUBJECTS, FROM JOPPA, OCTOBER 1, 1191.

RICHARD, BY THE GRACE OF GOD, KING OF ENGLAND, Duke of Normandy and Aquitaine, Earl of Anjou, to N., his dearly beloved and faithful subject, greeting!

Know that after the taking of Acre and the departure of the King of France, who so basely abandoned the purpose of his pilgrimage and broke his vow, against the will of God to his eternal shame and the shame of his realm, we took the road to Joppa. We were nearing Arsuf when Saladin swept down on us with a mighty host of Saracens. But by the mercy of God we lost no knights on this day save one. This was James of Avesnes, a man dearly beloved by the whole army, and rightly so, for he had proved himself during many years' service in the Christian army, a man of great valour, vigorous and devout in holiness and sincerity of the faith, so that he was like the mainstay and support of the whole army.

So, through God's will, we came to Joppa, which we fortified with a ditch and a wall, because it was our purpose to defend the interests of Christianity to the utmost of our power. On the second day, the Vigil of the Nativity of the Blessed Mary, Saladin lost an infinite number of great men, and being put to flight, in the absence of all help and counsel, he laid waste the whole land of Syria. On the third day before the defeat of Saladin, we were ourselves wounded on the left side with a javelin, but by the grace of God we have now recovered from the wound. Know also that with God's grace we hope within twenty days after Christmas to recover the holy city of Jerusalem and the Sepulchre of our Lord, and after this we will return to our own land.

Witness our own hand at Joppa, the first day of October.

Richard's letter to his subjects in England and France took the form of a brief war bulletin, sketchy and incomplete, with just enough information to whet their appetites. Once Jerusalem was conquered, he intended to return to the West. The hope and the passion lay in the words, "We hope within twenty days after Christmas to recover the holy city." He was giving himself a little more than three and a half months to conquer the city. By Easter his own Crusade would come to an end, and others would take over the command of the Christian army.

A war bulletin must be reasonably concise and factual, and there are usually important omissions and evasions. What Richard was really thinking was conveyed in a letter written on the same day to the abbot of Clairvaux, urging that the greatest possible aid be sent to the Holy Land, and hinting that unless the aid was forthcoming, the results might be disastrous. Here is the letter he wrote in a more chastened mood, full of Christian feeling and with obvious devotion to the abbot.

A LETTER FROM RICHARD I, COEUR DE LION, KING OF ENGLAND, TO THE ABBOT OF CLAIRVAUX, FROM JOPPA, OCTOBER 1, 1191.

RICHARD, BY THE GRACE OF GOD, KING OF ENGLAND, Duke of Normandy and Aquitaine, Earl of Anjou, to the venerable and most dearly beloved friend in Christ, the Abbot of Clairvaux, health and a succession of continued prosperity.

After the mournful and universally bewailed loss of the holy city of Jerusalem, the city of the living God, in favor of which His name was invoked, the earth was alarmed and trembled, because the King of Heaven had lost His own land, the land upon which His feet had trod. But the blessing of God being diffused from the Apostolic See throughout the whole earth, the friends of the Cross of Christ, as Your Holiness is not unaware, vying with each other, pressed onward to assume the sign of the Cross on their foreheads and on their shoulders, and to avenge the injuries done to the Holy Cross.

These people and ourselves shared the task of serving the living God when they took the sign of the Cross for the purpose of defending the scenes of His death which had been made holy by His precious blood, and which the enemies of the Cross of Christ had hitherto disgracefully profaned. . . .

. . . The road between Acre and Joppa is a very long one: we reached Caesarea with great hardship and lost many men. Saladin also—for he marched alongside us—lost many men. After the Christian army had rested for a while at Caesarea, we followed the road to Joppa. Our vanguard had pitched their tents at Arsuf when Saladin attacked our rearguard with a mighty host of Saracens. By the favoring grace of the divine mercy he was put to flight by only four battalions who faced about and set themselves against him, and for a whole league he was pursued in his flight by the entire Christian army. Thus there came about the slaughter of many of the emirs Saladin brought with him, at Arsuf, on the vigil of the Nativity of the Virgin Mary. Never in all his forty years had there been a day like this. . . .

Since the day when Saladin was thoroughly discomfited, he has not dared to do battle with the Christians, but like a lion in his den, he has been secretly lying in ambush on higher ground in order to slay the friends of the Cross as though they were sheep for the slaughter.

And so, through God's guidance, we reached Joppa, and strengthened it with a trench and a wall, making it our purpose to strengthen and promote the interests of Christianity to the utmost extent.

Meanwhile Saladin, hearing that we intended to march on Ascalon with great speed, gave orders that it should be levelled to the ground, and he has deserted and set at nought the whole land of Syria, as though he were utterly bereft of good councillors. For this reason we have hope that in a short time, by the mercy of God, the inheritance of the Lord will be entirely recovered. And since the inheritance of the Lord has already in some measure been recovered, and we have in this recovery endured all the heat and burden of the day, and have now exhausted all our money, and not only our money, but our strength and body as well. Therefore we say to your brethren that we cannot remain in Syria after the coming Easter.

The Duke of Burgundy and the Franks placed under his command, Count Henry with his troops, and the other earls, barons, and knights who, in the service of God, have expended their means on behalf of God, will all return home unless you by your skill in preaching can bring timely assistance to us, in men by whom the land may be peopled and defended, and in money, which they may expend more freely in the service of God.

Falling at the feet of Your Holiness and shedding tears, we proffer our humble entreaties and do most earnestly beseech you that, according to your duty and your honor, you will do everything possible to induce the princes and nobility of Christendom, and the rest of the people of God, to offer their services to the living God and make sure they do so.

After Easter it will be their turn to protect and defend the Kingdom of the Lord, and by that time, with God's mercy, we shall have gained possession of much more of the Holy Land. And may you act so earnestly on our behalf that nothing may be lost through neglect on your part concerning the common advantage that all Christendom so ardently awaits. It is for this reason that in these early days we address to Your Holiness our letters touching the interests of Christianity to the end that we may not be reproached with sloth or negligence, as we would rightly be if perchance we had failed to forewarn a person of your position and of so holy a life concerning the urgent needs of Christendom. Even before we resolved to go on this Crusade, you encouraged us and the rest of the people of God to enter the service of God, and to restore His inheritance to Him, so now also does the most urgent necessity call you to arouse the people of God to act as I have mentioned.

Witness ourselves at Joppa on the first day of October.

Richard's letter to the abbot of Clairvaux reveals the true situation as distinguished from the war bulletin issued to his subjects. He was saying to the abbot, among other things, that everything depended on him. He was asking the abbot to become another Urban II.

A great many things were going wrong with the Christian army. A large number of soldiers and many knights had slipped away by sea to Acre, and Richard himself had to take ship to Acre and order them back to Jaffa again. In Cyprus, too, there were mounting troubles, as the Viceroy, Robert of Turnham, confronted a rebellion by men still loyal to Isaac Comnenus. Richard decided to sell the island to the Templars on the grounds that they alone were capable of exerting the discipline to keep the native Cypriots in subjection and they alone could afford to pay for it. Conrad of Montferrat, the husband of Queen Isabelle, was conspiring with the help of the Genoese to become master of the kingdom. Reports came that Conrad was negotiating with Saladin.

At the same time Richard himself was carrying on ineffective negotiations with Saphadin, Saladin's brother. His ambassador was Humphrey of Toron, the first husband of Queen Isabelle, by now a considerable Arabic scholar and a practiced negotiator. Richard reposed a great trust in him. Humphrey, speaking for Richard, made an outright demand for Jerusalem and all the territory west of the Jordan, together with the return of the Holy Cross. Saphadin demurred. The Holy Cross was perhaps subject to negotiation but Jerusalem belonged to Islam.

Warming up, Richard made new proposals: Saladin should give all the disputed lands, and immediately afterward Saphadin should marry Joanna, the Dowager Queen of Sicily. As a dowry Joanna should receive all the coastal cities at present in the hands of the Crusaders. Saphadin and Joanna should rule from Jerusalem. In this way Richard hoped to make his favorite sister Queen of Jerusalem. It was a brilliant and impractical solution to an insoluble problem. Richard forgot to ask Joanna whether she approved of the idea, and he was a little surprised to learn that she had not the least intention of becoming the wife of a Muslim. She was adamant. The plan, which had seemed so hopeful, was abruptly discarded. Richard, seeing that his vision of peace had been an illusion, decided upon war. He would attack Jerusalem.

The news of the forthcoming attack reached Saladin within a few days. He was ready for it. From his camp at Ramleh he sent a small army against Richard's forces outside Jaffa. The attack failed, and Richard pursued the attackers and drove them back to the plain of Ramleh. In heavy armor, brandishing sword and lance, carving off limbs and heads like a trained butcher, he sometimes appeared to be a one-man army.

Richard alternated between pressing his advantages and withdrawing to consolidate his forces. The skirmishes on the plain of Ramleh continued, and once he rode close enough to Saladin's tent to salute it. On another occasion, a foraging party which included the earl of Leicester and the count of Saint-Pol, together with an escort of Templars, was surprised and surrounded by a large body of Turkish cavalry. The Templars dismounted, formed a square, and prepared to fight to the last man, with little hope that there would be any survivors. Richard, who had a habit of arriving providentially when his troops were in extreme danger, rode up just in time. Warned that he would almost certainly be killed if he entered the battle, he turned to his escort and said, "I sent these men here. If they die without me, may I never be called king again!" Then he spurred his horse and charged against the enemy, his sword flashing and his gold crown gleaming. The enemy scattered. Among the Crusading kings, Richard alone followed heroic words with heroic acts.

He was still planning to conquer Jerusalem when he met once more with Saladin's envoys and arranged to hold a conference with Saphadin at Lydda. The conference took place in a large tent; gifts were exchanged; minstrels sang; Syrian dancing girls performed; and there were protestations of eternal friendship on both sides. Saladin was also negotiating with Conrad of Montferrat, who was prepared to offer Acre to the Saracens in exchange for Sidon and Beirut. Saladin's envoys were impressed by his arguments until it occurred to them to ask him whether he was prepared to fight Richard. Conrad demurred.

At Christmas, Richard set up his headquarters at Latrun, on the edge of the Judaean desert. Joanna, Berengaria, and Guy of Lusignan, with their retinues, celebrated Christmas with him. When the army moved up to Beit Nuba, only twelve miles from Jerusalem, there was wild enthusiasm, for the Holy City, though hidden behind a fold in the hills, seemed to be within reach. The sick and wounded in Jaffa were carried up to Beit Nuba in the hope that they would soon be brought to the Holy Sepulchre, where their sicknesses would be cured and their wounds healed. The soldiers sang hymns, prayed, and prepared themselves for the assault on Jerusalem. Richard studied plans and listened to his spies, and at last concluded that Jerusalem was nearly impregnable; even if he was able to capture the city, he would be unable to hold it for more than a few days.

Winter storms raged. The land was under water, the tent poles sometimes broke in the high winds, the rain rotted the soldiers' salted pork and rusted their coats of mail. It was decided to carry the sick and wounded back to Jaffa; but along the way nearly all of them were massacred. Christmas week, which had begun so hopefully, ended disastrously.

Jerusalem, so close, was still a dream. Richard was compelled to retreat to the coast. The retreat was accompanied by the worst storms anyone could remember. Baggage carts floundered in the mud; men sank to their waists in the marshes; horses were drowned. A dispirited army at last reached Ascalon. Urgent messages were sent to Jaffa for provisions, for there was no harbor at Ascalon and ships riding offshore had been dashed to pieces. Richard, who knew a good deal about shipbuilding, ordered that all the flotsam and jetsam should be carefully collected and used for building new ships.

When the army arrived at Ascalon, they found a city Saladin had reduced to rubble; they had to climb over heaps of stones to enter it. Richard set everyone to work. Knights and esquires, laymen and clerics, masters and servants, and great noblemen found themselves new occupations as masons and bricklayers. Richard himself carried stones to the walls. He was determined to rebuild the city, to make it a bastion of Crusader strength in the south.

Meanwhile, Guy of Lusignan and Conrad of Montferrat were still quarreling over the kingship. Guy was in Acre, supported by the Pisans. Conrad remained in Tyre, and the Genoese in Acre supported him. The people of Acre were battling in the streets on behalf of their favorites. When Conrad set sail for Acre, the Pisans got word of it, and when his ship approached the seawalls of the city, the Pisans let fly with their mangonel and kept up their bombardment for three days. Richard was in Caesarea when he heard that Conrad's ship was being bombarded from shore batteries. He set spurs to his horse, reached Acre the same night, and immediately called for a truce between the rival kings. After meeting Conrad, he concluded that Guy had a more legitimate right to the throne. Richard returned to Ascalon, ill-at-ease.

Though he was deeply respected, as the one truly legitimate king in the Holy Land, Richard was not the ultimate arbiter. The barons and chieftains met in council and decided that Conrad should have the kingly powers because he had all the makings of a war leader, while Guy was irremediably tainted by his failure at the battle of Hattin. The councillors did not know that Conrad was in secret correspondence with Saladin and voted for him with a clear conscience.

Neither they nor Saladin had the opportunity to find out what sort of king Conrad would have made because only a few days later, on April 28, 1192, while returning at night from the bishop's palace in Tyre, he was stabbed to death by hired assassins.

The Old Man of the Mountain

HE murder of Marquis Conrad of Montferrat, King of Jerusalem, was one of those acts that confound the historian because the real motive behind it cannot be discerned. It may have been the result of a private quarrel, for he was a man who would think nothing of insulting high officers on his staff. Some believed that the assassination was ordered by Richard Coeur de Lion, and Saladin's envoy in Tyre reported that the assassins under torture confessed that the king of England had instigated the murder. On the other hand, Ibn al-Athir, who possessed a healthy dislike for Saladin, wrote that Conrad was murdered at Saladin's orders by arrangement with the Old Man of the Mountain, the head of the order of zealots known as *Hashishiyun*, or Assassins. Ibn al-Athir believed that the plan was to murder Conrad and Richard simultaneously, but Richard was too well protected. Others say that neither Richard nor Saladin had anything to do with it, and the murder was ordered by the Old Man of the Mountain for his own reasons.

If, as we may suppose, the assassination was ordered by the Old Man of the Mountain, we must ask ourselves what he hoped to achieve by it. Clearly the assassination was not a deathblow to the Crusaders, who could survive the death of Conrad by the simple expedient of replacing him with someone else. Conrad's power derived from the fact that he was the lawful husband of Queen Isabelle. If the queen had been assassinated too, it would have placed the crown in jeopardy, since, except for King Guy of Lusignan, there was no claimant to the throne who possessed any valid rights. By striking at Conrad, the Old Man of the Mountain was accomplishing at some risk something that scarcely advanced his cause. There was a rumor that Saladin paid him a large sum of money to procure the murder of both Richard and Conrad, but this can be dismissed because it was not in Saladin's nature to procure the murder of kings. Just as easily can we dismiss the story told by some local barons that Conrad had somehow intercepted a ship belonging to the Assassins, stolen the rich cargo, and was struck down in punishment for robbery. The Old Man of the Mountain would not have lowered himself so far. He murdered in order to enforce high political designs or on behalf of abstract principles.

A LETTER FROM THE OLD MAN OF THE MOUNTAIN TO LEOPOLD, DUKE OF AUSTRIA, FROM THE CASTLE OF MASYAF, SEPTEMBER 1193.

MANY KINGS AND PRINCES beyond the seas have accused Richard, the king and master of England, of killing the Marquis. I swear by the God who reigns eternally and by the laws we obey, that he is not guilty of the crime. What really happened is the following: One of our brethren coming by ship from Salteleya was thrown by a tempest into the port of Tyre. The Marquis had him arrested and killed, and he took possession of the large sum of money the man was carrying. We sent envoys to the Marquis, asking that the money should be returned to us and that we should be given recompense for our brother's death. The Marquis blamed Renaud, lord of Sidon, for the man's death. We who care so much for our friends were able to learn the truth, and the truth was that the Marquis had killed him and taken the money.

We then sent a second envoy named Ewris, and the Marquis wanted to have him thrown into the sea, but we had friends who arranged for him to leave the city, and he came to us and he told us the true story. From that moment we decided to kill the Marquis. We sent two of our brethren to Tyre, and they killed him openly and as it were in the presence of all the people. This is how the Marquis met his death.

We declare to you that the lord Richard, King of England, had nothing whatsoever to do with this affair. Those who say otherwise have done much harm to him; there is no grounds for their accusation. Know that we shall never kill for money or for any kind of payment except when harm has been inflicted on us. Know, too, that this letter has been written in our residence, the castle of Masyaf, in the middle of September, in the fifth year of Pope Alexander.

Was it really an act of revenge? It is more likely that Conrad was killed for no reason except to spread terror, confusion, and doubt among the Crusaders. The act of terror was probably designed to make all the high officers of the kingdom aware that their lives were in the keeping of the Old Man of the Mountain and that he could destroy them whenever he wished. The assassination was a warning, a call to order.

The Crusaders missed the message, at least partly because Conrad's death caused little lamentation. There followed a brief struggle for the succession, with the duke of Burgundy claiming the kingdom on behalf of the king of France; he demanded that Isabelle renounce all her rights and surrender Tyre to him and his army. It was an absurd demand, and she rejected it outright. She was pregnant by Conrad and would soon be delivered of a baby girl, her first-born. She was in no mood to renounce the throne. Tyre was her largest city; it was well defended and the duke of Burgundy, though quite capable of violent stratagems, was in no position to capture the city in defiance of Isabelle, Richard, and the captains of the Crusader army.

Help was at hand in the person of Count Henry of Champagne, the feudal lord of the wealthiest and most civilized province of France. He happened to have a talent for military command; he also happened to be a nephew of both Richard and King Philip. He was in Acre when he learned of the assassination of Conrad. He immediately set out for Tyre without the least intention of marrying the young widow but simply in order to be present as the representative of Richard, who was then fighting the Saracens in the region of Ramleh. The barons would meet; great decisions would have to be taken; and there was the funeral of Conrad to be held in the cathedral of Tyre.

But as he rode through Tyre decisions were being made for him. He was so young, so handsome, and held himself so well that the people acclaimed him and shouted that he should be the husband of Isabelle. It appears that he had never met the queen, and was startled by their sudden enthusiasm. When he did meet her, he was a little put off by the idea that she would soon be bearing Conrad's child; if a boy, this child would one day inherit the throne.

The thought had also occurred to Richard, who wondered whether Count Henry would accept her. Count Henry, as a dutiful nephew, sent messengers to Richard asking for advice, for the king was his liege lord and he would do nothing without his lord's permission. Richard was all for the marriage; so was Isabelle, who had fallen head over heels in love with Count Henry.

One day she came to him with a ceremonial offering: the keys of the city of Tyre. He accepted them, and they were married in the cathedral. The wedding took place on May 5, 1192. Exactly a week had elapsed since the assassination of Conrad.

Count Henry's first action was to secure all the castles and fortifications of the kingdom in his name and in the name of the queen. Although the chroniclers sometimes refer to him as King Henry of Jerusalem, he appears never to have been crowned. He ruled as Count of Champagne, or as Count-Palatine of Troyes, and as husband of the queen. He was one of those who preferred the substance of power to its gilded trappings.

Within a few days of the wedding he led his army back to Acre as the first step of a journey that would take him to Ascalon. We are told by Ambrose that sixty thousand armed men marched out of Acre to greet him and the queen. In the Arab fashion, the citizens hung carpets and tapestries from their windows, and in every window and outside every house were censers burning incense. The people gave themselves up to feasting and celebrations, for in their eyes Count Henry had been granted to them by God to strengthen the kingdom.

While the wine flowed and flowers were pelted at the count and his pregnant bride, there were also indications of a new purposefulness among the barons and in the army. Count Henry's arrival in Acre was an affirmation of power, and a signal of Crusader intentions. It was a very solemn occasion and the priests accordingly took him in hand, led him to the cathedral, showed their most sacred relics to him, and bade him kneel before the jeweled Cross, which was then in their keeping, and kiss it, before permitting him to rest in the palace.

Henry's army advanced by slow stages to Ascalon, where they learned that Richard was attacking Daron with huge siege engines. The defenders held out bravely against the incessant battering by huge rocks, stones, and javelinlike rods that were catapulted into the air and fell with tremendous force inside the castle walls. After five days of this, the defenders offered to surrender. Richard was in an implacable mood and said they must surrender unconditionally. He dismissed any suggestion that they be allowed to leave Daron as free men. So they fought on. Richard sent sappers to mine the walls under one of the great towers. When the tower crumbled with a sound like an explosion, the defenders retreated into the citadel, and the Christians poured through the broken walls. The Saracens then experienced a bloodbath: their throats were slit, they were thrown down from high walls, they were beheaded or cut to pieces. Only a few were permitted to become slaves. Richard gave the castle to Henry of Champagne.

From time to time Richard still thought of conquering Jerusalem, though the prospect seemed to him increasingly difficult. It was not only that Saladin had strongly fortified the city, and had scoured the countryside to prevent the Christians from gaining any advantage from the terrain—trees had been cut down, the wells were poisoned—but Richard seemed, for the only time in his life, to be genuinely fearful, as though he sensed that Jerusalem would be his grave. On the morning of June 12, when he was hurrying with an escort after a Muslim patrol, he caught sight of the city in the distance and immediately lifted his shield to cover his eyes, saying that he would not gaze longer on the Holy City until he had conquered it.

A week later, hearing that a rich Muslim caravan was coming from Egypt, he decided to go in pursuit of it. Accompanied by the duke of Burgundy and five hundred knights, all wearing keffiyas to disguise themselves as Bedouin, he raced through the night in the direction of an oasis in the Negev desert, where his real Bedouin spies told him the caravan had halted. The Mameluke guards, the camels, the unloaded merchandise, the cattle and the treasure, were all gathered around a watering place called the Round Tank. The guards were sleeping. It was one of the most pleasant sights he had ever seen, and on that warm night after a race across the sand dunes, the prospect of seizing so much wealth was exhilarating. At dawn he attacked. The Mameluke guards and the caraveners fled into the desert, leaving behind so much gold, silks, purple stuffs, copper bowls, Damascene armor, ivory chessmen, bales of sugar, and spices that Richard and his company scarcely knew what to do with it.

This was a triumph to gladden the heart of the Christian army, but there were no more triumphs of this kind. Richard decided to attack Beirut, which was in Muslim hands. In this way he hoped to extend the little strip of coastal territory still belonging to the Crusaders. Saladin watched his movements, and on the day Richard reached Acre, Saladin swooped out of Jerusalem and attacked Jaffa with a formidable army of three divisions. On the second day of the siege the wall near the Eastern Gate fell. When the Saracens advanced over the broken wall, they found garrison troops with the courage to fight an overwhelmingly superior enemy, but there was a limit to how long they could withstand the assault.

Urgent pleas for help had been sent to Richard in Acre. Right away, he sent the Templars and Hospitallers down the coastal road to Jaffa, filled some Genoese ships with his own troops, and took command of a fleet of fifty vessels. Off Mount Carmel, the fleet was becalmed for a few hours, filling Richard with impatience and even despair. But the wind rose, and at dawn on the following day the fleet stood off Jaffa.

It was characteristic of Richard that, no sooner was his flagship anchored, than he jumped overboard into waist-high water, his shield about his neck, his Danish battle-ax in his hand. His knights captured the seawall and spread havoc among the Muslims, who had spent the night looting the houses of Jaffa. The knights liberated the garrison troops; and their combined forces were sufficient to clear the Muslims out of Jaffa, and then to advance on Saladin's camp. Saladin fled as far as Assir. With only two thousand seaborne troops Richard had won Jaffa back from the Saracens.

However, with the aid of his spies, Saladin was able to keep a close watch on Richard who was camped outside the walls of Jaffa, indifferent to danger, very much at ease. Hoping to take Richard and all his camp by surprise, Saladin attacked. A Genoese sailor, wandering at night over the plain, saw the glint of armor and sounded the alarm. Richard mounted his horse, gave orders that the crossbowmen should be posted between the spearmen, and waited for the Muslims to advance. The Saracen cavalry charged, but could make no breach in the Crusader lines. The Christians counterattacked with such violence that the Muslims reeled back and became increasingly demoralized. The battle lasted all day. It was said that Saphadin, the brother of Saladin, observed that Richard was fighting on a wretched horse long past its prime and sent him two magnificent Arab horses, "because it is wrong that a king should fight on foot." Richard accepted the present gracefully and went on fighting until nightfall. During the night, Saladin's army slipped away. A few days later, at Jaffa, Richard fell seriously ill. Saladin heard of his illness, and with Muslim courtesy, sent him peaches and sherbet cooled with the snows of Mount Hermon. Richard accepted the gift with his customary graciousness. He spoke of concluding a truce with Saladin, of one last effort to wrench Jerusalem from the Saracens, of sailing for England, which was threatened by his brother John and by King Philip of France. He spoke, too, of leaving the Holy Land and returning with a much larger force in 1193. He did, in fact, conclude a three-and-a-half-year truce with Saladin based on the present boundaries: the Christians retained the coastal zone from Jaffa to Tyre, the Saracens kept the rest. One important provision of the treaty gave the Christians permission to make pilgrimages to Jerusalem as they pleased.

A little more than a month after signing the treaty Richard left the Holy Land forever. He had performed many good deeds and given orders for many massacres; he had been by turns cruel, heartless, chivalrous, hot and cool; he had the strongest sword-arm in Christendom. He had shown himself by far the most courageous and, after Baldwin III, the most intelligent of the kings who held power in the Holy Land. He sailed from Haifa on October 9, 1192, still a sick man, weary of war, hoping to reach England by the quickest possible route. By misadventure he fell into the hands of Leopold of Austria and was kept in prison until he was ransomed for 50,000 marks. During the last five years of his life he waged war continuously in England and France, dying at last when besieging the castle of Châlus. We know him as Richard the Lion Heart. Richard was only forty-two years old when he died in 1199. He left no children, but for centuries after his death Arab children were told when they were naughty, "Be quiet, or England will come after you!"

Saladin died early in the morning of March 3, 1193, at the age of fifty-four. His death convulsed the Muslim East, for his heirs were his seventeen sons, who watched each other vigorously and fought among themselves. Most of them were voluptuaries and lacked their father's enthusiasm for poverty. In Saladin's possession at the time of his death were one Tyrian dinar and forty-seven silver dirhams: he had given all of his great fortune away.

Saladin lived on in memory and in legend, honored by Muslim and Crusader alike. His sword was buried with him, and the Muslims believed that he alone would enter Paradise with his sword in his hand. Dante wrote of him as a strange figure standing alone in the sunlight, a man apart: *solo e da parte vidi il Saladino.* All agreed that he alone of the Muslim kings had been capable of forging the unity of Islam. With his death, Islam fell once more into its separate parts.

VII

THE DOGE IN HIS SPLENDOR

The Vermilion
Galley

O NE day in November 1199, Thibault, the young count of Champagne, entertained friends at his castle in the Ardennes on the River Aisne. Tents were erected in the fields, there were tournaments and feasts, and guests came from all over Champagne, Blois, the Île-de-France, and Flanders, for the count was related to nearly all the noble families of the region. The chief guest was his cousin Louis, Count of Blois. Thibault was twenty-two years old, his cousin was five years older. Their maternal grandmother was Queen Eleanor of Aquitaine, and their mothers were half sisters of King Philip and King Richard. Young, rich, possessing vast estates, with royal blood in their veins, they belonged to the *jeunesse dorée* of their time and could have lived out their lives with no more excitement than could be provided by hunting, jousting, and entertaining their friends.

Exactly why Thibault assembled his friends for a tournament at the castle of Ecry so late in the year is unknown. Perhaps it was merely an excuse for a great gathering of friends. But we do know that Thibault had spent a good deal of his short life thinking and dreaming about the Crusades. His father, Henry, Count of Champagne, had taken the Cross in 1178. He journeyed to the Holy Land, fought in many battles, was captured by the Turks, was thrown into prison, and was released through the intervention of the Byzantine emperor in 1181. He returned to Champagne but died soon after. Thibault's elder brother, also named Henry, had also taken the Cross. His fate was very different, for he was the Henry who married Isabelle, Queen of Jerusalem, and became *de facto* King of Jerusalem. After ruling the kingdom intelligently for five years, he died as the result of an accidental fall down a balcony. It was probably inevitable that Thibault should feel honorbound to follow in the footsteps of his father and elder brother. In any event, he announced at the end of the tournament that it was his intention to ask all the nobles and knights present to join him in a Crusade.

In Thibault's summons, there was honor but there was also a private
fantasy. It is likely that he saw himself as another Godfrey, another Baldwin, or another Henry of Champagne, husband of the queen of Jerusalem.
Although there is no doubt that Thibault was the man who gathered his
friends together to announce the Crusade, it is possible that his cousin
Louis was equally responsible. Louis's father, too, had been a Crusader; he
died in 1191 at the siege of Acre.

This was a time when the Crusading fever was rising again. A hundred
years had passed since the troops of Godfrey, the count of Toulouse, and
Bohemond scaled the walls of Jerusalem. Now the Christian Kingdom of
Jerusalem was in ruins, and the surviving Crusaders were clinging to a few
towns on the coast, like men clinging to a rocky precipice. The genius of
Saladin had shattered the kingdom, but with Saladin dead, there was hope
that the kingdom would rise again.

The recently elected pope, Innocent III, had called, albeit somewhat
halfheartedly, for the recovery of the Holy Land. A parish priest known as
Master Fulk of Neuilly, in the archbishopric of Paris, had been addressing
his flock and everyone else who would listen as he called upon men to
renounce vice in the name of the Holy Spirit. Finally in 1198, the Papal
Legate, Cardinal Peter Capuano, authorized him on behalf of the pope to
preach the Crusade. Master Fulk no longer attacked corruption in high
places; his audiences were now told of the benefits that accrued to the
faithful when they left everything they possessed and journeyed to the Holy
Land. He died at Neuilly in May 1202, worn out by his travels, but he was
long remembered.

Master Fulk's passion for the Crusade sprang out of his knowledge of
vice and corruption in Paris and the provinces. He saw the Crusade as an
instrument for cleansing people of their sins and setting them on the road
to Paradise. Thibault, Count of Champagne, had entirely different interests. The Crusade, for him, was part of his heritage, a devotional adventure
and an aristocratic privilege. There were not many people who could claim
such a close association with Jerusalem. We have no evidence that he ever
met Master Fulk or listened to his sermons, and it is unlikely that the young
nobleman would have anything in common with the unruly parish priest.
As conceived at the castle of Ecry, the new Crusade was to be led by the
count of Champagne and his noble friends.

There existed at one time a complete honor roll of the men who played
prominent parts in the Crusade. Both Geoffrey of Villehardouin and
Robert of Clari, the two principal chroniclers of the Crusade, recite the
names in very nearly the same order according to the provinces they come
from. About a hundred names are mentioned. The most important addition to the list of Crusaders was made on February 23, 1200, when Count
Baldwin of Flanders and Hainault formally took the Cross at Bruges. He
had married Mary, the sister of Thibault. His family had a long connection

with the Crusades. His mother's brother, Philip, Count of Alsace, had died at Acre in 1191. Other relatives, near and distant, had also taken the Cross. Thibault, Louis, and Baldwin, all closely related by marriage, assumed the responsibility for leading the Crusade.

It appears that they were in no hurry. Every two months or so, they held meetings with bishops and the baronage to discuss the practical problems of launching the Crusade: the day when they would assemble the army, the route they would take, the raising of funds, questions of shipping and administration, and the strategies to be employed. They sought out the nobles who had taken part in previous Crusades. There were meetings at Soissons and Compiègne, but there was little action until the end of the year when the three leaders decided to send six envoys to Venice to discuss the cost of transporting the troops by sea. Each of the three leaders chose two envoys. Villehardouin was one of the men chosen by Thibault; in his chronicle he makes it quite clear that among the envoys he was first among equals. He did most of the talking and was therefore largely responsible for what happened later. The envoys were given letters of credence signed and sealed by the leaders. According to the letters the doge of Venice was asked to treat the envoys as plenipotentiaries empowered to make arrangements which would be binding on Thibault and his two cousins.

The doge at this time was Enrico Dandolo, descended from one of the most illustrious Venetian families. He had lost the full use of his eyes in an accident in Constantinople and thereafter came to hate the city.

The six envoys were politely welcomed in the Doge's Palace. After briefly explaining their purpose, they were told to wait for four days until the doge could assemble "the Council of Six," who would listen to their request at greater length. This delay enabled Dandolo to make enquiries about the envoys through his extensive intelligence service, and to study their behavior in Venice.

On the fourth day the envoys were received by the council. "They had come," they said, "on behalf of the high barons of France who had taken the sign of the Cross to avenge the shame of Jesus Christ and to reconquer Jerusalem, if God wills it." The reference to the battle cry of the First Crusade was clear and precise. They asked the doge to act with diligence and to come up with a figure within their means; they were told to come back in eight days.

The doge had twelve days in all to study the envoys and their request. They wanted transport for forty-five hundred horses, nine thousand squires, forty-five hundred knights and twenty thousand foot soldiers, together with fodder and provisions for nine months. He named his price: four marks for a horse and two marks for a man. The total sum, therefore, was eighty-five thousand marks. In addition, the doge promised to provide fifty armed galleys, on condition that Venice would share equally with the Crusaders whatever territory or treasure they succeeded in capturing. The envoys spent the night discussing the proposal, and in the morning they agreed to the harsh terms.

After a high mass at St. Mark's, attended by thousands of Venetians, the doge invited Villehardouin to speak. He said they had been commanded, as envoys of the baron, to fall on their knees in supplication to the people of Venice. Whereupon the six envoys knelt before the high altar, tears streaming down their faces, their hands lifted in the traditional attitude of suppliants. This was playacting of a not very subtle kind, rehearsed and choreographed, in a brilliant setting, in the light of candles and the gleaming mosaics on the walls. The doge advanced toward them, lifting them up one by one, like a king bestowing mercy, and according to Villehardouin he was weeping with tears of joy. Soon all the people in the church were weeping excitedly, waving their arms, and shouting, "We consent! We consent!" "There was such a great tumult and uproar that it was as though the earth was being torn asunder," Villehardouin wrote many years later.

We have no reason to believe that he exaggerated the importance of the occasion. He, together with the blind doge, was responsible for the solemn covenant that was signed on the following day. On that day, too, it was announced to the grand council that the Crusade would sail for Cairo, because Cairo offered the best opportunity for destroying Turks, but the general public was not to be informed that the Crusade was bound for Egypt: the public would be told only that the Crusaders would be going overseas. The Venetians had very good reasons for not publicizing the fact that the fleet was bound for Cairo.

They drove a hard bargain: the entire sum of eighty-five thousand marks was to be paid in installments, the last payment of fifty thousand marks to be paid at the end of April, 1202, a year after the covenant was signed. The first payment of fifteen thousand marks was due on August 1, 1201, the second of ten thousand marks on November 1, and the third of ten thousand on February 20, 1202, the Day of the Purification of the Virgin. It was agreed that the Crusaders should set sail on the Day of St. Peter and St. Paul, June 29, 1202, more than a year away, unless the date would be changed by common consent.

There was more weeping when the doge presented the covenant to the councillors. The doge wept; the envoys wept; someone brought holy relics into the council chamber and everyone swore, in the presence of the relics, to observe the terms of the covenant. Messengers were sent to Rome with a copy of the covenant for the pope's approval.

When Villehardouin returned to France to give the good news to Thibault, Count of Champagne, he was horrified to discover that the count could not possibly lead the Crusade. He was dying. Still, Thibault was so overjoyed that arrangements had been made for the Crusade that he rose from his deathbed and mounted a horse. It was the last time he ever rode on horseback. He died a few days later, leaving in his will a sum of money to be spent as the leaders of the Crusade saw fit and another sum to be divided among friends who had promised to join the Crusade. Villehardouin observed bitterly that a surprisingly large number accepted the money but did not join the Crusade.

With the death of Thibault, Villehardouin sought another great lord to replace him. He went with a small delegation to Odo, Duke of Burgundy, urging him to accept command of the Crusade. The duke refused. Geoffrey of Joinville was sent as an envoy to Thibault, Count of Bar-le-Duc, who also refused. A parliament was held at Soissons to discuss whom they should approach. Villehardouin, who had taken upon himself so many burdens on behalf of the Crusade, suggested that Boniface, Marquis of Montferrat, would be an excellent candidate. He had met the marquis somewhere in Italy while he was journeying from Venice to Troyes and he seems to have known already that the marquis would enjoy leading the Crusade. "If you should ask him to come here," he declared before the parliament, "and if he should take the sign of the cross and assume the place of the Count of Champagne, and if you should offer him command of the army, he would take it soon enough."

What was needed, in Villehardouin's eyes, was a man of commanding presence, experienced in arms, belonging to a high order of nobility, perhaps having a connection with the royal House of Jerusalem. The marquis seemed to fulfill all these requirements. His eldest brother, William Long-Sword, had married Sibylla, the daughter of King Amaury of Jerusalem, and fathered King Baldwin V. Another brother, Renier, had married Maria, the daughter of the Emperor Manuel Comnenus, who had given him the deeds to the Little Kingdom of Thessalonica. Renier had died of poisoning in Constantinople. A third brother, Conrad, had preceded Henry, Count of Champagne, as the husband of Queen Isabelle of Jerusalem. All Boniface's brothers were now dead, and he was the inheritor of the marquisate. He had close ties with both Constantinople and the Holy Land.

But where his brothers were strong, Boniface was weak: he was one who would inevitably choose his own advantage above the public good. He was about fifty, given to easy living, gracious toward women and to poets, whom he cultivated at his court, and without any more military experience than could be obtained by skirmishes in Sicily or by stamping out the communes of Lombardy. Villehardouin was attracted to the splendor of his name and person; he could scarcely have chosen a man less capable of leading the Crusade.

In August 1201, Boniface attended the parliament at Soissons to be invested with the command of the Crusade. Some of the ceremonies took place in the orchard belonging to the abbey of Our Lady of Soissons. Boniface promised faithfully to accept the heavy burden now laid on him, and the bishop of Soissons, who had also taken the Cross, then attached the little square of cloth, with the cross sewn on it, to his shoulder. Boniface turned to the assembled counts and barons and asked them where they intended that he should lead the Crusade. They answered that it would be directed against Alexandria or Cairo because these places were "in the very midst of things and where most could be done." Boniface agreed. He appears not to have heard of the solemn covenant made with the doge for conveying the Crusaders to the East, for he immediately spoke about sending envoys to Genoa, Pisa, and Venice to see where suitable ships could be found. Half the fifty thousand livres left by the count of Champagne toward payment for the Crusade was now given to Boniface to do with as he saw fit.

By this time the Crusade had acquired its own momentum, its own purpose, and its own ambiguities. Its leader was ignorant and almost insanely proud, without faith, without scruples, without remorse. He would lead the Crusaders where he wanted to lead them.

Like many totally unscrupulous people, Boniface could be played upon by those who were equally unscrupulous; the doge of Venice learned, without too much sorrow, that all the wealth of the Crusaders did not amount to the sum needed for renting and provisioning the ships. By the terms of the shipping agreement the Crusaders were lacking thirty-four thousand silver marks. Instead of paying this sum, the Crusaders were required to help capture the city of Zara, which had rebelled against Venice and now belonged to the Kingdom of Hungary. Zara was a large and important seaport, two hundred miles southeast of Venice on the Adriatic coast, which had previously served as a supply base for the Venetian fleet. Since Zara was rich, the contents of its treasury would serve to balance the Crusaders' budget, and there would be a good deal left over for the Venetians.

The pope heard of the secret agreement and protested vigorously. It was an unconscionable offense against morality for a Christian city to be attacked by a Crusader fleet. His protests went unheard. The doge, and the Venetians with him, had often angered the pope without suffering any dire consequences. In a state of great excitement, before a high mass in the Church of St. Mark, the doge himself ostentatiously took the Cross, and proclaimed himself the leader of the expedition. At that moment power— real power—had slipped from the Crusaders. The blind doge commanded. The Crusade, which had begun with the young and idealistic count of Champagne, was now falling into the hands of the doge, a man of extraordinary willpower and immense ability, who surpassed the marquis of Montferrat in the arts of war and conspiracy. He was the war leader, but he had not the least intention of attacking Cairo or of aiding the shattered Kingdom of Jerusalem or of rescuing the Holy Sepulchre. His single aim was to establish an empire under the Republic of Venice, which would permit the Venetians to become "Lords and Masters of a Quarter and a

Half-quarter of the Roman Empire." In all this he succeeded brilliantly, and in doing it, he destroyed the Crusade.

The doge had a flair for the drama of conquest. For the Crusaders he became a legend, a mysterious and powerful force capable of commanding the destiny of kingdoms and empires.

About this time another mysterious and powerful force stepped on the stage briefly. The young Prince Alexius Angelus was the son of the Byzantine Emperor Isaac II. The brother of the emperor, also called Alexius, had been ransomed from Turkish captivity, and on his arrival in Constantinople he promptly seized the emperor, blinded him, and threw him into prison. One Alexius became emperor and the other, a fugitive, made his way to Italy and then to Germany, to the court of Philip of Swabia, who had married his sister. Then he settled in Verona, proclaiming himself the rightful emperor. He sent messages to the marquis of Montferrat and to other Crusading princes at Venice, urging them to help him regain his father's throne, promising great rewards from the treasury of Byzantium.

Prince Alexius Angelus thus provided with superb timing the provocation the doge and the marquis had been looking for. The young prince soon offered a prospectus of the coming rewards. He would offer the Crusaders the money they needed to pay the Venetians, he would assume the entire cost of the conquest of Egypt, and he would provide an army of ten thousand Byzantine soldiers and pay for the maintenance of five hundred knights. Finally, he offered to ensure that the Orthodox Church would submit to Rome. This last offer, if it had been carried out, would have plunged Constantinople into civil war. These breathtaking offers came from a mind at least as conspiratorial as the minds of the doge and the marquis. They were calculated to please the pope and the entire Crusading host. The pope, who had met the young prince and found him to be a braggart and a nincompoop, was not averse to receiving the submission of the Orthodox Church. But he was averse to bloodshed, and wrote that it was intolerable that Christians should kill Christians except under exceptional circumstances. In the eyes of the doge and the marquis, now firmly committed to the destruction of Zara and the sack of Constantinople, the "exceptional circumstances" already existed.

The Christian army, now fretting under close guard on the island of Lido, knew nothing about this. They were being manipulated by the doge, the marquis and a Byzantine prince. Most of the knights and foot soldiers believed they would be sailing to Egypt or the Holy Land. Because there were signs that the Crusade was about to begin, the soldiers on the island of Lido tied torches to their lances and paraded around their camp.

But there were more delays. The doge was in a conquering mood, and he decided that the time had come to demand the submission of Trieste and Moglie. Accordingly, part of the Venetian fleet set sail for these cities; they were invested and, finally, they surrendered. Only when they returned could the combined fleet attack Zara. Robert of Clari, standing on the poop of one of the great galleys, was overwhelmed by the sight of the great fleet sailing down the Adriatic, led by the galley of the doge, painted in bright vermilion with a canopy of vermilion silk spread over his throne, the drummers beating on their drums and four trumpeters sounding the notes that could be employed only in the doge's honor. The noise was deafening, for there were a hundred more trumpeters on the other vessels. When the trumpets died down, the priests and clerks sang *Veni creator spiritus*, weeping with joy at the prospect of sailing to the Holy Land. Even at this late stage there were very few who were in on the secret.

Long before the fleet dropped anchor in the harbor, the people of Zara had been warned of the coming invasion. They had taken precautions. The walled city had crosses set up along the whole length of the walls, to remind the invaders that the city belonged to Christians. In addition, they acquired from the pope a formal statement that anyone who made war on them would be excommunicated. With its strong walls and its navy, Zara could, in the ordinary course of events, keep invaders at bay, but the Crusader fleet led by the doge represented force on a massive, unprecedented scale. The Zarians saw they would have to capitulate. The doge had set up a pavilion outside the walls, and here came ambassadors from the city, offering to surrender on condition that their lives be spared. The doge was not content with their answer. The people must be punished for having deserted the Venetian cause; a suitable number of people must be massacred, a vast indemnity must be paid, Zara must never again be in a position where it could defy the power of Venice.

The chiefs of the Crusading army were of two minds: those who had no trouble with their conscience were all for attacking Zara; those with a more tender conscience asked themselves how they could avoid taking part in the conflict. What the Crusading soldiers thought of making war against a city whose battlements were crowned with crosses may only be guessed at, but they cannot have been pleased to discover that they had been lured into an adventure over which they had no control whatsoever.

The attack on the city was organized by the Venetians, who brought up wooden towers and mangonels for hurling huge stones at the city walls. Sappers mined the walls. From the masts of ships in the harbor, ladders reached out to the top of the walls. For five days the Venetians battered the city into submission; the city fathers, realizing that further resistance was impossible, surrendered. Their property and valuables now belonged to the conquerors, who formally entered the city and took possession of it. The Venetians kept the lion's share: the port, the warehouses, the shipyards, and the ships. To the Crusaders was granted the rest of the town, and they lodged in the houses of the citizens, who were reduced to slaves. Three days later, toward evening, the Crusaders, feeling that they might be the next victims, because they were hemmed in by the Venetians, rose in rebellion, and attacked the Venetians wherever they could find them. There was scarcely a street in Zara where there was not fierce fighting with swords, lances, crossbows, and javelins. The fighting lasted all night. By morning the doge and the Crusader knights had established a kind of peace, but there was sporadic fighting for another week. The expedition was in danger of wasting all its energies in civil war within a conquered city. "This was the greatest misfortune to overtake the army," wrote Villehardouin, "and it very nearly resulted in the total loss of the army. But God would not suffer it."

By harsh measures the rebellion was stamped out, the doge reestablished his position as commander, and two weeks later Boniface, Marquis of Montferrat, arrived to conduct discussions with the doge. A few days later, Philip of Swabia, brother-in-law of Alexius, sent a message to Boniface with the terms of a treaty to be agreed upon by Alexius and the leaders of the expeditionary force. The treaty was not signed immediately, and was kept secret until the last possible moment. The Crusading soldiers had no way of knowing what was happening, but they were restless and querulous in their winter quarters, while supplies ran low and there were limits to the exploitation of the Zarians.

Villehardouin, who consistently took the side of the doge, says there were forces at work to disband the Crusading army. Five hundred soldiers escaped from Zara by ship, and Villehardouin notes with satisfaction that the ship capsized and they were all drowned. Others escaped into the hinterland, and again Villehardouin notes with satisfaction that the peasants massacred them. In order to escape from Zara, some knights begged to be allowed to go to Syria on an embassy in one of the vessels belonging to the fleet; they never returned. Villehardouin was incensed by their ingratitude. The army was rapidly dwindling, for the good reason that the soldiers did not trust their commanders, and because the papal ban of excommunication was taken very seriously indeed. Accordingly, four ambassadors, two knights and two clerks, were sent to Rome to urge the pope to grant absolution to the conquerors of Zara. In a moment of weakness the pope granted it.

The long winter was followed by a short spring. Alexius arrived at Zara on April 25 and was received with the honors due an emperor. He seems to have been a youth of about fourteen, handsome, modest, easily manipulated. With his coming, there was no longer any doubt that the doge was determined to sack Constantinople as he had sacked Zara, using the young claimant to the Byzantine throne merely as a tool. The huge fleet, led by the doge's vermilion galley, sailed out of Zara with a fair wind, while the pipers and the trumpeters filled the air with their tumultuous music. They put in at Durazzo for provisions, and here, according to Villehardouin, Alexius received the acclamation of the people as the true emperor of Byzantium. Then they put in at Corfu, where the army rested in tents and the horses were removed from the transports and put out to pasture. They were on their way to commit one of the greatest crimes in history.

The Burning City

THE sack of Constantinople can be explained only by sheer lust for conquest, at whatever the cost in lives and treasure. It was accomplished by treachery in the modern manner, in cold blood, without any regard for the consequences, which inevitably included the weakening of the Byzantine empire, an empire that had for so long been a bastion against the Turks. The pope had promulgated that the Christians should not fight Christians except when one party was hindering the success of the Crusades. The Byzantines were not hindering the success of the Crusades; they were, and had been for a long time, helpful to the Crusaders. The excuse that they were about to attack Constantinople in order to put young Alexius on the throne was a fiction concocted by the doge, the marquis of Montferrat, and Philip of Swabia. They did not even have an interest in recovering the Holy Land; they wanted loot.

During the First Crusade, the Crusaders had found themselves at odds with the Emperor Alexius Comnenus, who had not permitted them to sack the imperial city. When they attacked the walls of Constantinople, he fought them to a standstill. When, with the help of the Byzantine army, Nicaea was captured, the emperor had again refused them permission to sack the city, the second most important in his empire. He demanded from them an oath of loyalty, which they gave him reluctantly with the secret reservation that they would break it whenever they pleased. The relations between Byzantium and the Crusaders were always strained, and this was due largely to the fact that in the eyes of the Crusaders, the civilization of Byzantium was a dying one ready for plunder. They did not know that great civilizations can die many times and be reborn many times. Before the Arabs poured out of Arabia, the Byzantine empire stretched all over Asia Minor, Syria, Palestine and Egypt. Byzantium was still an imperial power, and would endure for many more years. Even after the sack of Constantinople, even after Frankish kings ruled from the jewel-studded imperial throne, there remained in the eyes of the Byzantine people the firm promise of a *restoratio*, a new birth, a revival of the Byzantine spirit.

Except for the Venetians, those who were determined to sack Constantinople were in a minority. At Corfu, where the battle plans for the attack on the city were finally worked out, the commanders of the Crusaders found themselves with a revolt on their hands. Many of the knights protested the Venetian plans, and they were not alone. The foot soldiers set up the cry, "Go to Acre!"—"*Ire Accaron!*" There was a plot to ferry troops from Corfu to Brindisi, which was in the possession of Count Walter of Brienne. Count Walter would see that they reached the Holy Land safely. "More than half the army," Villehardouin admits, "was of this mind." They had suffered atrociously at Zara, and they had been under heavy guard on the island of Lido, and the Venetians had amused themselves by charging extravagant sums for bread and provisions. Now, at last, they had seen through the Venetian pretensions.

In a formal act of rebellion the Crusaders struck their tents and marched inland into another valley at some distance from the city, to separate themselves from the doge and his army; they hoped that ships from Brindisi would rescue them from their plight.

Boniface, Marquis of Montferrat, decided upon desperate measures. He would abase himself before the Crusaders, he would promise everything they demanded, and at the same time he would cajole a rebellious army with promises and half-promises he had no intention of keeping. He was the supreme commander of the Crusaders, and his staff included Baldwin, Count of Flanders, Louis, Count of Blois and Chartres, and the count of Saint-Pol. With them, and with a retinue of bishops and abbots, and with the young Alexius, he rode to the valley where the Crusaders were in camp and presented himself to them while they were holding a mass meeting. At some distance from the camp he dismounted, and all the others dismounted, to show that they had come on a peaceful errand.

Walking up to the Crusaders he threw himself abjectly down on the ground. All those who accompanied him did the same. There were about twenty people on their knees. It was a *coup de théâtre*, a spectacle so incredible that the Crusaders were surprised out of their wits. Boniface announced that he would remain on his knees until they had listened to him, that he had many things to say to them, and the most urgent of all was that the army must remain intact and follow the Venetians to Constantinople; all the rest was negotiable. He was a master of oratory. He implored, begged, pleaded. The young emperor was presented to them. It was right and proper that the Christian army should restore him to his throne; it was their Christian duty, and once they had performed this duty, then of course, with his permission and blessing, the Crusaders would sail to the Holy Land.

At first the Crusaders could scarcely believe their ears. Their leaders drew a little apart, out of earshot of the strangers who had come to visit them so dramatically with such finely wrought supplications. They asked themselves whether they could believe what they had been told. How could they trust this man who had lied to them so successfully in the past? His chief argument, as Robert of Clari remembered it, was purely pragmatic. "What shall we do in Babylon or Alexandria," he asked, "when we have neither provisions nor money to enable us to go there? Better for us before we go there to secure provisions and money by some good excuse than to go there and die of hunger. Moreover the emperor offers to come with us and maintain our navy and our fleet a year longer at his own cost." This meant of course that, once Alexius was established on the throne, his treasury would be placed at the service of the Crusaders. The diversion would be only temporary; the entire population of Constantinople would be eager to welcome their rightful emperor, there would be little or no fighting, and the troops would soon be released for more important duties in the Holy Land.

When the deputation of Crusaders returned to confront Boniface, their minds were made up. They agreed to go to Constantinople, but only on condition that they be released from their engagement after a fixed period. It was now about April 19. They demanded that by Michaelmas, which was September 29, they would be free to demand and to receive, within fifteen days, ships and provisions that would enable them to reach Syria. They demanded, too, that a solemn agreement be drawn up, and signed in the presence of holy relics, to the effect that Boniface would give them what they asked for "in good faith and without trickery" and "at whatever hour he might be summoned to do so." Boniface, Alexius, the counts of Flanders, Blois and Saint-Pol all signed the document.

Boniface, by abasing himself and by signing a document he had no intention of carrying out, had won the biggest gamble of his life. By his presence, and by the presence of the young Emperor Alexius, he quelled the rebellion of the Crusader army and in this way prepared the army for the conquest of the Byzantine empire and the vast territories he would later claim as his own.

Yet the marquis's real motive was not so much desire for conquest as for personal revenge. His brother Conrad had been in Constantinople in 1187. He had fought valiantly for the emperor, quelling a rebellion and personally killing the rebel leader. But Boniface believed that Conrad had been dealt with most treacherously by the emperor.

The ships in the huge armada that sailed from Corfu to the Dardanelles came like conquerors and wore the dress of conquerors. But the vast, honey-colored walls of Constantinople were also impressive, cogent physical evidence of the city's power and splendor. Villehardouin was not exaggerating when he wrote:

You should know that people who had never before set eyes on Constantinople were astounded, for never had they imagined that so rich a city could exist in the world, and as they gazed at the high walls and noble towers that ringed it around, and the splendid palaces and the towering churches—there were so many of them that no one could possibly believe it until they saw it with their own eyes—they were amazed by it, and especially by the height and breadth of the city, which was sovereign above all other cities. You should know, too, that there was not a single man among us whose flesh did not tremble at the sight of it; and it was no wonder, for never was so great an enterprise undertaken by any people since the creation of the world.

This was a bold claim, but Villehardouin had his own reasons for believing that the fleet was engaged in the greatest of all enterprises. He was himself high in the counsels of the leaders of the expedition; he was an arch-conspirator; he rejoiced in the prospect of sacking the greatest city in the world. He had much to gain from the enterprise.

The ordinary soldiers and sailors were not yet sure they would gain anything. They were suffering hardships, for food was running out again. Even the doge was beginning to behave with extreme caution. On June 23, his ship anchored in the Sea of Marmora opposite the Abbey of St. Stephanos, about twelve miles southwest of Constantinople. The doge and most of the leaders of the expedition were rowed ashore and a solemn council was held in the abbey church. There was a long debate, many arguments were heard, and at last the doge rose and laid down the strategy to be followed. It was a characteristically Venetian strategy, which depended upon sea power. Armies were not to be landed in the countryside for an attack on the land walls, because they would soon be dispersed and the enemy had the advantage of numbers. Also, the soldiers would immediately go foraging, and all foraging was useless effort when there was food available in the Sea of Marmora itself. There were islands that could be attacked; all their corn, all their grain, and all their provisions could be expropriated. The fleet had mastery of the straits and the islands were at the mercy of the ships.

Their present aim was to gather all the food on the Princes' Islands, but when a southerly wind sprang up, making a journey to the islands dangerous, the fleet found itself coasting pleasantly off Constantinople very close to the seawalls, so close indeed that they were able to shoot at the guards manning the walls and the towers. The wind carried the fleet to Chalcedon on the Asiatic shore. Here they found one of the many palaces of the emperor, "one of the most beautiful and delectable ever seen," and the leaders of the expedition came ashore and took up lodgings in the palace, while the soldiers lived in a tent city that sprang up outside the palace walls. The horses were brought to land, and only the sailors remained on the ships.

They had discovered that it was unnecessary to go to the islands. The Asiatic shore was undefended, for the emperor had pulled back all his forces to protect Constantinople. After resting at Chalcedon for two days, the Venetians and the Crusaders returned to their ships. They were well fed, the corn had just been reaped and was standing in sheaves in the fields around Chalcedon, and the soldiers had been busy carrying the corn to the waiting ships. Then the fleet continued up the straits to anchor off another imperial palace at Scutari. The horses taken off the transports at Chalcedon rode along the shore to Scutari. The massed might of the Crusader army stood at Scutari, ready to pounce on Constantinople.

The emperor had already sent envoys to demand the intentions of the invaders, although by this time he was well aware of their intentions, but he had some hope of reaching an accommodation. If they wanted gold or silver, he was prepared to give it to them. He was told bluntly that they wanted his empire, that he was a usurper and young Alexius was the rightful heir to the Byzantine throne. His envoys returned to Constantinople with the knowledge that it was impossible to argue with the Crusaders, and the city would have to be defended by force.

The doge, who had a keen sense of the uses of propaganda, thought up a ruse intended to mortify his enemies. Ten of the most splendid Venetian galleys would approach Constantinople under a flag of truce; in one of these galleys, sitting on a throne, would be the young Alexius arrayed in imperial robes. The people would be asked whether they recognized their emperor. The doge felt sure there would be some malcontents in the city ready to swear allegiance to a new emperor.

The ruse proved to be spectacularly unsuccessful. The Venetian fleet passed in procession under the walls of Constantinople, and to the cry, "Do you recognize the young Alexius as your lord?" the people shouted back, "We don't recognize him and we don't know who he is." The verdict of Constantinople was unanimous, and the Crusaders learned that there was no nest of spies fighting for them in the city. The outcome of the battle was now in doubt, for the people of Constantinople seemed well able to defend themselves.

For nine days, the Venetians and the Crusaders remained at Scutari. A good deal of time was spent in gathering supplies from the hinterland and in debates on the best method of attack. The knights assembled on horseback in a field and held a parliament, but in fact all the major decisions were made by the doge or by Boniface. The Crusader army was divided into seven main groups, with Baldwin of Flanders at the head of the vanguard and Boniface in command of the rear guard. To Boniface went the Tuscans, the Lombards, the Germans, and the soldiers from southern France. The doge commanded that the Crusaders should attack by land and the

Venetians should attack by sea. The land and sea operations were to be carefully orchestrated.

At dawn, under a clear sky, the Crusaders were ferried across the straits from Scutari to Galata at the mouth of the Golden Horn. During the night, all the soldiers confessed and received communion; the army was blessed; and the knights with their horses entered the transports, which were shaped like modern landing craft, with a door opening to permit horse and rider to ride off the ship onto the land. Two hundred trumpeters sounded the advance and there was a dreadful noise of drums. There was a small detachment of imperial troops at Galata, but they were soon overwhelmed. A Venetian ship called the *Aquila* succeeded in breaking the chain across the mouth of the Golden Horn—a chain so heavy and so well made that it was believed to be impregnable. One end of the chain was attached to the walls of Constantinople and the other to a fortresslike tower at Galata. A flotilla of Greek ships was anchored in front of the chain. The tower and the Greek ships were captured, and the Crusader army moved up the shore of the Golden Horn until they reached the famous bridge, which the Greeks defended as well as they could, at last retreating behind the city walls. After crossing the bridge, the Crusaders set up their tents outside the city walls facing the Blachernae Palace. They were following the scenario laid down during the First Crusade when an exactly similar maneuver had been attempted. During the First Crusade, the attempt had failed. This time, it was successful.

The doge or his naval staff had conceived new and extraordinarily powerful weapons. These were flying bridges attached to the high masts of the galleys, which could be made by a system of tackles and counterbalance weights to reach up to the parapets of the high walls. These flying bridges were sturdily built: three men abreast could walk across them in full armor. Hugh of Saint-Pol says the bridges were a hundred feet long, which may be true if we consider that they resembled a T with the mast forming the centerpiece. We are told that these bridges were protected against Greek fire with hides, which also protected them from arrows. Some of these bridges seem to have been built to form tunnels, so that a man could clamber along them and feel safe until he set foot on the parapet of the walls of Constantinople.

The emperor of Constantinople had not lost hope. He believed he could defend the city. The Varangian Guard, which consisted mostly of Danes and Englishmen who were fanatically loyal to the emperor's person, could be relied upon. The Pechenegs, recruited from southern Russia, were unlikely to go over to the enemy. The emperor's main strength lay with the Greek army within the walls, which gave a good account of itself. Constantinople had become a fortress from which the Greeks, the Pechenegs, and the imperial guard could make sorties from the well-defended gates. There were many sorties, most of them from the Romanus Gate and from other gates near the Blachernae Palace. The Crusaders were forced to construct a palisade around their camp. "The Greeks," wrote Villehardouin "never ceased to attack from one gate or another with the result that the whole army was called to arms six or seven times a day." The Crusaders found the continual attacks punishing. In addition, they were running out of provisions. They lived on flour, and salted pork, and their dead horses. The Crusaders lost many of their best knights but captured Constantine Lascaris, who was one of the best Byzantine generals. And so the fighting continued for ten days, the Crusader army failing to penetrate the walls of Constantinople.

But all this amounted to no more than a test of strength, with the Greeks demonstrating that they were perfectly capable of defending their city if the battles were fought in the customary way, with crossbows, swords, and lances. Now, quite suddenly, the Venetians, who had been making little use of their fleet while the fighting was going on near the Blachernae Palace, captured some of the towers and sent scouting parties into the city, by means of the flying bridges. None of these scouting parties seems to have progressed very far into the city, but it was not necessary to do so in order to employ their secret weapon. They set fire to a large area of the city. And the fire accomplished what all the weaponry of the Crusaders had failed to do: it conquered the city.

Villehardouin gives a clear description of what happened. The fires were lit deliberately by the Venetians, who saw they were hopelessly outnumbered by an advancing Byzantine army. "When the emperor saw that the Venetians were in the city," he wrote, "he sent his people against them in such numbers that we would be unable to endure their onslaught. So they set fire to the buildings between them and the Greeks, and the wind blowing from our side, the flames rose so high that the Greeks were unable to see our people, who fled to the towers they had seized and conquered." The flames that saved a small army of Venetians who had climbed over the walls destroyed about a quarter of the city. The two great palaces remained untouched, but the flames reached the Church of Sancta Sophia, where the porch with the mosaics of the patriarchs was destroyed, and then they leaped along the Hippodrome and down to the seawalls. All through the night the high winds fanned the flames.

Seeing the city in flames, the people lost heart, and the emperor, who had fought well and sometimes brilliantly, lost courage. During the night of July 17, he gathered up the imperial diadems and all the other treasure belonging to the court, including a thousand pounds of gold, and slipped out of the city. He rode to a place called Develtos on the shores of the Black Sea. He made no secret of his plans; he told everyone that he hoped in due course to raise an army and reconquer Constantinople. If he lost courage, it was because everyone else in Constantinople had lost courage. They were in a state of shock, traumatized, incapable of any further fighting, seeing the city burning to the ground.

The Devastastion of Constantinople

WHEN morning came, one emperor had fled, and another, the blinded Isaac II, sat on his throne in the Blachernae Palace with his empress beside him. Surrounded by court officials and ladies-in-waiting, they were conducting business as though nothing had happened. Villehardouin, who was sent as an envoy from the Crusader camp, observed that the emperor wore his most sumptuous robes, and the empress, the sister of the king of Hungary, was one of the most beautiful women he had ever seen. On the previous day the courtiers had bowed and genuflected before another emperor. This day they gave no indication that they were living in a conquered city that was still burning.

Villehardouin reminded the emperor, who had been released from prison during the night, that he wore his sumptuous robes at the pleasure of the Crusaders, who were the real rulers. He made his demands. First, Isaac must give surety for the covenants signed by his son, the young Alexius. The emperor was surprised: he had never heard of these covenants. Villehardouin issued an ultimatum. The emperor must accept the supremacy of the pope. He must give 200,000 marks to the Venetians and the Franks, together with enough provisions to support them for a year; in addition he must send ten thousand troops on his own ships and at his own expense to assist in the projected invasion of Egypt. Finally, during his lifetime, he must maintain five hundred knights in the territories about to be conquered.

Isaac pointed out that the demands being made on him were very onerous, and he did not see how they could be implemented. Nevertheless, since his son had signed the covenant, he could not refuse. Some time later in the day the blinded emperor and the son quarreled, the son saying that it was absurd that the empire be ruled by a blind man; he, Alexius, should be crowned emperor. Isaac lost the argument and abdicated in favor of his son.

On August 1, 1203, Alexius was crowned Emperor. Isaac continued to

hold court, blind and half-mad, devoting himself to prayers and prophecies, dreaming that power would one day be restored to him and that his
son would turn away from Frankish vices. Meanwhile, Alexius, believing
all the promises whispered into his ears by the doge and the marquis of
Montferrat, suffered from the illusion that he was a real emperor. In fact he
was merely a pawn who would be swept off the chessboard when the doge
and the marquis had no further use for him.

According to the covenant, the reigning emperor of Byzantium must
offer submission to the Pope of Rome. Alexius did so, and in due course
received a commendatory letter from the pope, who showed his gratifica-
tion by absolving Alexius of all the sins he had committed in the past, and
by exhorting him to make sure that the entire Orthodox Church follow his
example. The supremacy of the papacy was of importance to the pope, but
of very little importance to the Greeks, who continued to worship in the
old way.

For a short while, the conquered city of Constantinople enjoyed a
precarious peace. Under Alexius, an army went out in search of the other
Alexius who had taken refuge at Develtos where the Crusaders joined the
young emperor, demanding, as might be expected, an exorbitant fee for
their services. The emperor was forced to pay them whatever they asked for,
but there came a time when it became necessary to stop payment.

One of those who was prepared to defy the invaders was a certain Alexius
Ducas nicknamed "Murzuphlus," because of the heavy eyebrows growing
across the bridge of his nose. He belonged to an aristocratic family which
had given two emperors to Byzantium. Until recently he had been in
prison; the young emperor ordered his release and made him chief steward.
Murzuphlus was totally uncompromising. He hated the Crusaders and the
Venetians. The young emperor, on the other hand, delighted in their
company, and was once seen wearing the cloth cap of a Crusader to whom
he had loaned the imperial tiara. He enjoyed gambling with the Crusaders
and enjoyed visiting them in the camp they had set up across the harbor in
the region called Estanor. But Murzuphlus had a winning and powerful
personality, and he prevailed upon the emperor to such an extent that the
doge grew alarmed and summoned the emperor into his presence. "Will
you pay?" the doge asked. The emperor replied that he had paid enough. It
was becoming clear that the fighting between Crusader and Greek wasn't
over.

This time, the Greeks possessed some advantages. It was winter now, not
the best time for employing flying bridges to scale the walls. The currents
of the Bosphorus were treacherous. The Crusader army was starving again.
Murzuphlus ordered the construction of fire ships: they were small boats
filled with fats, oils, and dry kindling, to be let loose against the Venetian
fleet when there was a favorable wind. If, as it happened, they did little
damage, the fire ships still threatened the entire existence of the fleet.

Meanwhile, the army was living on dry biscuits, and the cost of an egg had risen to two pennies. The conquerors were beginning to feel the strength of the conquered.

Since the young emperor had signed the covenant, placing Byzantium in debt to the invaders, Murzuphlus decided that the time had come to destroy the emperor. This was easily done. He simply went to the palace with an armed guard, strangled Alexius with a bowstring, and proclaimed himself emperor. Then he saw to it that a letter was shot from the city into the Crusader camp, announcing that he was the reigning emperor. A little later he sent another letter in the same way, announcing that as emperor of Byzantium he could no longer tolerate the presence of the invaders, who were ordered to vacate their camp within a week or face the consequences. The barons defied him, answering that they intended to punish him for murdering Alexius and that they would not rest until they had reconquered Constantinople and received the money the former emperor had promised them.

Murzuphlus, now the Emperor Alexius V Ducas, was a man of feverish energy and ferocious ambition. Realizing that the barons seriously intended to reconquer the city, he commanded that the towers and walls be strengthened. He was exceedingly brave, and when he heard that Count Henry of Flanders had gone off with a foraging party to the town of Philea, he led his troops out of Constantinople in an effort to head off the foraging party when it returned to the Crusader camp. He wore the imperial golden helmet and carried the icon of the Virgin, which the Greek emperors carried into battle. Count Henry of Flanders was a far more experienced soldier than Alexius V Ducas, who was outgeneraled and forced to flee the battlefield. In his flight he lost the golden helmet, the imperial standard, and the icon of the Virgin. Count Henry exulted in his victory, and arranged that the captured treasure should be shown to the people of Constantinople. A galleon moved up and down the straits with the helmet, the standard, and the icon roped to the masthead. For the new emperor the loss of the symbols associated with his command over the Byzantine empire was ominous to the highest degree.

The barons were already discussing the partition of the empire. They would elect an emperor who would possess a fourth part of the empire and a fourth part of the city as his own; the remaining three parts would be divided between the Venetians and the rest. They swore on relics that they would bring all the gold, silver, and precious cloths to a central pool, where everything would be divided according to this rule. They also swore on relics that they would despoil no women of their garments—anyone who did so would be condemned to death—and that they would not lay a hand on monks or priests, or break into churches and monasteries. Once they captured Constantinople, all these admirable oaths would be forgotten.

The siege, they knew, would be difficult. Alexius V Ducas, with a demoralized army, no navy, an empty treasury, and a burned city, was nevertheless a man to be reckoned with. He strengthened the land gates, and the wooden towers built above the stone towers were covered with hides. His people were well armed and determined; even the soldiers, demoralized by so many sudden changes of rulers, and the nobles, who detested him because he had murdered his way to the throne, recognized him as their commanding general. The emperor set up his vermilion tent on high ground that permitted him to see what was happening beyond the walls of the city. From this vantage point, he could give orders by means of trumpeters who were able to be heard all over the city.

The first serious attack took place on Friday, April 9, when the Venetians lined up their fleet and attempted, with their catwalks attached to the masts, to land men on the walls, while the Franks attempted to mine the walls. The Venetians failed to climb over the walls because they were too high, and the Greeks dropped heavy stones on the Frankish miners. According to Robert of Clari, Alexius V Ducas ordered his trumpeters to proclaim a triumph, and he said, "See, my lords, am I not a good emperor? Did you ever have so good an emperor? Have I not done well? We need fear them no longer. I will have them all hanged and dishonored!"

While Alexius V Ducas exulted, the Venetians and the Franks could scarcely believe their misfortune. They spent Sunday at prayers; they received communion and listened to sermons in which the priests celebrated the righteousness of their cause and the need for Constantinople to bow down to their just conquerors. On Monday, the attack was resumed, with the ships lined up in front of the seawalls along the Golden Horn.

There was no battle that day, just a long and difficult effort to take possession of one of the towers. Only four or five ships had masts tall enough for this purpose. Two of these ships, tied together, were the *Paradisus* and the *Peregrina*, belonging to the bishops of Soissons and Troyes. From one of them, a knight called Andrew of Dureboise succeeded in entering a tower, crawling on hands and knees; because he was in armor, the defenders of the tower were unable to kill him. While the defenders fled to a lower floor, he was able to lash the catwalk to the tower, and many more were able to join him. Another tower was captured soon afterward. But while the capture of the towers lifted the morale of the Venetians and the Franks, the real breakthrough came from the small groups who landed on the little strip of land between the wall and the sea. In peaceful times there were sea gates, which were now bricked up. The men who landed attempted to cut their way through these sea gates with picks. They surmised rightly that the brick fills were only a few feet deep, whereas the walls themselves were much thicker. They had found the weakest element in the complex system of defense. While they worked, the Greeks poured boiling pitch, Greek fire, and heavy stones on them. But the work continued. Axes and swords were used; so were knives. Anything that could tear through brick was brought into play. The fate of Constantinople depended on how quickly men could break down a sea gate.

Aleaumes of Clari, the brother of the chronicler Robert of Clari, was the first to see daylight on the other side. Robert, observing his brother's determination to enter Constantinople, hung on to his legs, but to no avail; Aleaumes insisted on climbing out of the hole and singlehandedly confronting the Greeks, who were so amazed at the sight of a man covered with brick dust that they did nothing but gape at him. He drew his sword and lunged at them, and they fled. Aleaumes called back; "Hurry, my lords! I see them drawing back afraid and beginning to run away!" Through the tunnel carved in brick came ten knights and sixty sergeants. The emperor's trumpets were giving orders to stop the invaders, and the emperor himself, a stone's throw away, spurred his horse and rode at them. But then he thought better of it and turned back in the direction of his vermilion tents, where his guards were waiting to defend him. It was his worst mistake.

While all this was going on, there was fighting on the walls. Peter of Amiens, in command of the group that broke through the bricked-up wall, saw another sea gate nearby and sent some of his men to attack it. When this gate was opened, transports were brought up, and knights in armor rode off the gangplank and entered the city, as though they were on holiday. Soon there were hundreds of knights inside the walls, but there was no enemy in sight. Alexius V Ducas had fled, leaving behind his vermilion tents and his coffers full of treasure, which Peter of Amiens claimed by right of conquest.

The emperor had taken refuge in the Bucoleon Palace. Early the next morning, he slipped out of the Golden Gate, hoping to make his way to Thrace and to mount an attack on Constantinople another day. Meanwhile the Venetians and the Franks who had entered the city remained in the region of the monastery of the Pantepoptos—the monastery of the All-Seeing Christ—with their weapons at the ready, for they expected the Greeks to attack during the night or at first light.

When morning came, there was only a great silence. At last some priests came, and some soldiers of the Varangian Guard. They brought strange news. The emperor and his army and most of the rich people had fled, leaving only the poor people behind. Constantinople was open to them. They could do as they pleased with it: they could destroy it or plunder it or use it for whatever purposes they saw fit. The news stunned the invaders, who had expected hard fighting.

The great nobles chose the greatest houses for themselves. The marquis of Montferrat chose the vast Bucoleon Palace and the Church of Sancta Sophia and the nearby houses of the patriarchate. Count Henry of Flanders chose the Blachernae Palace. The soldiers set up house in the mansions of the rich until they were thrown out by unruly noblemen who wanted the mansions for themselves. It was understood that for three days all would have license to rape, murder, and pillage. Anarchy reigned. The churches were profaned; libraries were sacked; bronze statues dating back to classical Greece were overturned and then carried away to be melted down. The high altar at Sancta Sophia was covered with a sheet of gold and encrusted with jewels. The invaders tore out the jewels with their daggers. A prostitute was set up on the patriarch's throne to sing and dance. Since neither the Venetians nor the Franks possessed any respect for the Orthodox Church, they sometimes regarded the churches as pleasure halls and entertained themselves before the altars. Three churches were converted into storehouses for the gold and silver and costly cloths that were set aside for the barons. The rank and file, although promised treasures of their own, received very little; and those who took gold and silver valuables were summarily executed. The barons regarded the city as their own private property. When the massed treasure of all the palaces and churches of Constantinople was valued, the barons received 450,000 marks and only 100,000 marks was reserved for lesser ranks. Each knight received 20 marks, each priest and knight's servant received 10 marks, and each foot soldier received 5 marks. It was not a very generous distribution of the spoils.

This mindless looting, although most ferocious during the first three days, continued for years. The libraries of Constantinople contained great collections of the literary works of the Golden Age of ancient Greece; all, or nearly all, went up in flames. There were no Greek scholars among the Crusaders, no one to recognize the works of Aeschylus, Sophocles, and Sappho in the libraries. What we have now is merely a small part of the wealth of Greek literature that existed up to the sack of Constantinople.

What was most terrible of all was the mindless cruelty of the invaders. They murdered for fun, or to provide a spectacle, or for no reason at all. When Murzuphlus, the emperor, was finally captured, the new emperor, Baldwin, the former count of Flanders, wondered about a suitable punishment. The doge observed that he was too tall a man to be hanged. "I will tell you what to do with him," he said. "In this city there are two high columns, each of which is at least fifty or sixty *toises* in height. Let us make him climb to the top of one of them and throw him down to the ground." The barons agreed, and accordingly Murzuphlus climbed up the column, and was thrown down; his body was dashed to pieces.

Not all the Crusaders went in search of conventional treasure; relics were another much sought-after acquisition. The chronicler Robert of Clari was among the notable collectors of relics. He was on the staff of Peter of Amiens, a nobleman attached to the army of Hugh, Count of Saint-Pol, and his book *La Conquête de Constantinople* is an official history written with the aid of official documents. His search for relics was aided by his high connections. He amassed a considerable treasure, including a piece of the True Cross measuring four inches by three inches together with four smaller fragments, some thorns from the Crown of Thorns, the Sudarium, the Sponge, half of the girdle of the Blessed Virgin, the arm of St. Mark, and the finger of St. Helena. He also brought back to Corbie a part of the loincloth worn by Christ on the Cross. Altogether he acquired more than forty relics, which he gave to the church of St. Peter at Corbie.

Thus the Fourth Crusade came to an end, with nothing to show for it except the devastation of a great and once-proud city. Though quite properly counted by historians among the Crusades, since many who took part in it believed they were sailing to the Holy Land, the Fourth Crusade was little more than a successful effort to overthrow an empire and to gather its spoils. If the doge or Baldwin or Boniface had thought they had taken possession of the Byzantine empire on behalf of Venice and the West, if they had thought they could build up a wall against the encroachments of the Turks, there might have been some reason in their lunacy; but they did not think in these terms. They thought of plunder, toll gates, commercial privileges. They were colonizers who sought to extract the utmost from their colonies. They offered nothing in return for the bondage and enslavement of the local population.

Even Innocent III, who had no tender conscience, was aghast at their actions. There came from him, in letter after letter, cries of helpless rage. How was it possible that anyone could be so unreasonable, so inept, and so absurd as to conquer Constantinople? Were not the Turks on the march, and was it not certain that Byzantium served as a bastion against them? They had professed to be Crusaders who would march into Palestine had protect the Holy Sepulchre, and they were no more than thieves and robbers who had put aside the holy mission entrusted to them for the sake of lucre. Innocent anathematized the Venetians, who shrugged their shoulders and wondered why anyone should be disturbed by the distant echoes of papal thunder.

The sack of Constantinople was a disaster of the first magnitude. At a time when help was desperately needed by the Kingdom of Jerusalem, a great invasion fleet had been diverted from its proper course to serve the ambitions of the Venetians, who henceforth called themselves masters of "a half and a quarter of the Roman empire." They gained great wealth by plunder, but it was not to gain great wealth that the Crusades had come into existence. The inexhaustible rapacity of the Venetians harmed the Crusaders as nothing else had harmed them. The Muslims saw once more that the Crusaders were treacherous and never more treacherous than when they fought among themselves.

VIII

THE WASTING OF THE TREASURE

The Children's Crusades

THE moral force that brought the Crusades into existence ultimately derived from something very simple: the worship of Christ. A Crusade was a many-tongued act of prayer. It answered the need to come close to Christ, to be intimately aware of his abiding presence. While he was present as a living force in every church and cathedral, he was all the more present in the open spaces of the Holy Land, where men could walk where he had walked and see the landscapes he had seen. To go on pilgrimage or to take up arms in defense of the Holy Sepulchre were acts without ambiguity, and their very simplicity shaped the course of the adventure. Ambiguities came about when the leaders sought to take possession of new principalities and when merchants sought profits. Still, the great majority of the Crusaders went to the Holy Land for the glory of God. In them a pure flame burned brightly. But sometimes the flame bent backward and burned them, destroying them utterly.

Such was the Children's Crusade of 1212, when everything went wrong. The Crusade arose from the same impulses as the other Crusades: the rituals of pilgrimage were obeyed; the ceremonies of the Catholic Church accompanied the children; the leader, even though he was a child, was strong-minded and eloquent. The children were unarmed because they had no intention of fighting the Saracens: they hoped to convert the heathen by the force of their example, perhaps by their very youthfulness. Like the soldiers of the First Crusade they were exalted and determined, strangely remote from the ordinary affairs of the world. They believed that they would take possession of the Holy Sepulchre.

The leader was a boy of about fifteen called Stephen, born in the village of Cloyes, which is only a short walk from Fréteval, where King Philip of France was defeated by Richard Coeur de Lion in 1194. A boy wandering over the fields would find rusted helmets, swords, lances, and chain mail lying about, and the unburied skeletons of dead soldiers. In that wide valley of green meadows and shady willows a boy would feel the presence of their ghosts, and dream.

When Stephen came to Paris in May 1212, he had a strange story to tell. While he was tending his sheep at Cloyes, a stranger had come to him in the fields, saying that he had come from the Holy Land. He asked for food; Stephen gave it to him and listened to his stories; as the stories continued, Stephen became convinced that he was talking with Christ. The stranger at last announced that he was Christ and gave him a letter to deliver to the king of France. He also urged the boy to lead a Children's Crusade, which would succeed where mailed warriors and proud barons had failed. In Paris Stephen was regarded as a true visionary; the king received him; the children flocked to his banner, which was a copy of the sacred oriflamme given to the reigning king by the abbot of the Abbey Church of Saint-Denis whenever the kingdom was at war. Stephen was known as "the Prophet," and those who joined him were known as "minor prophets." With his clear, compelling voice Stephen soon had hundreds of children enthralled by the thought of embarking on a Crusade.

Processions formed through the streets of Paris with the Prophet or one of the minor prophets holding up the gold cross to which the oriflamme, a banner made of red silk with a scattering of golden flames, was attached. As more and more children came to listen to Stephen and take part in the processions, the king realized that steps would have to be taken to bring order to the city. He ordered the children to return to their parents; they refused; and he was confronted with the difficulty of rounding them up. He appears to have thought that their enthusiasm would soon melt away in the heat of summer. Instead, it increased. Now, all over France and Flanders, children were preparing to go on the Crusade; and the movement had spread to Germany where a boy called Nicholas, born near Cologne and even younger than Stephen, was calling upon children to follow him to the Holy Land.

Stephen disappeared from Paris. Having chosen Vendôme, which was not far from Cloyes, as the place of assembly for all the children, he returned to the Orléanais and set about the organization of the Crusade. Everything was happening very quickly. By the end of June the children, probably eight or nine thousand strong, were on the march. Their destination was Marseilles. Stephen rode in a cart provided with a canopy to protect him from the sun, with a bodyguard of armed youths riding with him. Many young priests accompanied the long procession, which arrived in Marseilles in the middle of August. The people knew of their coming and prepared provisions for them. They were accepted by the community, although they were kept outside the walls.

At first Stephen may have believed that the sea would open for him and that he would be carried in some mysterious way with all his followers to Jerusalem, but it soon became evident that the sea was indifferent to their prayers.

A certain Hugh Ferreus, who is known to have had a trading post in Acre, together with William of Posquères, who was in business with him, offered to carry the children to the Holy Land. They owned their own ships; they were widely known in Marseilles; they were apparently trustworthy. Seven ships were placed at the disposal of the children. When they were two days out, a storm blew two of the ships onto the island of Recluse and all the children on these ships were drowned. The five remaining ships were taken to Bougie, on the African coast directly south of Marseilles, and to Alexandria. Bougie and Alexandria had large slave markets and the children were sold into slavery.

About the same time that Stephen was leading his flock to Marseilles, the ten-year-old boy called Nicholas was leading a flock of children through Germany and Switzerland and over the Alps into Italy. According to the chronicler, an infinite multitude of boys and girls and young women with babes at their breasts followed Nicholas during his expedition, believing that they had been summoned by an angel and that when they had arrived in the Holy Land they would rescue the Holy Sepulchre from the detested hands of the Saracens. The "infinite multitude" was perhaps seven thousand. We know that some of them were lost while climbing the Alps. The survivors reached Genoa on August 25. Here they asked to be allowed to rest for a week, but were permitted to remain only for a single day. Then they were off again, marching south through Pisa and Rome, and the remnant of them finally reached Brindisi, where the expedition ended in squalor and terror. No shipowners offered to take them to the Holy Land. Instead, a certain Friso the Norwegian took charge of them. He sold the girls into brothels and the boys into slave markets.

The Children's Crusades were not legendary. They were recorded briefly by more than thirty chroniclers. They happened quickly, and the children vanished just as quickly, almost before the world knew of them.

The Plagues
of Egypt

MONG those who took part in the Crusades there are only five who wrote with a sense of mastery over their material. They were Raymond of Aguilers, William of Tyre, Geoffrey of Villehardouin, James of Vitry and John of Joinville. Although James of Vitry was perhaps the least of these five chroniclers, he was the one whose character emerges most clearly in his works. His was not an altogether pleasant character, for he was moralistic to a fault, pompous, self-assured, and apoplectic. His hatred bordered on biting contempt. Heretics, schismatics, half-castes, lawyers, usurers, and women dressed in finery received violent tongue-lashings from him. He raged so much against the vices of his time that he sometimes became incoherent. He had reason to rage in the Holy Land, for he was among the first to detect the fatal flaw of the Crusaders in the thirteenth century: the deadening of the soul.

James of Vitry was born in Argenteuil, outside Paris, about 1175. He became a canon regular in the monastery near Liège. His preaching attracted the attention of the bishops who were directing the Crusade against the Albigenses; and he accompanied the armies that invaded the Languedoc with fire and sword at the direct invitation of Pope Innocent III. The fame of his preaching grew. It reached Acre, where the bishopric was vacant, and the canons wrote to the pope, urging that James of Vitry be appointed Bishop of Acre. In 1216 he was solemnly inducted. He seems to have accepted the appointment as a duty, without too much enthusiasm, and he found very little to please him in the Holy Land. Twelve years later, he abandoned his see abruptly, and returned to the obscurity of his monastery at Oignies in Belgium. Although James's virtues as a chronicler are erratic and elusive, they include a warm humanity and a sense of place. In the intervals between raging against corruption a sentence or a page of his *History of the Crusades* brings the Holy Land to life. He is quirky, loves marvels, adores miracles and old wives' tales. When he talks of what he saw with his own eyes, he is completely convincing, as when he describes the

Christian army setting out from Acre in November 1217 under the command of the kings of Jerusalem, Cyprus, and Hungary, for none of whom had he any use. He reserved his admiration for Duke Leopold VI of Austria with his martial bearing and his obvious competence.

This was the largest army seen in the Holy Land since the time of the Third Crusade, numbering at least fifteen thousand knights and three or four times as many foot soldiers. Its purpose was to engage the Saracen forces in the region of the Sea of Galilee. It was a motley army, lacking in discipline, and ill led, for each of the three kings regarded himself as the sole commander. John of Brienne, King of Jerusalem, led the Frankish forces; King Andrew II of Hungary commanded the Austro-Hungarian forces; King Hugh of Cyprus led his Cypriots. The masters of the Temple and of the Hospitallers led their own forces, and there were therefore at least five command centers. James of Vitry says of the kings, "No divine gifts having been given to them, it is unnecessary to relate their accomplishments." Here James of Vitry describes two expeditions in which he took part:

> The scouts were sent ahead, and soon we saw the great cloud of dust raised by the enemy. We had no way of knowing whether they were coming toward us or going away from us. On the following day as we were marching among the mountains of Gilboa, the mountains on our right and the marshes on our left, we came to Bethany, where the enemy had pitched their tents, but when they saw the coming of the army of the living God marching in good order and apparently in vast numbers they fled after folding their tents, leaving to Christian horsemen the ravaging of the land.
>
> ... we made two stops along the shores of Lake Galilee to see the sights associated with our Lord who deigned to work miracles and to converse with men, whom He honored with his bodily presence. We came to Bethsaida, the town of Andrew and Peter, now reduced to a pathetically small village. We saw the places where Christ summoned the disciples, and walked on water, and fed the multitude in the desert, and where He climbed up in the mountain to pray, and the place where He ate with the disciples after the Resurrection; and then we came to Capharnaum and we returned to Acre, mounting our sick and poor on beasts of burden.
>
> During our second cavalry expedition we came to the foot of Mount Tabor. We thought at first there was no water there, but we dug deep and found water in abundance. Our leaders thought there was no way we could climb the mountain. They deliberated, and a Saracen boy told them how the castle could be taken. And so on the first Sunday after our arrival, while the Gospel was being

read aloud: *"Ite in castellum quod contra vos est*: Go into the village over against you,"* the Patriarch marched ahead, bearing the Cross, followed by the bishops and the priests all praying and singing, and we made our way according to the slope of the mountain; and although it was very high and steep, and although it was nearly impossible to climb except by way of a narrow path, the knights and the foot soldiers, and all those who rode on horseback or walked, all of them made the ascent with enthusiasm.

John, King of Jerusalem, followed by the army of the Lord, overwhelmed the castle's governor and an emir with the first onslaught. The castle guards who poured out of the gates with intrepidity in order to defend the approaches, fled ignominiously, being seized with terror. King John behaved admirably as he raced up the mountain but he came down ingloriously. While the enemy remained shut up within the castle, the kings of Jerusalem and of Cyprus together with the Master of the Hospital and the other barons retired shamefully on one side of the mountain to decide on the proper course to take. The noble Duke of Austria, who took no part in these deliberations, was fighting the infidels on the other side of the mountain, and he could not find us, for we were already at the top. . . .

The castle on Mount Tabor fell to the Christian army; large numbers of prisoners were taken, and James of Vitry, the Bishop of Acre, had the pleasure of baptizing many Saracen children who fell into his hands either by gift or because he paid for them with gold coins. What is remarkable in his account of the expedition is its casualness, the sense of things happening haphazardly, without order and without logic. We see the clouds of dust—are they coming or going? The duke of Austria vanishes around the other side of the mountain, and it appears that no one is attempting to find out what happened to him. The first expedition disintegrates into a sightseeing tour.

Yet there were deeply serious purposes in these marches through the Galilee. The Crusaders were testing the enemy's mettle; they were gathering intelligence; they were deciding on the next point of attack. The Templars were the chief strategists, and their opinions on military matters were always listened to with respect. The master of the Temple hoped to attack Nablus, as a stepping stone to the recapture of Jerusalem. At some time in the winter or the early spring, the attack on Nablus was abandoned and it was generally agreed that an attack on Damietta would be more rewarding.

Meanwhile one of the kings was departing. This was King Andrew II of Hungary, who ruled over a vast territory comprising present-day Hungary,

Dalmatia, Croatia, Bosnia, and Galicia. He announced that he had come on pilgrimage and the pilgrimage was over. He had acquired the head of St. Stephen, and he had also acquired one of the jugs used at the marriage feast at Cana. He announced his departure without warning; the patriarch of Jerusalem flew into a rage, but the king was adamant. He marched north to Armenia, received a safe-conduct from the Turks as far as Constantinople, and another safe-conduct through Byzantine territory until he reached his own capital. The Christian army at Acre was incensed: they had hoped for so much more from the king, whose wealth was said to be greater than that of any other king in Europe.

Meanwhile the Crusaders were busy strengthening their fortifications. At the orders of John of Brienne, King of Jerusalem, and with the help of Duke Leopold of Austria, the fortifications at Caesarea were vastly improved, and the Templars and the Teutonic Knights, with the help of thousands of pilgrims, set about building on a spit of land jutting into the sea about ten miles south of Haifa the great fortress they called Chastel Pèlerin, the Castle of the Pilgrims. It was a perfect site, impregnable by land or by sea, and the fortress they built was so strong that it was never successfully besieged. On both sides there were shelving bays where ships could berth. Fishing boats sailed out from the fortress, and returned with their catch. Because it jutted out from the land and was visible for many miles around, Chastel Pèlerin represented the presence of Frankish power to remarkable degree.

Chastel Pèlerin was built on the ruins of an ancient Phoenician fortress. Construction of the fortress had been going on for seven weeks when workmen came upon a hoard of Phoenician gold coins. These coins, which they regarded as a gift from God, came to the Templars at a time when they were wondering how they could afford to build so vast a building. Thereafter, work went on at an increased pace: all the walls and towers, and most of the interior, were completed within a year. While still under construction, it was attacked by Malik al-Mu'azzam's army. (Al-Mu'azzam was the king of Damascus.) Siege engines were brought up; flaming arrows were shot over the walls; every device of warfare was employed to compel the Templars to surrender.

A month later, having accomplished nothing at all, Malik al-Mu'azzam abandoned the effort. He was like a man throwing tennis balls at a plate of steel; he made no dent in the fortress.

In May 1218, with the arrival of the long-promised Frisian fleet, the affairs of the kingdom suddenly improved. The pope, who had summoned the fleet into existence, had called for the utmost speed; the fleet commanders had spent a year on the journey from the Frisian Islands to Acre, stopping at Dartmouth, Brest, Lisbon, and various other places on the way. Originally the fleet consisted of over 220 ships, almost certainly the largest armada put together up to this time. Some of these ships were built in shipyards along the Rhine. While they were being built, according to James of Vitry, strange and compelling signs appeared in the sky. In the Frisian Islands, in the province of Cologne, and in the diocese of Münster, men saw three Crosses in the sky, one white and turned to the north, another also white and turned to the south, and between them a Cross of many colors on which they could make out the shape of Christ with outflung arms, his hands and feet nailed down, and his head bent forward.

Nearly half the Frisian fleet arrived at the end of May. Most of these ships came from the Rhineland. The Kingdom of Jerusalem had a small fleet of its own, and there were therefore about a hundred ships lying at anchor in the Bay of Acre. The Germans and Frisians had brought provisions and supplies. The shock that followed the departure of the king of Hungary and his army was wearing off and the Crusaders were of good heart again.

In retrospect, they could see that they had lived through a terrible winter. Although the expeditions through the Galilee had been important for testing the enemy's strength, they had accomplished nothing else of value. There had been a feeling of acute distress, the crops had failed, they had few horses, and the expectation of reinforcements from Europe were not being fulfilled. The mood of the Crusaders before the arrival of the fleet is clearly revealed in a letter written by William of Chartres to the pope at some time during that long winter.

EXCERPTS FROM A LETTER FROM WILLIAM OF CHARTRES, MASTER OF THE TEMPLE, TO THE POPE HONORIUS III, FROM ACRE SOMETIME IN THE WINTER OF 1217.

TO THE VERY REVEREND FATHER IN CHRIST, the Lord Honorius, by the Providence of God Supreme Pontiff of the Holy Roman Church, Brother William of Chartres, humble master of the poor chivalry of the Temple, proffereth all due obedience and reverence with the kiss of the foot.

... [I]n these parts corn and barley and all the necessities of life have become extraordinarily dear. This year the harvest has utterly disappointed the expectations of our husbandmen, and has almost totally failed. The natives, indeed, now depend altogether on the corn imported from the West, but as yet very little foreign grain has been received, and to increase our uneasiness nearly all our knights are dismounted and we cannot secure enough horses to replace those which have perished. It is therefore all the more important, O Holy Father, to warn all those who deign to assume the Cross of this scarcity that they may furnish themselves with plentiful supplies of grain and horses.

Before the arrival of the King of Hungary and the Duke of

Austria we had decided to march against the city of Naplous and to bring the Saracen chief Coradin to an engagement with our forces, and we have all now decided to undertake an expedition into Egypt by sea and by land, and by destroying the city of Damietta we shall be able to command the road to Jerusalem.

The strange belief that Damietta controlled the road to Jerusalem had become by this time an obsession of the Crusaders. Damietta was in fact a place to be avoided, a place of misery and pestilence, certain to be the graveyard of innumerable soldiers. William of Chartres died a few months after writing this letter in the pestilential camp near Damietta.

Once the council of war, which consisted of John of Brienne, King of Jerusalem, Duke Leopold of Austria, and the masters of the Temple, the Hospital, and the Teutonic Knights, had decided upon attacking Damietta, there was no turning back.

Although they were still expecting the rest of the Frisian fleet, it was decided that with a hundred ships they could safely attempt an attack on Egypt. The fleet set sail without a commander in chief. It assembled off Chastel Pèlerin, saluting the impregnable fortress, which shone like a white headland. They were about to set sail for the south when the wind dropped. Only a small part of the fleet was able to catch any wind. This small part succeeded in sailing south and anchored off the Damietta mouth of the Nile to await the main fleet. Six days later, when it arrived, John of Brienne, King of Jerusalem, assumed the role of commander in chief.

There had already been a landing and the Christian army had put up tents on the west bank of the river two miles from Damietta. But heavy chains moored on one side of the river to a small fortress blocked the only navigable channel. The chronicler Oliver of Paderborn thought of a simple scheme for attacking the fortress. He lashed two ships together, built a high mast equipped with scaling ladders, and covered mast and ships with skins so that they could not be set on fire. In his chronicle he lovingly describes the making of this floating fortress.

Prayers were recited, and Ralph of Merencourt, Patriarch of Jerusalem, lay prostrate in the dust before a portion of the True Cross which he had brought from the Church of the Holy Sepulchre. Success depended upon capturing the fortress. To Oliver's delight his floating fortress was able to grapple with the fortress on land. The Egyptians realized they were in danger. They succeeded in setting fire to the floating fortress, but the Christians put out the fire; and went on, with the help of a flying bridge, to batter their way into the interior of the fortress. The surviving Egyptians, numbering a hundred men, surrendered to the Duke of Austria and were held prisoner.

With the fortress captured, it was an easy matter to cut the chains. The advance on Damietta now began.

If the Christians had sailed up to the walls of Damietta, they might have captured the city, which was still unprepared for a frontal assault. Instead they waited for reinforcements, deliberated, and were cautious to excess.

The capture of the fortress took place in the middle of August. In the middle of September, the Papal Legate, Cardinal Pelagius, arrived on the scene, claiming that he had been appointed commander in chief by the pope. A Spaniard with a sharp satirical mind, harsh, obdurate, singularly ignorant of warfare, and always tactless, he went out of his way to insult King John of Brienne, insisting that he, the cardinal, would lead the army, hitherto ill led, to victory, and he pointed to the failures of the Crusaders as a sign that a new commander was long overdue.

Cardinal Pelagius had brought a small army with him, and at about the same time a French and English contingent had arrived to swell the ranks of the Crusaders. Among the Englishmen was Ranulf, Earl of Chester, an extremely brave but also a most bloodthirsty man.

In November a tempest nearly drowned the Crusaders. In the middle of the night the waters rose, tents floated away, food supplies were ruined, and when the floods subsided, they saw "the fishes of the sea and of the river fearlessly penetrating our sleeping quarters and we were able to catch them with our hands, a delicacy we would cheerfully have foregone." So wrote the chronicler Oliver of Paderborn.

With the tempest came the plague: fever, pains in the legs and arms, rotting of the teeth and gums, and soon parts of the body turned black. Men died in agony, with faces, arms, and legs eaten away. Oliver of Paderborn says that those who survived until the spring were given back their health, but perhaps a fifth of the Crusaders died in that long, cold winter.

In February 1219, Cardinal Pelagius ordered an attack on al-Adiliya, where the Sultan al-Kamil had his headquarters. The attack was called off because they found themselves riding into a blinding rainstorm. A few days later advance patrols discovered that the sultan had abandoned al-Adiliya, but if anyone thought the sultan had abandoned this stronghold for fear of the Christians he was mistaken; he was in fact fleeing from his own lieutenants who were conspiring against him. The plot was quickly uncovered, the sultan executed the conspirators, and marched his troops to Ashmun-Tannah, where he was met by the army of his brother al-Mu'azzam, King of Damascus. He was now in a much better position to fight the Christians, or so it seemed.

But the capture of al-Adiliya had given heart to the Christians. They were well entrenched, and they were beginning to understand the language of dykes, canals, rivers, and waterways. On Palm Sunday the Muslims attacked al-Adiliya, but to no avail. Every available person was thrown into the battle. The Crusaders fought with extraordinary determination. The women of the camp brought water, wine, and bread to the soldiers, and carried heavy stones to the front lines. The priests served as doctors and nurses, bandaging wounds and blessing injuries suffered in battle. There was no time for the processions and parades associated with Palm Sunday. "Our crossbows, bows and arrows, lances, swords and shields were our palms," Oliver wrote proudly.

Yet no one had gained a victory, and Damietta with its triple walls, its innumerable shops, gardens, orchards, factories, and mosques, remained untaken. Nevertheless Damietta, had the Crusaders known it, was ripe for conquest. Famine and pestilence stalked the city. They were suffering from the same plague that still ran through the Christian camp. While the Sultan al-Kamil promised that they would soon be relieved, he was unable to come to their rescue. Prices rose alarmingly. A fig was sold for eleven bezants, a princely sum. Too weak to mount the walls and keep guard, the soldiers of Damietta shut the city gates and allowed no one to go in or out. The Christians could only guess how deeply they were suffering.

Sporadic attempts were made to rush the walls, but without success. At last on the night of November 5, 1219, King John of Brienne directed an assault, and the city was taken "without resistance, without treachery, without violent pillage or turmoil." The reason why it was so easily taken became clear when they entered it. The streets were strewn with the bodies of people dead of famine or pestilence. Oliver of Paderborn wrote:

> As we entered the city, we encountered an intolerable stench and an appalling sight. The dead had killed the living. Husbands and wives, fathers and sons, masters and slaves, had killed each other with the odor of corruption. Not only were the streets full of the dead, but corpses lay in the houses, in the bedrooms and on the beds. When a husband died, then his helpless wife also died and his son died near him, and a handmaiden died near her mistress, having wasted away. "The young children ask bread, and no man breaketh it unto them." Infants clung to their mothers' breasts, embraced by the dead. Rich men raised on dainty food died of hunger amid heaps of wheat, desiring in vain their familiar melons, garlic, onions, fish, poultry, fruit and herbs. In them was fulfilled the words of the prophet: "Instead of a sweet smell there shall be stink."

Eighty thousand men, women, and children had perished during the siege. Only three thousand remained alive when the Crusaders entered the city, many of them dreadfully ill. Of these, three hundred were taken captive. These were the surviving dignitaries and their families, who might be ransomed off to the sultan, or sold in a slave market, or even baptized.

The mosque of Damietta was converted into a church dedicated to the Virgin. The wealth of the city was distributed among the knights and the clerics. Cardinal Pelagius contended that the city belonged to the Church, not to the Crusaders. On this subject he was adamant until King John of Brienne threatened to abandon the army and sail back to Acre. Thereupon the cardinal relented, declaring that he would permit the king to be the temporal ruler until the coming of Frederick II, the Hohenstaufen and Holy Roman Emperor, who was believed to be planning a great expedition to the East for a final confrontation with Islam. But Frederick delayed and the confrontation between the Holy Roman emperor and the sultan of Egypt was indefinitely postponed.

In Palestine things were going a little better, although al-Mu'azzam attacked Caesarea—most of its inhabitants escaped—and he went on to attack the great fortress of Chastel Pèlerin, again without success. The walls of Jerusalem were torn down, evidence that the Saracens believed the Christians might recover it. Acre was in danger, and for a while King John of Brienne abandoned the canals and waterways of Egypt to superintend its fortifications. In November al-Mu'azzam retired to Damascus to watch the events in Egypt from afar.

Soon after the fall of Damietta, the Christians captured Tanis, an important town a few miles to the east. The castle of Tanis was protected by a double moat and seven strong towers, but when the defenders saw the army coming, they panicked. Although there were only a thousand troops, the garrison at Tanis thought they were only the vanguard of the main army. The Egyptians may have shown weakness by fleeing from the castle of Tanis, but they possessed hidden reserves of strength. Peter of Montague, writing after the fall of Damietta and Tanis, was well aware of the dangers of the Egyptian adventure.

EXCERPTS FROM A LETTER FROM PETER OF MONTAGUE, MASTER OF THE TEMPLE, TO THE BISHOP OF ELY, FROM ACRE, OCTOBER 1220.

BROTHER PETER OF MONTAGU, Master of the Knights of the Temple, to the reverend brother in Christ, N, by the grace of God Bishop of Ely, salvation!

. . . The Sultan of Egypt is encamped at a short distance from Damietta at the head of a vast army, and he has recently built bridges across both branches of the Nile, to impede the progress of the Christian army. He remains there, quietly awaiting our approach; and his soldiers are so numerous that the faithful cannot leave their trenches around Damietta without great danger. Meanwhile we have surrounded the town and the two camps with deep trenches and we have strongly fortified both banks of the river as far as the seacoast, hoping that the Lord will console and comfort us with speedy aid.

The Saracens have perceived our weakness. . . . Be it known to you that Coradin, Sultan of Damascus, has gathered a large army of Saracens and attacked Tyre and Acre. As the garrisons of these places were weakened in order to strengthen our forces in Egypt, they can with difficulty sustain themselves against his attacks. Coradin has also pitched his tents before the fortress called Chastel Pèlerin, and has put us to enormous expense to defend this place. He has besieged and captured the castle of Caesarea.

For a long time now we have been expecting the arrival of the Emperor and all those other noble personages who have assumed the Cross and by whose aid we hope to be relieved from our dangers and difficulties and to bring our exertions to happy fruition. If we are disappointed of the aid we expect next summer (which God forbid), all our newly acquired conquests together with the places we have held for ages past will be left in a very dubious state. We ourselves, and others in these parts, are so impoverished by the heavy expenses we have incurred in prosecuting the affairs of Jesus Christ that we shall be unable to contribute the necessary funds, unless we speedily receive succour and subsidies from the faithful.

Such letters, sent from the master of the Temple in Acre, were dispatched throughout Europe. They were not universally welcomed. Rumor pointed to an increasing misuse of the money sent to the Crusaders. The pope came to know about it, and he set up an inquiry. He wrote to Pelagius, the Papal Legate, and to the patriarch of Jerusalem, and the masters of the Temple, the Hospital, and the Teutonic Knights. He received, as might be expected, a ringing refutation of the calumnies heaped upon the financial agents of the Crusaders. There had been no embezzlement: every penny sent to the Holy Land could be accounted for. To the bishops of France, England, and Sicily—the countries where the rumor was widespread—the pope wrote vehemently that the military orders in the Holy Land were financially respectable and were incapable of committing financial crimes. But he provided no accounting of the enormous cost of the Crusade.

Peter of Montague had written the letters at a particularly bad time. It was a period of stalemate. The loss of Caesarea had disheartened many of the Crusaders; some knights had been withdrawn from Damietta and sent to stiffen the resistance at Chastel Pèlerin, which remained unconquered. But the army at Damietta could not afford the loss of a single man. Yet throughout this time knights were continually abandoning the battlefield and returning home to manage their own affairs. They were free agents; they could not be compelled to stay; like King Andrew of Hungary they could simply leave.

The stalemate, the diminishing number of knights, and the presence of

Pelagius all contributed to making life intolerable for the Christian army. And Frederick II deeply affected the atmosphere of the times: his repeated promises that he was about to come to the East finally wore people down. They lost hope. The pope also lost hope. Frederick had been crowned by the pope in Rome in November and had promised to embark on a new Crusade in the spring, but he was still busy suppressing uprisings in Germany. He would come in his own good time.

Little known, and not yet perceived as a great and towering force, was the Mongol leader Genghis Khan, who swept into Azerbaijan in that same year. There he destroyed an army led by King George of Georgia, thereby reducing the military power of the Christian state to zero. Eventually, the Mongols would ally themselves with the Christians, but that was yet to come.

At this time, if Cardinal Pelagius had ordered an attack on Cairo after Damietta and Tanis had been captured, he might have won a great victory, for al-Kamil was in a mood of despair. The longer the stalemate continued, the more eagerly did al-Kamil prepare his defenses, recruit more soldiers, and build more ships. The cardinal raged against the inertia and drunkenness of his own soldiers, but could do nothing. There were frequent skirmishes, small towns changed hands, the Christians learned to maneuver among the canals, and a number of strange, prophetical books appeared. These books, perhaps manufactured in the feverish court of Frederick II, were full of prophecies about a great king coming from the West and meeting another great king from the East, who was perhaps King David, the son or nephew of Prester John, the mysterious Christian emperor believed to be lurking in central Asia or Ethiopia. These apocalyptic prophecies, based on Revelation, were too precise to be ignored. Letters from King David also appeared, promising succor to the Christians. In the light of these letters and prophecies the cardinal saw himself as the forerunner of the kings of the East and West.

Toward the end of July 1221, the cardinal decided to throw his whole force against the sultan. Reinforcements had arrived from Genoa and Apulia. Matthew, Count of Apulia, the viceroy ruling over Frederick II's territories in southern Italy, came with eight galleys. Hundreds of pilgrims had also arrived, and they could be used as laborers and water-carriers. King John of Brienne, who disputed the cardinal's generalship and who had returned to Acre, was summoned to take command of the army. He did so reluctantly, quarreling with the cardinal to the very end. By July 20 the Christians were in Sharimshah, a city halfway between Damietta and Mansourah, which had been abandoned by the enemy: the sultan had given orders that his own palace in Sharimshah should be destroyed. The cardinal believed that the way was now open for the march on Cairo.

He could not have been more mistaken. Al-Kamil, too, had received reinforcements. A vast army of Nubians and the army of Syria had joined his own forces. He did not really need them. He had a weapon denied to the Christians. He opened the sluices, and the Christians found themselves floundering in water up to their knees. Stores, baggage, horse-drawn carts, tents, and animals floated away in the night, while the enemy attempted to break up the army and send it into deeper water. Meanwhile the fighting went on. The Crusaders had sport with some of the untrained Nubians and made them "jump like frogs"; the Templars and Hospitallers attacked them on horseback and killed many of them. But it was all to no avail. The waters rose, food gave out, the road to Damietta was blocked, and soon the cardinal was forced to ask for terms of surrender.

Al-Kamil's terms were surprisingly lenient. In exchange for Damietta, he offered an eight-year truce and the return of the True Cross and all Christian prisoners. The army would be allowed to go free, and since most of its stores and provisions were lost, the sultan offered to feed them. While the agreement was being worked out, hostages were exchanged. King John of Brienne was entertained at a huge feast. Quite suddenly the Crusaders and the Muslims were at peace.

The Crusaders left Egypt, having accomplished nothing in their long months of fighting. Oliver of Paderborn attributed the defeat to mutiny, luxury, and ambition. There were other reasons: the cardinal's blundering, an uncertain knowledge of the topography, belief in high places in the validity of prophecies and letters from the mysterious King David. The True Cross, promised by al-Kamil, was never received: no one could find it.

According to Oliver of Paderborn the treaty concluded with al-Kamil contained the words, "This treaty will be observed unless the crowned king who is coming should wish to change it." Al-Kamil appears to have accepted these words with good grace. He was in secret communication with Frederick II and knew what manner of man he was. They had much in common, the sultan of Egypt and the fiery Holy Roman emperor. They had taken each other's measure, and together, very briefly, they would establish a new direction in the wars between the Muslims and the Crusaders.

IX

FREDERICK, EMPEROR OF THE ROMANS, EVER GLORIOUS

The Stupor
of the World

IT was Matthew Paris, the English historian, who gave Frederick II the appellation of *Stupor Mundi*. It fitted him so well that ever since then he has been called by this name, as if it were one of his legal titles. It was how he saw himself: the man who stupefied the world by his conquests and by his far-reaching intelligence and imagination; the viceroy on earth of both Alexander the Great and Christ himself. There was no end to his ambitions. He defied emperors and popes and acted as though he alone knew the art of kingship. Matthew Paris called him *Stupor Mundi et immutator mirabilis*—Stupor of the world and marvelous changer of things. Actually, he changed very little and the Hohenstaufen dynasty collapsed with his death.

Yet in a sense what Matthew Paris claimed for Frederick II was true. He was a new kind of man; he saw the world in a new way. He was a man of the Renaissance long before the Renaissance came into existence. His imagination was precise and jewel-like; and while there was no limit to his ambitions, there was also no limit to his belief in the perfectibility of man and in man's power to understand the world around him. He could say that he alone among the European kings and emperors conquered Jerusalem without the use of military force; he alone would claim that it was due to his own presence in the Holy Land.

Frederick II, Emperor of the Romans, King of Sicily and Apulia, and King of Jerusalem, was a short, nearsighted, beardless man, with red-gold curly hair, and without natural grace except when he was riding on horseback. He liked to say that he ruled firmly in order to bring order to the world, but in fact he ruled chaotically, relying on sudden impulses and sudden changes of mood rather than on his formidable intelligence. He was cold, cruel, selfish, and unrelenting in his pursuit of those he regarded as his enemies. Although he claimed to be the viceroy of Christ, charged to bring heaven to earth, he had very little religious feeling and no regard whatsoever for the pope.

Frederick II puzzled and amazed his contemporaries, largely because of the strange electric excitement which accompanied him wherever he went. He seemed to be in rebellion against the world, against all constituted authority. Though he acquired all his crowns legitimately, by direct descent from an emperor and a king, he acted throughout his life with the cunning of a pretender or the malice of a usurper. He was uncomfortable to be with. He liked to say that his whole life was devoted to the quest for inner and outer peace, but no one could have been more noisy, more raucous, more desirous of trumpet music.

On July 25, 1215, Frederick was crowned at Aix-la-Chapelle in the presence of most of the nobility of Germany. He was twenty-one years old, already a seasoned warrior. He sat on the throne of Charlemagne; his grandfather, Frederick Barbarossa, had been crowned on the same throne. He swore to defend the empire and the Church in the name of the Father, the Son, and the Holy Ghost, to love justice and hate iniquity, to judge the rich and the poor equally; and when the long and exhausting ceremony came to an end, he announced from the throne that he intended to lead Christendom on a new Crusade to rescue the Holy Sepulchre from the infidels. No one had expected him to say this. The knights acclaimed him with enthusiasm; he asked them all to join him, and if he had set out for the Holy Land at that moment they would have followed him. All through the following day, at the orders of the young emperor, the nobility listened endlessly to Crusade sermons.

Wearing a red cross sewn onto the shoulder of his imperial robes, Frederick resembled a Crusader-emperor to perfection. His call to arms was a political act of the first magnitude: it excited the Germans, intimidated the pope, who had also called for a Crusade, and it placed him in a position of extraordinary authority. At that moment he seemed to be the destined leader of Europe.

But there was something about Frederick that made the pope wary. He realized that if Frederick led a Crusade, he would inevitably attempt to carve out for himself an empire in the East; at the very least he would want to be King of Jerusalem.

Still, in November 1220, Frederick, following the tradition set by Charlemagne, was crowned again, by the pope at St. Peter's. He was anointed, received into the brotherhood of the Canons of St. Peter, and given a sword which he brandished three times, thus becoming a *miles beati Petri*, a soldier of the blessed Peter. By becoming a soldier of the pope, he was sworn to defend the pope and the Church. It remained that he should become a *miles Christi*, a soldier of Christ.

Once again he announced that he would lead a Crusade. He even gave a date when the Crusaders would set sail: August 1221. Whether he had any real intention of keeping his promise is unclear. He was a man who enjoyed making vast plans for the future, but he was also a man who lived from day to day. There were problems in Sicily (in those days this meant most of southern Italy together with the island of Sicily), which was in a state of chaos because of a large Saracenic colony. The trouble was stamped out, and the Saracenic prisoners were transferred to fortified camps in Apulia, where they tilled the land and could sometimes be called upon to serve in Frederick's army. It was during this period that he began to learn Arabic and to study science and philosophy, astronomy, astrology, and the physical sciences. He was preparing himself for the day when he would speak with Saracenic princes on equal terms and in their own language. He was also behaving more and more like the king of a Saracen country, with his vast harem and his oriental panoply. He was treated like a divinity by his court.

In March 1223, an extraordinary conference was held at Ferentino to discuss once more the question of the Crusade. Present at this conference were the pope, Honorius III, who was angry with Frederick for delaying the Crusade, the masters of the temple and the Hospital, Hermann of Salza, who was the grand master of the Teutonic Knights, John of Brienne, King of Jerusalem, Ralph, Patriarch of Jerusalem, and Pelagius, the papal legate who had commanded the Christian army in Egypt. It was as though the pope had decided to gather together the corporate leadership of the Christian army in the Holy Land in order to discuss the ultimate Crusade. But gradually, as they talked and argued, it became obvious to all that there was no possibility of raising enough money and enough troops for another two years. But out of these debates one new idea emerged: Frederick should marry Isabelle, the daughter of John of Brienne and heiress through her mother to the throne of Jerusalem. It was an idea that pleased Frederick, for it meant that he would become king of Jerusalem without any more effort than was needed to attend a marriage ceremony. The pope was pleased with the idea because it bound Frederick to the Holy Land, and John of Brienne was pleased because his daughter would become an empress while continuing to be queen of Jerusalem.

Isabelle was fourteen. Frederick was thirty. They were first married by proxy in the Church of the Holy Cross at Acre. A certain Bishop James of Patti represented Frederick. There followed in the cathedral at Tyre the solemn coronation of the young queen, and for fifteen days there was feasting and celebration. Then at last she was placed on an imperial galley bound for Brindisi, with a guard of honor consisting of many notables of the kingdom. At Brindisi the emperor married the newly crowned queen of Jerusalem. Within a few days of their wedding, he announced that the title of King of Jerusalem was rightfully his and that John of Brienne was henceforth merely his subject. He issued grants in the name of "Ysabella, my beloved wife, empress of the Romans, queen of Jerusalem and Sicily." In this way he ruled the Kingdom of Jerusalem from afar.

From this marriage Isabelle gained very little personal happiness. On their wedding night he seduced one of her ladies-in-waiting. Frederick kept Isabelle at a distance; she was merely the instrument by which he obtained his new kingdom. In 1228, when she was seventeen, she gave birth to a son, who was called Conrad. She died a few days later.

Although the pope refused to recognize Frederick as King of Jerusalem, and continued to address John of Brienne by that title, the barons of Jerusalem believed that there was need for a strong, high-minded king. They believed that Frederick would bring power and authority to the Holy Land. If they had known him well, they might have thought otherwise.

Frederick was a Christian only because in the West it was probably not possible for anyone in his time not to be caught up in the vast stream of Christianity; Frederick's greater sympathies lay with Islam. He surrounded himself with Saracenic attendants and eunuchs, his harem was full of Saracenic women, and even his habits of mind were authoritarian in a peculiarly Saracenic way. The caliphs of Islam were learned men with a passion for knowledge and scientific invention; they were extremely sophisticated, and at home in the physical world. Frederick resembled them in his flair for the decisive act, and in his self-glorification.

Because he was believed to be so powerful, it puzzled the barons that he had not entered the Holy Land earlier. They had been waiting for him for a very long time. Nor were the barons in any way dismayed by his claim to be the lawful king of Jerusalem. By law and by tradition, the crown of Jerusalem passed, in the absence of male heirs, through the female line. The husband of the queen became king. So it had happened for Guy of Lusignan, Conrad of Montferrat, and Henry of Champagne. But the law expressly stated that the king must appear in his kingdom within a year and a day of inheriting the title. The marriage in Brindisi took place on November 9, 1225. Frederick therefore had until November 10, 1226, to set foot on the Holy Land. It was totally characteristic of him that he should delay his arrival, thereby defying the orders of the pope and the laws of Jerusalem.

One of the principal reasons Frederick continually delayed his Crusade can be found in his secret correspondence with the sultan of Egypt. Embassies were exchanged; trade treaties were signed; the sultan and the emperor exchanged presents. All this came to the attention of the pope, who quite naturally wondered how the peace-loving emperor could make war on a friendly sultan.

Frederick continued to promise that he would lead the Crusade. At last, in the early summer of 1227, it became clear that he intended to carry out his promise. From England, Sicily, Apulia, Lombardy, and farther Germany, the crusading army could be seen converging on Brindisi. The German army was commanded by the Landgrave Louis of Thuringia and Duke Henry of Lemburg. Forty thousand English knights and soldiers arrived under the bishops of Exeter and Winchester. This formidable army reached Brindisi and found that Frederick had made only a very slight effort to welcome it. Food supplies were low, lodgings for the knights were inadequate, there was scarcely any sanitary facility to be seen on the campsites for the soldiers, and there was only a handful of ships in the harbor. There had been cloudless skies all through the summer, the heat was terrible, and the land was parched. Then the plague came, killing thousands, and both the emperor and Louis of Thuringia caught the fever. Soon the plague was being carried through Italy by troops who, having deserted the Crusade, were desperately attempting to reach their own lands.

Frederick could say that he was not responsible for the summer heat or for the plague, but in the eyes of the pope the plague was God's punishment on him. Although weak with fever, Frederick superintended the embarkation of some of his troops, believing that it was better that they should leave the plague-ridden city than die of the fever, and he sailed for the Holy Land. When he was two days out from Brindisi, Louis of Thuringia died of the plague. Terrified, Frederick put into the port of Otranto, buried his friend, and rushed off to the baths of Pozzuoli on the advice of his physicians, who counseled a moderate diet and frequent bathing in the springs.

Pope Gregory IX was an old man, crusty, handsome, strong-minded, with a great liking for the panoply of the Church and an even greater liking for power. Learning that Frederick had abandoned the Crusade and was now wallowing in the baths at Pozzuoli, he was incensed. There had been too many postponements, too many delays, and now, it seemed, Frederick had played the devil's game. In a state of fury the pope charged him with crimes he had not committed: he had deliberately chosen Brindisi as the staging ground for the Crusade, knowing how ill-favored the place was; he had had secret communications with the Saracens; he had never intended to go to the Holy Land. These were offenses that warranted excommunication. And without further ado the pope excommunicated the emperor.

Frederick was described as the beast who had torn the side of Mother Church, the cursed enemy of Christ, the most damnable enemy of mankind. With the solemn rites of excommunication performed, in the eyes of the church Frederick was a dead man. Not only was he cut off from the sacraments of the church, but no Christian could have any dealings with him. If he died he could not be buried in consecrated ground.

Frederick protested that he still intended to take the Cross; he had been delayed by illness, nothing else. He offered to perform whatever penance the pope demanded of him. The pope continued to curse him, accused him of poisoning Louis of Thuringia, and refused under any conditions to lift the ban of excommunication.

Frederick had wanted to lead the Crusade in August because he believed on the evidence of his correspondence with the sultan of Egypt that it would be possible by then to negotiate a treaty by which Jerusalem, or a large part of it, could be retained in Christian hands. He had his own *bailli* in the Holy Land, acting as viceroy. This was Thomas of Aquino, who was astute and forceful. He also had his own troops there, for the duke of Lemburg had sailed from Brindisi with eight hundred knights and ten thousand infantry. Frederick was already a presence, issuing orders, in command of armies, while the pope fulminated that he was a procrastinator who had never intended to set foot in Palestine.

Frederick announced that he would leave Brindisi in May; he left in June. He had only forty ships with him, and they cruised close to the coast, past Corfu, Cephalonia, Crete and Rhodes. Three weeks after leaving Brindisi the imperial galleys put into the harbor of Limassol in Cyprus. Evidently, he wanted to add the kingdom of Cyprus to his possessions, which could take a few weeks. Then he would sail to the Holy Land.

No one in Cyprus particularly wanted to come under the German emperor who was also king of Apulia, Sicily, and Jerusalem. Cyprus was then being ruled by John of Ibelin, Lord of Beirut, who acted in the name of the eleven-year-old King Henry of Lusignan. The boy's mother, Queen Alix, was regent and had the enjoyment of the revenues. Frederick would have liked to sweep Queen Alix, King Henry, and John of Ibelin aside. It would not be easy, for John of Ibelin was one of those lords who walk with great assurance through the labyrinths of diplomacy and politics and are very calm at moments of great danger. He was half-French and half-Greek, and was also related to the young king, Henry of Lusignan. He was about fifty years old, and at the time of Frederick's arrival on the island of Cyprus he was mourning the death of his brother Philip.

From Limassol Frederick summoned the entire court to appear before him. The court was at Nicosia. There was a good deal of discussion about whether they should obey the summons of an excommunicated emperor who was bound to create trouble on the island and further trouble when he sailed off to the Holy Land. It was suggested that they should reply diplomatically to the emperor that they were too busy raising the army which would follow Frederick to Syria. John of Ibelin realized that Frederick was not likely to believe any of these arguments; the better course was simply to obey him and to use every kind of argument to prevent him from taking complete possession of Cyprus. Philip of Novara, who was a Crusading knight, a lawyer of some eminence, and at various periods John of Ibelin's secretary, was present during these discussions and he remembered the words of the man who was commonly known as "the old lord of Beirut":

> We have counselled loyally and lovingly together, but I prefer to be captured or slain and to suffer what God has in store for me rather than consent that anyone should say that through me and my house or through the people on this side of the sea there was

any lack or delay in the service of God and the conquest of the Kingdom of Jerusalem.

For I do not wish to do ill to Our Lord, nor do I wish that people will say throughout the world: "The Emperor of the Romans came across the sea in great force and would have conquered everywhere he went but the Lord of Beirut and other disloyal men in Outremer loved the Saracens better than the Christians, and therefore they revolted against the Emperor and did not wish that the Holy Land should be recovered."

So they rode to Limassol, taking the young king with them. Frederick received them warmly at first, asking that as a favor to him they should remove the black gowns they wore in mourning for Philip of Ibelin. They granted him this favor and accepted the scarlet gowns and robes he had prepared for them. Frederick had taken over a palace that had formerly belonged to Philip of Ibelin, and invited them all to meet him there for a feast on the following day. During the night, sailors and armed men from his fleet came secretly to the palace. According to Philip of Novara, there were about three thousand men hidden in the stables and the guardrooms.

The feast opened in great splendor, with all the nobility of Cyprus in their scarlet robes, and the emperor explained that it was his habit to appoint cupbearers and bowlbearers in his own court, and he therefore designated John of Ibelin's two sons, Balian and John, to these high positions. He had also arranged that the tables were arranged in such a way that everyone had a clear view of the high table where the emperor sat next to John of Ibelin.

Suddenly about a hundred armed men emerged from hiding, and every Cypriot found a sword or a dagger held against his back. No one moved. Frederick announced that he had two claims to make, and a wise man would hasten to accept them. John of Ibelin said, "I will obey you willingly, so long as I believe the demands to be just and honorable." Frederick's demands were simple: the lordship of Beirut must be given to him, together with all the revenues of Cyprus for the last ten years. John of Ibelin replied that he held Beirut because it had been granted to him by Queen Isabelle, "who was my sister through my mother and daughter of King Amaury," at a time when the city was in ruins and the Templars and Hospitallers and barons of Syria had rejected it, and he had rebuilt the city with his own money, and all this was according to the laws of Jerusalem. As for the revenues of Cyprus, Queen Alix had disposed of them, as she was entitled to do according to the laws of the kingdom. The courts, not the emperor, must decide.

Frederick, confronted with a lawyer's brief, flew into a rage. He shouted that he had been told that John of Ibelin was well known for sweet words and cunning phrases. John of Ibelin answered that he had been told that

Frederick was well known for his deeds and he had come to Limassol with the intention of sentencing him to death or to imprisonment. Frederick became incoherent; he might have executed John on the spot if some religious men had not pacified him. At last he agreed to abide by the laws, but only on condition that twenty of the most prominent nobles were given to him as hostages until such time as the courts could hand down their decision. Balian of Ibelin was one of the hostages. Characteristically Frederick told John of Ibelin, "I know that Balian is your heart, and as long as I have him I have you." Even more characteristically he ordered the hostages to be trussed on an iron cross, so that they could move neither hands nor legs.

John of Ibelin's party had put up tents just outside the city. They had horses and arms; the emperor had no horses. John of Ibelin rode off to Nicosia during the night, and when a few days later Frederick brought his own army there, the royal family, John of Ibelin, and their troops raced to the north of the island and took refuge in the castle of Dieu d'Amour, 2,300 feet above Kyrenia. The castle was built on the two prongs of the mountain and across the valley between them, and resembled one of those romantic castles in children's fairy stories. John of Ibelin had previously provisioned it, and he had the satisfaction of knowing that it was very nearly impregnable. On the northern flank there was a sheer drop of 1,500 feet.

Winter was coming on. John of Ibelin remained at Dieu d'Amour, and Frederick stayed in Nicosia with the men of his fleet, which was still at anchor in the harbor of Limassol. John of Ibelin was advised that he had only to descend from his mountain stronghold with his army and he would be able to drive Frederick into the sea. He answered that there were better things to do than to wage war against an emperor. He would wait for a few weeks and see what happened, knowing that Frederick was a man singularly lacking in patience.

Frederick had to act quickly because the papal armies were invading Apulia, helped by King John of Brienne. He must also go to the Holy Land, because he had given the most solemn promise that he would do so. His relations with Sultan al-Kamil of Egypt were not faring well, and this was one more reason to hurry to the Holy Land. One of the more ridiculous aspects of the affair was that there were now three kings of Jerusalem: John of Brienne, the baby Conrad, and Frederick, who claimed the title both for himself and his son.

At last what John of Ibelin had expected came to pass. Frederick sent ambassadors to Dieu d'Amour, virtually agreeing to everything that John of Ibelin had asked for. The hostages would be returned, the regency of Queen Alix would be confirmed, no one would be asked to perform an act of homage. Instead, they would swear an oath of fealty, which would create a lesser bond between them. Above all, they would swear to keep the peace and sail together to the Holy Land.

John of Ibelin may have had second thoughts when his favorite son, Balian, was returned to him. Balian had been kept in prison and then made to work as a galley slave on one of Frederick's ships. Similar treatment had been given to all the hostages. Balian, like his father, was a master of tact, and when the emperor asked him to become a member of his staff he readily agreed.

At last on September 3, 1228, Frederick set sail for the Holy Land, having spent forty-three days in Cyprus. With all his wealth, his intelligence, and the regal panoply that surrounded him, Frederick seemed to be a man hounded by his demons. He reached Jerusalem, comported himself for a few hours like a conqueror, and then departed. What he would accomplish seemed grandiose in the extreme, but it is possible he knew in his heart that he accomplished nothing at all.

Brief Victory

FREDERICK's showmanship stood him in good stead. He had announced that he was on his way to the Holy Land to take his part as the leader of the Crusade, and the Saracens were properly respectful. They knew him well and saw elements of themselves in him. They, too, were intelligent, sensual, capable of sudden changes of mood, loving panoply and showmanship. There were some who said he was more Arab than the Arabs, being a Muslim in disguise. Frederick was not the first to have been enchanted by the Muslim culture. The Kingdom of Jerusalem had been ruled by men with a talent for luxury and high living. They were in love with the refinements of life in the East and were deeply influenced by Muslim culture, so that we find them sitting cross-legged on carpets and leaning on cushions, wearing the same embroidered silk garments worn by the Turkish emirs and chieftains. The East had seduced them, and granted them a way of life totally dissimilar to anything found in Europe. The Arabs cultivated gentleness but they were never harder than when they appeared most effeminate. Ascetic priests arriving from northern France or Flanders were thrown off balance when they saw Crusaders imitating the morals of the Arabs. Frederick II was the prime example of this seduction.

Frederick's fleet, seventy ships strong, sailed into Acre with about a thousand knights and eight or nine thousand pilgrims of all kinds. His army looked formidable, for he was accompanied by his own retinue and most of the knighthood of Cyprus.

At Acre Frederick was received with great ceremony, but there could be detected a curious sullenness among the people, who knew his reputation, feared him, and expected nothing good from him. The Pisans and Genoese generally favored him, the Venetians were neutral, the Templars and Franciscans were hostile.

About the time that Frederick landed at Acre, two Franciscan fathers arrived with a papal declaration that anyone who assisted Frederick in any way—by attending his court, offering homage, bearing arms for him, or taking part in negotiations with him—would be rendered liable to excommunication. It was the pope's duty to see that Frederick's dominions should be taken from him and given to others who were more obedient to the Church. The pope's declaration with its clear and implied threats meant that Frederick would have to act very quickly in order to acquire authority in the Holy Land.

This authority could only come from Sultan al-Kamil, who had recently taken possession of Jerusalem and had gone on to invest Damascus. Al-Kamil was in a position of ascendancy. Now he did not need Frederick, but Frederick was in desperate need of al-Kamil, the old friend with whom he had exchanged many embassies.

At this moment al-Kamil was encamped with his army at Nablus in Samaria. He had promised Jerusalem to Frederick if the emperor would help him take Damascus. But Frederick had come too late to the Holy Land, for Damascus had already been taken. He had nothing to offer al-Kamil except his friendship and some expensive gifts. If he had any use for Frederick at all, it would be as leader of the Christian army against a threatened invasion of the Khwarismian Turks. The Khwarismians had reached the Upper Euphrates. Al-Kamil was certain they would advance sooner or later into Syria; and sooner rather than later. He was therefore disposed to regard Frederick as an ally in the coming war with the Khwarismians, and if he had to surrender Jerusalem to the emperor, it would be for this reason and no other. Jerusalem would be returned to the Crusaders because armies of tribesmen were breaking out of central Asia, threatening the whole of the Middle East.

Frederick made his temporary capital in Jaffa, where he fortified the castle and waited for supplies, which failed to come. Jaffa was close to famine. The Templars and Hospitallers refused to fight for him; the Cypriots could not be depended upon; only the Italians he had brought from Brindisi and the Teutonic Knights under the Grand Master, Hermann of Salza, would stand by him. He had a force of about six thousand knights and perhaps eight thousand foot soldiers; it was pathetically small when compared with the army of the sultan of Egypt.

His real strength lay in the past, in the stream of letters and gifts he had exchanged with al-Kamil. Thomas of Aquino and Balian, Lord of Sidon, were sent as ambassadors to Nablus, and the learned Fakhr ad-Din came to Frederick's camp outside Jaffa. One of Frederick's letters to al-Kamil has survived in an Arab translation:

> I am your friend. You are not ignorant of how far I am above all the princes of the West. It was you who bade me come here. The

kings and the pope know of my coming here. If I return empty-handed, I shall lose all respect in their eyes. After all, was it not Jerusalem that gave birth to the Christian religion. You have destroyed it, and it is now reduced to the utmost misery. With good grace give it back to me even in its present state, so that I may lift up my head before kings. I renounce in advance all the advantages I might gain from it.

This letter from an emperor to a sultan begged too many questions to be entirely credible. He implied that the pope knew of his coming and approved of his mission. He implied, too, that Jerusalem was nearly worthless because the walls had been torn down. That he would renounce all the advantages he might gain from it was entirely beyond belief. Al-Kamil, in his reply, spoke of the inherent difficulties of surrendering Jerusalem: public opinion throughout the entire Muslim world would be aroused, there would be insurrections, his dynasty might be swept away. Nevertheless he sent Fakhr ad-Din on another embassy with an immense array of gifts—silks, jewels, Arab mares, racing camels, and elephants—to arrange an agreement, which was signed at Jaffa on February 11, 1229.

This agreement was one of the most spectacular accomplishments of Frederick's spectacular life, for it gave him nearly everything he wanted and seemed to ask nothing in return. Jerusalem, Bethlehem, and Nazareth, together with Lydda, Ramleh, and Emmaus, were restored to the kingdom. The roads from Jaffa to Jerusalem and from Jerusalem to Bethlehem were surrendered to the Christians; a large slice of the Galilee, Sidon and Toron, the villages between Nazareth and Acre were also restored. In Jerusalem the Temple Area, including the Dome of the Rock, was reserved for the Muslims, who were to have their own courts. Franks might enter the Temple Area provided they showed proper respect for the dignity of the holy sites. No new fortresses were to be built by the Egyptians. Antioch and Tripoli were excluded from the treaty, and since they were in the possession of Bohemond IV, Prince of Antioch and Count of Tripoli, Frederick seems to have hoped that al-Kamil might in his own good time take possession of them. Certainly the exclusion was deliberate. There would be a complete exchange and restoration of prisoners. The truce would last for ten years, five months, and forty days.

The treaty was almost too good to be true. It was largely the work of Frederick and al-Kamil themselves, and it was therefore a personal document testifying to an enduring friendship. Frederick on behalf of the Christians renounced all efforts to conquer Egypt, and it was this aspect of the treaty that seemed in the eyes of the Christian clergy the most alarming. Gerold, Patriarch of Jerusalem, also objected strongly to the fact that the Muslims would be allowed to worship in Jerusalem. But these objections were a form of quibbling. What the pope objected to most of all was that an excommunicated emperor had succeeded where better men had failed. For the first time in forty-two years, Christians were free to make the pilgrimage to the Holy Sepulchre. Frederick now claimed the right to be crowned King of Jerusalem. On Saturday, March 17, he entered the Holy City, and all through that day and night preparations were made for the coronation. The archbishops of Capua and Palermo were by his side, but when he asked them whether they could perform a coronation mass they refused, being too fearful of the ban of excommunication. The coronation ceremony was very simple. The crown was laid on the altar; a thousand candles burned; Frederick, wearing his richly embroidered imperial robes, marched up to the altar, seized the crown was laid on the altar; a thousand candles burned; Frederick, wearing his richly embroidered imperial robes, marched up to the altar, seized the crown, and placed it on his own head. Thereupon Hermann of Salza read out a long speech in celebration of the event, in which God, David, Christ, and Frederick were mystically united. Frederick, who wrote part of the speech himself, declared that he had come to Jerusalem by divine intervention as a prince of peace. The same themes can be heard in a letter sent to all the sovereigns of Europe the same day.

EXCERPTS FROM A LETTER FROM THE EMPEROR FREDERICK II, KING OF JERUSALEM AND SICILY, TO KING HENRY III OF ENGLAND, FROM JERUSALEM, MARCH 17, 1229.

FREDERICK, BY THE GRACE OF GOD, the August Emperor of the Romans, King of Jerusalem and Sicily, to his well-beloved friend Henry, King of the English, health and sincere affection.

Let all rejoice and exult in the Lord and let those who are correct in heart glorify Him who, to make known His power, does not make boast of horses and chariots, but has now gained glory for Himself in the scarcity of His soldiers, that all may know and understand that He is glorious in His majesty, terrible in His magnificence, and wonderful in His plans for the sons of men, changing seasons at will, and bringing the hearts of different nations together; for in these few days, by a miracle rather than by strength, that business has been brought to a conclusion which for a length of time past many chiefs and rulers of the world amongst the multitude of nations have never been able until now to accomplish by force, however great, nor by fear. . . .

. . . At length Jesus Christ, the Son of God, beholding from on high our devoted endurance and patient devotion to His cause, in His merciful compassion for us, at length brought it about that the Sultan of Babylon restored to us the holy city, the place where the feet of Christ trod, and where the true worshippers adore the Father in spirit and in truth. . . . [N]ot only is the body of the aforesaid city restored to us, but also the whole of the country extending from thence to the seacoast near the castle of Joppa, so that for the future pilgrims will have free passage and a safe return to and from the sepulchre, provided however that the Saracens of that part of the country, since they hold the Temple in great veneration, may come there as often as they choose in the character of pilgrims, to worship according to their custom, and that we shall henceforth permit them to come, however, only as many as we may choose to allow, and without arms, nor are they to dwell in the city, but outside, and as soon as they have paid their devotions they are to depart.

Moreover, the city of Bethlehem is restored to us, and all the country between Jerusalem and that city; the whole of the district of Turon, which is very extensive and very advantageous to the Christians; the city of Sidon, too, is given up to us with the whole plain and its appurtenances, which will be more acceptable to the Christians the more advantageous it has till now appeared to be to the Saracens, especially as there is a good harbor there, and from there great quantities of arms and necessaries might be carried to the city of Damascus, and often from Damascus to Babylon. And although according to our treaty we are allowed to rebuild the city of Jerusalem in as good a state as it has ever been, and also the castles of Joppa, Caesarea, Sidon and that of St. Mary of the Teutonic Order, which the brothers of that order have begun to build in the mountainous district of Acre, and which it has never been allowed the Christians to do during any former truce; nevertheless the sultan is not allowed until the end of the truce between him and us, which is agreed upon for ten years, to repair or rebuild any fortresses or castles. . . .

. . . Given at the holy city of Jerusalem, on the seventeenth day of the month of March, in the year of our Lord one thousand two hundred and twenty-nine.

One might have expected Frederick to linger in Jerusalem for a few days to savor the delights of kingship. He stayed only one more day. After crowning himself, he held court in the Palace of the Hospital, and toward evening he visited the Temple Area, admiring the Dome of the Rock, which still carried on its summit the crescent of Islam. He saw a Christian priest begging for alms while holding a gospel in his hand. Incensed, the emperor bore down on the priest and buffeted him so that he almost fell to the ground. "Pig!" shouted the emperor. "The Sultan has graciously granted us permission to come here on pilgrimage, and already you are begging alms!" The emperor was not being insensitive: he had a duty to protect the Temple Area from Christians. To the accompanying Islamic dignitaries he said, "My chief purpose in coming to Jerusalem is to hear the Muhammadans, at the hour of prayer, calling upon Allah by night." Frederick seems to have known large sections of the Koran by heart. Al-Kamil had given orders that the words of the Koran denouncing the polytheists should not be uttered from the minarets of the al-Aqsa Mosque, in honor of Frederick, who believed or pretended to believe in the Trinity. Frederick noticed that they had been omitted and sternly rebuked the Islamic scholar who walked by his side. "You must not change your religious rites because of me," he said. "This is a great mistake."

Frederick was truly sympathetic to Islam. At Lucera in Apulia he had built up a whole town of Muslims, with a mosque and religious schools, and he had studied the Islamic rites carefully with the help of his Arab teacher.

The pope would not have been amused by the spectacle of Frederick crowning himself in the Church of the Holy Sepulchre. The pope, of course, only learned of the coronation many weeks later. But by a curious coincidence, the papal interdict on Jerusalem arrived on the day following the coronation.

Only a very enraged pope would have the temerity to place an interdict on the Holy City. He went further. He wrote letters to the Templars, Hospitallers, and the sultan of Egypt demanding that Frederick be destroyed, speaking as though the emperor was the Whore of Babylon, who must be stamped out because he represented all that was evil. It is possible that Frederick was later shown the letter sent to the sultan, but he had more than enough reasons to hate the pope, whose armies were ravaging Apulia.

Frederick decided to leave Jerusalem, where he had spent altogether about forty-eight hours. He rode off to Jaffa, and exactly a week later he was in Acre. His first act there was to order the destruction of the patriarch's palace and the Templar fortress. Siege engines were brought up, the Teutonic Knights and the Pisans who were his allies attempted to storm the buildings, and Frederick looked forward to a general massacre of the Templar forces and the execution of the patriarch. He was quite capable of doing these things. But the troops attached to the patriarch's palace fought back, and the Templars, who were more disciplined than the Teutonic Knights, were masters of the towering fortress facing the sea at the southwest corner of the city. All this time, on the orders of the patriarch, the friars were running through the streets of Acre reminding the people that anyone who supported the emperor would fall under an interdict. He could not be baptized or wedded; all the sacraments were denied to him; he could be buried only in unconsecrated ground. Frederick might regard an interdict as a matter of small consequence but the common people took such things seriously. After five days the attack on the palace and the fortress was called off.

Frederick was now hated and despised by the Church, by the Frankish barons, by the Genoese and the Venetians, and by the common people of Acre, who saw no reason to be ruled by an absentee emperor. There was no doubt that Frederick would soon be returning to Italy; he might never return to the Holy Land, and obviously had no profound interest in it. He existed in the radiance of imperial glory, but the radiance was more likely to blind him than those who came into his presence. To the Teutonic Knights and the Pisans he granted charters with sweeping powers in reward for their loyalty. He appointed a certain Amaury Barlais, a lifelong enemy of John of Ibelin, to be *bailli* of Cyprus. At all costs, even at the cost of civil war, he was determined to leave his stamp on the Holy Land. Civil war was perilously close during those last days of April, when he was settling his affairs and preparing to leave for Italy.

On May 1, at dawn, accompanied by his guards, Frederick left his palace at Acre and rode down to the port and the waiting ships. On the way they passed through the Street of the Butchers, famous for the formidable old women who kept watch over the street from the upper windows on behalf of their sons and grandsons. Learning that Frederick would soon be passing through the streets with all his retinue, they laid up their weapons during the night—stones, rocks, offal, dung, sheep's entrails. All this was poured on the heads of the horsemen as they passed below. Frederick made no effort to punish the women: there was no time. He hurried to his ship. On the wharf, John of Ibelin was waiting for him. It was a brave act, for although John was heavily guarded, Frederick had a great desire to make him a prisoner. John of Ibelin bade him a courteous farewell, while Frederick cursed him.

Such was the Crusade of Frederick, Emperor of the Romans, ever glorious, the excommunicated King of Sicily, Apulia and Jerusalem, who alone among Western monarchs acquired Jerusalem for the Christians.

The Disaster at La Forbie

KINGSHIP in medieval times was a thing apart, remote from ordinary human preoccupations, touched with divinity. A king did not walk or talk like ordinary mortals; still less did he make decisions like them, for he saw himself walking with God at his side. While the emperors of Byzantium were most keenly aware of their divine power, even the kings of small states like Cyprus believed they were especially blessed. As a consequence, the king stood at the greatest possible distance from his subjects. He rarely knew what they were thinking, and rarely cared.

From the very beginning the pope had hoped that kings would lead the Crusade. Their splendor, their majesty, their semi-divine powers were needed as much as their armies were for the final conquest of the Holy Land. Their mystical armor preserved them from the arrows of the Saracens. In the imagination of the Vatican, the kings always rode ahead of their knights and infantrymen, and there was always a papal legate beside the king to warn, to console, to bless, and to guide.

In 1234, at the midpoint of the truce arranged between the Emperor Frederick and Sultan al-Kamil, Pope Gregory IX found himself once more putting his trust in a Crusade of kings. He appealed to the kings of France, England, Aragon, Castile, and Portugal. He wanted all of them to assemble their armies in Italy and then to sail off to the Holy Land in order to secure the Kingdom of Jerusalem finally and unalterably. The appeal was urgent, for the principalities in Palestine were dangerously unstable, capable of drowning each other in a sudden bloodbath. Bohemond V ruled over Antioch and Tripoli, but without his father's flair for vigorous government and legal scholarship. Various members of the Ibelin family ruled over Beirut, Arsuf and Jaffa. In Acre, the merchant colonies of Genoa, Pisa, and Venice elected consuls whose administration extended over the greater part of the city, which was nominally the capital of Richard Filanghieri, whom Frederick had appointed as his viceroy. Tyre was in the hands of

Philip of Montfort. The Templars and Hospitallers also had their independent principalities, which consisted of vast chains of fortresses dotted across the length and breadth of Palestine. The Holy Land was fragmented, and its two kings, Conrad and John of Brienne, were both in Italy.

The pope's call for a Crusade of kings produced only one king. This was Thibault IV, Count of Champagne, who became, in 1234, king of Navarre. He was a faithful servant of the Church, (he burned heretics). He was witty and improvident, generous to a fault, but without much talent as a war leader. He had one virtue as a military commander: he was cautious not out of cowardice, but because he wanted to save as many lives as possible.

Before taking part in the Crusade, the king of Navarre wrote to the barons of the Kingdom of Jerusalem and asked some sensible questions. He wanted to know whether they regarded the truce to be valid; whether the new Crusaders would be welcomed; which were the best ports of departure; and whether he would be able to find supplies in Cyprus. They answered that the truce was invalid, for the Saracens attacked whenever they pleased; the best ports were Genoa and Marseilles; there were plentiful supplies in Cyprus. Moreover, once they reached Cyprus, they were in a position to strike at Syria or Egypt according to the opportunities at the time of their arrival. He would be warmly welcomed, and they hoped he would come soon.

The army reached Lyons in the summer of 1239. The muster roll included some of the most prominent names of French chivalry, Hugh IV, Duke of Burgundy, among them. The king of Navarre had planned to lead his army across Italy and to set sail from Brindisi, but the pope and Frederick were still quarreling bitterly and he had no desire to be caught in the middle. The army, numbering about twelve hundred knights and eight or nine thousand foot soldiers, marched down the Rhône Valley, some taking ship at Marseilles and others at Aigues-Mortes.

All went well at the beginning. However, as they approached the Holy Land, the ships were scattered by a sudden storm; some were blown onto the shores of Cyprus, while others drifted all the way to Sicily. But the portly figure of the king was seen stepping off his flagship at Acre on September 1, 1239, with the walls streaming with banners and the crowds cheering.

The Sultan al-Kamil had died in March, 1238. He had led his army against Damascus in January, captured it, and then set about organizing his empire, which stretched from southern Egypt almost to the Euphrates. But the effort was too much for him. His death at the age of sixty precipitated another civil war. A nephew, al-Jawad, seized power in Damascus, while his elder son, as-Salih Ayub, marched against Damascus with the help of Khwarismian tribesmen and quickly put an end to the rule of al-Jawad. As-Salih Ayub's younger brother, al-Adil II, formerly viceroy of Egypt, appointed himself Sultan at the time of his father's (al-Kamil's) death. Enamored of a handsome young Negro, al-Adil II surrendered most of his powers to the youth, which would later bring about the enmity of the emirs and most of the population. In May 1240 the tent of the sultan and the youth would be surrounded, and they would both be killed. As-Salih Ayub, who would lose Damascus to his uncle, as-Salih Ismail, would then become sultan of Egypt. With one as-Salih in Cairo and another in Damascus, the civil war between the two branches of the family would begin in earnest, complicated by the presence of marauding Khwarismian tribesmen.

By dying, al-Kamil had made civil war inevitable; and by inviting Khwarismians to enter his army, his elder son had made it inevitable for those hordes of tribesmen to sweep across the country.

On the surface it might have seemed that the war between Damascus and Cairo was favorable to the Christians. But the Christians were themselves engaged in smoldering, haphazard civil wars, which flared up at intervals and subsided quietly: between the followers of Frederick and the Frankish barons who detested him, between the Temple and the Hospital, and between the local principalities. The king of Navarre was not the powerful charismatic leader capable of welding the kingdom into a single fighting force. The kingdom resembled an animal with too many heads and too many legs. The Arabs could survive their civil wars; it was becoming increasingly doubtful whether the Christians could survive theirs.

In an unhappy time, the king of Navarre did his best. His coming coincided with two events of considerable significance. Jerusalem fell to al-Nasir Daud, King of Transjordania. This was believed to be the fault of Richard Filanghieri, Frederick's viceroy, who had neglected to fortify the city or had done so only halfheartedly in the belief that the truce of Jaffa would be maintained. That the siege lasted as long as twenty-seven days testified to the determination of the garrison troops. That it took place at all testified to the lack of leadership at Acre. No attempt was made to send a relief force. No arms or provisions were sent. Al-Nasir allowed the Christians to go free but none were allowed to remain in Jerusalem; and he dismantled the Tower of David. The fall of Jerusalem seemed to take place in a strange silence, without anyone being aware of it.

The second event which took place at this time was the fall of Damascus to as-Salih Ismail. This was not an event that could possibly pass unnoticed. As long as al-Kamil's elder son remained alive, he could be depended upon to stir up civil war. At this time, al-Adil II, degenerate and luxury-loving, was still ruling Egypt. In these circumstances, the King of Navarre, with his small council of advisers, had to decide whether to attack Egypt or Damascus. The council consisted of the master of the Temple, the patriarch of Jerusalem, the bishop of Acre, the master of the Teutonic Order, and Gauthier IV of Brienne, Count of Jaffa, the nephew of John of Brienne, King of Jerusalem. Gauthier, who was married to the daughter of

Hugh I of Lusignan, King of Cyprus, was coming into prominence as one of the leading barons of the kingdom.

The decision of the council was to attack Egypt first and Damascus second. An attack on Jerusalem was discussed briefly, and there was even some talk of a foray against Safed, overlooking the Sea of Galilee. But the general opinion was that an attack on Alexandria or Damietta would be most profitable, since it was known that al-Adil II was unpopular with his people. The former empire of al-Kamil was in ruins, but the various pieces of it were still formidable. The king of Navarre was aware that an attack on Egypt presented grave problems, and his most important task was to keep his army intact. He would not, if he could possibly avoid it, permit any of his officers to engage in reckless adventures. The lesson of Hattin had finally been learned.

On November 2, the king's army marched out of Acre with the intention of attacking the Egyptian outposts of Ascalon and Gaza. The army numbered about four thousand knights and about twelve thousand foot soldiers; and although the foot soldiers were comparatively few, this was one of the largest armies that had ever set out against the Saracens. Some of the local barons took part; the Templars and the Hospitallers were also represented; the army was well armed, but there were not enough horses, and many of the knights were forced to walk; provisions were low, but spirits were high. To ride against the enemy under a king was an experience the Crusaders had not enjoyed for many years.

While they were marching on Jaffa, Peter of Dreux, Count of Brittany, learned from a spy that a rich caravan was moving up the Jordan Valley toward Damascus. Included in the caravan was a great herd of cattle and sheep intended to provision Damascus in the event of a Crusader attack, which as-Salih Ismail had been expecting for some time. The count of Brittany decided that the herd could be put to better use by the Crusaders. Without asking permission of the king of Navarre, he detached about two hundred knights from the main army to form a raiding party. He rode off into the hills the same evening, and at dawn found himself close to the castle where the caravan, which was well guarded by bowmen and cavalry, had camped for the night. The spy had given the count of Brittany an accurate report of the castle and the approach roads, and it was therefore possible to set up an ambush. One of the approach roads entered a narrow defile, and the count hoped that the caravan would pass through the defile. He divided his troops, posted himself in the defile, and gave Ralph of Nesles command of the alternate road. What was certain was that the caravan would have to pass along one of those roads.

The caravan came along the road that led to the defile, and here the count of Brittany pounced upon it. There was some savage hand-to-hand fighting, during which the count of Brittany was nearly killed. The bowmen were too close to the Crusading knights to be able to discharge their arrows, and the knights were always at their best in close combat. There were probably fewer than three hundred men in the raiding party, and only half of these were attacking in the defile. The horn was sounded. Ralph of Nesles brought up his troops in time to decide the battle. The enemy fled to the castle, pursued by the knights, who seized the herds of cattle and sheep, killed many of the defenders, and made others captive. For the rest of the day, and for two more days, the Crusaders guarded the herds on the way to Jaffa.

Meanwhile the king of Navarre learned that the sultan of Egypt had sent an army to Gaza. Al-Adil II was not witless; he had large armies and was prepared to use them; and he was well aware of the threat posed by the king's arrival in the Holy Land. Some of the knights, dazzled by the success of the count of Brittany's raiding party, began to think of a raid on Gaza. Hugh IV, Duke of Burgundy, was one of those who favored the raid, and his standing among the knights was almost as high as that of the king of Navarre. When the ever-cautious king of Navarre discovered this plan, he objected strongly. So did the Templars and Hospitallers. But it appeared that there were only a thousand enemy troops at Gaza and, according to the conspirators, it would be easy to overwhelm them. Let them go forward, attack Gaza, and if the signs were propitous, march into Egypt. The king of Navarre insisted that the army should move forward as a single unit. The count of Brittany and the heads of the military orders protested just as strenuously. The king reminded them that they had all taken an oath to obey him as their military leader. They were rebellious and refused to listen.

The rebels rode off with Count Henry of Bar in command. The king held a council of war, where it was decided that at first light the main army would march south in the hope that they would be able to protect these foolhardy knights.

From Jaffa the rebels rode all night, swept past Ascalon, reached the brook that formed the frontier of the Kingdom of Jerusalem, crossed it, and continued along the coast in the direction of Gaza. It was a bright moonlit night, very beautiful, and every shrub or tree stood out clearly among the shimmering sand dunes. They took no precautions at all. They spread cloths on the sand and sat down for supper, while others slept and still others groomed their horses. They had sent out no patrols and they were totally unaware that they were being watched at every moment. Suddenly there was an uproar. The Egyptian army came out above the dunes, bowmen and slingers shouting at the top of their voices.

Even then it was possible to make decisions. Gauthier of Brienne and the duke of Burgundy believed they could still fight their way back to Ascalon. Count Henry of Bar and Amaury of Montfort argued that they must stand firm, because only the cavalry could escape and they had no intention of abandoning the foot soldiers. Gauthier of Brienne and the duke of Burgundy and a small handful of knights slipped away. The rest fought under appalling conditions. There were wild skirmishes in the sand. Count Henry used his bowmen well, but they were no match for the enemy. Amaury of Montfort saw a steep passage between two dunes where he thought he could take shelter from the enemy bowmen. He threw his cavalry into the passage defended by Egyptian infantry. The cavalry cut down most of the infantry, but at the other end of the passage the Egyptian cavalry was waiting for them. The Egyptian cavalry then performed a classic maneuver. They fled, with the Frankish knights in full pursuit. Then the Egyptians blocked the passage with their infantry, and their cavalry swung around and charged the knights.

This was the end of the battle of the dunes. For miles around the sands were strewn with the dead. Count Henry of Bar was killed, Amaury of Montfort was taken prisoner, and eighty knights were captured. Altogether twelve hundred Crusaders were killed and half as many were taken prisoner.

There was madness in the moonlit battle, and when the king of Navarre reached Ascalon and met Gauthier of Brienne and the duke of Burgundy, he quickly became aware that everything had happened as he thought it might—a disaster that was totally senseless and totally explicable.

At Ascalon he held a council of war which ended in tentative decisions: to advance, to retreat, to wait for more information? What happened, perhaps inevitably, was that they did all these things. Finally the king decided to advance across the brook in order to help the scattered fugitives. Then he advanced deeper to see the battlefield and to make contact with the enemy, and when the enemy pulled back, the king's forces withdrew all the way back to Acre. The king himself was inclined to attack Gaza, but the Templars and Hospitallers pointed out sensibly that the enemy would probably cut the throats of all the prisoners if they did so. The prisoners had become hostages for the good behavior of the king's army.

It has been suggested that the king of Navarre had no reason to retreat to Acre, and it might have been better if he had strengthened the fortifications of Ascalon, or captured Gaza, or made one last effort to take possession of Jerusalem. The Rothelin manuscript, a document that details these events, describes the misery of the people as they watched the great cavalcade on its way back to Acre. "In all the places they passed through there was great weeping and great crying out because so many great Christians were returning after having accomplished nothing at all." It was precisely because of this sense of futility that they returned to Acre, the largest and most powerful city belonging to the Crusaders.

There was also another reason for returning to Acre. The interminable wars between Damascus and Cairo were about to begin again with undiminished fury. As-Salih Ayub had taken refuge in Kerak with al-Nasir Daud, King of Transjordania. His uncle, as-Salih Ismail, had Damascus completely under his control. Suddenly in May 1240, with the assassination of al-Adil II and the return of as-Salih Ayub to the Egyptian throne with the help of the king of Transjordania, it was clear that there would be a fight to the death between uncle and nephew. By moving back to Acre, the king of Navarre was placing himself at an equal psychological distance from Cairo and Damascus so that he could bargain with both of them, extract concessions from them, and perhaps arbitrate between them.

The political map of the Saracenic Near East at this time showed remarkable fragmentation. Between Damascus and Cairo there were about a dozen principalities. Some were at war with one another; others were searching for allies; still others were quite capable of abandoning their alliances at a moment's notice. In this way it happened that Muzaffar, Prince of Hama, having fought a border war with the prince of Aleppo, sent an ambassador to Acre, promising that, in exchange for help against Aleppo, he would give the use of his castles to the Christians and all his people would become Christians. The prince of Hama wanted the King of Navarre to send troops to his aid, or at least to make a show of force. The King of Navarre led his troops northward along the coastal road to Tripoli, and he seems to have intimidated the prince of Aleppo. Although the prince of Hama reneged on his promise to let the Crusaders use his castles and convert his subjects, there were indications that more useful alliances would soon be formed.

A few weeks later, when the king of Navarre's army was encamped at Sephoria in the Galilee, an ambassador arrived from as-Salih Ismail of Damascus with an offer to surrender the castles of Belfort, Tiberias, and Safed, and large areas of the Galilee and the hinterland of Sidon, in exchange for an agreement that the Christians would make no truce with Egypt and that they would defend Jaffa and Ascalon against the Egyptian forces. The king of Navarre agreed to these terms, and marched to Jaffa, where, strangely enough, his army was met by a large detachment of the army of Damascus.

What happened at Jaffa has never been satisfactorily explained. The army of Damascus seems to have melted away after some desultory fighting with the Crusaders, who had meanwhile occupied most of the Galilee and its powerful fortresses. Then as-Salih Ayub, now sultan of Egypt, sent an embassy to win the Franks over to him, with an offer to release all the prisoners taken in the moonlit battle at Gaza and to confirm that the Crusaders had possession of Jerusalem and Bethlehem.

Like Frederick II, the king of Navarre had accomplished by diplomacy what he had failed to accomplish by force of arms. The Kingdom of Jerusalem had been restored to its historical limits, except for the regions around Nablus and Hebron. The king had accomplished his purpose. He rode to Jerusalem to pay his respects to the tomb in the Church of the Holy Sepulchre, and then returned to Acre for a last meeting with the barons before sailing back to Spain. Somewhere in the Mediterranean, his small fleet would pass the much larger fleet of Richard, Earl of Cornwall and brother of King Henry III of England, who would take the king of Navarre's place as the acknowledged leader of the continuous Crusade.

Richard, Earl of Cornwall, was one of those curious men who go through life wearing great titles they can never live up to. His uncle was Richard the Lion Heart; his father the lackluster King John; his mother Isabelle of Angoulême, who after her husband's death married Hugh of Lusignan, Prince of the Galilee; his sister, another Isabelle, was married to the Emperor Frederick. He therefore had wide family connections with the Holy Land, and since he came as a kind of royal legate on behalf of his brother, King Henry III of England, he seemed to be invested with kingly power and the barons of Jerusalem accepted him as they had accepted the king of Navarre.

He was intelligent and affable, and he had very few illusions about the Kingdom of Jerusalem. In one of his letters home he wrote, "In the Holy Land peace has been replaced by discord, unity by division, concord by civic loathing. The two fraternal orders, although they were brought into being in defence of their common mother, are swollen with pride because they have an excess of wealth, and they quarrel mercilessly in her breast." Apparently the relations between the Hospitallers and the Templars were strained to the breaking point. The Hospitallers were concentrated at Acre, the Templars at Jaffa. The Hospitallers favored Egypt, while the Templars were in alliance with Damascus. Richard, who had brought eight hundred knights with him, represented a third force, which held the balance of power.

November saw a turning point. Richard threw in his lot with the Hospitallers and came to an understanding with Sultan as-Salih Ayub of Egypt, who confirmed the agreements reached with the king of Navarre. There was a brief period of euphoria. It seemed that the kingdom was secure and that all the disruptive forces might be held in check. Richard was the balance wheel. For a few months he represented the power and might of the Crusader army, the more powerful because it was in alliance with Egypt.

Actually it was Frederick II who was acting behind the scenes, although Richard became the beneficiary. During that winter, Frederick sent two ambassadors to as-Salih Ayub. They came with a retinue of a hundred men, laden with expensive gifts for the sultan. This embassy was greeted as no other embassy had ever been greeted before. The sultan ordered that everyone in Cairo should welcome the ambassadors and their retinue, who were given Nubian horses from the sultan's own stables. The streets and the public buildings were illuminated. There were parades and audiences and celebrations, and the sultan spoke kindly to the ambassadors and their retinue, lodged them in his palaces, and gave them mountains of gifts. The members of the embassy were invited to go on hunting expeditions, to practice with their crossbows, to amuse themselves as they pleased. Winter is always the best time of the year in Cairo, and as-Salih Ayub seemed determined to impress Frederick with his liberality and generosity in a good season.

Richard, well aware of the success of the embassy, seems to have felt that his services were no longer needed. He fortified Ascalon, did his best to resolve the quarrels of the barons, and in May 1241 he returned to England, taking his knights with him.

With the balance wheel gone, the barons of Jerusalem leaped at each other's throats: The Templars fought the Hospitallers, there were murderous raids by the Templars into the territory of al-Nasir Daud, and by the Hospitallers against Aleppo; Richard Filanghieri, the imperial viceroy, was thrown out of Tyre by a consortium of barons, who were incensed when he attempted to organize a *coup d'état* in Acre. Balian of Ibelin was emerging as the chief of the barons. Neither King Conrad, who reached the age of fifteen in 1243, nor the aging John of Brienne were able to exercise kingship in the Holy Land, and the barons decided that the title Queen of Jerusalem should be granted to Queen Alix of Cyprus, who became regent. The barons were in the ascendant, with no king of Navarre or earl of Cornwall to curb their recklessness, their stupidity, or their avarice. Each was prepared to defend his own property against all comers. The Kingdom of Jerusalem scarcely existed, there was only the sum of its parts.

If the barons had been united under a war leader of proven excellence—another Godfrey, another Leper King, another Richard the Lion Heart—it would have made very little difference during the days that followed the departure of the earl of Cornwall. The forces confronting the kingdom were vast and incalculable, and even the Templars, with their network of spies and secret agents in Damascus and Cairo, could not measure the extent of the horrors about to be visited on them.

In June 1244, the Khwarismian horsemen swept out of the Hauran, invaded the Galilee, captured Tiberias, put all the Christians to the sword, and then swung toward Nablus and Jerusalem. This long column, more than ten thousand strong, had crossed the Euphrates in boats made of animal skins earlier in the year. They had been summoned by Sultan as-Salih Ayub, who wanted them to create havoc in their southward march, join the Egyptian army at Gaza, and then march north against the Christians along the seacoast and east against Damascus. With the help of the Khwarismians, he hoped to destroy both the Christians and the armies of his uncle, as-Salih Ismail.

The Khwarismians were mercenaries, out for plunder, living off the land. They wore wolfskins and sheepskins; they survived on boiled herbs, water, milk, and a little meat. They were admirable bowmen, skilled lancers; they were quick, with their short hunting knives, at cutting throats. They brought their women and children with them, and the women fought beside the men. They sacked Tiberias and Nablus, but these were small towns. Jerusalem was not so easily sacked by wild tribesmen.

The Christians had been slow to realize the danger. Robert, Patriarch of Jerusalem, now hurried to the holy city with the masters of the Temple and the Hospital, hoping there was time to put the defenses in order. Part of the Christian population was evacuated. Then, on July 11, 1244, the Khwarismians broke into the city, murdering and plundering as they raced through the narrow streets. They reached the Church of the Holy Sepulchre, desecrated the tombs of the kings of Jerusalem, and cut the throats of the priests who were celebrating mass at the high altar. They opened the graves of the kings, searching for treasure; they found only bones, which they threw into a fire. But the garrison held out for a few weeks. The Crusaders made a surprisingly vigorous defense, and they did not surrender until August 23. The Khwarismians then offered to let the Christians go free. About eight thousand survivors of six weeks of murder and pillage took the road to Jaffa.

They had gone only a little way down the road when they looked back and saw Frankish flags waving on the walls. Thinking that Jerusalem had somehow been recaptured by the knights, they turned back, only to fall into an ambush carefully laid by the Khwarismians, who had had second thoughts about letting the Christians go free. They amused themselves with another massacre. The Arab tribesmen in the neighborhood smelled blood. The Christians who survived the massacre were hunted down by the tribesmen and killed. Only three hundred survivors, out of the eight thousand, reached Jaffa.

In this way Jerusalem fell finally and completely into the hands of the Muslims. Except for an anomalous six-month period in 1300, 673 years would pass before a Christian army would enter the city again. On December 9, 1917, the Turks surrendered the city to General Sir Edmund Allenby.

The Khwarismian invasion brought about changes in the fragile system of alliances. The barons threw in their lot with Damascus; the king of Transjordania and the prince of Hims joined the Christians; the Templars and the Hospitallers seemed to bury their quarrels. When the prince of Hims arrived in Acre, he was welcomed with enthusiasm and jubilation; cloths of gold, silks, and carpets were spread out before him wherever he walked or rode through the city. He was known to be an excellent soldier and a master of diplomacy; and he liked and understood the Christians.

Gauthier of Brienne, Count of Jaffa, and Philip of Montfort, Lord of Tyre, commanded the expedition, which consisted of about a thousand knights and six thousand foot soldiers; the prince of Hims brought two thousand cavalry, and the king of Transjordania about an equal number of Bedouin. A real alliance had been forged: the Christians and Muslims marched together in good spirits; there was no bickering as the three columns drove toward Gaza, where the Egyptians and the Khwarismians were waiting for them.

The armies met near the village of La Forbie on the sandy plains northeast of Gaza. Gauthier of Brienne became commander in chief of the allied forces. A young Mameluke officer, Baibars, formerly a slave, commanded the combined Egyptian-Khwarismian army. The opposing armies were about equal in numbers and equipment. The best military strategists on the field were Baibars and the prince of Hims.

At a war council before the battle, the prince of Hims insisted that they should take up defensive positions and transform the camp into an armed fortress. The Khwarismians generally avoided fortified strongpoints. Confronted by an unyielding wall of knights and foot soldiers, they could be expected to melt away, and the Egyptian army was too small to attack without them. But Gauthier of Brienne, always quick to act, decided upon an immediate attack.

The Franks were massed on the right wing, near the sea; the prince of Hims with his detachment of Damascenes occupied the center, and the king of Transjordania with his mounted Bedouin were on the left. The battle lasted two days, from the morning of October 17, 1244, to the afternoon of the next day. During the first day, the knights made repeated charges against the army of Baibars, which held its ground. There were skirmishes with the Khwarismians, thrusts and sallies all along the line. On the following day the Khwarismians attacked the Damascenes in the center, and this concentrated attack of extraordinary ferocity punched a hole in the allied line which could never be filled up. The Damascenes fled. Then the Khwarismians wheeled around against the Bedouin and cut them to pieces. The army of the prince of Hims fought well, almost to the last man. Seventeen hundred of them fell to the Khwarismians, and the prince of Hims rode off the field with only 280 men. Having disposed of the Damascenes, the cavalry of the prince of Hims, and the Bedouin, the Khwarismians turned on the Christians with the relish of men who, having feasted well, look forward to the sweetmeats at the end of dinner.

Sandwiched between the Khwarismians and the Egyptians, the Franks were torn to shreds. They charged and were thrown back, and every charge produced a mountain of dead horses and dead riders. Over five thousand Christians died in the sands. The losses at La Forbie were even greater than the losses on the Horns of Hattin. Only thirty-three Templars, twenty-seven Hospitallers, and three Teutonic Knights survived the battle. Eight hundred prisoners were taken, including Gauthier of Brienne. The Khwarismians tortured him and then surrendered him to the Egyptians in the hope of a large ransom. He died in a dungeon in Cairo, murdered by some merchants who felt that he had raided too many caravans moving between Cairo and Damascus.

The losses among the great officers of the kingdom were staggering. The Master of the Temple, the archbishop of Tyre, the bishops of Lydda and Ramleh, and the two cousins of Bohemond of Antioch, John and William of Botrun, perished; their heads were cut off to decorate the gates of Cairo. Philip of Montfort and the patriarch of Jerusalem, who had carried the True Cross into battle, escaped to Ascalon. The Egyptians celebrated in Cairo with a triumphal procession, fireworks, illuminations, and a grand parade in which the captured emirs of Damascus were seen roped together with their heads bent low and their faces grey with despair. Cairo went wild with joy.

The disaster at La Forbie signified the end of the Crusaders' offensive military power. They would continue to hold castles and fortified cities for a little while longer, but never again were they able to put a large army in the field. They had been bled white at La Forbie; the body politic had suffered so many shocks that it seemed to be dazed, exhausted, without willpower.

One more king, arrayed in the mysterious panoply of majesty, would come to the Holy Land and attempt after more terrible defeats to put its affairs in order. Meanwhile the Crusaders, crouched behind their fortress walls, murdered each other, sent occasional raiding parties into the hinterland, and sometimes they managed to believe that the kingdom was in the care of the Holy Trinity and would endure for eternity.

X

THE SAINT
IN HIS
TOILS

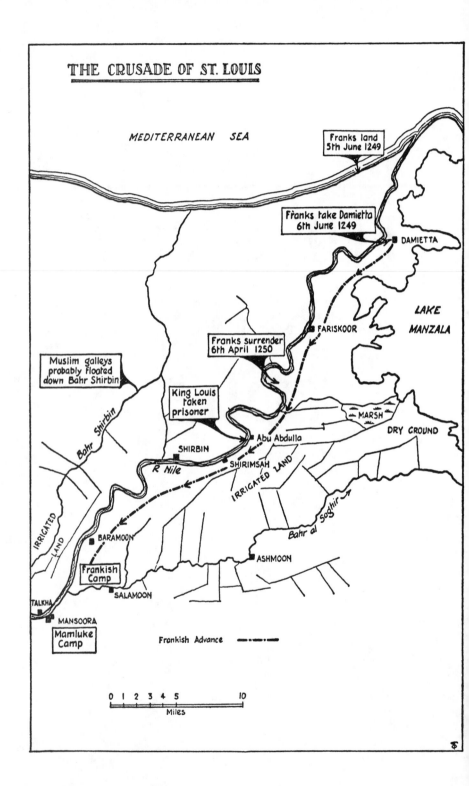

THE CRUSADE OF ST. LOUIS

MEDITERRANEAN SEA

Franks land
5th June 1249

Franks take Damietta
6th June 1249

DAMIETTA

LAKE
MANZALA

FARISKOOR

Franks surrender
6th April 1250

Muslim galleys
probably floated
down Bahr Shirbin

MARSH

DRY GROUND

King Louis
taken
prisoner

Abu Abdulla

Bahr Shirbin

SHIRBIN

R. Nile

SHIRIMSAH

IRRIGATED LAND

Bahr al Soghir

IRRIGATED

LAND

BARAMOON

ASHMOON

Frankish
Camp

TALKHA

SALAMOON

MANSOORA

Mamluke
Camp

Frankish Advance ▬ ▬ ▬

0 1 2 3 4 5   10
Miles

The Pilgrimages
of St. Louis

ONLY one of the kings of France became a saint. Although in all his acts he exhibited a peculiarly French grace and courtesy, his temperament was profoundly Spanish. His mother, Queen Blanche of Castile, instilled in him a love for devotional practices, and he was very young when he wore his first hair shirt. He had a Spaniard's abject fear of mortal sin and a Spaniard's habit of harsh meditations. He was crowned at the age of twelve at Rheims. His mother ruled France until he came of age; and even when he became the sole ruler, he sought his mother's advice so often that even the clerics who half-worshipped him wondered who was in command.

The monks called him "Friar Louis," and there was something monkish in him; yet he was very well aware that he was king of France. Moreover, since the day of his coronation, he felt he was king not so much by divine right but by a singular blessing of God. He prayed a great deal; in his prayers he seemed to lose—and find—himself. He was devoted to the poor, the sick, and the maimed. He would go to hospitals and work there like the commonest of nurses; he would even empty out the bedpans.

One day he asked one of his companions, "What would you rather be—a leper or in mortal sin?"

"I would rather have committed thirty or forty mortal sins than be a leper," his companion replied.

The king said nothing at the time, but on the following day the man was summoned into his presence.

"Come and sit at my feet," the king said. "Yesterday you spoke rashly, for all the ills of the body are cured in a little while when a man dies, but if the soul is tarnished and if you are uncertain whether God has pardoned you, the evil will last forever as long as God sits in Paradise."

The king disliked ostentation, and usually wore a brown taffeta tunic under a dark blue mantle of coarse cloth, and it may not have occurred to him that the dark tunic brought out the highlights of the bright yellow

335

hair that reached to his shoulders. Although usually clothed modestly, he counseled his sons to dress well. "You should clothe yourselves well and decently," he told them, "so that your women will love you more and your household will respect you, for the wise men say we ought to dress and arm ourselves in such a manner that neither shall the good men of the world blame us for extravagance nor the young blades for meanness." On ceremonial occasions he delighted in wearing a sumptuous vermilion surcoat edged with ermine.

He was paradoxical: a meditative man who loved action, a reasonable man who believed in the sanctity of improbable relics, a profoundly gentle man who could be mercilessly cruel on occasion. His pride and humility were in harmonious balance.

He collected relics with avidity, including the Crown of Thorns and a portion of the True Cross, both of which he purchased in Constantinople for vast sums. Eventually he built the famous Sainte-Chapelle to house them.

In time he acquired the Holy Lance and the Holy Sponge and the Holy Nails, the Purple Robe, a piece of the Holy Shroud, a portion of the Napkin used by Mary Magdelene to wash Christ's feet, a phial of the Virgin's Milk and another of the Precious Blood. Avaricious of relics, he acquired the Virgin's blue mantle and the swaddling clothes of the Christ-child. Having exhausted the available treasures of the New Testament, he went in search of the treasures of the Old Testament. He acquired the Rod with which Moses struck the Rock and all manner of strange objects from the ancient past: there was no end to the inventiveness of Venetian and Byzantine merchants.

More than any of his contemporaries, Louis IX possessed the means to buy relics and the faith necessary to worship them. He seems to have felt that relics formed a kind of celestial economy that could be brought down to earth. Heaven was in the relics, and the more relics he possessed the more of heaven lay in his possession.

There remained the ultimate relic: the empty tomb in the Church of the Holy Sepulchre. Indeed, for him the Holy Land was itself a relic, a place of surpassing holiness, and he was determined to conquer it.

At last, when Sainte-Chapelle had been completed, he set out on his Crusade with every intention of recovering the Holy Sepulchre for the Christians. He left Paris on June 12, 1248, marched by slow stages to Lyons, where the baggage trains were transferred to barges and the great war-horses were walked along the river bank. Near Valence, the king paused long enough to attack the castle of La Roche-Glun, whose lord preyed on all pilgrims and merchants who passed below the castle walls. It was a very hot summer; the earth was parched and the sky cloudless. When they reached Aigues-Mortes, which means "dead waters," the Crusaders were exhausted. At Aigues-Mortes, the sea came right up to the walls, and one could step out of the town and board the ships at the watergate. Thirty-eight ships from Genoa and Marseilles were waiting for the Crusader army, which numbered about twenty thousand men, of whom about four thousand were armed knights. King Louis was accompanied by his wife, Marguerite of Provence, one of the four beautiful daughters of the count of Provence. King Henry III of England married Eleanor, Richard of Cornwall married Sanchia, and Charles of Anjou, King of Naples, married the youngest, Beatrice. The four daughters were all high-spirited, intelligent, and resourceful, and they were able to influence events.

On August 25, the great fleet assembled at Aigues-Mortes was ready to sail, the horses battened down in the hatches, the knights taking their places in the forecastles and the sergeants and bowmen on the deck aft. Two days passed before the wind caught the great sails. Then, with all its banners flying, the armada made its way toward Cyprus.

Both King Louis and his chronicler, John of Joinville, were bad sailors. The king was often seasick; he had a horror of the sea. John of Joinville describes with a cold passion what it was like to be out of sight of land:

> Soon the wind filled our sails and carried us out of sight of the land, so that we saw nothing but sky and water; and every day the wind carried us further from the country where we were born. I tell you these things so that you will understand how foolhardy it is for a man to run such grave risks, especially if he is in possession of something that belongs to someone else or if he is in mortal sin. For when you go to bed at night on shipboard, you do not know whether you may find yourself in the morning at the bottom of the sea.

Three weeks after leaving Aigues-Mortes, the fleet dropped anchor in the harbor of Limassol on the southern coast of Cyprus. Immediately, there was a council of war. King Louis wanted to sail at once to Egypt, but the Cypriots and most of his knights preferred to delay the attack until the following spring. So they wintered in Cyprus, building up the fleet, amassing armaments and provisions, and quarreling with one another, while a surprisingly large number of French barons died of disease. The historian De Nangis says that two hundred and forty nobles and knights died. Charles of Anjou, the king's brother, suffered from a quartan fever. It was a bad omen. The king, however, remained in good spirits; he was so busy adjudicating the quarrels of his subjects and of the princes of the Near East that he had no time to brood.

The king of Armenia was quarreling with the prince of Antioch. The king bade them settle their quarrel with a two-year truce, and then prudently aided the prince of Antioch with a present of six hundred bowmen to fight off the marauding Turks. The Cypriots quarreled with the French;

the rival archbishops of the Latin and Greek rites stirred up dissension; and in spite of an outward show of agreement, the king of Cyprus was not always on friendly terms with the king of France. The king's financial troubles were increasing, because so many of the knights simply could not afford to spend a long winter in Cyprus. John of Joinville soon exhausted his money. He went to the king, who gave him 800 livres, "which was more than I needed." It is fortunate that he did so, for otherwise John of Joinville would have been compelled to return to France and his *Chronicle of the Crusade of St. Louis* would never have been written.

Toward Christmas there arrived in Nicosia, where the king had his headquarters, two envoys called Mark and David, both of whom were Mongols and Nestorian Christians. They represented Aljighidai, the Mongol viceroy of Persia. Guyuk Khan, the nephew of Genghis Khan, ruled all of northern Asia from Peking to the Crimea and beyond, and Aljighidai was one of his most powerful advisers. The envoys brought news that Guyuk Khan, Aljighidai and most of the Mongol army had been converted to Christianity, and that the Mongols hoped for an alliance with the Franks against the hated Saracens. Mark and David were watched carefully, but there was not the least doubt that they were Christians; they attended mass, made the proper responses, and spoke very seriously with the Dominican friar, Andrew of Longjumeau, who was in attendance at King Louis's court, and who happened to be one of the greatest experts in the West on the Mongols. Friar Andrew spoke Persian, the court language of the Mongols in western Asia, and was able to authenticate the documents produced by the Nestorian Christians.

It was an exciting moment, this first confrontation between a European king and envoys representing the Mongol horde. The king was aware that everything about the meeting was fraught with heavy consequences. An alliance between the Mongols and the Franks promised the destruction of Saracen power in the Near East: Baghdad, Damascus, and Cairo would fall; Mongols and Christians would rule over the Holy Land. Nor was this prospect merely a visionary dream. The kingdom of Armenia in Cilicia was already a vassal state of the Mongol empire; Hethum I, King of Armenia, who had married the granddaughter of a former queen of Jerusalem, had traveled across nearly the whole of Asia to present himself at the Mongol court in Karakorum at a time when the Great Khan was thinking seriously of converting to Christianity. The Mongols were closer to Jerusalem than people realized.

Mark and David, the two Mongol envoys, remained in Cyprus for over five weeks. The king sent an embassy to Aljighidai, the most important ever sent by Christendom to the Mongols. It included Andrew of Longjumeau, two more Dominican friars, two clerks, and two sergeants-at-arms. With them were sent many jewels and a tent-chapel of scarlet silk, embroidered with scenes depicting the life of Christ so that it resembled a church with stained glass windows, mosaics, and paintings. Aljighidai died before they reached him. The embassy went on toward Mongolia only to find that Guyuk Khan had also died. The empire was being administered by his widow, Ogul Gamish, who showed no interest at all in a Franco-Mongol alliance. She received the ambassadors graciously, gave them gifts in return, and sent them back to King Louis, calling upon the king to send tribute of gold and silver "as much as may win you our friendship," and threatening to destroy him if he did not do so.

With the coming of spring, the king's problems increased. He needed more ships for the invasion fleet; his money was running out; the quarrels of the Genoese and Pisans were getting out of hand; some of the Frankish soldiers were sailing to Cilicia to join forces with the king of Armenia, who was fighting the Turks in Asia Minor; the Templars were engaged in secret negotiations with the sultan of Egypt in spite of the king's determination that no negotiations should take place. During the previous winter the sultan had captured Hims and was thus in a position to threaten many of the coastal cities of the Crusaders. The worst of these tribulations was the quarrel between the Genoese and the Pisans, which led to a ferocious civil war lasting twenty-one days in Acre. The king wanted the ships moored in the harbor of Acre to sail to Limassol, to serve as transports for the descent on Egypt, but none came.

At last, on May 13, 1249, the fleet was assembled. There were about 120 galleons, 80 smaller ships, and a host of pinnaces, supply boats, and small craft. It took more than two weeks to provision the ships, and finally the ships were ready to sail. But just at the moment when the king was attending his last mass on the island of Cyprus, there came a tempest from the south so violent that two-thirds of the fleet, brought together at such vast expense and with so much ingenuity and care, was scattered by winds of hurricane force and dispersed throughout the eastern Mediterranean. If God were saying to King Louis, "Go back to France, your journey is doomed, save what can be saved," he could not have said it more clearly.

Oddly enough, the king who worshipped relics was not a man to pay attention to signs and portents. As soon as the storm had abated, he collected his remaining ships and gave orders to sail straight for Damietta. He had about a third of his army with him. Many of the ships scattered by the storm would reach Damietta later.

By this time it had, by constant repetition, become an article of faith that the road to Jerusalem lay through Egypt. Jerusalem would be free when the power of Egypt was destroyed, when the Christians were established in Alexandria, Damietta, and Cairo. The Crusader passion for doing things the hard way received its ultimate benediction in this obsession with Egypt. The unmapped and treacherous tributaries of the Nile Delta offered no easy passage; the deadly heat of the Egyptian summer, the sandstorms, the Nile floods, the pestilences, the interminable sandy deserts, all these would have suggested to any sensible Crusader that there were better ways to safeguard Jerusalem. But the Crusaders were not sensible; they expected miracles, and sometimes King Louis provided them. At other times, he provided them with overwhelming disasters.

As-Salih Ayub, Sultan of Egypt, was the grandnephew of Saladin and the son of the wise al-Kamil by a Sudanese slave woman. He was cruel, imperious, covetous of the wealth of his emirs, and strangely addicted to drowning his enemies. He was not a cultured man: He detested reading, knew nothing about the sciences, and was at home only in the camp or in the audience chambers of his palaces, where he gave orders crisply to his terrified subjects. No high officer dared to make any move without his express permission. Yet he was a good soldier who understood battlefields, lines of force, and the deployment of reserves as well as any Christian prince or general. He had thought the Franks would attack Syria, which showed his intelligence. When he heard, through spies on the island of Cyprus, that the Franks' real objective was Damietta, he hurried back to Egypt. He had to be carried on a litter because he was in an advanced state of consumption and suffered horribly from ulcers. While he was being brought back to Egypt, the defense of the country was in the hands of Fakhr ad-Din, the former ambassador to the court of Frederick II.

No Egyptian warships were waiting for the French fleet when it arrived off Damietta, the triple-walled city with many towers and a wide moat on the landward side, so designed that it was very nearly impregnable. The Egyptian army was waiting for the Christians on the shore some distance away. There was no attempt to prevent the landing. In the distance the Crusaders could see the Egyptian cavalry, their weapons gleaming like gold in the hot sunshine. The noise of their drums, cymbals, and horns was deafening, but they did not attack. John of Joinville, puzzled because the expected massive attack never came, learned later that the Egyptians had sent carrier pigeons to Ashmun-Tannah, a town on one of the Nile tributaries, where the sultan was staying. Three times the carrier pigeons were sent off, but there was no reply. The Egyptian generals concluded that the sultan was dead or dying. Having never been empowered to make decisions, the generals were irresolute.

But while there was no attack, there were many skirmishes. Here and there along the coast the Egyptians fought off the invading ships by plunging into the sea, cavalrymen attacking the armed boatmen with swords and lances.

Seeing these skirmishes from the poop of his flagship, the *Montjoie*, King Louis could not resist the excitement. He leaped into the water and, his shield hanging from his neck and a lance in his hand, he strode ashore. As soon as he saw the enemy, he set his lance at his shoulder and his shield in front of him, and he would have charged the Egyptians if wiser men had not held him back.

The French landed on the morning of June 4, and by evening they had won the beachhead. On the following evening, the Egyptian troops withdrew from the city, very quietly, and the next morning there came a renegade Egyptian to the French camp, saying that the city had been abandoned. The bridge of boats across the moat was left intact. During the afternoon, the Christians marched into the city in force and planted the king's banner on the highest tower.

The sultan was incensed when he heard of the abandonment of Damietta. Some emirs were hanged, and Fakhr ad-Din was in danger of his life.

So little damage was done to the Christian forces by the Egyptians, so easily and quickly did Damietta fall to the Christians, that people like Guy of Melun, who fought in the ranks, thought a miracle had taken place through the intervention of King Louis.

EXCERPTS FROM A LETTER FROM GUY, A PILGRIM, TO HIS FRIEND IN PARIS, FROM DAMIETTA, 1249.

. . . [A]fter a few days a sudden tempest drove us over a wide expanse of the sea. Several of our vessels were driven apart and scattered. The Sultan of Cairo and other Saracen princes, informed by spies that we intended to attack Alexandria, had assembled an infinite multitude of armed men at Cairo as well as at Damietta and Alexandria, and awaited us in order to put us to the sword. One night we were borne over the waves by a violent tempest. Toward morning the sky cleared, the storm abated, and our scattered vessels came together safely. An experienced pilot who knew all the coast and who was considered a faithful guide, was sent to the masthead. After he had carefully examined all the surrounding country, he cried: "God help us, God help us, we are before Damietta!"

All of us could see the land. Other pilots on other vessels had already made the same observation. The King, assured of our position, endeavoured to reanimate and console his men. "My faithful friends," he said to them, "we shall be invincible if we are inseparable in our charity. It is not without the divine permission that we have been brought here to a country so powerfully protected. I am neither the King of France nor the Holy Church; you are both. I am only a man whose life will end like other men's when it shall please God. Everything is in our favor, whatever may happen to us. If we are conquered, we shall be martyrs. If we triumph, the glory of God will be thereby exalted—the glory of France, yea, even of Christianity will be exalted thereby. Certainly it would be foolish to believe that God, who foresees all things, has incited me in vain. This is His cause, we shall conquer for Christ, He will triumph in us, He will give the glory, the honor and the blessing not unto us, but unto His name. . . ."

. . . We lost only a single man by the enemy's fire. Two or three others, too eager for the combat, threw themselves into the water too quickly and perished there. The Saracens gave way and retired into their city, fleeing shamefully and with great loss. Several of them were mutilated or mortally wounded.

We followed them closely but our chiefs who feared an ambuscade held us back. While we were fighting, some slaves and prisoners broke their chains, for the jailers came out to fight us. Only the women, children and old men remained in the city. These slaves and prisoners were full of joy and rushed up to us, crying: "Blessed is he who cometh in the name of the Lord." These events happened on Friday, the day of our Lord's passion; we drew from it a favorable augury. The King disembarked joyfully and safely, as well as the rest of the Christian army. We rested until the next day when, with the aid and the guidance of slaves who knew the country and the roads, we took possession of what remained to be captured of the land and shore. During the night the Saracens who had discovered that the prisoners had escaped, killed those who remained. They thus made of them glorious martyrs of Christ, to their own damnation.

The following night and Sunday morning, as they lacked weapons and troops, the Saracens seeing the multitude of the Christians who were landing, their courage and firmness, and the sudden desolation of their own city, departed with their chiefs, taking their women and children and carrying off everything movable. They fled from the other side of the city by little gates which they had made long before. Some escaped by land, others by sea, abandoning their city filled with supplies of all kinds. That same day, at three o'clock, two prisoners who had escaped by chance from the Saracens, came to tell us what had happened. The King, no longer fearing an ambuscade, entered the city at nine o'clock without hindrance and without shedding blood. Of all who entered only Hugo Brun, Count de la Marche, was severely wounded. He lost too much blood from his wounds to survive.

I must not forget to say that the Saracens, after having decided to flee, hurled at us a great quantity of Greek fire which was very injurious to us, because it was carried by a wind that blew from the city. But the wind suddenly changing carried the fire back upon Damietta where it burned several persons. It would have consumed more property if the slaves who had been left behind had not extinguished it by a process which they knew, and by the will of God.

The King having entered the city amidst cries of joy went immediately into the temple of the Saracens to pray and to thank God whom he regarded as the author of what had taken place. The Te Deum was chanted, and after the temple had been purified, mass was celebrated. We found in the city an infinite quantity of food, arms, engines, precious clothing, vases, gold and silver utensils and other things. In addition we had our provisions and other necessary objects brought from our vessels.

By the divine glory the Christian army, like a pond which is greatly swollen by the torrents pouring into it, was added to each day by members of the Teutonic Order, by Templars and Hospitallers, without speaking of the pilgrims who arrived at every moment. The Templars and Hospitallers did not want to believe in such a triumph. In fact, nothing that had happened was credible. All seemed miraculous. . . .

Victory and Defeat at Damietta

HEY would say of King Louis IX that he was a man who rarely showed emotion, that he maintained in his everyday life the calm of a prayerful man, and that he never spoke ill of anyone unless he was a traitor or an infidel. All this was true of the outer man, who always succeeded in maintaining his royal dignity, but the inner man was in constant turmoil: his desire for sanctity was at war with his desire to be remembered as a warrior and as a prince who governed well.

All the evidence goes to show that he believed the abandonment of Damietta came as a result of his own generalship and in answer to his prayers. He was not surprised or even elated; it was what he had expected all along. What he did not know was that the city was a trap; and he fell into it.

He made his solemn entry into Damietta on June 6. The great gates opened on a city from which everyone had fled. The houses, shops, and palaces were intact; the granaries were filled with wheat, barley, and rice; the armories were filled with weapons; the oil vats were full of oil.

Within a few days Damietta was transformed into a Christian city. The king lived in the sultan's palace, the papal legate lived in the nearby fortress of the former military commander, the great mosque was transformed into a church, and fifty-three Christian prisoners found in the dungeons were given their freedom. The army was lodged outside the city, because the king feared an imminent attack by the sultan. For a few days there were no attacks except by marauding Bedouin who galloped up to the city at night in the hope of acquiring a few Christian heads, the sultan having promised ten bezants for every head presented to him. But the Christians were on guard, the crossbowmen generally kept the Bedouin at a distance, and, when too many of them succeeded in passing the guards, the king ordered a palisade to be erected around the camp. Later the palisade was transformed into earthworks, and the camp became a small fortress.

The Nile was about to overflow, as it always does in June. Between June and September, fighting in the Nile Delta was very nearly impossible. The king decided to dig in for the long summer and prepare for an attack on Cairo, which was over 100 miles to the south of Damietta. The count of Brittany and most of the barons would have preferred to besiege Alexandria, where there was an excellent port, so that provisions could be brought to the army whenever needed, but Robert, Count of Artois, the king's brother, was adamant that they should march on Cairo. The king relied heavily on this brother, who regarded himself as the military expert in the family. The decision to march on Cairo would turn out to be suicidal and would lead to the destruction of the entire Christian army.

The long summer itself, after its brilliant beginning, became a nightmare. The tremendous heat, the snakes, the insects, the sense of isolation in a foreign land, all these affected the foot soldiers cooped up behind the earthworks. The knights, of course, could enter the city at will. The lords lived well, the soldiers complained bitterly; by the time the king began to march on Cairo, he was commanding troops whose morale had been shaken by nearly five months of enforced inactivity, boredom, and misery.

Robert, Count of Artois, reasoned that the best way to kill a snake was to smash its head. This statement might have made more sense if accurate maps had been available. The Crusaders did not know how to reach Cairo, the political head. But the capture of Cairo would have been of little use to them, since in any event the real head was the Egyptian army, which was lying in wait for them at Mansourah, and which they would have to destroy before they could reach Cairo. In the plans of the king and his brother there was no element of surprise, no feints, no cunning. The huge, unwieldy Christian army was ordered to move southward among the canals and rivers; it was visible to spies, who were able to report all its movements. As it marched further and further into marshy land, there was the possibility that at any moment retreat would be cut off.

And always, there were delays. Just as they had wasted a winter in Cyprus and a long summer in Damietta, so they allowed the autumn to pass, and it was winter again when they left Damietta, leaving Queen Marguerite and the patriarch of Jerusalem in the walled city with a small garrison to protect them. A few days later they received news that the sultan was dead. They also heard that the sultana and Fakhr ad-Din had assumed power, while waiting for the arrival of the heir to the throne, the sultan's son Turanshah, who was viceroy in the Jezireh. Turanshah was a long time coming, and this too portended good fortune for the Christian army. King Louis could not bring himself to believe that a woman could rule Muslim country, though he was perfectly content to let his mother, Blanche of Castile, rule over France in his absence.

They left Damietta on November 20, and another month passed before they reached the main defensive positions of Mansourah. There were the

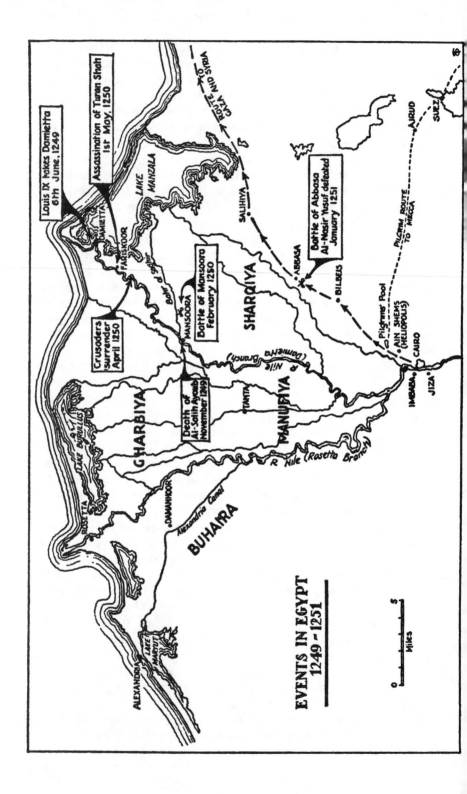

EVENTS IN EGYPT
1249 – 1251

Louis IX takes Damietta 6th June, 1249

Assassination of Turan Shah 1st May, 1250

Crusaders Surrender April 1250

Death of Al-Salih Ayoub November 1249

Battle of Mansoora February 1250

Battle of Abbasa Al-Nasir Yusuf defeated January 1251

ALEXANDRIA

LAKE MARYUT

ROSETTA

LAKE BURULLUS

DAMANHOOR

Alexandria Canal

BUHAIRA

R. Nile (Rosetta Branch)

GHARBIYA

TANTA

MANUFIYA

DAMIETTA

FARISKOOR

LAKE MANZILA

Bahr al Saghir

MANSOORA

R. Nile (Damietta Branch)

SHARQIYA

SALIHIYA

ABBASA

BILBEIS

Pilgrims' Pool

AIN SHEMS (HELIOPOLIS)

CAIRO

IMBABA

JIZA

PILGRIM ROUTE TO MECCA

AJRUD

SUEZ

TO ROUTE AND SYRIA
GAZA

0   5
Miles

N

usual skirmishes on the way. The king gave orders that skirmishes were to be avoided wherever possible, but when five hundred Egyptian cavalry fell on the Templar vanguard, the Templars in their fury decided to teach them a lesson. Their horses were fresh; the Egyptian horses were already weary; and in the general charge no Egyptians survived, for they were either cut down or they fell into the river and were drowned.

In such forays, involving small numbers, the Templars always gave a good account of themselves. They were assault troops, trained for sudden raids, improvisations, hit-and-run attacks. Their chief fault was that they defied the rules, while the chief fault of the king was that he obeyed the rules even when they were absurd.

On February 8, 1250, in a grey misty dawn, the Templar vanguard, with Robert, Count of Artois, in command, was to cross a ford, thereby outflanking the Egyptian position before Mansourah. The ford had been conveniently pointed out by a renegade Muslim, who was rewarded with fifty bezants for his pains. For once there would be the element of surprise. The knights would make their way over the ford and then wait for the main army under the duke of Burgundy to come up. They were to hold the bank, while the bowmen came running over a pontoon bridge. Until the whole army had crossed over, there must be no movement, no sallies, no attempt to engage the enemy. The king wanted to be sure that the attack against the enemy would be a massive one, carefully choreographed.

The army was now very close to the walls of Mansourah. Robert rode across the ford with the Templars, saw the Egyptian cavalry in front of him, heard the horns and trumpets of the enemy, and with his retinue hurled himself against them. The Templars tried to stop him but, being unsuccessful, they decided to join him in order to protect his life. There was a wild skirmish.

Fakhr ad-Din was in his bath, having his hair dyed with fiery red henna. Hearing the dreadful noise, he jumped out of the bath, threw a robe over himself, leaped on a horse, and charged into battle, soon to be cut to pieces by knights in armor. But the Egyptians had prepared a trap by leaving one of Mansourah's gates open. The open gate was altogether too inviting. The Templars and the count of Artois charged through it. It was a stupid and dangerous move. They soon lost themselves in the narrow streets, huge beams were thrown down on them, and they were unhorsed. Trying to fight their way out of the city, they were reduced to hand-to-hand combat with swords, maces, and knives, and were overwhelmed by sheer numbers. Three hundred knights and nearly three hundred Templars were killed in the maze of Mansourah's narrow streets.

The king could be seen fighting between Mansourah and the river, wearing a golden helmet and wielding a sword of German steel, and at one point he was surrounded by six horsemen and escaped by hacking at them with his sword. The French bowmen, for some inexplicable reason, had not yet crossed the river, while the Egyptian bowmen were busily killing off the French horses. The rest of the day passed in heavy skirmishing, until late in the afternoon, when the full force of the Christian bowmen came up and most of the Muslim cavalry retreated behind the walls of Mansourah. The king slept that night in the camp of Fakhr ad-Din, who had died in the battle. This was a victory of sorts, but small skirmishes continued through the night. That evening the king heard about the death of his favorite brother. With the knowledge that Robert of Artois had disobeyed him by his reckless ride into the city, and met a miserable death, all he could say was that God had been exceedingly good to him.

God, however, seemed to have forgotten the Christian army and failed to provide King Louis with military intelligence. A new leader had arisen to take the place of Fakhr ad-Din. This was Baibars al-Bundukdari, now a young Mameluke emir, who had been the officer in charge of the combined Egyptian and Khwarismian forces which had utterly destroyed the Christians at the battle of La Forbie. The defense of Mansourah was now in his hands, and he was more relentless and more pitiless than any Muslim commander had ever been. For the first time since Saladin, the Crusaders were confronted with a military commander of genius.

The king and his army remained outside the walls of Mansourah for eight weeks, hoping that another miracle would happen. It did not. Baibars was conserving his strength, hoping the French would perish of their own perversity. Sultan Turanshah, having at last arrived in Egypt from an extended holiday in Damascus, was nominally in command, but Baibars was already commander in chief of the army, and it seems to have been Baibars who organized the fleet of light ships which suddenly appeared in the waterways between Damietta and Mansourah, thus cutting off the Crusaders' supply ships. Baibars's ships were carried on camelback in sections, and were sufficiently well equipped when put together to form another army behind the Christian army.

The king should have fought his way back to Damietta as soon as the first ship appeared. He lost more than eighty ships, and on March 16 a convoy of thirty-two ships was intercepted. Now, the king's army could neither move backward nor could it move forward. Adding to this insolvable problem, there came famine, and then pestilence. Scurvy, typhoid, dysentery were rampant. The plagues of Egypt had returned.

So many of the knights died that the grooms wore their armor and stood guard at points of danger; and so many priests died that there were not enough of them to minister at the altars. The king himself fell ill. He sent Philip of Montfort to the sultan, offering to surrender Damietta to the Egyptians in exchange for Jerusalem and other places in the Holy Land that had recently fallen into Muslim hands. It was an offer that was too late by two months, for the Egyptians knew that he was in a hopeless position and that his whole army was at their mercy.

On April 5, the king at last gave the order for the retreat to Damietta. The Egyptians were on the alert. They attacked the Christians on all sides, massacring the defenseless, killing the knights weakened by pestilence, making prisoners of those who might be expected to pay heavy ransoms. They claimed afterward that they killed or captured fifty thousand men. The king escaped only because Geoffrey of Sargines, in charge of the bodyguard, succeeded in leading him to an abandoned village. Now very ill, the king lay in one of the village huts, while the chief of his bodyguard kept watch on horseback, charging along the village street at any Saracen who dared to show himself. The king was alone in the hut, and Geoffrey of Sargines was alone in the street: and those two lonely men symbolized the strange alteration that had come upon the great army that set out from Damietta.

A few days later, the king surrendered. At about this time disaster also struck the young Sultan Turanshah. He was weak and self-indulgent; he was afraid of Baibars's Mamelukes, who had all the important positions in the army, and he was in the process of reorganizing the army and giving high commands to soldiers from the Jezireh when Baibars struck at him. On the night of May 2, while he was entertaining emirs in his tent, he heard a commotion outside, and a moment later Baibars burst into the tent at the head of a small group of army officers. Wounded in the hand, the sultan escaped to a wooden tower beside the river. Some of the emirs came with him.

Baibars and his fellow conspirators followed. Greek fire was hurled at the tower, which burst into flame. Turanshah jumped down and ran along the riverbank, until someone hurled a spear, which caught him in the ribs. Trailing the spear, he threw himself into the river, and the conspirators went swimming after him, while bowmen fired arrows at him. He was already dying when Baibars himself leaped down the bank and plunged a sword into him. The Arab historians who describe the event observed that he died three deaths: by fire, by iron, and by water.

The strange thing was that the death of Sultan Turanshah was observed by John of Joinville and by King Louis, who were being held on a galley moored in the river. A few minutes later a Mameluke general, Faris ad-Din Octai, came on board the galley, his hand blood-stained, for he had just cut out the sultan's heart. Addressing himself to King Louis, he said, "What will you give me? For I have slain your enemy who, had he lived, would have slain you." The king answered with a long silence.

A little while later some thirty Mamelukes came on board the galley, drawn swords in their hands and Danish axes hanging from their necks. The prisoners imagined they would be put to death. Instead, they were thrown into the hold where they were packed in tightly.

The next morning most of the prisoners, all of them knights or great officers of state, were released in order to discuss the terms of an armistice.

Before King Louis would agree to the treaty, a good deal of time was spent in wrangling about the nature of the oath to be sworn by the Egyptian emirs. It was necessary that the oath should be binding on the Egyptians, and with the help of Nicholas of Acre a curious diplomatic formula was decided upon. The emirs agreed that they would carry out the terms of the armistice or they would be as dishonored as a Muslim who eats swine's flesh, or goes uncovered on a pilgrimage to Mecca, or leaves his wife and then comes back to her again, for according to Muslim law such a man may not return to his wife unless he has seen her in another man's arms.

When the terms were arranged to the satisfaction of the emirs, it was agreed that Damietta should be surrendered to the Egyptians and that the Christians should pay 400,000 livres tournois as an indemnity, half to be paid in Damietta, and half when the king reached Acre. The French for their part would receive all their siege engines and all their supplies of salted pork and their ships; the prisoners would be restored to them; and they in turn would surrender the few prisoners in their power. The king asked for Jerusalem in exchange for Damietta, which was held by a small garrison force aided by Genoese and Pisan sailors. Characteristically, the king refused to swear an oath. The Egyptians were incensed, and to punish the king they tortured the patriarch of Jerusalem by tying him to a post and binding his wrists in such a fashion that his hands swelled to the size of his face. The eighty-year-old patriarch faced the ordeal bravely, and at last they untied him and let him go free.

The torturing of the patriarch in front of the king was idle malice, for the Egyptians knew that the king would not change his mind. They were half in awe of him, and they considered giving him Jerusalem. There were even some who thought that, if he were converted to Islam, he would be a worthy sultan of Egypt. All through those confused negotiations we are aware of the king's calm decisiveness, his passionate self-abnegation.

He had cause for self-abnegation, for he knew that the disaster at Mansourah was due to his own follies, and most especially to his caution, the long weeks and months during which he ordered the army to stay put in Cyprus, in Damietta, and outside the walls of Mansourah. Because of him, perhaps fifty thousand men had died of pestilence or were butchered on the battlefield. A vast treasure had been squandered, and a huge ransom was being paid, equal to the entire yearly revenue of the king of France. The worst was the carnage: the canals swollen with the dead, the fields carpeted with the dying. None of this would have happened if he had been a better soldier. He found consolation in the thought that the dead would be received in heaven by a merciful God, but there were times when he fell into long fits of depression.

He was wretchedly ill, sometimes he had to be carried about by a servant, and for a while, until someone gave him a rough gown to hide his nakedness, he had no clothes. Later the Egyptians gave him a gown of silk and miniver, so that he could attend the meetings of the armistice commissioners in proper attire.

Damietta was surrendered to the Egyptians. There was no difficulty in raising half the ransom money, but the king's brother, Alfonso, Count of Poitou, had to remain at Damietta as surety for the remaining half of the ransom, which was to be paid in Acre. When at last, early in May 1250, the king and his retinue of knights sailed for Acre, he was carried on board the galley on the same mattress he had used in prison. He was still very ill, but the sea air seemed to revive him. Once, while on shipboard, he saw some knights gambling at backgammon; he was so angry that he threw the board into the sea and gave the knights a sermon on the sin of gambling on a Crusade.

The king, of course, was the greatest gambler of them all. He had gambled with human lives on a prodigious scale, recklessly and imprudently, with little understanding of the enemy or of the geography of the Nile Delta. His monumental ignorance of the enemy and the enemy's land was fatal to his cause, and in his own way he contributed to the final defeat of the Kingdom of Jerusalem.

Scorn for his misbegotten endeavors imbues this ironic Arab poem:

> May God reward you for having brought to death the
>   adorers of Jesus the Messiah.
> You came to Egypt with the idea of conquering this
>   kingdom,
> And you believed you would meet here only hautboys
>   and cymbals,
> But instead by your imprudence you have led your men
>   to the gate of death!
> Fifty thousand men, and there is not one of them who is
>   not dead, wounded, or in prison
> God be merciful to you for such an enterprise!

St. Louis in Acre

OW many defeats could the Crusaders withstand? It was as though a curse lay upon them, as though in some mysterious way they found themselves attracted to disaster, like men desperate to destroy themselves. Hattin, La Forbie, and Mansourah were calamities of the first magnitude, and all of them could have been averted with a little common sense or with a fourteen-year-old boy's knowledge of warfare. The Christian commanders were astonishingly ignorant, inept, and careless; they rarely looked at maps; they underestimated the strength of their enemies; while the knights were well cared for, they paid little attention to the provisioning of the foot soldiers; they allowed the enemy to choose the battleground. Into these death traps the Crusaders fell in the thousands.

Nor was it difficult to discover why they acted so precipitately, so unheedingly. They despised the Saracens, knew very little about them, believed that God was on their side, and were quite certain that their civilization was far superior to the civilization of the Arabs at a time when it would have been clear to a visitor from another planet that Arab civilization was in the ascendant. In the sciences, philosophy, theology, medicine, and poetry, the Arabs were far more advanced than the West. They knew where they were going; they had a social system which, in spite of its authoritarian character, was remarkably responsive to the wishes of the people. Their society was stable, while Western society was in flux, the feudal state giving place to the nation state, the cities dissolving into communes, the state itself dissolving into its commercial allegiances. The West was changing at a dizzy pace, but the East was changeless.

The Crusaders were, by their very nature, the inhabitants of a theocracy. If the theocracy sometimes took the form of the government of Acre, part princedom, part commune, part colony, this was because its ultimate ruler was the pope, who understood very little about its inner mechanisms; and even if they had been explained to him, he would not have understood them. Acre was in a state of perpetual civil war, with the Pisans, Genoese, and Venetians at each other's throats. Even when they were not fighting one another with weapons, they hated each other so vigorously that they were rarely capable of coming to any agreement.

When King Louis IX arrived in Acre, the people, having seen his flag flying from the mast, came down to the sea in procession to meet him. The clergy led the procession, the church bells pealed, and in the churches candles were lit for his safe arrival. Once more there was a king in Acre, and once more the business of the Crusades could go on.

At first, he seems to have had no intention of remaining in the Holy Land for any length of time. His mother was beseeching him to return to France; France and England were at loggerheads and war seemed imminent; people in France were protesting against the tithes spent on the upkeep of the Holy Land; and the queen was even sterner than her son, the king. He was needed in Paris, but he was also, as he saw clearly, needed in Acre. "If I depart," he told his councillors, "this land is lost, for all those who are in Acre will follow after me, none daring to remain when the people are so few." This was not a boast; it was the truth. By kingly power he could hold what was left of the kingdom together; without that power, the kingdom was almost certainly doomed.

He allowed his councillors eight days in which to come to their conclusions. When they met the king in council, nearly all of them agreed that he should return to France because the people were so few that it would be necessary to recruit another army in order to hold the Holy Land, even the little cliff-edge of it that remained. Only a few councillors, including the chronicler John of Joinville, thought he had a bounden duty to remain. There was another meeting eight days later, and the king announced that he was staying indefinitely, as long as he could be useful.

He felt responsible for the men who were still in captivity in Egypt; he felt a greater responsibility for Jerusalem, which he hoped, in spite of the defeat at Mansourah, to reclaim for the Christians; and he felt that perhaps his greatest responsibility was to strengthen those fortresses that still remained in Christian hands, so that the kingdom could endure. Repairing and building fortresses became his constant preoccupation: and so at Acre, Jaffa, Caesarea, and Sidon he could be seen mingling with the masons, carrying stones and baskets full of quicklime. The Saracens were making frequent forays near Acre, and he took part in repulsing them.

He was war leader, chief justice, prince, and gravedigger. He regarded himself as the only person allowed to make treaties, and when the master of the Temple made an agreement with the sultan of Damascus about some land on the borders of the kingdom, he was incensed because he had not been consulted. The sultan's ambassador was invited to the king's tent, the treaty was given back to him unsigned, and he was then invited to watch a long procession of Templars, headed by the master, all of them barefoot, their heads bowed in penitence. Thereafter, the sultan of Damascus knew who signed treaties.

While he was in Acre the king entertained envoys from the Old Man of the Mountain, who still maintained the stronghold at Masyaf, and still sent out Assassins to murder kings. Indeed the murdering of kings was one of his major occupations. He had a long Danish ax, the haft silver-plated with many knives affixed to it, which would, on ceremonial occasions, be carried before him by a herald, and everyone would know that those were the knives the Assassins had used when they struck down kings.

Louis was prepared to receive envoys from Masyaf: such receptions were dangerous, but it was also dangerous not to receive them. There were three members of the embassy. First, there was the ambassador, a man of high position. Behind him was a young man who held in one hand a knife that consisted of three knives, two of the blades being inserted in the handles of other knives. This three-bladed knife was an offering signifying defiance in the event that the king refused to accede to their demands. A third youth carried a winding sheet of coarse linen cloth wrapped around his arm; this, too, was intended as a present for the king if he disobeyed the orders of the Old Man of the Mountain. The Assassins went to some pains to cultivate terror.

The king had cautiously arranged that the ambassador should sit immediately below his throne, with the youths sitting behind the ambassador. He knew the reputation of the Old Man of the Mountain and was taking no chances.

The ambassador began by asking the king whether he knew the Old Man of the Mountain. The king replied that he had heard of him but had never met him.

"Well then," said the ambassador, "since you have heard of him, I marvel greatly that you have not sent him such gifts as would assure his friendship. The Emperor of Germany, the King of Hungary, the Sultan of Egypt, and all the rest, send gifts to him every year. They know very well that they live out their lives only at my lord's pleasure. And if it does not please you to do this, then at least acquit him of the tribute he has to pay to the Hospitallers and the Templars, and he will be quits with you."

The king was infuriated by the conduct of the ambassador and by the fact that he had brought the two aides bearing the symbolic instruments of murder and death. Nevertheless, the king kept his temper. He told them he would see them in the afternoon, after he had given some thought to the matter.

In the afternoon he met them again, and this time both the master of the Temple and the master of the Hospital were in attendance on the king, standing beside his throne. The ambassador repeated what he had said earlier in the day. The two masters were incensed. They told the ambassador that if it were not for the king's honorable intentions in receiving them, they would be thrown into the sea outside Acre. Instead they were to be sent back to the Old Man of the Mountain, from whom they must return within fifteen days with suitable letters and jewels to be offered to the king in order to appease him. The king rejected the threats implied in the three-bladed knife and the winding sheet, and wanted something better.

The ambassador returned within fifteen days. We hear no more about the two youths. This time he came with more suitable offerings: the Old Man's shirt—"This has been closest to me, and therefore I present it to you," and a gold ring of very fine workmanship bearing his name— "With this ring I espouse you, and we shall be one." In addition there were many jewels, crystal animals and fruit, and various table games. All these presents were heavily scented with ambergris tied to them with fine gold thread. The king, in return, sent the Old Man of the Mountain a chest full of jewels, rolls of scarlet cloth, horse snaffles of silver, and cups of gold.

In this way, the French king who was to become a saint formed an alliance with the murderous Old Man of the Mountain, whose real name was Najm ad-Din. It was a strange confrontation.

The king was intrigued by the character of the prince of the Assassins. He sent his own interpreter, Yves le Breton, to stay at Masyaf, and to report on the beliefs and political prospects of the strange community living on top of the mountain.

The report is lost, but Joinville was able to obtain some portions of it or he remembered what Yves le Breton told him. Joinville knew the interpreter well and had a high regard for him. He belonged to the Order of the Preaching Brothers. His task was to convert the Saracens to the Christian faith, and for this purpose he spoke Arabic. He was one of the few Christians who had any interest in Islam. Yves le Breton told Joinville one day about his encounter with an old woman who wandered down the street with a dish full of fire in her right hand and a bowl full of water in her left hand. "What are you doing with these things?" he asked her. She answered that with the fire she would burn up Paradise until nothing remained of it, and with the water she would put out the fires of Hell until nothing remained of them. "Why would you do this?" Yves asked her. She answered, "Because I want no one to do good in order to receive the reward of Paradise, or from fear of Hell; but solely out of love for God, who is wholly worthy and can do all manner of good to us."

Yves le Breton's mission marks something new in the minds of the Crusaders: a general interest in Muslim beliefs, an effort to understand the aspirations of a people long considered simply as mortal enemies. Instead of blind hatred there was a tentative reaching out, a searching of hearts. One of the things the Crusaders were beginning to know was that Islam, far from being a monolithic religion, with orderly hierarchies, absolute doctrines, and unchanging forms, was riddled with sects. The Old Man of the Mountain, for example, belonged to an offshoot of the Shi'a sect, which had its origins in Persia. They venerated Ali, the son-in-law of Muhammad, more than they venerated Muhammad. Those who obeyed the law of Ali regarded those who obeyed the law of Muhammad as miscreants or heretics worthy of death. There was an unbridgeable gap between them.

Yves le Breton went up to Masyaf and stayed there for some time. He attempted to convert the Old Man of the Mountain to the Christian faith, an attempt that was doomed to failure. Yet the Old Man remained cordial. Yves le Breton was invited into his bedroom, where there were many books, including an old Gnostic *Acts of Peter* which had been translated into Arabic. The Old Man said he had often read the book and delighted in it. He said, "I have a great liking for my lord St. Peter; for at the beginning of the world the soul of Abel, when he was killed, went into the body of Noah, and when Noah died it went into the body of Abraham; and from the body of Abraham, when he died, it went into the body of St. Peter at the time when God came down to earth."

Yves le Breton, as a true member of the Order of Preaching Brothers, had no patience with the works of the Gnostics, and said so. The Old Man of the Mountain was not offended. He remained a Shi'a Muslim who venerated Ali and delighted in St. Peter.

One of their discussions concerned the beliefs of the Shi'a sect as understood by the Assassins. The Old Man of the Mountain said:

> Know that one of the rules of the law of Ali is that when a man is killed in the service of his lord, his soul enters a more pleasant body than it had before; and therefore the Assassins do not hesitate to get themselves killed when their lord commands because they believe they will be in more pleasant circumstances after they are dead.
>
> And there is another rule: they believe that no one dies except on the day appointed for him; and no one should hold this belief, for God can prolong or shorten our lives. But the Bedouins support this rule of the law of Ali, and thus they refuse to put on armor when they go into battle, for otherwise they believe they would be acting against the commandment of their law. And when they curse their children, they tell them: "May you be cursed like the Franks, who put on armor for fear of death."

When Yves le Breton came down from the mountain, he had acquired more knowledge about the Assassins than any foreigner before him. Almost from the beginning, the Crusaders had encountered the Assassins, but never so intimately.

Louis knew the Old Man of the Mountain was friendly to him only because the Old Man was on bad terms with the sultan of Damascus. On his side, the king's embassy to the Old Man was part of a larger plan. Once again the Crusaders were forced to attempt to bring about a balance of power between Damascus and Cairo. The task of the Christians was continually to keep the two Muslim powers on the edge of war, in order to be certain that they would not waste their energies attacking the Christian strongholds. Fast footwork was necessary, and the king had always to give the impression that he commanded a larger army than he possessed.

About the end of November 1252, Blanche of Castile, regent of France during the king's absence, died in Paris. In the last year of her life she had to deal with the strange Crusade of the Shepherds, led by the half-mad Master of Hungary, a pale, bearded ascetic who acquired a following of poor shepherds and farmworkers. The Master of Hungary spoke of leading his flock to the Holy Land, but as he moved across France he seemed to be more interested in killing priests and looting than in bringing about a real Crusade. He performed sacraments in his own way, healed the sick, inveighed against the rich, argued vehemently with university students, and established himself as a dangerous popular leader with the power to lead a peasant army wherever he wished.

Queen Blanche at first found him appealing and loaded him with presents, believing or half-believing that he carried a letter written by the Virgin Mary. Soon it became clear that the Master of Hungary wanted to be master of France. Sometimes he wore royal robes, sometimes he wore the flowing gown and miter of a bishop. He wanted to be king, and he wanted to be pope; and his sermons were filled with invective against the royal family and the papacy. The movement became too powerful and had to be stopped. At the orders of Queen Blanche the army was sent out to destroy him, and at the battle of Villeneuve-sur-Cher the Master of Hungary was killed. His body was found in the mud of the battlefield, easily recognizable by his magnificent long beard.

Louis IX did not hurry back to France when he heard of his mother's death. He would later ask about the death in its most minute particulars, but it happened while he was immersed in important diplomatic maneuvers in the Holy Land.

Like Frederick II, Louis knew how to flatter the Saracens into accepting his terms. The heads of the Crusaders killed at La Forbie had become trophies on the walls of Cairo. He arranged that they should be taken down, placed in boxes, and brought to the Holy Land, where they were given a decent burial. He arranged for the cancellation of the second half of the ransom and the release of all the remaining prisoners, even those who had been converted to Islam, even those who had been captured as children. He signed a treaty with Cairo which would have brought Jerusalem into Christian hands, together with most of the land up to the Jordan River, but the treaty was conditional on aid given in the war against Damascus and Aleppo, and these conditions were never completely met. He signed another treaty with Damascus to the same effect. He made clever use of his kingly authority, and although there were many skirmishes, no serious

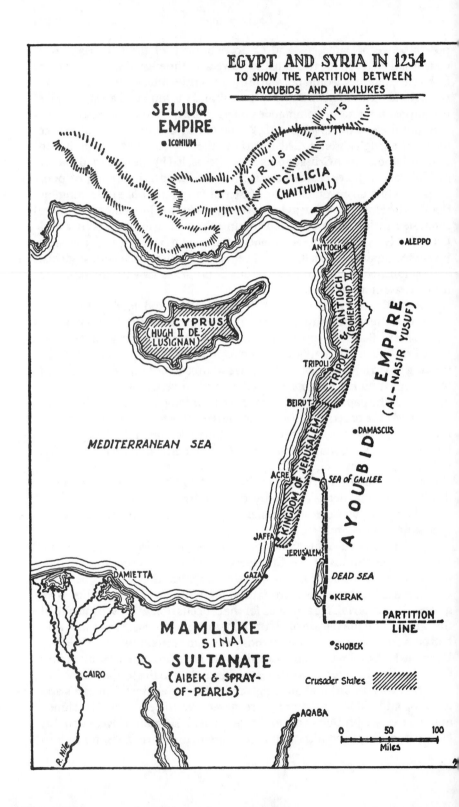

EGYPT AND SYRIA IN 1254
TO SHOW THE PARTITION BETWEEN
AYOUBIDS AND MAMLUKES

SELJUQ
EMPIRE
• ICONIUM

TAURUS MTS

CILICIA
(HAITHUM. I)

• ALEPPO

ANTIOCH

CYPRUS
(HUGH II DE
LUSIGNAN)

TRIPOLI & ANTIOCH (BOHEMOND VI)

TRIPOLI

BEIRUT

MEDITERRANEAN SEA

• DAMASCUS

AYOUBID EMPIRE
(AL-NASIR YUSUF)

ACRE

SEA of GALILEE

KINGDOM OF JERUSALEM

JAFFA

JERUSALEM

DEAD SEA

DAMIETTA

GAZA

• KERAK

PARTITION
LINE

MAMLUKE
SINAI
SULTANATE
(AIBEK & SPRAY-
OF-PEARLS)

•SHOBEK

CAIRO

Crusader States ///////

• AQABA

R. NILE

0   50   100
Miles

war with the Muslims took place during his four-year reign over the Holy Land.

He was a man who had changed much since he set sail from Cyprus to Damietta. His shoulders were bent, he wore a full beard, he ate little and was weighed down with cares. He had become even more religious, more determined to obey the inscrutable will of God. Finally, after long self-questioning, having put all his affairs in order, he concluded that God's will demanded that he should return to France, which he had not seen for nearly six years.

On April 24, 1254, he set sail from Acre with his queen, who had borne him three children in Egypt and the Holy Land. Nine galleons and nine galleys were all that was left of the great fleet which had left Aigues-Mortes. The king's ship was caught on a sand shoal off Cyprus. The king, a bad sailor, who trusted the sea no more than he trusted the Saracens, flung himself down on the ship's deck, barefoot and wearing only a tunic, to implore God's aid. The ship floated off the sandbank, but a few hours later they were in the middle of the storm. This gave rise to long discussions about God's intentions when he let loose storms at sea. Was it punishment for their sins? Was it a warning or a threatening? Was it God's anger or God's love? Neither the king nor John of Joinville, an equally bad sailor, could quite bring themselves to believe that a storm was a manifestation of God's love.

Although Louis questioned himself and was given to penance, he would at times be unsparing with others. Once three galleys from the fleet put in at Pentellaria to find fruit for the royal children. They spent such a long time in the island, while the main fleet was anchored off shore, that the king thought the galleys had been captured by the Saracens, who claimed the island. When at last the galleys sailed out of the harbor, the king learned that six gentlemen had been so well entertained at lunch that they had forgotten they were committing *lèse majesté* by keeping the king waiting. In his fury the king ordered them to be cast into one of the trailing rowboats, where for the rest of the journey they would be half-drowned. The six gentlemen begged for pardon, but the king remained adamant.

At last, after some ten weeks at sea, the king's fleet landed at Hyères in Provence, and all made their way by slow stages to Paris. He had hoped to return as a conqueror. Instead he returned as a king who had lost more troops and weapons than any Frenchman before him, a fact redeemed only by four years of arduous work as the uncrowned king of Jerusalem.

People saw in him a strangeness which was not of this world. His rages, even his indecisiveness, worked for him in the eyes of the people. His physical beauty attracted people to him, his pallor and frailty were to his advantage. He was a priestly man, and a priest-ridden king. He was the last Western king to lead a Crusade.

The Death
of St. Louis

BY 1270, when Louis IX set out on another and his last Crusade, there existed in France a growing realization that the adventure was senseless and futile. The chronicler John of Joinville concluded that a Crusade, far from being pleasing to God, was a mortal sin. Having no illusions about the nature of the Crusade, he refused to embark on it, and his account of it was written at second hand with the help of witnesses, letters, and official documents.

There were many in France who believed Louis's last Crusade was doomed to failure. The English historian Matthew Paris wrote that, after the disaster at Mansourah, when almost his entire army was lost, "the name of the French king began to be held in very small esteem in that kingdom, and to become hateful and disreputable amongst both the nobles and the common people." The Franciscan historian Salimbene wrote in even stronger terms, saying that people cursed the preachers who begged alms for the Crusade. If an itinerant preacher came along, they would give money to a poor man instead of to the preacher, and say, "Take this in Mahomet's name, for he is stronger than Christ."

Above all, there was the growing realization among the people that the Crusades accomplished nothing except to fill the coffers of the king and the Church. There was also increasing sympathy for the Muslims, whose lands were being attacked for no good reason and with very little profit. Crusaders who set out with high hopes for Jerusalem had found the expedition deflected by unscrupulous leaders who had their own reasons for going elsewhere.

Thus it happened that Charles of Anjou—a younger brother of King Louis IX, a violently ambitious man, who was also capable of feigning deep religious emotion—managed to enter the good graces of Pope Urban IV. The pope offered him the kingdom of Naples and Sicily after the downfall of Conrad and Manfred, the sons of the Emperor Frederick II. Charles of Anjou succeeded in maneuvering King Louis into leading a

Crusade not against the Holy Land but against Tunis. Charles had great financial interests there, and if the Crusade was successful, he had hopes of becoming the ruler of a kingdom which stretched over southern France, southern Italy, Sicily, and Tunisia.

Charles of Anjou was well aware that his brother had been planning to lead a Crusade to the Holy Land since 1267. Ships were being acquired, Catalan mercenaries and Provençals were being enrolled, provisions were being stockpiled, and money was being collected for another attack on Egypt. Charles of Anjou would have preferred an attack on Constantinople, where there were prospects of booty.

Pope Urban IV died in 1264, but his successor, Clement IV, was equally gracious to Charles of Anjou, King of Sicily, until, toward the last months of his life, he began to realize that he had reaped the whirlwind. Clement IV died very conveniently in 1268. For three years after that Charles of Anjou, by bribery and by intrigues with the cardinals, succeeded in blocking the election of a new pope.

He dreamed of being ruler of all Italy, but what Charles of Anjou would have liked most was to be the leader of a purely mercantile Crusade, whose single purpose was to extend the bounds of his Mediterranean empire. Mustansir, Emir of Tunis, was ripe for conversion; he needed only a little prompting to be brought to the true faith. The prompting could be supplied providentially by the crusading army, and soon all of North Africa would belong to Christianity, as in the days of St. Augustine, Bishop of Hippo.

The argument was specious, but Charles of Anjou was a vehement and determined prosecutor of his own interests. King Louis was impressed by the argument, but kept the destination of the Crusade secret. It was learned later that some of the Crusaders had sent banker's drafts to Acre, intending to cash them when they arrived.

Early in the spring of 1270, everything was ready for the Crusade. The king had been in failing health for some time, but he seemed to have recovered. He drew up his will, leaving the greater part of his fortune to hospitals, leper houses and orphanages. His executors were clerics, and he appointed Matthew of Vendôme, the Abbot of Saint-Denis, to be regent in his absence. He trusted clerics, rewarded them handsomely, and felt uncomfortable if there was no priestly person in sight. He set out for the Crusade in a deeply religious mood.

But habit of procrastination was deep in him. And so he went to the Abbey Church of Saint-Denis, took down the brilliant gold oriflamme from above the altar, and prayed earnestly for victory. Then he took ten days to reach Sens, which is only seventy miles from Paris. He visited the great abbey of the Cistercian monks at Cîteaux; he was at Mâcon at Easter, and it took him seventeen more days to reach Lyons. He paused for ten days at Nîmes, and set out for Saint-Gilles, the small town beloved by Count

Raymond of Toulouse. Saint-Gilles was only twenty-five miles from Aigues-Mortes. The Crusaders marched in slow motion, as though they knew they were going to their deaths.

A large part of the fleet, many of the knights and foot soldiers, and most of the provisions had already arrived at Aigues-Mortes. With nothing very much to do, weary of waiting for the king, the Provençals and the Catalans picked a quarrel with the French, and were soon at each other's throats. In no time, all the troops bivouacked near Aigues-Mortes and within the city were in arms. There was so much havoc that the Crusade was in danger of being destroyed before it had begun. The king was finally moved to hurry from Saint-Gilles to Aigues-Mortes, and by his orders all the leaders of the riot were hanged.

There were more evil omens when the fleet finally set out from Aigues-Mortes on July 1, 1270. Just as, many years earlier, when his fleet left Cyprus, it was buffeted by a storm, so now once again, not long after they left the seaport, a storm struck the fleet and scattered it. But the storm abated, and seven days later most of the fleet limped into the harbor of Cagliari, the capital of Sardinia, and within the next few days all the remaining ships reached port. Here the king held a council of war with his three sons, King Thibault of Navarre, who was his son-in-law, and his nephew, the young Robert of Artois. The count of Flanders and the count of Brittany also took part. At the conclusion of the council, it was announced that the Crusade would not venture to the Holy Land but would go to Tunis.

The secret had been well kept but came as a shock to the lesser ranks. The king who always acted cautiously had taken certain precautionary measures. Although he had previously proclaimed that he was going to the Holy Land, he had drawn up contracts with the Genoese shipowners in such a way that he could order the ships to go to one port, and then reembark and go to another port without further charge. If he had been going to the Holy Land, he would have arranged to stockpile provisions in Cyprus, as he did in his first Crusade. He had made no formal arrangements with the king of Cyprus, but he was expected in Acre, which desperately needed help, for Baibars had already conquered Jaffa and Antioch, and it was evident that Acre would fall unless a powerful army arrived from the West.

The saintly king was perfectly capable of duplicity, if it served his purposes.

The fleet set sail from Cagliari on July 15 and arrived near Carthage three days later after an easy passage with a following wind. It was the worst time of the year for campaigning. The heat was so terrible that it was impossible for a man to wear armor for more than an hour, and the nights were nearly as bad as the days. The Crusaders captured the harbor of

Carthage, moved along the coast a few miles, and set up their tents under the walled city. Charles of Anjou had promised to send another fleet; it failed to come, and the French, Provençals and Catalans waited outside the walls of Carthage, just as they had waited outside the walls of Mansourah. There were a few skirmishes but no pitched battles. The French were safe behind their trenches and the Muslims were safe behind their walls. The French had little fresh water; the Muslims had as much as they wanted. The Muslims did not bother to attack. Their strategy was simply to wait until the French had been destroyed by the heat or the pestilence. There were about ten thousand men in the army, and by the middle of August, when the pestilence began to spread wildly through the camp, half the troops were incapacitated.

The King's last-born son, John Tristan, who had been born at Damietta, died of the pestilence. Another son, Philip, the heir to the throne, seemed to be dying. The papal legate died. The king realized that he too was dying and prepared himself. He dictated the famous document, known as the *Enseignements,* for the spiritual education of the heir to the throne. Prince Philip was encouraged to love good and to eschew evil, to love priests, to be tender toward the poor and miserable, and never to stray from the path of righteousness. At last, shortly before his death, the king asked to be carried to a bed sprinkled with ashes, received the last sacraments, was anointed with oil, and was able to recite in a clear voice the seven penitential Psalms.

At about the same time that King Louis was dying outside the walls of Carthage, the fleet of Charles of Anjou was sighted at sea. He had come just in time to reap the fruits of a dubious victory, for with his coming the situation changed. The emir, looking down from the high towers of ancient Carthage, saw fresh troops running along the beach, well fed, free of the pestilence, well armed with catapults and ballistas and all the machinery of war, and realized that, while it had always been the practice of King Louis to play a waiting game, Charles of Anjou was of a different temperament.

Charles hurried to the bedside of the dead king, whose body was still warm; he fell on his knees, prayed, wept, and gave orders. King Louis's body was to be boiled in wine and water until the flesh came off the bones, which were to be placed solemnly in a casket. The bones would be taken to the Abbey Church of Saint-Denis, the heart and entrails would be buried in the great cathedral of Monreale in Palermo. He was on his way to sainthood.

Charles went to see the new king, Philip III, who would be known as Philippe le Hardi, though there was no hardiness in him. The young king was still weak and feverish, unable to command the army, and Charles of Anjou made the gestures of attacking Carthage. This put him in a position to negotiate with the emir, who offered to pay 210,000 ounces of gold to be rid of the invaders. Charles also negotiated an exchange of prisoners and signed a treaty by which Christians were permitted to live, work, trade, and worship in Tunis.

These negotiations were concluded in late October, and on November 15, 1270, four and a half months after the fleet came to berth at Carthage, it set sail again—Charles, who knew very little about the sea, having decided to sail across the Mediterranean narrows at the worst time of the year. When the fleet was sailing close to Trapani on the west coast of Sicily, a violent storm arose, many ships were damaged, some were sunk, and some of the sailors and soldiers were swept out to sea. So many were drowned that it was believed to be a warning from God, a premonition of worse things to come.

XI

THE AX
FALLS

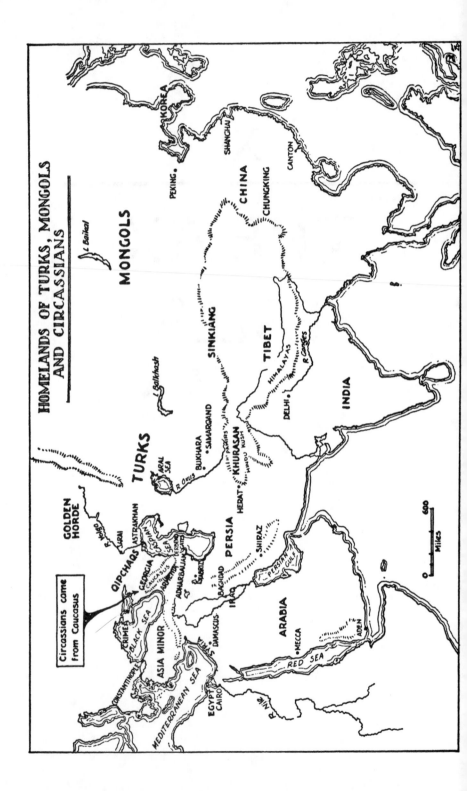

HOMELANDS OF TURKS, MONGOLS AND CIRCASSIANS

MONGOLS

TURKS

GOLDEN HORDE

Circassians came from Caucasus

QIPCHAQS

L. Baikal

KOREA

PEKING.

SHANGHAI.

CHINA

CHUNGKING

CANTON

SINKIANG

TIBET

HIMALAYAS

R. Ganges

DELHI.

INDIA

L. Balkhash

BUKHARA •SAMARQAND

ARAL SEA

R. Oxus

•Pamirs

KHURASAN

HINDU KUSH

HERAT•

ASTRAKHAN

GEORGIA CASPIAN SEA

CAUCASUS

AZERBAIJAN

TABRIZ

PERSIA

•SHIRAZ

•Hamadan

BAGHDAD

IRAQ

PERSIAN GULF

R. Volga

SARAI

CRIMEA

BLACK SEA

CONSTANTINOPLE

ASIA MINOR

DAMASCUS

MEDITERRANEAN SEA

EGYPT CAIRO

R. NILE

ARABIA

•MECCA

RED SEA

ADEN

0   600
Miles

Baibars

THE Sultan Baibars al-Bundukdari was a tall, heavy-set Circassian with ruddy cheeks, brown hair, and blue eyes, and he was born on the shores of the Black Sea. Sold into slavery, he was taken to Damascus where, because he was handsome and powerfully built, he was bought for eight hundred copper coins. As a Circassian, he had no loyalty to the sultans; he carved his way to power by the simple expedient of murdering everyone in his path. He killed Sultan Turanshah and went on to kill Sultan Qutuz, who had refused to make Baibars governor of Aleppo. Qutuz was stabbed in the back. It was an especially unpleasant murder. Immediately afterward, there was a great deal of confusion, with people milling about and not knowing what to do. At last a court attendant pointed to the throne and said, "The power is yours."

Baibars sat on the throne like a man who had been expecting it all his life. Sultans usually gave themselves titles intended to describe their own characters and the future accomplishments of their reigns. Baibars's first thought was to call himself "the terrible" or "the one who inspires terror." He thought better of that, and chose "the victorious" instead. Both titles suited him.

He had a curious white spot in one of his eyes, and a penetrating gaze, both of which inspired fear. He condemned people to death with equanimity. He forbade prostitution—on pain of death. He forbade the drinking of alcoholic beverages—also on pain of death, for the Circassian sultan embraced fundamentalist Islam with fervor. In the camp and in the palace his loud voice could be heard denouncing the evils of his time. His secretary complained that he was always on the move. "Today he is in Egypt, tomorrow in Arabia, the day after in Syria, and in four days in Aleppo."

Baibars provided Islam with something it had not possessed since the time of Saladin: a core of iron, a relentless determination. But they were men of totally different characters: Saladin was a rapier compared with

367

Baibars's exuberant battle-ax. Saladin had a conscience; Baibars had none. Saladin could murder in hot blood; Baibars could murder at any time of the day and for any reason or for no reason at all. Baibars did not destroy the last crumbling vestiges of the Kingdom of Jerusalem, but he opened the way.

In the summer of 1266, Baibars appeared outside the walls of Acre with a large and well-armed army. He had spies in the city from whom he learned a good deal of disappointing news. He learned, for example, that the garrison had recently been reinforced from France and was not likely to surrender on any terms. He learned, too, that the double walls with their great towers had been strengthened and that a much greater army than he had, with a vast quantity of powerful siege engines, would be needed to destroy them. He therefore withdrew from Acre and marched on the Galilee. Here, by a ruse, he captured the castle of Safed, overlooking the Sea of Galilee. Having promised the garrison that it would be allowed to go free, he then reneged on his promise and had them all beheaded as they marched out. His chief weapons were treachery and terror. He gave orders to his army to murder any Christians they came upon; and he marched through the Galilee like a red-hot rake.

Meanwhile Qalawun, the best of his emirs, was fighting in Cilicia. King Hethum of Armenia knew that Baibars's Mameluke army was advancing, and he hurried to the court of the Ilkhan in Tabriz to seek reinforcements for his army. In his absence, in a series of lightning raids, the Mamelukes captured Adana and Tarsus and sacked Sis, the capital of the Armenian kingdom. The palace was plundered, the cathedral was burned to the ground, and the inhabitants were slaughtered or taken prisoner. King Hethum returned from Tabriz to find his capital in ruins, his son Leo, the heir to the throne, a captive, and another son, Thoros, slain. It is significant that Hethum had with him a small company of Mongols. For the first time the Mongols and the Christians were acting in unison.

Baibars may have thought that his campaign against the Armenian cities of Cilicia had put an end to Hethum's kingdom. If so, he was mistaken. The Armenians continued to fight and to maintain an alliance with the Mongols, who were now well established in Persia up to the Euphrates and could draw on immense reserves of troops throughout central Asia.

In the autumn of 1266, Baibars sent an army to attack Antioch but failed to penetrate the city's defenses. He was not present; his generals had gathered so much booty that they felt no need to gather more; and it is possible that the Antiochenes were able to bribe the generals to lift a siege which had lasted only a few days. Baibars was incensed by the failure of the army at Antioch.

In May 1267, he led his army right up to the walls of Acre. He used a ruse that always pleased him. Possessing so many captured uniforms, lances, and banners of the Crusaders, he could outfit thousands of troops to resemble a Crusader army. In this disguise, his troops rode through the orchards around Acre, killing Christians in the nearby villages, and destroying everything in their path. But they could not destroy Acre because the guards in the watchtowers had seen them coming and, realizing that they were Muslims in disguise by the way they rode and by their darker features, had sounded the alarm. The attack was repulsed, and Baibars withdrew to his castle at Safed. When envoys came to Safed to sue for a truce, they found the castle encircled by Christian skulls.

When, occasionally, Baibars's deceptions failed him, he resorted to terror. Massacre appealed to him, and whenever he attacked a city he always threatened to massacre the inhabitants unless they surrendered immediately. In February 1268, he attacked Jaffa, which resisted heroically for twelve long days. He massacred the inhabitants but allowed the garrison to go free. This unusual event may be explained by the fact that the fortress was well defended and the siege of the stronghold would have cost many Egyptian lives if it had been permitted to continue.

From Jaffa, Baibars marched to the castle of Beaufort, which had passed into the hands of the Templars. After ten days of violent bombardment, the castle was forced to surrender. With unaccustomed mercy, Baibars offered to let the women go free, but the Templars were sold into slavery.

Then it was the turn of Antioch, which had been in Christian hands for more than 170 years. Bohemond VI, Prince of Antioch and Count of Tripoli, had left the city in the care of the Constable, Simon Mansel, who was quickly captured when he led a column of troops against the advancing Mamelukes. Simon Mansel was ordered to command the garrison to surrender. The garrison refused. There was heavy fighting, and on May 18, 1268, Baibars ordered a general assault. The Mamelukes succeeded in breaching the walls, the garrison troops fought bravely, and the inhabitants surrendered. Baibars was encouraged by their surrender to order another general massacre, after closing the gates so that none could escape. Those who survived the massacre were given out as slaves to his soldiers. Christian Antioch vanished, never to be reborn.

Because he despised Bohemond VI, Baibars wrote him a strange, taunting letter, which is a masterpiece of venom and invective.

EXCERPTS FROM A LETTER FROM THE SULTAN BAIBARS AL-BUNDUKDARI TO BOHEMOND VI, PRINCE OF ANTIOCH, FROM ANTIOCH, MAY 1268.

THE GLORIOUS COUNT BOHEMOND, magnificent and magnanimous, having the courage of a lion, being the glory of the nation of Jesus, the head of the Christian church and the leader of the people of the Messiah, who no longer bears the title of Prince of Antioch, since Antioch has been lost to him, but is reduced to a mere count, may God show him the way and give him a good death and help him to remember my words.

. . . We took Antioch by the sword on the fourth hour of Saturday on the fourth day of Ramadan, and we destroyed all those you had chosen to guard the city. All these men had possessions, and all their possessions have passed into our hands.

Oh, if only you had seen your knights trampled by our horses, your houses looted and at the mercy of everyone who passed by, your treasure weighed by the quintal, your women sold in the market-place four for a gold *dinar*. If only you had seen your churches utterly destroyed, the crucifixes torn apart, the pages of the Gospels scattered, the tombs of the patriarchs trodden underfoot. If only you had seen your Muslim enemy trampling down your altars and holy of holies, cutting the throats of deacons, priests and bishops, the patriarchate irremediably abolished, the powerful reduced to powerlessness! If only you had seen your palaces given over to the flames, the dead devoured by the flames of this world before being devoured by the flames of the next world, your castles and all their attendant buildings wiped off the face of the earth, the Church of St. Paul totally destroyed so that nothing is left of it, and seeing all this you would have said: "Would to God that I were dust! Would to God! Would to God that I had never received the letter with these melancholy tidings!"

If you had seen these things, your soul would have expired with sighs, and the multitude of your tears would have quenched the devouring flame. If you had seen those places which were once opulent reduced to misery, and your ships captured by your own ships in the port of Seleucia—your ships at war with your ships—then you would have realized without the least doubt that God, who once gave Antioch to you, had now taken it away from you, that the Lord who gave you this fortress had withdrawn it from you and wiped it off the face of the earth. You must know that by God's grace we have regained the castles formerly lost to Islam. Know that we have removed all your people from the country; we took them, as it were, by their hair and dispersed them hither and thither. The only rebel now is the river that flows through Antioch:* it would change its name, if it could; its waters are tears, once pure and limpid, now stained with the blood we have shed.

---

*The Orontes, called *al-'Asi*, "the rebel," by the Arabs, because it flows from south to north.

This letter is sent to congratulate you that God has seen fit to preserve you and to prolong your days. All this you owe to the fact that you were not in Antioch when we captured it. If you had taken part in the battle, then you would either be dead, or a prisoner, or riddled with wounds. You must take great joy in being alive, for there is nothing so joyful as escaping from a great calamity. Perhaps God gave you this respite so that you could make amends for your former disobedience toward Him. And since no one from your city survived to tell you the news, it has fallen upon us to give you these tidings; and since also no one from your city is in any position to congratulate you on your own survival, this too has been left to us. Nor can you accuse us of saying anything false, nor do you need to go elsewhere to learn the truth.

The spectacle of the victor crowing over his victory is not a pleasant one. What is chiefly remarkable about the letter is Baibars's enduring rage, his almost incoherent vituperation. Yet there is something in his screaming that suggests that he is the victim, not the perpetrator, of the crime.

The reason for his rage is not hard to discover. To enjoy the vengeance he desired, it was necessary to have physical possession of the prince, to kill him or to torture him, to see him suffering, to see him dead; but the prince of Antioch had escaped his net.

Baibars thought of himself as the man destined to sweep the Christians out of the Holy Land. He had conquered Antioch and Jaffa, he had succeeded in weakening Armenia, he had made a near-desert of the Galilee, and he had wrested the castle of Beaufort from the Templars. But these were small things compared with what he wanted. The once-proud edifice known as the Kingdom of Jerusalem resembled a palace riddled with mortar fire and without a roof, with its cornices blown off and large areas reduced to rubble. He wanted the palace destroyed utterly.

The strange kingdom actually possessed a king. He was Hugh III, King of Cyprus and Jerusalem, who had been crowned in Nicosia on Christmas day, 1267. There were other contenders for the throne, including Maria of Antioch, the daughter of Melisende of Lusignan. Later she would sell her claim to the throne to Charles of Anjou. The following year, Charles executed Conradin, the grandson of Frederick II, who claimed the titles of King of Jerusalem and of Sicily, and Duke of Swabia, and whose crime was that he had attempted to regain his Italian inheritance.

Like Conradin, Hugh III was young, vigorous, and sweet-tempered. He was the grand conciliator, the one man who could ensure that the little princedoms would live at peace with one another. He arranged truces, mollified the more quarrelsome of the vassals, and continually appealed for help from the West. The Templars and the Hospitallers distrusted him, and so did the Commune of Acre, which had no patience with kings. He relied often on the advice of Philip of Montfort, the most accomplished of the barons, and he was devastated when Philip was murdered by the Assassins at the instigation of Baibars.

By his ferocious cruelty Baibars had at first outraged the Crusaders, but soon he inspired a fear that threatened to overwhelm them. They remembered the circle of skulls around the fortress at Safed. The blue-eyed sultan, without a trace of Egyptian blood in him, in love with murder, was more like a destructive force of nature than a man. Having no ultimate loyalties, he destroyed as he pleased.

The Kingdom of Jerusalem was now reduced to a handful of cities clinging to the seacoast. And for the first time we hear a note of total despair in the voices of the Crusaders. We hear it in the letter written by Hugh of Revel, the Master of the Hospital, to his friend, the prior of Saint-Gilles in Provence.

EXCERPTS FROM A LETTER FROM HUGH OF REVEL, MASTER OF THE HOSPITAL, TO FARAUD OF BORRAS-SIO, PRIOR OF SAINT-GILLES IN PROVENCE, FROM ACRE IN THE FORTNIGHT OF PENTECOST 1268.

BROTHER HUGH OF REVEL, by the Grace of God humble master of the Holy House of the Hospital of St. John of Jerusalem, and guardian of the poor of Jesus Christ, sends greetings and sincere love to his dearly beloved in Christ Brother Faraud of Borrassio, Prior of St. Gilles, and to all the brethren attached to that priory.

We know not to whom we should complain and show the wounds of our heart, so pierced and so anguished, if not to those who to our knowledge are moved by deep compassion for our sufferings. Nor do we need to describe the hardships we have endured in the Holy Land for such a long period of time nor the magnitude of our losses in property and lives. We believe that almost all of this must be known to you. These sufferings, these losses, do not appear to be coming to an end; instead, they increase and multiply daily. . . .

. . . [Y]ou know very well what comes to us from overseas. We have received nothing from Spain except for a few animals. From Italy and especially from Apulia we expected aid, but our hopes have been shattered by the behavior of Brother Philip of Glis, who used up everything we had for his own purposes as he pleased, and because of this same Brother Philip of Glis everything we possessed in Sicily has been ruined and devastated just because he led the brothers of our Order in armed conflict with those who were fighting Charles of Anjou. The houses we possessed in Sicily were therefore razed to the ground, our fruit trees were cut down, our vines were uprooted, the contents of our houses were stolen. I am sure you are aware of our war in Tuscia and how everything we possessed in that region has been destroyed, and therefore little or nothing is sent overseas to us from Italy. From the priory in France it is impossible to obtain anything useful by reason of the debts contracted by the aforesaid Brother Philip—debts that he promised to settle but failed to do so. The priory of England, which formerly provided considerable aid and assistance, has greatly reduced the sending of revenues by reason of the wars going on there.*

Consider therefore how we can meet our expenses from the small revenues we receive from your priory and from the priory in Auvergne, which is all that remains to us except for the revenues from England, and there is nothing from Germany. We are not bringing these matters to the attention of the brotherhood for any other reason except to warn you not to be surprised if we inconvenience you by asking for your help. Yet there is another reason: Whatever fate is reserved for our fortresses—let us hope that they are spared the worst fate—or whatever fate befalls our land—and much is spoken about this—you must excuse us for having assumed these responsibilities, we and our house, since only a small number of Christians remain here and we lack the strength to resist the unspeakable power of the Saracens. We are quite certain that the city of Acre could not be properly defended even if all the Christians beyond the seas were here to defend it.

Because of the losses sustained by the Christians and the losses they continue to sustain daily, they are so distressed that they lack confidence in themselves to resist the enemy. This year the city and fortress of Joppa were captured in an hour. The fortress at Caesarea, a great stronghold, held out for only two days when attacked by the Sultan. Safed, the pride of the Templars, gave up after sixteen days. They said the fortress of Belfort was so strong that it would hold out for a year, yet it fell in less than four days. The noble city of Antioch was captured. . . .

Such is the condition of our land, and such is the peril that overwhelms us! God will declare what shall become of us. But for God's sake be moved to pity us with all your heart. Pray God to grant us as much aid as possible. . . .

Hugh of Revel's letter is a classic of its kind, at once a desperate plea for

---

*He is referring to the long-drawn and bitterly fought Welsh wars of King Henry III.

help and an acknowledgment that help was beyond hoping for—and that if it came, it would probably come too late.

When Hugh of Revel complained that the West had lost interest in the affairs of the Holy Land, he was speaking in relative terms. In the autumn of 1269, there came the Crusade of King James I of Aragon, who sailed out of Barcelona with a powerful fleet. It had scarcely left the harbor when it was scattered in a storm. The king abandoned the enterprise but sent his two sons with a much smaller fleet. The two sons reached Acre at a time when Baibars was once more attacking the city. The small Spanish army, thirsting to attack the Mamelukes, was prevented from fighting because it was felt the soldiers were untrained and less useful in the field than in the garrison. In a few weeks the Spaniards returned to Spain in disgust.

The English also sent their Crusaders under the command of Prince Edward, son of Henry III and heir to the throne. He left England in the summer of 1271, with only a thousand men. Like the Spaniards he wanted action, and he took part in a daring raid into the Plain of Sharon. He was the first Englishman to send an embassy to the Mongols: Reginald Russell, Godfrey Welles, and John Parker went to the court of the Ilkhan to seek aid, which was promptly forthcoming. A Mongol army swept out of Anatolia and captured Aleppo. Baibars, with a huge army, set out from Damascus to give battle to the Mongols, who withdrew wisely. But the Mongol alliance had been strengthened and there was hope that they would return at a suitable time.

Prince Edward was handsome, restless, fond of jousting, capable of compromise, yet utterly merciless against declared enemies. When he became King Edward I, he attacked Scotland so implacably that he became known as the "Hammer of the Scots." But in Palestine he was kindly and efficient, and like King Hugh III he attempted to unite the Crusaders, who were so often at each other's throats. Baibars, who saw him as another Philip of Montfort, a man with the power to dominate and unite, ordered his assassination. An Assassin, disguised as a Christian pilgrim, stabbed him with a poisoned dagger. He had a strong constitution and recovered from the wound; but at about this time he heard that his father, King Henry III, was dying. He returned to England to be crowned. In England, he continued to give long-range support to the Christian alliance with the Mongols.

Baibars continued his depradations. He conquered the Templar fortress called Safita and went on to conquer Krak des Chevaliers, which even Saladin had found impregnable. He invaded Anatolia, brushed against the forces of the Ilkhan, and retired to Syria. Fortunately, and to the satisfaction of the Christians, he died of poison in the summer of 1277, having accidentally drunk from a poison cup he had prepared for someone else. But he was succeeded by his chief general, Qalawun, who was equally determined to sweep the Christians out of the Holy Land. It would be easier, now that Baibars had conquered so many places.

In the last days of the kingdom a madness descended on the Crusaders. Knowing that they must unite against the overwhelming force of the Mamelukes, they fought each other instead, and contrived to weaken each other with conspiracies and treacheries, thus playing into the hands of their enemies. The kingdom was being destroyed from within long before it was destroyed by the enemy. Blindly and voluptuously, the little princes who retained title to the seaports on the Palestinian coast hurled themselves on one another without any purpose except private vengeance.

In January 1282, Guy II Embriaco, Lord of Jebail, outfitted three ships to transport a small army consisting of twenty-five knights and four hundred foot soldiers to Tripoli. He hoped to take Tripoli by surprise and to capture Bohemond VII, who had succeeded his father Bohemond VI in 1274, and put him to death. He left Jebail at night and reached Tripoli before dawn, anchoring his ships near the house of the Templars and coming ashore in the darkness. With all his men, who were mostly Genoese, he entered the house of the Templars. He had his agents there, including the Templar commander Reddecoeur, but for some reason the commander was absent. Perhaps Reddecoeur no longer wanted to take part in the plot, or perhaps there was a simple misunderstanding about the time they would meet. Guy II Embriaco panicked, hastily left the house of the Templars, and took refuge with his knights in the house of the Hospitallers.

Dawn came up. The alarm bells were rung. Bohemond VII was informed about the strange behavior of these visitors from Jebail, who had taken possession of one of the towers of the house of the Hospitallers and threatened to sell their lives dearly. All of Tripoli now gathered at the foot of the tower, clamoring for the death of the invaders. The commander of the Hospitallers offered to act as mediator. Before the tower could be stormed, an agreement was reached that Guy's life and the lives of all his knights would be spared if they surrendered. Guy would serve a five-year sentence of imprisonment, and at the end of that period all his possessions would be restored to him.

Guy might have known that this was only a ruse to make him descend from the tower, for Bohemond VII had given orders that the Genoese should have their eyes put out. Guy and his brothers John and Baldwin, and his cousin William, were kept in prison for six weeks while Bohemond considered the various forms of punishment suitable for such an occasion. Then they were taken to Nephin, where they were set down in a ditch. A wall was constructed around them, the ditch was filled with earth, and they were left to die of hunger.

John of Montfort, Lord of Tyre, an ally of the lord of Jebail, marched with all his knights to Jebail, hoping to protect the city from the vengeance of Bohemond. He found that the city had already been captured and the fires of victory were burning on the battlemented walls. He returned to Tyre in disgust, realizing that his city might fall to Bohemond before it fell to the Mamelukes.

The Pisans in Acre were overjoyed when they learned the fate of the Genoese expedition to Tripoli. They celebrated with music, dancing, and fireworks. It pleased them especially that Guy II Embriaco had been buried alive; and their pleasure was a sign of the corruption of spirit that affected all these coastal princedoms. None was immune. The Hospitallers hated the Templars, who were also hated by Bohemond VII and by the king of Cyprus and Jerusalem.

Vast triumphs and absolute disaster were close companions in those times. To the north and east, a new power was entering the scene. A huge Mongol army, numbering a hundred thousand men, was preparing, in alliance with King Leo of Armenia and the Hospitallers, to do battle with the Mamelukes. Qalawun commanded the Mamelukes, Mangu Timur commanded the Mongols, and Leo commanded the Armenians. The battle of Hims, which took place on October 30, 1281, was one of the bloodiest ever known. A quarter of a million men took part in it. When the advantage seemed to be going in the direction of the Christian-Mongol forces, Mangu Timur was wounded. He panicked, and gave orders for a retreat. Qalawun's army had suffered too much to be able to follow the Mongols beyond the Euphrates, so there was neither victory nor defeat. Leo distinguished himself during the long and difficult retreat to Armenia. The Mongols could fight another time and choose their own battlefield.

On the night of March 30, 1282, Charles of Anjou received the greatest shock of his life. The Sicilians, exasperated by the behavior of the French army of occupation, rose up and massacred every Frenchman they could lay their hands on. The Sicilian Vespers came as an inevitable result of Charles's depradations, arrogance, and incompetence. With this uprising, his dreams of a Mediterranean empire, with himself as emperor of Byzantium and king of Jerusalem, crumbled. Charles would no longer play any role in Crusader affairs.

Meanwhile, Qalawun continued to ravage the Christian outposts in the Holy Land, capturing the great Hospitaller castle at Marqab, but was not yet ready for the final assault on Acre. He watched from a distance while the kings of Jerusalem succeeded one another. King Hugh III died. His eldest son, John, a graceful and delicate boy of seventeen, followed him. John died a year later, and his younger brother Henry was crowned at Tyre on August 15, 1286. His coronation was attended by elaborate festivities. Henry was fourteen, handsome, gracious, very brave, and an epileptic. In less than five years he would see the downfall of his kingdom in the ruins of Acre.

The End of
the Kingdom

THERE were men who said Acre was one of the oldest cities of the earth, or at least as old as any city on the Palestinian coast. It appears on the conquest list of Thutmose III, which was drawn up about 1500 B.C. It is mentioned in the Amarna tablets of the heretical Pharaoh Akhenaton. In the third century B.C. Ptolemy II Philadelphus founded it afresh and gave it his name—Acre or Akka became Ptolomeis. In the ninth century A.D. Ahmed ibn-Tulun, the Governor of Egypt, conquered Syria and decided to fortify the city with a great seawall. The Franks conquered it and changed its name to Saint-Jean d'Acre. It grew and flourished under the Franks until toward the end of the thirteenth century it was, after Constantinople, the richest city in the region, with huge towers and walls dominating the landward approaches, an inner and outer harbor, a large customs house where the customs officers sat on carpets and dipped their pens in inkwells of ebony and gold. There were squares and open spaces in the city, shaded from the sun by huge painted cloths stretching from wall to wall. Workmen and artisans lived in the center of the city, and here, too, were the shops and the marketplaces. There were thirty-eight churches, and when, on Sunday, all the church bells rang, they could be heard for more than a mile out to sea.

Acre was a mercantile town, trading with all the countries of Europe and with Egypt and the East. Lombards, Pisans, Genoese, Venetians, and Germans had their own warehouses and what corresponded to chambers of commerce. They were continually quarreling with one another, so that it became the custom to erect barricades in the narrow streets at the first sign of fighting. It was said that there were 14,000 prostitutes to serve a population of perhaps 120,000, of whom half were Muslims. Since the Muslims lived in the city, there was very little about the government and the military which was not quickly known in Damascus and Cairo. Acre lived off its traders; it had few factories, but more warehouses than anyone could count. Furs from Russia, turquoises from Persia, silks from China, rubies from India could be bought in the enormous marketplaces. The popes thundered against the vice and luxury of the great seaport but could do nothing to change it. Acre lived according to its own momentum.

In theory, the city was ruled by Henry II of Lusignan, King of Cyprus and Jerusalem. In fact it was ruled by a multitude of rulers, most of them exiles from the lost Kingdom of Jerusalem. The papal legate, the grand master of the Temple, the grand master of the Hospitallers, the grand master of the Teutonic Knights, and various princes who had taken refuge in Acre when their lands and estates passed into the hands of the Saracens— all had something to do with the government of the city, which was divided into twenty-seven districts, each one largely self-governing. In such a city, government works awkwardly. There were too many rulers and too many things that could go wrong.

In a situation so complex and so difficult, it was disastrous when foreigners came into the city. They upset the balance of forces, and massacred Muslims, thus giving the sultan a ready-made pretext to attack the city and destroy it stone by stone.

Pope Nicholas IV received an urgent appeal for more soldiers. He was able to enroll a few hundred peasants and unemployed laborers under the banner of the Cross. They came from Lombardy and Tuscany, and were shipped off to Acre in Venetian vessels under the command of Nicholas Tiepolo, the son of the reigning doge. The papal treasury provided three thousand gold pieces to pay for the expedition. Five galleys owned and outfitted by King James of Aragon accompanied the new Crusaders, who arrived in Acre toward the end of August, 1290.

It was the season of festivities; there had been a superb harvest in the Galilee; Damascus merchants were once more sending their produce to the marketplaces of Acre. The prince of Tyre, the brother of the king of Cyprus, was in residence in the royal palace, and he received Nicholas Tiepolo with all the honor due his rank. There was always the fear that Sultan Qalawun would attack, but the relations between the Franks and Egypt seemed to be improving. Suddenly, in that peaceful summer, there were signs that there might not be any more summers.

A few days after they arrived at Acre, the Tuscans and Lombards went on a rampage. Apparently they had not been paid, they were unruly after the long sea voyage, and they had no understanding of the habits and customs of a Levantine city. Acre flaunted its wealth; they had none, or so little that it scarcely counted. They thought they had come to fight the Saracens, and there were Saracens all around them. Bernard, Bishop of Tripoli, had been placed in charge of them by the pope, but had no control over them. Debauched, drunken, without roots in the country, seeing themselves as foreigners in a strange land, despised by the people of Acre, and without any resources of their own, they raced through the streets in murderous fury, killing every Muslim they encountered. They killed men, women, and children indiscriminately, but they had a special hatred for bearded Muslim merchants. They swept through the marketplace in the center of the city and out into the suburbs. Since many Christians wore beards, they too were killed. The riot started so quickly that the police, the soldiers, and the knights were taken by surprise. Some Muslims were dragged to safety in the castle, others found refuge in private houses. The Lombards and Tuscans were rounded up, but many escaped. It was as though a hurricane had appeared out of a cloudless sky and killed about a thousand people in the city.

The government, knowing that the news of the massacre would soon reach Egypt, immediately offered its apologies to Qalawun. But Qalawun was in no mood to listen to apologies. He sent his representatives to Acre to demand that all the men responsible for the outrage should be handed over to him for punishment, which meant execution. The city councillors met and debated the sultan's demand at some length. The grand master of the Temple suggested that the matter could be settled very easily by sending all the prisoners in the city jails to Egypt. This was a characteristic Templar solution. The idea of a general scouring of the prisons was abandoned; no better ideas were advanced; and the councillors announced that the massacre was at least partly the fault of the Muslims and they hoped the sultan would accept their apologies and forget the matter.

The sultan did not forget. Incensed by the massacre, and also by the high-handed attitude of the councillors, he resolved to destroy Acre. He summoned his jurists and asked them for advice. He had signed a treaty with the king of Cyprus. Could he break it, and on what grounds? One jurist advised him that he had the power to break or maintain the treaty at his pleasure, but he was more impressed by the argument that the treaty had been broken by the Christians, who had failed to obey the clause by which all Muslims within Acre were under the protection of the civil government and every offense against them must be punished by the Christian magistrates. This had not been done, and accordingly a state of war existed between Egypt and the Latin Kingdom.

Qalawun was so delighted with the latter argument that he issued an immediate order for a vast number of trees at Baalbek and in the region between Caesarea and Athlit to be cut down for making siege engines. The Christians quickly learned that the trees were being cut down and began to raid the places where the woodcutters were at work. When winter came, the work of the woodcutters was made difficult by both the intense cold and the raids of the knights.

The master of the Temple had for some time traditionally enjoyed a secret correspondence with Qalawun. This correspondence was now coming to an end. Qalawun wrote to the master saying that he had come to an irrevocable decision: Acre must be destroyed, it was useless to hope he would receive envoys, his mind was made up. The Master, William of Beaujeu tried one last, desperate appeal.

Qalawun relented. He offered to spare Acre for a ransom of one Venetian sequin from each inhabitant of Acre. Sequins were gold coins, worth about ten dollars, and the ransom therefore amounted to about $600,000. This was a huge sum for the time, but not beyond the ability of the citizens to raise. William of Beaujeu summoned a meeting of the citizens at the Church of St. Cross to listen to the demand for ransom. Instead of agreeing to pay the ransom, they laughed in his face, hurled abuse at him, accused him of being a traitor for having secret correspondence with the enemy, and would have killed him if he had not escaped in time.

The councillors of Acre decided to send one more embassy to Cairo. When they reached Qalawun's court, he refused to see them. They were either murdered on the spot or thrown into prison. Nothing more was ever heard of them.

At the end of the year, Qalawun sent messages to all the Arab states, proclaiming that, as a result of innumerable violations of the treaty by the Christians, he was resolved to destroy Acre. In a letter to King Hethum of Armenia, he wrote that he had sworn on the Koran that not one single Christian would be left alive in that accursed city.

The Christians, too, were sending out proclamations and appeals. Letters were sent to the pope, to friendly kings, to the Templars and Hospitallers in the West, and to the king of Cyprus, urgently demanding aid. In Acre the Patriarch Nicholas, John of Grailly, and an extraordinary knight called Otto of Grandson formed a military command, and at once gave orders to repair all the towers and battlements, which had recently been strengthened by King Henry of Cyprus. The city was in a good state of defense. It could hold off a large army almost indefinitely, if there was good leadership, because it could be provisioned and supplied by sea. Able men were in command of some sectors of the wall, but there were others commanded by men who were cowardly and without resolution.

Suddenly, the city councillors heard that Qalawun had died soon after marching out of Cairo, and they exulted. They thought the danger was past. But with his dying breath, the seventy-year-old sultan had commanded his son al-Ashraf Khalil to continue the expedition against Acre, and not to rest until the city was in ruins. He also commanded his son to leave his body unburied until the day Acre fell.

About 40,000 cavalry and 160,000 foot soldiers converged on Acre. Huge mangonels, called "black oxen," were dragged through the mud and sleet of a particularly hard winter. There were two hundred of them, more than had ever been gathered together against a single city. Two towering siege engines called "the Victorious" and "the Furious," which took the form of giant catapults, were also brought to Acre on carts drawn by a hundred pairs of oxen. By sheer force of numbers, and by the weight of his military machinery, Khalil expected to overwhelm the last fortress of the Crusaders.

The siege of Acre began on April 5, 1291, when Khalil arrived before the city with great pomp. The defenders were vastly outnumbered by Khalil's army, yet during the first weeks of the siege they fought brilliantly. Sometimes they opened the great gates, thus taunting the enemy to enter. They refused to play the defensive role the enemy assigned to them, and they often made small sorties outside the city walls. On the night of April 15, under a full moon, a small army of Franks attacked the camp of the prince of Hama, who was taken by surprise. Most of the Franks were Templars, who fought with their accustomed fury. Many lost their lives, but the Muslims also suffered. With the first light, the prince of Hama had the pleasure of stringing together the heads of some of the Crusaders and placing them like a wreath around the neck of a captured horse and sending it as a present to Khalil. The Crusaders could have done the very same thing with Muslim heads.

A few days later, the Hospitallers made a sortie through the Gate of St. Anthony. It was a very dark night, the Hospitallers moved stealthily, and they were about to spring on the camp when suddenly the night was made bright by thousands of torches held in the hands of white-robed Muslims. Khalil's men had got wind of the affair, and they sprang a surprise on those who had hoped to surprise them. There followed a fierce battle by the light of torches, with two thousand slain on each side. Such sorties proved to be too costly and were discontinued.

On May 4, a new commander arrived in Acre. He was King Henry II of Lusignan and Cyprus, brother of the prince of Tyre, who came with forty ships from Cyprus. He had about a hundred horsemen, two thousand foot soldiers, and plentiful supplies. He was greeted with processions and hymns, as though he were the destined savior of Acre.

Khalil heard of his coming and deliberately increased his fire, pounding the walls with rocks and launching a vast quantity of Greek fire. His sappers were at work attempting to undermine the tower named for the king. Other towers were also being mined. The noise inside the city was deafening. The walls trembled, and the booming of the sultan's kettle-drums could be heard throughout the city. Against the enemy mines, the Franks built countermines; sometimes the mines met, and there would be fierce hand-to-hand fighting deep beneath the city walls.

King Henry decided upon one last effort of diplomacy. He sent two envoys, William of Cafran and William of Villiers, to Khalil to ask for an armistice, and also to ask why he had broken the truce. What were his real grievances? Could the war be stopped?

Khalil refused to answer any questions. Standing outside his tent and surrounded by his generals, he announced that only one thing interested him: Had they brought him the keys to the city? "It is more than our lives are worth to ask our citizens to surrender," they answered. Khalil declared that he wanted the city, not the people in it, who could go free. Out of his admiration for the king's courage, he was prepared to let the people of Acre take their possessions with them when they left the city. Just at that moment a stone flung from a catapult mounted on the Tower of the Legate fell close to Khalil's tent. Khalil was so enraged that he drew his sword, and was ready to kill the envoys. One of his chief emirs restrained him, saying it was unworthy of Khalil "to stain his sword with pig blood." The knights returned to Acre with the certain knowledge that the siege would continue.

The city of Acre was provided with all the defensive machinery known up to this time. A double row of walls, each row provided with towers, faced inland. These walls followed a somewhat jagged line, with a sharp angle which was considered to be the weakest link in the chain. Here the towers proliferated. There was the Tower of the Countess of Blois, the English Tower, the Towr of King Hugh and the Tower of King Henry II. They were all on the outer wall. On the inner wall was the Accursed Tower, which faced the Tower of King Henry II directly. This section was under the command of the prince of Tyre, the brother of the king. On his right were French and English knights under the command of John of Grailly and Otto of Grandson, and beyond these were the militia of the Venetians; then came the Pisans, and then the army of the commune of Acre. The defense was well coordinated, and there was a system of communication by trumpet that was as effective as any modern system of communication.

Khalil's main task, as he saw it, was to break through the fortifications at their weakest point. The English Tower and the Tower of the Countess of Blois were mined. The Tower of St. Nicholas, on the southern line of defenses, was also mined. One by one, the towers were falling; sections of the outer wall were crumbling under the impact of the huge rocks hurled by the siege engines; the rubble was filling the ditches between the two walls.

On May 15, the Tower of King Henry II, which had been recently built on the king's orders, crumbled, and the Muslims entered the ruins and took possession of it. An attack on St. Anthony's Gate was repulsed with heavy losses on both sides. Matthew of Clermont, the Master of the Hospital, took the leading part in the bitter fighting at the gate, where the Templars distinguished themselves. That they were able to throw back the Muslims seemed a miracle. But the army was exhausted; time was running out; and every day the Muslims were gaining another tower, another strip of wall. The fighting men left in the city were outnumbered by Khalil's men, twenty to one.

May 17 was an ominously quiet day. Khalil was preparing his troops for a general assault. Thirty thousand troops were being amassed outside the walls, with another thirty thousand held in reserve. Khalil issued an order to his treasury to pay any Muslim who captured a Christian lance the sum

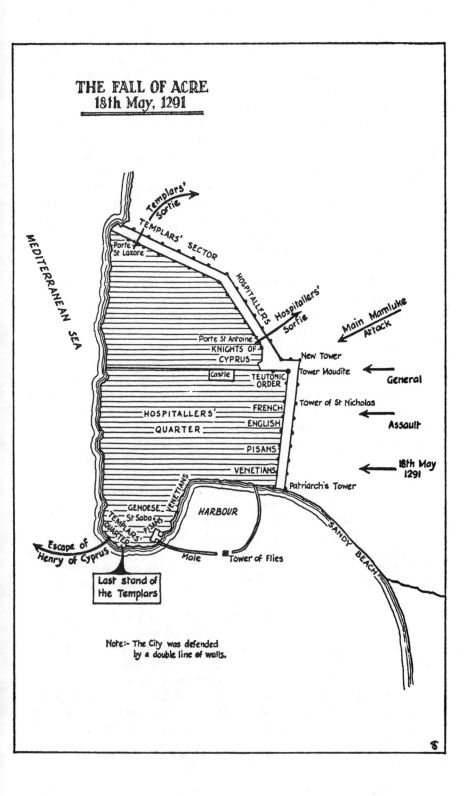

THE FALL OF ACRE
18th May, 1291

MEDITERRANEAN SEA

Templars' Sortie

TEMPLARS' SECTOR

Porte St Lazare

HOSPITALLERS

Hospitallers' Sortie

Main Mamluke Attack

Porte St Antoine

KNIGHTS OF CYPRUS

New Tower

Tower Maudite

General

Castle

TEUTONIC ORDER

Tower of St Nicholas

FRENCH

HOSPITALLERS' QUARTER

ENGLISH

Assault

PISANS

VENETIANS

18th May 1291

VENETIANS

Patriarch's Tower

GENOESE

St Saba

PISANS

HARBOUR

TEMPLARS' QUARTER

Escape of Henry of Cyprus

Mole

Tower of Flies

SANDY BEACH

Last stand of the Templars

Note:- The City was defended by a double line of walls.

of a thousand dirhams. Mullahs and dervishes brought the troops to a high pitch of excitement by promising them that Acre would be leveled to the ground and that no Christian would be left alive in the Holy Land.

Early the following day, May 18, a thick mist concealed the advance of Khalil's troops through the almond orchards. Their first objective was the Accursed Tower, set in the inner wall at the angle of the salient. Here King Henry II and the elite of the Crusader army steadied themselves to receive the brunt of the attack. Here too, the Templars and Hospitallers, always rivals, fought together—perhaps for the first time—in perfect harmony. But their efforts were unavailing. The Muslims captured the Accursed Tower.

Matthew of Clermont led a charge designed to free the tower from the Muslims, and was thrown back. In this counterattack, William of Beaujeu, Master of the Temple, was mortally wounded by an arrow that entered his armpit below the right shoulder.

The best died. Matthew of Clermont, who fought so vigorously at the Accursed Tower, set in the inner wall at the angle of the salient. Here King Henry II and the lite of the Crusader army steadied themselves to receive the great danger everywhere, he was killed before the day was out. Of the army of Templars only ten survived, and of the Hospitallers only seven. On that day when the Muslims poured through the narrow streets of Acre like avenging angels, massacring everyone in their path, the likelihood of any Crusader's surviving was infinitesimal. The city was burning, and Muslims were everywhere. King Henry II wisely permitted himself to be carried on board a ship for Cyprus, since a captured king was too great a gift to the enemy. The aged Patriarch Nicholas of Hanape was less fortunate. Followed by his flock, he went down to the harbor to be taken on a small skiff to a ship. But seeing the people crowding the shore, he felt pity on them and allowed them to come swimming out to his skiff. So many swam to him and clambered on board that it sank: the patriarch was drowned and so were all those who swam out to him. The dockside was crowded with women and children begging to be taken to Cyprus.

About this time Peter of Flor, a Catalan adventurer, who had fought with the Templars, took charge of a Templar galley and invited the rich noblewomen of Acre to accompany him to Cyprus, their passage money being all the jewels and all the gold they possessed. In this way he amassed the foundations of his immense fortune.

Earlier, on May 8, Khalil had ordered an attack on the fortresslike Temple, which formed a salient in the southwest corner of Acre, facing the sea. Crowded with refugees, men, women, and children, Pisans, Venetians, and Genoese, the Temple appeared to be impregnable, even in its last hours. It was heavily fortified, with many towers, all of them emblazoned with lions of hammered bronze, and with great gates which were thought to be impenetrable. The Temple would hold out for ten days. After two or three days Khalil offered terms. All who had sought refuge in the Temple could leave under a safe-conduct if they surrendered their weapons and took with them nothing more than the clothes they wore. Khalil sent them a white banner as a sign that they were under his protection, together with an emir and a regiment of soldiers to see that the terms of the surrender were carried out. It appeared that the last Christians in Acre would be able to depart peacefully, but that was not to be so.

The emir and his regiment of soldiers were allowed to enter the fortress. In full sight of the Crusaders, they began to maltreat the girls and boys they found. The Christians flew at the Muslims, murdering them all. The corpses were thrown into the street outside the Temple, and the white banner was tossed on the mound of corpses.

Such acts were not designed to please Khalil, who regarded all further resistance as an affront. He offered to negotiate with Peter of Sevrey, the Marshal of the Templars, and urged him to come with a small escort to his tent under a safe-conduct. The moment Peter reached the tent he was trussed up and beheaded, as were the members of his escort. All this could be seen from the walls of the Temple. The hapless survivors realized that Khalil had no intention of letting them go.

They defended themselves as best they could. Khalil had given orders that the landward walls of the Temple should be mined, and on May 18—the day of the general assault—part of the walls came crumbling down. The sappers planted great balks of timber to prevent any further damage to the Temple, so that the Muslims could rush in and massacre the Christians, while two thousand cavalry guarded the road outside to prevent anyone from escaping. But the balks of timber were not strong enough to support the huge building. The timbers collapsed and the whole Temple collapsed with them. As the Temple came crashing down, everyone in it, including the Muslim soldiers, was killed, and the cavalry guarding the road died under the weight of stone that fell on them. Within a few minutes, where there had been a huge edifice, there was only a vast mound of rubble and a great silence.

On this day, Friday May 18, 1291, with the destruction of its last outpost, the Kingdom of Jerusalem came to an end. The Crusades had ended as they began, in treachery and massacre.

There remained the mopping-up campaign, which Khalil entered upon almost casually. All the remaining fortresses along the seacoast surrendered without a struggle. Tyre, which had twice resisted Saladin's armies, was simply abandoned when the enemy approached. Sidon fell to the Muslims. Many of the people escaped to Cyprus, but many more were captured by the Muslims and were killed or sold in the marketplaces of Cairo and Damascus. The Templar castles of Tortosa and Athlit, and the cities of Beirut and Tortosa, all surrendered. There remained to the Templars only the waterless island of Ruad, two miles off the coast of Tortosa, which they retained for another twelve years.

The coast of Palestine became a desert. In their fury, the Muslims were determined to extirpate every trace of the Christians who had once dominated the seaports here. Where there had been orchards, they left only dead trees; where there had been buildings, they left only rubble. An Arab historian wrote that no Christian would ever set foot on these shores until Judgment Day.

The Crusades, however, were not quite over.

The Last Throw
of the Dice

FTER the fall of the Kingdom of Jerusalem in the Holy Land, shock waves traveled through Europe. Every bishop summoned the faithful to tell them that Christ's Sepulchre had been irretrievably lost to them. Among the people there was no rage, only a vague sense of loss. For two hundred years they had been hearing about the Crusades, their triumphs, and their failures, and they had little emotion left for the dead who lay buried among the ruins of Acre. The days of the Crusades were over, and they had other matters to attend to. Moreover, they were grateful that they were no longer to be taxed to pay for the Crusades.

But the Crusades were not yet entirely a thing of the past. To end the story with the fall of Acre is to leave out the last brilliant flaring-up of the Crusader spirit, the sudden emergence of a new, heaven-sent opportunity to establish God's kingdom firmly in the Holy Land. The Mamelukes might seem to be in total control; they had reduced most of the seacoast cities to rubble; they stabled their horses in Jerusalem; but they were not in any practical sense ruling over Palestine, which had become a desert. There remained Armenia, which would survive for 175 years, almost forgotten by the West, under Christian kings who descended from the family of Lusignan. There remained the armed Templars who had taken refuge on the island of Cyprus. There were not very many of them, but they could call upon the Templars in Europe to swell their ranks. Above all, there remained the Mongol army of the Ilkhan Ghazan, and this army, when well led, could sweep everything in its path. Ghazan had been converted to Islam, but he felt kindly toward the Christians and unkindly toward the Sultan of Egypt.

In the summer of 1292, a year after the fall of Acre, the Templars on Cyprus elected a new Master, Jacques de Molay, who was the Marshal of the Templar army, and expert in all military affairs from the construction of fortresses to tactics and strategy. His election was fraught with extraordinary consequences.

Jacques de Molay, who would bear an extraordinary weight of destiny on his shoulders, was a man almost without a history. He was born near Besançon in eastern France to a family of the minor nobility. He was about twenty-one years old when he entered the order, in 1265, at Beaune in the wine-growing region near Dijon. Thereafter, he spent his whole life in the service of the Templars. He was one of those steadfast soldiers who disappear into the army, for nothing very much was heard of him until he became Marshal.

He quarreled with King Henry of Lusignan, because he wanted to retain complete control of the Templars, while the king wanted to command all the forces on the island. The quarrel became violent, and in August 1298, the pope came out openly on the side of the Master. The pope urged Henry of Lusignan, King of Cyprus, to set aside his quarrels with the Templars, because it was beyond doubt that they contributed to the safety of the kingdom and an open break would only jeopardize the lives of everyone in Cyprus. Boniface VIII was not overstating the case on behalf of the Master of the Temple. The number of Templars on the island was probably no more than five hundred, but they were a disciplined force. Jacques de Molay was a fighting knight, and if the Crusaders ever fought again they would need someone like him to lead them.

For nearly seven years the Mameluke army remained quiescent, partly because Egypt was being ravaged by a plague and partly because the army needed time to absorb the treasure it had pillaged from Palestine. Then suddenly two fully equipped Mameluke divisions stormed Alexandretta and advanced into Cilicia to attack Sis and Adana, slaughtering as they went. One by one, the castles of Armenia were demolished. King Constantine of Armenia, acting on behalf of Hethum, the rightful king, who had been wounded in a palace intrigue, summoned the help of the Mongols. The Ilkhan Ghazan offered to lead a combined Armenian and Mongol army against the Mamelukes.

Messengers were sent to Cyprus to warn the king of the coming battles. A small army was hastily put together and ferried to the port of St. Symeon in the autumn of 1299. Here they made contact with Mongol forces encamped in the ruins of Antioch. Jacques de Molay was given command of thirty thousand Mongol soldiers. Hethum, recovered from his wounds, took command of the Armenian army. He had been partially blinded during the palace intrigue, but his sight had returned and he was able to see the immense army brought up by the Mongols. Altogether there were more than a hundred thousand troops: three or four thousand from Cyprus, perhaps fifteen thousand from Armenia, a small army of Georgians, all the rest Mongols. Ghazan decided that the time had come to rid Syria of the Mamelukes. .

Hethum, who knew the Mongol emperor well, and indeed was related to him—Ghazan had married a princess of the Armenian royal family—

accompanied the huge army on the march to Hims. Ghazan was very small and he had the wizened features of a Mongol. Hethum thought that in all his army there were not two thousand men as small as the emperor, and there were few who were as ugly; neither were there any so generous, brave, high-minded, or sweet-tempered. Ghazan told Hethum that his intention, once he had swept Syria and Palestine clear of the Mamelukes, was to give that land to the Christians.

Hims, halfway between Aleppo and Damascus, was a large walled town on the Orontes. It was well fortified, with walls of black stone, and was famous for its orchards and the beauty of its people. The Mameluke army was camped in and around the town, ready to do battle. The Mongol-Armenian-Christian army rode along the plain in the shadow of the Lebanon mountains until it was a day's march from Hims. Ghazan called a halt, saying he would remain there until his horses were fully rested. He set up his camp, busied himself with his own affairs, and seemed totally indifferent to the presence of the enemy a day's march away. There was an abundance of fodder and water, and provisions came from the surrounding villages.

The news that Ghazan was resting in his camp came to the ears of the Sultan at Hims on December 22, 1299. He decided to attack immediately, reached Ghazan's camp toward evening, and sent his cavalry to destroy the army of the Mongol emperor. Caught by surprise, Ghazan ordered his own cavalry to dismount. They were not to attack the enemy, but to use their horses as a wall and to shoot arrows at the enemy as soon as they came within range. The Mongols were superb archers. They broke the charge, and by nightfall the Mamelukes had fled.

During that night, the Mongols and their allies advanced on Hims. The battle was resumed at dawn, and this time the Mongols had no need to kneel behind their horses. Armenians, Templars, Hospitallers, and contingents of the Cypriot army, Georgians, and Mongols, spent the day slaughtering the Mamelukes until there was scarcely any part of the battlefield uncarpeted by dead bodies.

The allied losses were small; the Mamelukes lost three-quarters of their army. The sultan fled to Cairo with a small bodyguard of Bedouin, while the survivors fled in the direction of Tripoli and were cut down by Christians living in the mountains of Lebanon. The Sultan's treasure was found intact. Characteristically, Ghazan ordered that the spoils should be divided among the soldiers, and he kept for himself only the sultan's sword and a pouch containing the seals of the sultanate.

The army rested for five days and then advanced on Damascus. While they were on the march, the governor of Damascus sent ambassadors with costly presents and the keys to the city. Ghazan received the ambassadors, accepted their gifts, and told them he would set up his camp near the city and perhaps make it his capital. Capchik, a Saracen who had ingratiated himself with Ghazan, was made governor of Damascus, while Cotulossa, a Mongol chieftain, was made second-in-command of the army. Toward the end of February 1300, Ghazan had to return to Persia to put down an uprising. Before he left, he summoned King Hethum, and said the time had come for the Christians to take possession of their castles and restore them to fighting strength. Ghazan said he had given orders to Cotulossa to help them in every way.

For six months the Christians, with the help of the Mongol army, were in effective control of the Holy Land. Everything was restored to them. Dazed, they saw the country over which they had fought for two hundred years given back to them. Armenia belonged once again to the Armenians; the cities of the seacoast as far south as Gaza and Jerusalem itself belonged to the Crusaders. At Easter, services were held in the Church of the Holy Sepulchre. Templars and Hospitallers had entered the city in triumph, and no one had tried to stop them. Ghazan, before leaving Damascus, sent ambassadors to the pope and the sovereigns of Europe, urging them to pour men, money, and armaments into Palestine, which was his gift to them. He wanted an alliance between the Mongols and the countries of Europe against the Mamelukes, and he was prepared to back up the alliance with his vast army.

The Armenians drifted back to Armenia; the Christian knights surveyed the shattered seacoast cities and wondered whether help would come in time. There were less than five thousand of them now, and they realized that it was beyond the power of a handful of men to make a kingdom. Jacques de Molay sent out columns in all directions, pretending to have a force much greater than the one he possessed. The pope told the Mongol ambassadors that the time was not ripe for another Crusade, and the sovereigns of Europe said the same. Ghazan remained in Tabriz; Jacques de Molay took up residence in the Templum Dei in Jerusalem, and fretted over the impossibility of the task entrusted to him. The kingdom was in his hands, but where were the people to till the fields, guard the frontiers, rebuild the churches? The seacoast cities must be rebuilt brick by brick: towers, castles, gates, city walls. Where were the women? Where were the children? With a Mongol army to protect them, with thousands upon thousands of immigrants coming from Europe under the good offices of the pope and the sovereigns of Europe, the kingdom might be restored, but it would have to be done quickly and decisively.

It was the year 1300, the Jubilee Year commanded by Pope Boniface VIII, the most imperial of popes, to celebrate the achievements of the Church and his own power. Enormous crowds flocked to Rome, where the pope sometimes appeared in procession with two swords held before him, representing both spiritual and temporal power. In the Kingdom of Jerusalem, the few remaining Crusaders were desperately seeking help and the pope did not listen to them.

In Palestine the summer was unusually hot. The trees withered; the roads were thick with dust. As usual, there were conspiracies, counterconspiracies, secret agreements. Quite suddenly Jacques de Molay was confronted with a conspiracy designed to shatter his last hopes. Capchik, the Saracen governor of Damascus, the close and trusted friend of the Ilkhan Ghazan, who had innocently raised him to high position, entered into secret correspondence with the Mameluke sultan, offering to place Damascus under Egyptian sovereignty in exchange for a vast treasure, the sultan's sister in marriage, and the governorship of Damascus to be held by him and his family in perpetuity. Dictating his memoirs to his friend Nicolas Falcon seven years later, in a convent in Poitiers, the monk Haiton, formerly Hethum, King of Armenia, records in his rather haphazard manner the events of that summer and autumn:

> When Molay saw that the entire country was in a state of rebellion, he knew he would be unable to make headway with so few men, and that is why he rode to the kingdom of Mesopotamia by the shortest route, and related in great detail everything that had passed in the kingdom of Syria. Ghazan could do nothing because it was summer, but with winter coming up he made all his preparations on the banks of the Euphrates and sent Cotulossa with thirty thousand Tartar horsemen, ordering them, when they reached the country of Antioch, to send word to the King of Armenia and other Christians in the countries of the Orient and Cyprus to join him. While they were waiting for Ghazan himself to march into the kingdom of Syria with all his forces, Cotulossa followed the emperor's orders.
>
> Cotulossa reached Antioch with his thirty thousand Tartars and sent word to the King of Armenia to join him. The King agreed to march and went to find him; and the Christians in the kingdom of Cyprus, having heard of the arrival of Cotulossa, sent forces to the island off Tortosa. Among them was the Lord of Tyre, brother of the king of Cyprus, who was Generalissimo, and the men in charge of the Hospital and the Temple with their brethren. While they were all preparing themselves to do their Christian duty, there came the rumor that Ghazan was ill and the doctors despaired for his life.
>
> So it came about that Cotulossa returned to Ghazan with the Tartars, and the King of Armenia returned to Armenia, and the Christians who had assembled at Tortosa returned to Cyprus. In this way the expedition to save the holy land was totally abandoned. This happened in the year of Our Lord 1301.

This was not quite the end, because the Mongols and Armenians went on fighting. There were continual small battles and skirmishes, and then at last, in 1303, at Marj as-Saffar, a great plain twenty miles south of Damascus, the combined Mongol-Armenian army was defeated. The remnants of the army retired to Nineveh, where Ghazan received them, promising to continue to wage war against the Saracens and giving King Hethum a sum of money, sufficient to support a thousand Armenian horsemen and a thousand Mongol soldiers to be used in the defense of the kingdom of Armenia. The king returned to Armenia, raised an army and won a victory over the Mamelukes at Ayati, near Tarsus. It was a decisive victory. Of the seven thousand Mamelukes who took part in it, only three hundred survived. The sultan called for a truce. King Hethum was happy to give it to him. Thereupon, remembering that he had always wanted to be a monk, he set his affairs in order, put a nephew on the throne, and traveled to the West.

The monk Haiton was not entirely correct when he said that all the Christian forces returned to Cyprus. He left out of account the handful of Templars who had remained on Ruad. From this small waterless island, the last remaining possession of the Templars, Jacques de Molay had hoped to send landing parties along the coast to recover the Holy Land. The island was well fortified, it had a good harbor, a fine church, tanks for storing rainwater. One day in 1303, the Mamelukes sent twenty ships to the island with ten thousand soldiers. They forced a landing, massacred most of the Templars, and sailed away. Only a few of the Templars on Ruad were able to reach Cyprus.

With the battle of Marj as-Saffar and the fall of Ruad, the Crusades truly came to an end. There would be raids on Tortosa, Acre, and Alexandria by ships based on Cyuprus, and from time to time popes and kings would announce forthcoming crusades either because it suited them to do so for political reasons or because they genuinely felt that such things were possible. Whatever their intentions, these crusades never took place.

Throughout the Crusades there had been a strange sense of fatality, a sense of doom. Even when the Crusades were at their height, when the kings of Jerusalem appeared to be in full control, there seemed to be something wanting. Seen from the villages and cities of the West, Jerusalem appeared in men's eyes like a dream in shimmering Oriental colors, remote and inaccessible; and even those who walked through the streets of Jerusalem sometimes wondered whether they had really reached the place they had so desired to see. They had heard it called "Jerusalem the Golden," and they imagined a city made of gold and rubies and emeralds. Instead, it was a dusty place, though the stones were the rich color of crusts of bread. No city created by man could live up to Jerusalem's reputation. For two hundred years, proud men from the West fought a continuing battle for the city set on one of the mountains of the Judaean desert. For two hundred years, kings, princes, knights as well as the common people suffered from thirst and scorching heat to win and hold a city in the wilderness. Then at last they discovered that Jerusalem was not a geographical place. It was a place in the human heart.

Chapter Notes

REFERENCES are given in a shortened form. Thus Michaud I refers to the first volume of his *History of the Crusades* and MichaudB I refers to the first volume of his *Bibliothèque des Croisades*. Similarly HillR refers to Rosalind Hill's edition of the anonymous *Deeds of the Franks and the other Pilgrims to Jerusalem*, and William refers to the *History of Deeds Done Beyond the Sea* by William, Archbishop of Tyre. This work, together with René Grousset's *Histoire des Croisades et du Royaume franc de Jerusalem* and the magnificent compilation of documents known as the *Receuil des Historiens des Croisades*, compiled between 1841 and 1906 and produced in gloriously printed elephant-sized folios, were by far the most impressive works I encountered during the seven years I studied the Crusaders.

60   "'If I had all this treasure . . .'"   Comnena, 266
60   "'I never imagined . . .'"   Comnena, 266
61   "'He was a man . . .'"   Comnena, 267
69   "'As many of them . . .'"   HillR, 15
71   "'The women of our camp . . .'"   HillR, 19
81   EXCERPTS FROM A LETTER FROM STEPHEN . . .
     Translations, I, 4
85   ". . . They flayed the Turks"   (Source unknown)
88   "Knowing that no one was there . . ."   D'Aguilers, 52
89   "Do you not know . . ."   D'Aguilers, 53
90   "'Lord, who shall abide . . .'"   D'Aguilers, 55
92   "'I not only desire . . .'"   D'Aguilers, 100
96   "Those who were strong . . ."   D'Aguilers, 118
97   "'If you will attack . . .'"   D'Aguilers, 117
103 EXCERPTS FROM A LETTER FROM DAIMBERT . . .
     Translations, I, 4
119 "'they could be used . . .'"   Fulcher, 154
125 ". . . the Saracens . . . lie in wait . . ."   Munro, 67
136 "We who were . . ."   Fulcher, 271
144 "'a man of much wisdom . . .'"   William, II, 148
145 "'Would you like to see God . . .'"   Ousama, 177
158 "During the fighting . . ."   Odo, 118-120
159 "'From this time . . .'"   William, II, 196
168 "'We should pity them . . .'"   William II, 294
168 "'There is no record . . .'"   William, II, 294
171 "'with extreme unwillingness . . .'"   William, II, 321
186 "'a man of proven loyalty . . .'"   William, II, 418
188 "I thought of thee . . ."   Lane-Poole, *Saladin*, 155
192 "'I think that when . . .'"   Gabrieli, 101
192 "You, who are the bulwark . . ."   Gabrieli, 101
193 "Soft in gestures . . ."   *Chronicle*, 140
195 "'She sent to Saladin . . .'"   Grousset, II, 737
196 "'The leper child . . .'"   Gabrieli, 114
199 "'The new king will not last . . .'"   Raynaud, 135
199 "'Well then, I shall forgive . . .'"   Raynaud, 136
202 "'Tiberias is mine . . .'"   Grousset, II, 793
202 "'Have no faith, Sire . . .'"   Grousset, II, 793
205 ". . . we saw the tent . . ."   Oman, I, 331
206 "'I did only what princes . . .'"   HRC, *Le Livre des Deux
     Jardins*, 275
207 "'I am therefore not bound . . .'"   HRC, *Jardins*, 296
207 "I rode across the battlefield . . ."   HRC, *Jardins*, 272-3
207 "'This man is guilty . . .'"   HRC, *Jardins*, 276
208 "'men of pious and austere . . .'"   HRC, *Jardins*, 277

311 "'I will obey you willingly . . .'"   Novara, 78

312 "'I know that Balian is . . .'"   Novara, 81

315 "'I am your friend . . .'"   Grousset, III, 303

317 EXCERPTS FROM A LETTER FROM THE EMPEROR . . .
Peters, 162

318 "'Pig!' shouted the emperor . . ."   Grousset, 230

319 "'My chief purpose . . .'"   Grousset, 231

328 "'In the Holy Land . . .'"   Grousset, III, 393

335 "'What would you rather be . . .'"   Joinville, 141

336 "'You should clothe yourselves . . .'"   Joinville, 144

337 "Soon the wind filled our sails . . ."   Joinville, 167

341 EXCERPTS FROM A LETTER FROM GUY . . .
Translations, I, 4

349 "'What will you give me . . .'"   Joinville, 223

351 "May God reward you . . ."   Labarge, 131

353 "'If I depart . . .'"   Joinville, 240

354 "'Well then,' said the ambassador . . ."   Joinville, 248

355 "'This has been closest to me . . .'"   Joinville, 249

355 "'What are you doing . . .'"   Joinville, 246

356 "'I have a great liking . . .'"   Joinville, 251

356 "Know that one of the rules . . ."   Joinville, 250

360 "'the name of the French king . . .'"   Regalado, 41

360 "'Take this in Mahomet's name . . .'"   Regalado, 45

369 EXCERPTS FROM A LETTER FROM THE SULTAN
BAIBARS . . .   MichaudB, III, 507

372 EXCERPTS FROM A LETTER FROM HUGH OF REVEL . . .
Cartulaire, 291

391 "When Molay saw that . . ."   Haiton, 61

Select Bibliography

Addison, C. G. *The Knights Templars*. London: Longman Brown, Green, & Longmans, 1853.

Al-Isfahani, Imad Ad-Din. *Conquête de la Syrie et de la Palestine par Saladin*. Translated by Henri Massé. Paris: Librairie Orientaliste Paul Geuthner, 1972.

Ambroise. *The Crusade of Richard Lion-Heart*. Translated by Merton Jerome Hubert. New York: Columbia University Press, 1941.

Ameer Ali. *A Short History of the Saracens*. London: Macmillan & Co., 1899.

Andressohn, John C. *The Ancestry and Life of Godfrey of Bouillon*. Bloomington: Indiana University Press, 1947.

Arberry, A. J. *Sufism*. London: George Allen & Unwin, 1956.

Archer, T. A., and Charles Lethridge Kingsford. *The Crusades*. London: T. Fisher Unwin, 1894.

Atiya, Aziz S. *The Crusade: Historiography and Bibliography*. Bloomington: Indiana University Press, 1962.

Barasch, Moshe. *Crusader Figural Sculpture in the Holy Land*. New Brunswick: Rutgers University Press, 1971.

Barber, Malcolm. *The Trial of the Templars*. Cambridge: Cambridge University Press, 1978.

Barker, Ernest. *The Crusades*. London: Oxford University Press, 1923.

Belloc, Hilaire. *The Crusade: The World's Debate*. London: Cassell & Co., 1937.

Benvenisti, Meron. *The Crusaders in the Holy Land*. New York: Macmillan, 1970.

Bordonove, Georges. *La Vie Quotidienne des Templiers au XIIIe Siècle*. Paris: Hachette, 1975.

————. *Les Templiers*. Paris: Fayard, 1963.

Brand, Charles M. *Byzantium Confronts the West 1180-1204*. Cambridge: Harvard University Press, 1968.

Brion, Marcel. *Blanche de Castille*. Paris: Les Editions de France, 1939.

Broadhurst, R. J. C. *A History of the Ayyubid Sultans of Egypt*. Translated from the Arabic of al-Maqrisi. Boston: Twayne Publishers, 1980.

Brockelmann, Carl. *History of the Islamic Peoples*. London: Routledge & Kegan Paul, 1949.

Brundage, James A. *Richard Lion Heart*. New York: Scribner, 1974.

———. *The Crusades: A Documentary Survey*. Milwaukee: Marquette University Press, 1962.

———. *The Crusades: Motives and Achievements*. Lexington, DC: Heath & Co., 1964.

Byron, Robert. *The Byzantine Achievement*. New York: Russell & Russell, 1964.

Campbell, G. A. *The Crusades*. New York: Robert M. McBride, 1938.

———. *The Knights Templar: Their Rise and Fall*. New York: Robert M. McBride, n.d.

Cartulaire Générale de l'Ordre des Hospitaliers. Paris: Delaville Le Roux, 1894-1904.

Castries, le duc de. *La Conquête de la Terre Sainte par les Croisés*. Paris: Albin Michel, 1973.

Chalandon, Ferdinand. *Histoire de la Première Croisade*. Paris: Auguste Picard, 1925.

Charpentier, Louis. *Les Mystères Templiers*. Paris: Robert Laffont, 1967.

Clari, Robert of. *The Conquest of Constantinople*. Translated by Edgar McNeal. New York: Norton, 1969.

Clifford, Esther. *A Knight of Great Renown*. Chicago: University of Chicago Press, 1961.

Cohn, Norman. *The Pursuit of the Millenium*. New York: Oxford University Press, 1970.

Comnena, Anna. *The Alexiad*. Translated by Elizabeth A. S. Dawes. London: Kegan Paul, 1928.

Conder, C. R. *The Latin Kingdom of Jerusalem*. London: Palestine Exploration Fund, 1897.

D'Aguilers, Raymond. *Historia Francorum Qui Ceperunt Iherusalem*. Translated by John Hugh Hill. Philadelphia: American Philosophical Society, 1968.

Dailliez, Laurent. *Les Templiers et les Règles de l'Ordre du Temple*. Paris: Pierre Belfond, 1972.

———. *Jacques de Molay*. Paris: Robert Dumas, 1974.

Daniel-Rops, Henri. *Cathedral and Crusade: Studies of the Mediaeval Church 1050-1350*. 2 vols. Translated by John Warrington. Garden City: Doubleday, 1963.

David, Charles Wendell. *Robert Curthose, Duke of Normandy*. Cambridge: Harvard University Press, 1920.

De Morgan, Jacques. *The History of the Armenian People.* Boston: Hairenik, 1965.

Deschamps, Paul. *Au Temps des Croisades.* Paris: Hachette, 1972.

Duggan, Alfred. *The Story of the Crusades 1097-1291.* New York: Pantheon Books, 1964.

Dupuy, Pierre. *Histoire de l'Ordre Militaire des Templiers.* Brussels: Pierre Foppens, 1751.

Ehrenkreutz, Andrew S. *Saladin.* Albany: State University of New York Press, 1972.

Erbstrosser, Martin. *The Crusades.* New York: Universe Books, 1979.

Ernoul, Chronique d'. Edited by M. L. Le Mas Latrie. Paris: 1871.

Evans, Joan. *Life in Mediaeval France.* London: Phaidon, 1925.

Fedden, Robin. *Syria.* London: Robert Hale, 1956.

Fedden, Robin, and John Thomson. *Crusader Castles.* London: John Murray, 1957.

Franzius, Enno. *History of the Order of Assassins.* New York: Funk & Wagnalls, 1969.

Fulcher of Chartres. *A History of the Expedition to Jerusalem 1095-1127.* Translated by Frances Rita Ryan. Knoxville: University of Tennessee Press, 1969.

Fuller, Thomas. *The Historie of the Holy Warre.* Cambridge: Thomas Buck, 1639.

Funck-Brentano, Fr. *The Middle Ages.* Translated by Elizabeth O'Neill. London: William Heinemann, 1930.

Gabrieli, Francesco. *Arab Historians of the Crusades.* London: Routledge & Kegan Paul, 1969.

Gautier, Leon. *Chivalry.* New York: Barnes & Noble, 1959.

Gibb, Sir Hamilton. *The Damascus Chronicle of the Crusades.* London: Luzac, 1967.

————. *The Life of Saladin from the Works of Imad ad-Din and Baha ad-Din.* Oxford: Clarendon Press, 1971.

Gibbon, Edward. *The Life and Letters of Edward Gibbon with his History of the Crusades.* London: Frederick Warne, n.d.

Gray, George Zabriskie. *The Children's Crusade.* New York: Morrow, 1972.

Grousset, René. *The Epic of the Crusades.* Translated by Noel Lindsay. New York: Orion Press, 1970.

————. *Histoire des Croisades et du Royaume franc de Jerusalem.* 3 vols. Paris: Plon, 1934.

Guerdan, René. *Byzantium: Its Triumphs and Tragedy.* London: George Allen & Unwin, 1956.

Haiton. *Histoire Orientale, en Voyages Faits Principalement en Asie.* [Edited by] Pierre Bergeron. The Hague: Jean Neaulme, 1735.

Heer, Friedrich. *The Mediaeval World: Europe 1100-1350.* New York: World, 1961.

Henderson, Philip. *Richard Coeur de Lion.* New York: Norton, 1958.

Hill, John Hugh, and Laurita Lyttleton Hill. *Raymond IV Count of Toulouse.* Syracuse: Syracuse University Press, 1962.

Hill, Rosalind, and R. A. B. Mynors, eds. *The Deeds of the Franks and the other Pilgrims to Jerusalem.* New York: Thomas Nelson & Sons, 1962.

Hitti, Philip K. *History of Syria.* New York: Macmillan, 1951.

––––––. *History of the Arabs.* New York: Macmillan, 1946.

Hopf, Charles. *Chroniques Gréco-Romaines.* Berlin: Librairie de Weidman, 1873.

Hutton, William Holden. *Constantinople: The Story of the Old Capital of the Empire.* London: J. M. Dent & Sons, 1914.

Jeffery, Geo. *Cyprus Under an English King in the Twelfth Century.* London: Zeno, 1973.

Join-Lambert, Michel. *Jerusalem.* New York: Putnam, 1958.

Joinville, Jean de. *Memoirs of the Crusades.* Translated by Sir Frank T. Marzials. New York: Dutton, 1958.

Kantorowicz, Ernst. *Frederick the Second, 1194-1250.* Translated by E. O. Lorimer. New York: Ungar, 1957.

Kelly, Amy. *Eleanore of Aquitaine and the Four Kings.* New York: Vintage Books, 1962.

Kendall, Alan. *Medieval Pilgrims.* New York: Putnam, 1970.

King, E. J. *The Knights Hospitallers in the Holy Land.* London: Methuen, 1931.

Krey, August C. *The First Crusade: The Accounts of Eye-Witnesses and Participants.* Princeton: Princeton University Press, 1921.

Labarge, Margaret Wade. *Saint Louis: Louis IX Most Christian King of France.* Boston: Little, Brown, 1968.

Lamb, Harold. *The Crusades.* New York: Bantam Books, 1962.

La Monte, John L. *Feudal Monarchy in the Latin Kingdom of Jerusalem 1100-1291.* Cambridge: The Mediaeval Academy of America, 1932.

Lane-Poole, Stanley. *The Mohammadan Dynasties.* New York: Ungar, 1965.

––––––. *Saladin and the Fall of the Kingdom of Jerusalem.* Beirut: Khayats, 1964.

Lawrence. T. E. *Crusader Castles.* 2 vols. London: Golden Cockerel Press, 1936.

Le Febvre, Yves. *Pierre l'Hermite et La Croisade.* Amiens: Malfère, 1946.

Le Strange, Guy. *Palestine under the Moslems.* Boston: Houghton Mifflin, 1890.

Longnon, Jean. *Les Francais d'Outre-Mer au Moyen-Age.* Paris: Perrin, 1929.

Maillet, Germaine. *La Vie Religieuse au Temps de Saint Louis.* Paris: Robert Laffont, 1954.

Mayer, Hans Eberhard. *The Crusades.* Translated by John Gillingham. New York: Oxford University Press, 1972.

Meistermann, Barnabas. *Guide to the Holy Land.* New York: P. J. Kenedy & Sons, 1923.

Melville, Marion. *La Vie des Templiers.* Paris: Gallimard, 1951.

Michaud, J. F. *Bibliothèque des Croisades.* 4 vols. Paris: A. J. Ducollet, 1829.

———. *The History of the Crusades.* 3 vols. Translated by W. Robson. New York: Redfield, 1855.

Millingen, Alexander van. *Byzantine Constantinople.* London: John Murray, 1899.

Morgan, M. R. *The Chronicle of Ernoul and the Continuation of William of Tyre.* London: Oxford University Press, 1973.

Morrisson, Cécile. *Les Croisades.* Paris: Presses Universitaires de France, 1969.

Muller-Wiener, Wolfgang. *Castles of the Crusaders.* New York: McGraw-Hill, 1966.

Munro, Dana Carleton. *The Kingdom of the Crusaders.* Port Washington: Kennikat Press, 1966.

Nangis, Guillaume de. *Chronique.* In M. Guizot, *Collection des Mémoires relatifs à l'histoire de France.* Paris: J.-L.-J.-Brière, 1825.

Newhall, Richard A. *The Crusades.* New York: Holt, Rinehart & Winston, 1963.

Newton, Arthur Percival. *Travel and Travellers in the Middle Ages.* New York: Barnes & Noble, 1968.

Nicholson, Robert Lawrence. *Joscelyn III and the Fall of the Crusader States 1134-1199.* Leiden: E. J. Brill, 1973.

Norman, A. V. B. *The Medieval Soldier.* New York: Thomas Y. Crowell, 1971.

Novare, Philip de. *The Wars of Frederick II Against the Ibelins in Syria and Cyprus.* Translated by John L. La Monte and Milton Jerome Hubert. New York: Columbia University Press, 1936.

Odericus Vitalis. *The Ecclesiastical History of England and Normandy.* London: Henry G. Bohn, 1854.

Odo of Deuil. *De Profectione Ludovici VII in orientem.* Translated by Virginia Berry. New York: Norton, 1948.

Okey, Thomas. *The Story of Paris.* London: J. M. Dent, 1911.

Oldenbourg, Zoé. *The Crusades.* New York: Random House, 1966.

Oliver of Padeborn. *The Capture of Damietta.* Translated by John J. Garigan. Philadelphia: University of Pennsylvania Press, 1948.

Oman, Charles. *A History of the Art of War in the Middle Ages.* London: Methuen, 1924.

Ostrogovsky, George. *History of the Byzantine State.* New Brunswick: Rutgers University Press, 1957.

Otto of Friesing. *The Deeds of Frederick Barbarossa.* Translated by Charles Christopher Mierow. New York: Norton, 1955.

Ousama. *The Autobiography of Ousama.* Translated by George Richard Potter. London: George Routledge & Sons, 1929.

Pacaut, Marcel. *Frederick Barbarossa.* New York: Scribner, 1970.

Parker, Thomas W. *The Knights Templars in England.* Tucson: University of Arizona Press, 1963.

Parrot, André. *Golgotha and the Church of the Holy Sepulchre.* New York: Philosophical Library, 1957.

Pauphilet, Albert, ed. *Historiens et Chroniqueurs du Moyen Age.* (Robert de Clari, Villehardouin, Joinville, Froissart, Commynes) Paris: Bibliothèque de la Pleiade, 1952.

Payne, Robert. *The Holy Sword.* New York: Harper & Brothers, 1959.

Pears, Edwin. *The Fall of Constantinople.* New York: Harper & Brothers, 1886.

Pernoud, Régine. *Alienor d'Aquitaine.* Paris: Albin Michel, 1965.

_____. *In the Steps of the Crusaders.* New York: Hastings House, 1959.

_____. *The Crusaders.* London: Oliver & Boyd, 1963.

_____. *Un Chef d'Etat: Saint Louis de France.* Paris: J. Gabalda, 1960.

_____. *The Crusades.* Translated by Enid McLeod. New York: Capricorn Books, 1964.

Peters, Edward, ed. *Christian Society and the Crusades 1198-1229. Sources in Translation, including The Capture of Damietta by Oliver of Paderborn.* Philadelphia: University of Pennsylvania Press, 1971.

_____. *The First Crusade.* Philadelphia: The University of Pennsylvania Press, 1971.

Powicke, Sir Maurice. *The Christian Life in the Middle Ages.* London: Oxford University Press, 1966.

_____. *The Thirteenth Century.* London: Oxford University Press, 1962.

Prawar, Joshua. *Histoire du Royaume Latin de Jérusalem.* 2 vols. Paris: Editions du Centre National de la Recherche Scientifique, 1969.

_____. *The Crusaders' Kingdom.* New York: Praeger, 1972.

_____. *The World of the Crusaders.* New York: Quadrangle Books, 1972.

Queller, Donald E. *The Fourth Crusade: The Conquest of Constantinople 1201-1204.* Philadelphia: University of Pennsylvania Press, 1977.

_____. *The Latin Conquest of Constantinople.* New York: Wiley, 1971.

Raynaud, Gaston. *Les Gestes des Chiprois.* Geneva: Jules-Guillaume Fick, 1887.

Regalado, Nancy. *Poetic Patterns in Rutubeuf.* New Haven: Yale University Press, 1970.

(RHC) *Receuil des Historiens des Croisades.* Paris: Academie des Inscriptions et Belles Lettres, 1841-1906. This includes, under many editors:

Documents Armeniens, 2 vols., 1869-1906. *Historiens Grecs*, 2 vols., 1875-81. *Historiens Occidentaux*, 3 vols., 1844-95. *Historiens Orientaux*, 5 vols., 1872-1906.

Riant, Comte. *Archives de l'Orient Latin*. Paris: Ernest Leroux, 1881.

―――. *Exuviae sacrae Constantinopolitane*. 2 vols. Geneva: 1877-78. (Privately printed.)

―――. *Historia Constantinopolitana: Guntheri Alemanni*. Geneva: 1875. (Privately printed.)

Richard, Jean. *Le Royaume Latin de Jérusalem*. Paris: Presses Universitaires de France, 1953.

Robson, James. *Christ in Islam*. New York: Dutton, 1930.

Roger of Hoveden. *The Annals*. 2 vols. London: H. G. Bohn, 1853.

Roger of Wendower. *Flowers of History*. 2 vols. London: George Bell & Sons, 1899.

Rosebault, Charles J. *Saladin: Prince of Chivalry*. New York: Robert M. McBride, 1930.

Runciman, Steven. *A History of the Crusades*. Vols. 1 and 2. New York: Harper & Row, 1964-65.

―――. *A History of the Crusades*. Vol. 3. Cambridge: Cambridge University Press, 1966.

Sanutus, Marinus. *Liber Secretorum Fidelium Crucis*. Toronto: University of Toronto Press, 1972.

Saunders, J. J. *Aspects of the Crusades*. Christchurch: University of Canterbury, 1962.

Schlumberger, Gustave. *Byzance et Croisades*. Paris: Paul Geuthner, 1927.

―――. *Campagnes du Roi Amaury Ier de Jérusalem*. Paris: Plon, 1905.

―――. *Numismatique de l'Orient Latin*. 2 vols. Graz: Akademische Druck-u. Verlagsanstalt, 1954.

―――. *Renaud de Châtillon, Prince d'Antioche*. Paris: Plon, 1923.

Setton, Kenneth M., ed. *A History of the Crusades*. Vols. 1-4. Madison: University of Wisconson Press, 1969.

Sewter, E. R. A., trans. *The Alexiad of Anna Comnena*. Harmondsworth: Penguin Books, 1969.

Simon, Edith. *The Piebald Standard: A Biography of the Knights Templars*. London: Cassell, 1959.

Slaughter, Gertrude. *Saladin (1138-1193)*. New York: Exposition Press, 1955.

Smail, R. C. *Crusading Warfare, 1097-1193*. Cambridge: Cambridge University Press, 1956.

―――. *The Crusaders in Syria and the Holy Land*. New York: Praeger, 1973.

Smith, George Adam. *The Historical Geography of the Holy Land*. New York: Harper & Row, 1966.

Stevenson, W. B. *The Crusaders in the East.* Beirut: Librairie de Liban, 1968.

Stone, Edward Noble, trans. *Three Old French Chronicles.* Seattle: University of Washington Press, 1939. (Includes Ambrose, *History of the Holy War,* Robert of Clari, and *A Chronicle of Rheims.*)

Throop, Palmer A. *Criticism of the Crusade.* Amsterdam: N. V. Swets & Zeitlinger, 1940.

Translations and Reprints from the Original Sources of European History. Philadelphia: University of Pennsylvania, 1901, 1905. Vol. I, No. 4 (on all periods of the Crusades) and Vol. III, No. 1 (on Fourth Crusade).

Vasiliev, A. A. *History of the Byzantine Empire.* Madison: University of Wisconsin Press, 1961.

Villehardouin, Geoffroy de. *Memoirs of the Crusades.* Translated by Sir Frank T. Marzials. New York: Dutton, 1958.

Vitry, Jacques de. *Histoire des Croisades.* In M. Guizot, *Collection des Mémoires relatifs à l'histoire de France.* Paris: J.-L.-J.-Brière, 1825.

Watson, Sir C. M. *The Story of Jerusalem.* London: J. M. Dent, 1918.

Wilkinson, Clennell. *Coeur de Lion.* New York: D. Appleton-Century, 1932.

William, Archbishop of Tyre. *A History of Deeds Done Beyond the Sea.* 2 vols. Translated by Emily Babcock and A. C. Krey. New York: Columbia University Press, 1943.

Wright, Thomas. *Early Travels in Palestine.* New York: KTAV Publishing House, 1968.

Yewdale, R. B. *Bohemond I, Prince of Antioch.* Ann Arbor: University Microfilms, 1974.

Index

OTHER COOPER SQUARE PRESS TITLES OF INTEREST

AGINCOURT
Christopher Hibbert
176 pp., 33 b/w illustrations, 3 maps
0-8154-1053-0
$16.95

AUGUSTUS
The Golden Age of Rome
G. P. Baker
378 pp., 17 b/w illustrations, 8 maps
0-8154-1089-1
$18.95

GENGHIS KHAN
R. P. Lister
256 pp., 1 b/w illustration
0-8154-1052-2
$16.95

HANNIBAL
G. P. Baker
366 pp., 3 b/w illustrations, 5 maps
0-8154-1005-0
$16.95

HISTORY OF THE CONQUEST OF MEXICO & HISTORY OF THE
CONQUEST OF PERU
William H. Prescott
1330 pp., 2 maps
0-8154-1004-2
$32.00

THE LIFE AND TIMES OF AKHNATON
Pharaoh of Egypt
Arthur Weigall
322 pp., 26 b/w photos, 7 line drawings
0-8154-1092-1
$17.95